BUILDING ASSETS, BUILDING CREDIT

JAMES A. JOHNSON METRO SERIES

The Metropolitan Policy Program at the Brookings Institution is integrating research and practical experience into a policy agenda for cities and metropolitan areas. By bringing fresh analyses and policy ideas to the public debate, the program hopes to inform key decisionmakers and civic leaders in ways that will spur meaningful change in our nation's communities.

JAMES A. JOHNSON METRO SERIES

As part of this effort, the James A. Johnson Metro Series aims to introduce new perspectives and policy thinking on current issues and attempts to lay the foundation for longer term policy reforms. The series examines traditional urban issues, such as neighborhood assets and central city competitiveness, as well as larger metropolitan concerns, such as regional growth, development, and employment patterns. The James A. Johnson Metro Series consists of concise studies and collections of essays designed to appeal to a broad audience. While these studies are formally reviewed, some will not be verified like other research publications. As with all publications, the judgments, conclusions, and recommendations presented in the studies are solely those of the authors and should not be attributed to the trustees, officers, or other staff members of the Institution.

Also available in this series:

On growth and development

Edgeless Cities: Exploring the Elusive Metropolis
Robert E. Lang

Growth and Convergence in Metropolitan America
Janet Rothenberg Pack

Growth Management and Affordable Housing
Anthony Downs, editor

Laws of the Landscape: How Policies Shape Cities in Europe and America
Pietro S. Nivola

Reflections on Regionalism
Bruce J. Katz, editor

Sunbelt/Frostbelt: Public Policies and Market Forces in Metropolitan Development
Janet Rothenberg Pack, editor

On transportation

Still Stuck in Traffic: Coping with Peak-Hour Traffic Congestion
Anthony Downs

Taking the High Road: A Metropolitan Agenda for Transportation Reform
Bruce Katz and Robert Puentes, editors

On trends

Redefining Urban and Suburban America: Evidence from Census 2000, vol. 1
Bruce Katz and Robert E. Lang, editors

Redefining Urban and Suburban America: Evidence from Census 2000, vol. 2
Alan Berube, Bruce Katz, and Robert E. Lang, editors

On wealth creation

The Geography of Opportunity: Race and Housing Choice in Metropolitan America
Xavier de Souza Briggs, editor

Low-Income Homeownership: Examining the Unexamined Goal
Nicolas P. Retsinas and Eric S. Belsky, editors

Savings for the Poor: The Hidden Benefits of Electronic Banking
Michael A. Stegman

On other metro issues

Evaluating Gun Policy: Effects on Crime and Violence
Jens Ludwig and Philip J. Cook, editors

BUILDING ASSETS, BUILDING CREDIT

Creating Wealth in Low-Income Communities

Nicolas P. Retsinas
Eric S. Belsky
Editors

Joint Center for Housing Studies
Cambridge, Massachusetts

Brookings Institution Press
Washington, D.C.

Copyright © 2005
THE BROOKINGS INSTITUTION
1775 Massachusetts Avenue, N.W., Washington, D.C. 20036
www.brookings.edu

Library of Congress Cataloging-in-Publication data
Building assets, building credit : creating wealth in low-income communities / Nicolas P. Retsinas, Eric S. Belsky, editors.
    p.   cm.
Summary: "Examines the path from basic banking services to creditmaking decisions to mortgage lending that can give low-income individuals and communities the opportunity to build assets through credit, highlighting the need for transparency in the subprime market, buyer education, and borrower safeguards"—Provided by publisher.
Includes bibliographical references and index.
ISBN-13: 978-0-8157-7409-9 (paper : alk. paper)
ISBN-10: 0-8157-7409-5 (paper : alk. paper)
    1. Consumer credit—United States. 2. Low-income consumers—United States. 3. Home ownership—United States. 4. Mortgage loans—United States. I. Retsinas, Nicolas Paul, 1946– II. Belsky, Eric S. III. Title.
    HG3756.U54B85 2005
    332.024'01—dc22   2005017461

9 8 7 6 5 4 3 2 1

The paper used in this publication meets minimum requirements of the American National Standard for Information Sciences—Permanence of Paper for Printed Library Materials: ANSI Z39.48-1992.

Typeset in Adobe Garamond

Composition by Kulamer Publishing Services
Potomac, Maryland

Printed by R. R. Donnelley and Sons
Harrisonburg, Virginia

Contents

Foreword

One of the more significant social developments of recent years has been the increased access to credit for lower-income communities and people. Lending statistics for the 1990s show high rates of credit growth for low- and moderate-income households, much higher than comparable rates of growth for higher-income households. Homeownership rates over this period also increased smartly, especially for lower-income and minority households. And, many formerly downtrodden urban and rural neighborhoods have witnessed a marked resurgence spurred, at least in part, by growth in credit and homeownership.

The increased access to credit and expanded opportunities for homeownership (for households that previously might have been denied credit) has important democratizing benefits. Lower-income households now should be able to build wealth in the way that their higher-income counterparts have long done. Since homeownership induces households to maintain their properties better, homeownership gains also lead to neighborhood improvement.

But these social gains do not come without cost, and some social costs have accompanied the rapid extension of credit. For instance, some households may obtain more credit than they can properly manage and thus put themselves at risk of losing their homes or severely damaging their credit histories and future access to credit. Such actions may have spillover effects, which may adversely affect other residents of their communities. Further, it is unclear whether increased access to credit resolves all concerns regarding lending to lower-income communities and people. Worries remain about the terms and pricing of credit to such households, particularly when it is predatory in nature. Also, even though access to credit may have improved, some households may lack the knowledge to take advantage of the credit for which they may qualify.

The Joint Center for Housing Studies at Harvard University, in cooperation with the Ford Foundation, Freddie Mac, and the Neighborhood Reinvestment Corporation, recently sponsored a conference to examine these issues. Participants included industry analysts, community activists, regulators, and researchers from both the public and private sectors. The conference was organized around the presentation of nearly two dozen technical papers, but the structure of the conference allowed for considerable time for discussion and debate on the research and policy issues raised. This volume, *Building Assets, Building Credit: Creating Wealth in Low-Income Communities*, includes the revised versions of some of the prominent papers from this conference.

Part 1, Making Choices, addresses the consequences when some households rely on what is known as the alternative financial system, consisting primarily of payday lenders, pawnshops, and check cashers, all of which are much less carefully regulated than other financial institutions. Although the reach of the mainline institutions—including commercial banks, thrifts, and credit unions used by middle- and upper-income households—into the lower-income and minority communities has increased substantially over the past decade, a large share of lower-income households, and an even larger share of minority households, still rely on the alternative financial system for most or all of their credit and payment needs. A recent survey of low-income households identified barriers that may discourage such households from using the mainline financial system. One barrier identified involves the minimum balances necessary to open a bank account. In addition, the complexity of mainline accounts can lead to perplexing informational problems for low-income householders. The study does point out, however, that a surprising number of households deal with both mainline and alternative institutions.

Parts 2 and 3, Beyond Prime and Keeping Score, focus on the evolution of risk-based pricing in the subprime mortgage market. Among other topics, chapters explore the relationship between credit scores and mortgage rates, the relative penalties for having below-average credit, and how these penalties have changed over time. Also studied are the role of credit history in allowing individuals to obtain credit in order to buy a home and trends in credit quality across different populations. One prominent finding shows that renters appear to have had deteriorating credit records over the past decade or so. A chapter also explores the quality of the information maintained in credit bureau records and finds that the effects of data problems in these records on individual credit access are ambiguous. A particular type of data problem is likely to benefit some consumers and harm others. Of note, this study also finds that many data problems are mitigated by credit score modelers who have developed methods that eliminate many of the effects of errors.

Part 4, Role of Regulation, examines the role of regulation in the credit reporting system, noting that U.S. credit files, despite their limitations, are among the most accurate in the world and appear to support reasonably precise assessments of credit risk. Proposed changes to the rules to address data quality issues can often have unintended consequences and need to be considered in that light. On the mortgage side, one chapter compares several regulatory approaches used to overcome barriers to credit, such as requiring that all mortgage lenders report their loans to the credit reporting agencies, prohibiting lending discrimination and, of certain lending practices, requiring that lenders make loans to low- and moderate-income individuals or communities, and subsidizing mortgages in general. The authors here make the argument for a blending of regulatory approaches, but one could make the stronger claim that a multifaceted approach would be superior to exclusive use of any one particular approach.

Part 5, Working toward Solutions, deals with inclusive approaches that seek to induce lower-income households to make more use of mainline financial institutions. There is particular focus on new and different kinds of saving incentives and the use of more innovative technological approaches.

Taken together the chapters here convey an impressive array of knowledge in this burgeoning area, spanning all the important policy and research questions. There is plenty of grist for the academic mill—testable hypotheses galore. There are many new policy ideas, and many findings that challenge previously held policy ideas. The conference has already stimulated much academic and policy thought and debate, and this volume should stimulate much more.

EDWARD GRAMLICH
Federal Reserve Board

Acknowledgments

This book is the culmination of a conference exploring ways low-income Americans can build assets and the critical role that access to credit plays in making this possible. Principal funding for the symposium was provided by the Ford Foundation, Freddie Mac, and Neighbor Works America. We are indebted to these organizations for seeing the value of sponsoring an event dedicated to understanding these issues, and, especially, what can be done to improve low-income access to credit and asset-building opportunities.

A project of this magnitude involves the work of dozens of individuals. In our case, we were fortunate to have worked with an extraordinary group of colleagues all of whom contributed to making this project such a success. We would especially like to thank George McCarthy of the Ford Foundation, Edward Golding of Freddie Mac, and Ellen Lazar and Michael Collins of Neighbor Works America for the formative role they played in shaping the research questions addressed in this book.

At the Joint Center for Housing Studies, we would like to thank Pamela Baldwin, Rebecca Storo, Laurel Trayes, William Apgar, Elizabeth England, and Jackie Hernandez for their hard work and dedication to this project. Allegra Calder is deserving of special thanks. She was closely involved in every aspect of the work that led up to this book and was instrumental to the success of the endeavor. In addition, we owe a debt of gratitude to each of the following leaders in the field who gave freely of their time and shared with us ideas that we incorporated into the design of the conference : Michael Barr of the University of Michigan Law School; Stephen Brobeck of the Consumer Federation of America; Glenn Canner, a member of the Board of Governors of the Federal Reserve; John Caskey of Swarthmore College; Kent Colton of K. Colton, LLC; Marsha Courchane and Peter Zorn of Freddie Mac; Allen Fishbein of the Neighborhood Center for Community Change; Michelle Kahane of the Ford Foundation; Duncan Kennedy of the Harvard Law School; Prue Larocca of RBS Greenwich Capital; Andrea Levere of the Corporation for Enterprise Development; Moises Loza of the Housing Assistance Council; Michael Sherraden of the University of Washington at St. Louis; Michael Staten of the Credit Research Center at the McDonough School of Business; Andrea Stowers of VISA USA; and Ellen Seidman of ShoreBank Advisory Service.

Of course, this book would not have been possible without the exceptionally strong papers that were prepared by the contributors. We went to the best and the brightest in the field, and the result is a set of papers that is meticulously researched and cogently argued. Further, the moderators and discussants of the papers at the conference added enormous value and insight. In addition to the book's contributors, our thanks go to Gary Acosta of the National Association of Hispanic Real Estate Professionals, Ray Boshara of the New America Foundation, Malcolm Bush of the Woodstock Institute, James Carr of the Fannie Mae Foundation, Diane Casey-Landry of America's Community Bankers, Geoffrey Cooper of MGIC Investment Corporation, Robert Couch of the Mortgage Bankers Association of America, Frank DeGiovanni of the Ford Foundation, James Garner of the U.S. Conference of Mayors, Sharon Hermanson of the American Association of Retired Persons, Vada Hill and Barry Zigas of Fannie Mae, Jeff Jaffee of Citigroup, Bruce Katz of the Brookings Institution, James Laffargue of the Union Bank of California, Prue Larocca of RBS Greenwich Capital, Bill Longbrake of Washington Mutual, Heidi-Anne Loughlin of the Maine Family Development Account Program, Cathy Lesser Mansfield of Drake University, Frank Raiter of Standard & Poor's, Richard Riese of the Office of Thrift Supervision, Sandor Samuels of Countrywide, Michael Stegman of the University of North Carolina, Andrea Stowers of Stowers Consulting, and John Taylor of the National Community Reinvestment Coalition.

Lastly, we wish to express our deepest appreciation to Joan Retsinas and Cynthia Wilson for their abiding support and contribution to our lifelong learning.

Building Assets, Building Credit

1

New Paths to Building Assets for the Poor

ERIC S. BELSKY AND
NICOLAS P. RETSINAS

M ost poor people have no problem filling in the spaces on their balance sheets for income, debts, and expenses, but come up short in the space for assets. Apart from seniors who bought homes when their incomes were higher, few among the poor have many assets. In fact, when last measured in 2001, the median net wealth of renters with incomes of $20,000 or less was a low $900.

Indeed, assets for the poor among those who do not own homes seem an oxymoron. After all, low incomes coupled with high rents and other living expenses rule out savings. In some neighborhoods it is hard to find a bank branch, let alone one that offers accounts for those with minimal savings. Meanwhile, stocks and bonds are accessible to middle- to upper-income earners, as the other ephemera of wealth, like paintings and gold, are to high net worth households.

The Path More Traveled

Since poor people spend their money on daily living, how can they accumulate substantial wealth? In twenty-first century America, the answer is housing. People who buy homes are buying not just shelter, but also an asset, one in which they will build equity. Through the enforced savings of paying off a mortgage, homeownership can allow the poor to build assets even with little or no inflation in a home's value. But housing usually appreciates over time, matching or beating inflation, especially if a property is held long enough.

Housing has not always been seen as a vehicle for generating financial wealth. Throughout history people have prized and exchanged salt, diamonds, and even tulips, converting these items into mediums of exchange that could rise or fall in value. But houses were not bought and sold. Instead, they were inherited or eventually collapsed from neglect. Even today, in much of the world homeownership is considered socially desirable, but it is not a vehicle for wealth accumulation. For instance, poor people in Mexico own their homes, but since those homes have limited exchange value they are not assets that can be borrowed against or sold to build wealth.

A home is most definitely an asset in the United States. Home equity ranks as Americans' chief source of wealth, even among the majority of households who own stock. And as home values have risen, homeowners have drawn on the equity in their homes through refinances and home equity loans, cashing out $333 billion in this way from 2001 to 2003. Both tax-advantaged and secured by real estate, borrowing against home equity is typically much less costly than consumer credit. Owning a home, therefore, can be a path both to wealth accumulation and cheaper borrowing.

Credit for All

Just as certainly as housing is an asset in this country, it is only recently that low-income households, especially those with a history of missed payments (or worse, default), have enjoyed widespread access to the mortgage credit needed to buy homes.

Mortgages themselves are relatively new. Until the mid-nineteenth century, most home buyers paid the full cost through accumulated savings, leaving homeownership to the ranks of the wealthy or families who pooled years of savings. By the mid-twentieth century, banks opened homeownership to the middle class, launching the now classic 20 percent down, thirty-year fixed-rate mortgage. After World War II, this classic mortgage propelled thousands of families to the suburbs where they purchased capes and split-levels. Yet many low-income families (as well as a lot of middle-income families) could not afford this classic mortgage. Either the down payment or monthly payment was too high.

Just as crucial, many would-be borrowers found that their race, ethnicity, or religion restricted their choices. Lenders said no to borrowers, even solvent ones, if their skin color was wrong. Real estate agents respected "gentlemen's agreements" that restricted some neighborhoods to Christian Caucasians. With red pens, bankers drew exclusionary lines around neighborhoods, barring African American buyers. Even the Federal Housing Administration spawned restrictive covenants and redlining. This barrier to homeownership stymied the creation of wealth. Minorities and others could not buy homes and so could rarely build much wealth. It is largely due to this obstacle—as well as barriers to education, lower levels of pay for comparable levels of education, and labor-market discrimination—that the homeownership rate for minorities still stands more than 25 percentage points lower than that of whites.

Today nearly everybody, rich and poor, has access to mortgage and most other forms of credit. Now, even low-income Americans are able to buy homes with little money down, allowing them to capitalize on the substantial benefits of making a leveraged investment in an asset that is likely to appreciate in the long run. Another way to view it is that the alternative to making a 3 percent ($2,400) down payment on an $80,000 house is to invest it in stocks, bonds, or savings. Even if the home appreciates a mere 1 percent in value, in a single year the return on investment is 33 percent. And with programs now available that allow home buyers to pay only closing costs (which can be picked up by the seller), buyers can get an $800 return on no initial investment. While home buyers may be taking a risk that their house will go up in value between the time they buy and sell as well as if they can keep current on their loan, other paths to wealth accumulation are either blocked (minimum investment requirements), very risky (individual stocks whose values can rise and fall by large percentages in a single day), or very slow (low interest rates on savings accounts).

Importantly, however, access to mortgage credit is no longer on equal terms. Indeed, the world of lending has changed fundamentally over the past thirty years. From a one-size-fits-all strategy of underwriting and pricing loans—in essence offering credit only to modest, credit-worthy borrowers at a uniform price—lenders increasingly base pricing on the risk profile of applicants and now reach out to borrowers once flatly denied. The change began in the credit card industry in the mid-1970s, branched to the auto and consumer loan industry in the 1980s, and began to transform the mortgage industry by the late 1990s. Two key developments have made this industry transformation possible: the ascendance of statistical measures of past credit history (known as credit scores) and the growth of capital markets.

Long Arm of Credit Scores and Histories

Credit scores—grades on how well individuals have met their past credit obligations—are the principal reason for the growth of risk-based pricing. These scores are highly predictive of the severity and incidence of defaults. Nearly every credit decision now involves a credit score, even subtle decisions, like allowing a customer to open a checking account, which could leave a lender responsible for bounced checks. Credit scores give lenders comfort that the magnitude of the risk they are assuming is well measured and justifies a particular yield. But these scores exact a price from borrowers who do not have the established electronically documented credit histories that drive the scores. People who have not opened checking accounts, used credit cards, or obtained consumer loans are at a disadvantage in credit markets. Also at a disadvantage are those who borrow money from payday lenders or do not report to mainstream credit bureaus. And credit scores also exact a price from those who have had trouble making payments in the past.

Credit scoring relegates borrowers with tarnished credit histories to a subprime market where lenders charge higher rates to cover the added risk—and these rates are not published weekly in the newspaper, as are prime rates. Nor do disclosure regulations govern this market effectively. Only if combined rates and fees exceed a high threshold are special disclosures even required and very few practices are prohibited outright. Agents and brokers make commissions on the marketing of these mortgages and have no financial stake in the afterlife of these loans, so it does not matter if the buyer subsequently defaults. Poor people, especially minorities, often end up in the subprime market, paying more for the same mortgage than borrowers deemed more creditworthy. In low-income minority neighborhoods the subprime share of lending increased from only a few percentage points in 1993 to 13 percent of home purchase loans and 28 percent of refinanced loans in 2001.

The subprime market fills a niche, opening credit to people who might not get it otherwise. But an egregious offshoot of this market is the predatory lender, who issues mortgages at terms people cannot meet—indeed a lender who may profit when borrowers default. A foreclosure makes a mockery of the notion of a house as asset. When a lender forecloses, an owner loses any equity in the home. One particularly cruel scam depletes the equity a homeowner has amassed in the house: through home equity loans (again, available by phone), an owner ends up paying exorbitant fees and repeated refinances that escalate until the owner eventually loses the home to the lender.

Equally important, the centrality of credit scores to pricing decisions means that the long arc of past credit behavior governs access and pricing of mortgages. Hence a checking account or credit card, which electronically captures payment histories, can influence an individual's access to mortgage credit. Access is also influenced by how an individual handled past credit experiences. Therefore, success in building assets through homeownership starts long before a would-be home buyer walks in the door of a mortgage lender.

Two Faces of the Capital Markets

The second development that has transformed the world of credit is the ascendance of capital markets—markets where debts with maturities of a year or more are bought and sold. In the past, lenders held credit they extended in their own portfolios and serviced it as well. Over the past fifty years, loan originators increasingly have become separated from those ultimately investing in loans. In addition, loans have been pooled to back securities that bring added liquidity to the market. The efficiency of capital markets in matching debtors with certain risk profiles to investors with certain risk tolerances is unparalleled. But this efficiency comes at a cost: it requires heavy reliance on third-party agents to connect investors and debtors. In theory, these intermediaries work on behalf of investors and in the interests of debtors, but in reality their incentives may not be aligned with either one.

Nevertheless, a powerful aspect of the global markets that dominate modern mortgage lending is that in many respects they are blind to race, ethnicity, and religion. A neighborhood banker often no longer makes a face-to-face decision on how much to lend an applicant. Instead, the financial history of the applicant is usually fed into a computer, which renders a score that is a financial calibration of risk. Each day lenders (no longer just banks, but mortgage brokers, too) issue thousands of mortgages, which are then sold on the secondary market. Indeed, the global markets care only about risk and return, not race and religion. To the degree that the scores and other information used to underwrite loans predict risk accurately, and arrive at an interest rate that compensates investors for the level of risk assumed, investors are satisfied.

The blindness of the capital markets to much of what goes into credit decisions cuts both ways, though, as it has both positive and negative aspects. On the plus side, with the protections of better colorblind risk assessment and management tools, lenders have abandoned near-exclusive reliance on the classic 20 percent down, fixed-rate mortgage. Today, lenders offer a remarkable array of products to borrowers with a wide range of past credit histories, and even offer products to borrowers without documented credit histories. These products include: low to no down payments; adjustable-rate loans; hybrid loans that fix a rate for a number of years and then reset to current market rate; loans that require low or no documentation of income and assets; and loans that allow for larger ratios of debt to income. As a result, people with low incomes (and minimal savings) can get mortgages. People with major blemishes on their credit records can get credit. Indeed, the poor no longer face a scarcity of credit; they face a surfeit of it. With a few clicks on the computer mouse, or calls to toll-free numbers, a person can take a first step toward homeownership. Easy mortgages have made many Americans homeowners. And for most of them, homeownership has been the first step in the accumulation of genuine equity, giving them an asset to list on their balance sheet.

On the minus side of the ledger are several items that, if not addressed, could diminish the potential value brought by the revolutions in information technology and capital markets. First, investors in mortgage-backed securities are remote from the lenders or brokers that initially underwrote the loans. Thus discrimination and fraud can plague the system if investors fail to manage the risk that loan originators or servicers will not act in their interest. Second, investors do not care whether there might be better models that distinguish price risk more advantageously for low-income communities and minorities. Their main concern is whether borrowers are willing to pay mortgage interest rates that fairly compensate the investor. This can lead to charging borrowers for lax underwriting, servicing, and even fraud that suppliers may introduce into the system. As long as the borrowers are willing to cover the costs of those missteps or misdeeds in the form of interest rates and fees, investors are satisfied. Third, in a world in which mortgage products have proliferated to such a degree—and the price points for mortgages along with them—it becomes harder for consumers to know the best deal for which they qualify and easier for lenders to take advantage of this fact. Therefore, borrowers may be overcharged as a result of a lack of efficiency and accessible consumer information in the system. Furthermore, in a world in which loans have higher prices and fees than a conventional prime loan, opportunities to prey on hapless consumers mount.

As a result, not all homeowners have benefited equally (or at all) from opening the spigots of mortgage and other credit. Some owners have not been building wealth as much as they might because they are being overcharged. Others are getting credit even though they have high probabilities of missing payments and lack a safety net on which to fall back when they do. Other owners are building the asset-portfolios of an array of predatory lenders, brokers, and agents, rather than their own.

Regulation Matters

The world of lending has changed, but has the world of regulation changed with it? Without question, the legal and regulatory framework within which credit information is gathered and used, credit decisions are made, credit information is disclosed to the public, and capital flows are directed have all changed dramatically over the last half century. What is debatable is whether these regulatory changes have adequately protected consumers, educated and informed the public, and brought the greatest possible efficiency and fairness to the credit system.

Federal legislation, like the Fair Housing Act and Equal Credit Opportunity Act, barred discrimination in housing and mortgage markets. But barring discrimination by law is not the same thing as actually ending it. Signs that discrimination still exists in housing and mortgage markets are abundant. In fact, responsible banks themselves test for it in an effort to stamp it out. But some lenders, especially those not subjected to stiffer scrutiny by federal regulators, may tolerate it (or at worst, encourage it). The laws and their enforcement, though, have surely reduced discrimination. Some well-publicized lawsuits against banks in the early 1990s made bank boards recognize that it was their responsibility to better police their own organizations.

Perhaps equally important on the regulatory side have been the Home Mortgage Disclosure Act (HMDA) and Community Reinvestment Act (CRA). Together these two acts have resulted in expansion of credit to low-income and minority borrowers and communities. HMDA has demanded increasingly revealing disclosure of mortgage information from more and more types of lenders. CRA has created an affirmative obligation—and public grading—on banks and thrifts to supply mortgage credit to low-income communities. These acts armed advocates for low-income borrowers with information they could use to highlight potential problem areas in the lending practices of particular institutions and provided powerful regulatory and public relations incentives to reach out to low-income and minority markets once weakly served. To this day, the two acts are bulwarks of the new path to asset accumulation for low-income Americans. They are joined by aggressive affordable, special needs, and underserved area regulatory goals imposed by Congress on secondary mortgage market giants Fannie Mae and Freddie Mac. These regulatory goals also keep the focus on the credit needs of those borrowers who were once denied. All these regulations have seen recent changes: goals set by HUD as the mission regulators for Fannie Mae and Freddie Mac keep getting ratcheted higher; interest rates and fees, if they are over specified threshold, must now be reported under HMDA; and CRA was recently amended.

The Truth in Lending Act (TILA), Real Estate Settlements and Procedures Act (RESPA), and more recently passed Homeowners Equity Protection Act (HOEPA) are intended to provide important disclosures to borrowers in an effort to avert last-minute surprises and alert borrowers when they are getting especially high-cost mortgages. The disclosures signal greater need for caution on the part of the borrower. Of these, only HOEPA has been revised since the mid-1990s, but revisions to the others are under near-continual debate and review. The very recently revised Federal Credit Reporting Act (FCRA) is intended to ensure that credit information used to drive credit scores is accurately reported, though it does not mandate reporting by all creditors. This act has been both faulted and applauded for placing the onus on consumers for detecting and challenging credit reporting errors. Critics of the act charge it places a burden on consumers that is unfair and which they are ill-equipped to carry. Proponents counter that consumers are in the best position to judge whether credit information on them is accurate and that the system appropriately lowers costs of gathering literally billions of bits of information annually.

With predatory lending on the rise and even subprime lenders using practices that trouble many advocates, states have begun to take regulatory action in the absence of what some state legislators feel are adequate federal protections. States like North Carolina and cities like Chicago are stepping into the fray. As these laws multiply, calls mount for federal law to regulate mortgage-lending tactics more aggressively and to preempt potentially more aggressive (and certainly disparate) state laws.

Taking Stock

Against this remarkable backdrop of sweeping changes to the mortgage finance system and surging homeownership, the Joint Center for Housing Studies of Harvard University convened a conference to present new research on building assets and building credit in low-income and minority communities and among low-income and minority individuals. Researchers from across the country gathered to present papers on the extension of basic banking services and mortgage credit to low-income and minority individuals and communities. In attendance were business, government, advocacy, and community leaders. Many of them participated on panels, sharing their reactions to the new findings being presented. The healthy dialogue that ensued and its implications for business, policy, regulation, and advocacy is summarized in a proceedings produced by the center (Joint Center for Housing Studies, 2004).

The most important of these findings are found on the pages that follow in this remarkable look at the path that leads from basic banking services, to creditmaking decisions, then to mortgage lending, and at last to the chance for low-income people and communities to build assets through credit. Here we note only a few.

On the one hand, the growth of the subprime market has propelled millions of Americans into homes, and those homes are an asset. On the other hand, there are ways to steer more Americans into the prime market, as well as ways to discourage the predatory lenders.

First, the mainstream financial institutions must reach beyond middle-class depositors and investors. In 2001 almost 30 percent of poor people did not have transaction accounts (savings or checking accounts), hence the profusion of check-cashing storefront operations. Accounts give people experience with mainstream banks, and vice versa. They also allow people to save safely and establish electronic records of their payments, records that fuel the fires that stoke the credit-scoring engine that now permeates our economic lives. As many as one-third of people who borrowed from subprime lenders may have been eligible for better rates from prime lenders, suggests a somewhat dated study from the late 1990s, but the borrowers erroneously assumed that certain banks would not lend to them, so instead went to the ever-willing lender who knocked on the door or called them on the phone or sent them a compelling letter.

Second, there should be more transparency in the subprime market. Just as prime lenders publish rates and terms, we can ask the same of subprime lenders, so that the borrower can make an informed decision. Lawmakers can require brokers and agents to disclose their fees. Again, the predatory lenders are a subset of the subprime market. Transparency will highlight their scams.

Third, as a corollary to the transparency, policymakers can insist on and provide adequate funding for buyer education. There is evidence that such education, if done properly, can result in lower defaults. Yet right now the cost of providing that education is much higher than any lender has been willing to pay, even though it might ultimately pay for itself. And, the government has not helped much either. Funding for home buyer education is limited and the per-pupil amount offered is too low, even with counselors who themselves are often paid at or near a poverty wage.

Fourth, although our culture of ownership may encourage more and more Americans to trade their lease for a mortgage, without safeguards in place we may be saddling those people with more debt than they can handle. Instead of building assets, they will sink toward bankruptcy.

In sum, for most Americans homeownership constitutes a wealth-building strategy. For lower-income people, it is the only real wealth-building strategy. Right now, low-income Americans have unparalleled access to credit to buy a home. The challenge is to increase the chances that those homes become the new pathways to low-income asset building that everyone wants them to be. Low-income homeownership has been sold as a good thing to those putting their cash, homes, and credit records on the line. Let us all work to ensure that it succeeds for as many low-income Americans as possible.

2

Credit Matters: Building Assets in a Dual Financial Service System

ERIC S. BELSKY AND ALLEGRA CALDER

Since the publication in 1991 of Michael Sherraden's seminal book *Assets for the Poor,* efforts have intensified to document the extent of asset poverty and devise strategies for ameliorating it. Interest in the subject derives not only from the importance of assets to individual well-being and economic security, but also from the extreme disparities in wealth found in the United States, dispari-ties that eclipse even the wide income gaps between the rich and poor. By one measure of asset poverty, as many as 41 percent of all households in 1999 had inadequate savings or other liquid assets to cover their basic needs for three months (Caner and Wolff, 2004).[1] Among those with the lowest incomes, asset poverty is even more severe. Fully one-third of all homeowners and two-thirds of all renters in the bottom-income quintile, for example, had $500 or less in savings and other liquid assets at last measure in 2001 (see figure 2-1).

Attempts to build assets among the poor have concentrated on encouraging saving and promoting homeownership. Saving is seen as a necessary first step in building other assets and creating an individual safety net. Savings help insulate low-income households from temporary disruptions in income and spikes in expenditures, are necessary for making down payments on other assets, and

---

1. Caner and Wolff (2004) define a household (two adults and two children) as asset poor if the net worth of the current value of their marketable assets less the current value of their debts was less than $4,151. By this measure, 25.9 percent of families in 1999 were asset poor. Excluding home equity, the share rose to 40.1 percent.

Figure 2-1. *Savings and Liquid Assets of Low-Income Households, 2001*[a]

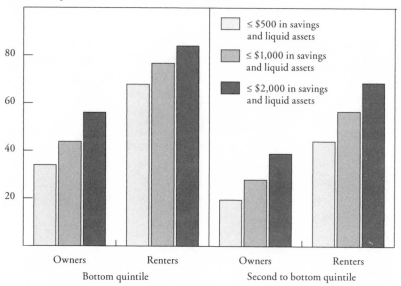

Households (percent)

Legend:
- ≤ $500 in savings and liquid assets
- ≤ $1,000 in savings and liquid assets
- ≤ $2,000 in savings and liquid assets

Owners   Renters   Owners   Renters
    Bottom quintile   Second to bottom quintile

Source: Survey of Consumer Finances (2001).
a. Liquid assets include transactions accounts, certificates of deposit, stocks, mutual funds, bonds, and savings bonds.

reduce reliance on costly short-term credit to make ends meet. Homeownership has been singled out for special attention for a variety of reasons as well. A highly leveraged investment, homeownership allows those with relatively small amounts of capital to earn large gains even if house price appreciation is only a few percentage points. Mortgage payments also constitute a form of enforced savings because a fraction of each payment goes to paying off the principal on the loan. In addition, homeownership provides opportunities to later borrow against equity at tax-advantaged and lower secured lending rates. On top of these attractions, well-situated housing can yield additional intangible benefits, such as access to jobs, better schools, and stronger social capital networks.[2]

Model of Influences on Mortgage Credit Terms

Because virtually every low-income household must borrow money to buy a home, the emphasis placed on homeownership as the foundation of low-income

2. Assets are often classified as tangible or intangible. Tangible assets are financial and durable goods such as savings, stocks, bonds, mutual funds, homes, and vehicles. Intangible assets increase access to life chances and contribute to the ability to earn income and thus acquire tangible assets. Education, work experience, and social networks are examples of such assets.

asset building elevates the importance of credit and the system by which credit risk is assessed and priced. Until the mid-1990s, the creditworthiness of mortgage loan applicants was typically assessed by a manual review of credit records supplied by one or more of the centralized credit repositories. The only applicants to receive mortgages were those who had no or only modest past repayment problems. Today, the creditworthiness of loan applicants is assessed by statistically modeling credit records and correlating the resulting scores with the likelihood and severity of default. Although credit-impaired mortgage applicants are still often rejected for lower-cost prime loan products, most can now at least qualify for higher-cost subprime products.

Mortgage credit access and pricing therefore rely on the quality of the systems that are used to collect and model credit information as well as the marketing strategies of subprime and prime lenders. In addition to these supply-side influences, credit access and pricing hinge on the capacity of low-income households to manage their finances and save despite their low incomes.

Figure 2-2 illustrates the interrelationships among incomes, assets, credit, and basic financial services. Volatility and level of household income (top left section of the figure) are important drivers of the ability to purchase a home, as well as of the credit terms for home purchase, refinance, and home equity loans (bottom section of the figure). Refracted through savings incentives, incomes influence savings and other wealth because they shape how much money remains (if any) to save or invest after expenses to cover basic needs are made.[3] Income and savings together shape demand for short- and long-term credit. The types and levels of past credit use in turn determine what information, if any, has been captured and reported to the credit repositories. Credit scores are then used alone or as part of mortgage scoring models to underwrite applications and price loans. In addition, faced with expenses that often equal or exceed their incomes, the capacity of low-income borrowers to repay loans depends to some degree on the availability of products that help them mitigate repayment risk, including savings incentives, financial education, and insurance products.

This simplified model does not cover all the influences that follow from income and savings to asset building through homeownership, such as regulations intended to ensure fair and equal access to credit. However, it does highlight some of the most important features.

Although the pathways through which income influences these outcomes are complex, the importance of loan pricing to wealth building is easily illustrated. The difference in interest paid between a 7 percent versus a 9 percent loan on a $100,000 home over 30 years is $239,825.

---

3. Though not shown in figure 2-2, additional influences on savings and wealth are intergenerational wealth transfers and the cost of outstanding credit.

Figure 2-2. *Influences on Low-Income Asset Building through Homeownership*

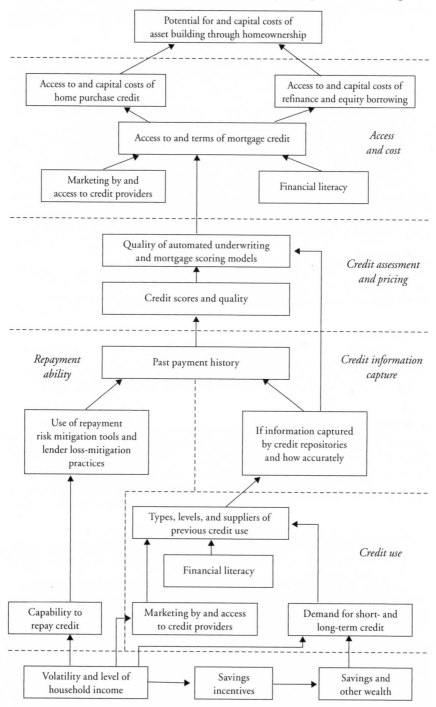

Homeownership as an Asset Building Strategy

Investing in a home is unlike investing in financial assets such as stocks and bonds. First, the costs of buying and selling homes are materially greater than the costs of trading stocks or bonds. Second, housing is a capital good that depreciates and so must be maintained. Third, housing is a necessity that must either be owned or rented while stocks and bonds are purely investments. Fourth, and perhaps most important, housing is typically a highly leveraged investment, which is not the case with stocks and bonds. As a result of these differences, investors in homes are slower to divest their homes when prices fall or better investment opportunities are perceived than are investors in financial assets. In addition, investors in homes have the opportunity to leverage small gains on their asset into large returns on their invested capital.[4] Thus while low-income home buyers place their hard-earned savings at risk, they stand to gain a great deal by investing in a home despite the fact that stocks have much lower transaction costs and may appreciate more in value than homes over longer holding periods.[5]

Among households in the lowest-income quintile, housing is second only to transaction accounts as the most commonly held appreciating asset. However, it is by far the larger of the two. Among all nonelderly (65 years of age and younger) households in this quintile, for example, the median value of transaction accounts in 2001 was $1,800, while for home equity it was $60,000. For elderly (over 65 years of age) households in this quintile, the median value of transaction accounts was $590 and of home equity was $73,000.

Homeownership rates of those in the lowest quintile lag those in the top quintile by about 40 percentage points (see figure 2-3). However, among those that do own, home equity is more important to homeowners in the lower reaches of the income distribution. Among nonelderly in the lowest quintile, home equity accounted for 78 percent of net wealth in 2001. This compares to 48 percent for homeowners in the middle quintile and 26 percent for those in

---

4. Thanks to advances in risk-assessment technology, it is now possible and common for home buyers to put as little as 3 or 5 percent down. If a borrower puts 5 percent down on a home that appreciates in value by 3 percent in a single year, the 3 percent growth will constitute a 60 percent return on invested capital.

5. A major conference held in 2001 examined the merits of low-income homeownership as a tool for asset building and catalogued the ways that low-income households can benefit from investing scarce savings in homes (Retsinas and Belsky, 2002). Homeownership promotes savings through paying down principal, allows homeowners to tap into home equity to finance other consumption and investment at lower and tax-advantaged rates, and may even improve child educational outcomes (Haurin, Parcel, and Haurin, 2002; Rohe, Van Zandt, and McCarthy, 2002). However, the conference underscored the considerable risks involved with homeownership and noted that a significant fraction of low-income homeowners would have been better off renting and investing in some other financial asset instead (Belsky and Duda, 2002; Goetzmann and Spiegel, 2002; Case and Marynchenko, 2002).

Figure 2-3. *Homeownership Rate by Race, Ethnicity, and Quintile, 2001*

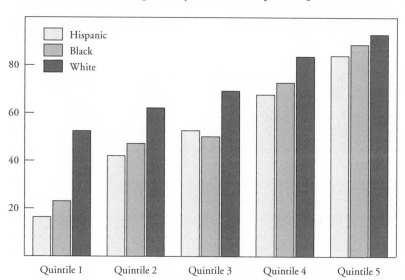

Source: Joint Center for Housing Studies tabulations of the March Current Population Surveys, 2001.

the highest quintile. Similarly, although minority homeownership rates lag those of whites, home equity accounts for a larger share of minority net wealth. For Hispanics of all incomes, home equity accounted for 63 percent of net wealth compared to 51 percent for African Americans of all incomes and 39 percent for whites of all incomes.

Portfolio Diversification Issues

While housing is an attractive investment, it is preferable to hold a diversified portfolio of assets. Controlling for income, initial wealth, and other factors, Hurst, Luoh, and Stafford (1998) found that holding a disproportionate share of wealth in home equity in 1984 reduced total wealth in 1994. Similarly, Ambrose and Goetzmann (1998) looked at low-income households in Atlanta in the 1980s and found that the optimal portfolio included no more than 35 percent allocated to housing.

While these studies confirm that a diversified portfolio is preferable to a concentrated one, for most low-income households the choice is not how much to invest in each asset, but instead whether they have enough to invest in a single asset. Low-income savers often fall short of the minimum investment requirements for stocks and bonds. Among those that could meet the minimum requirements, few would have enough left over to invest in a home as well. Furthermore, a portfolio composed primarily or entirely of individual stocks exposes households to at least as much risk as a portfolio consisting only of a

home. Finally, financial assets do not result in forced savings through amortization the way a mortgage does. Perhaps for these reasons there is no comparable
push to increase low-income households' ownership of stocks, bonds, or mutual
funds.

Asset Ownership

The difference between the net wealth and asset ownership of low- and high-
income households is stark. At just $7,900 dollars in 2001, the median net
wealth of households in the bottom-income quintile was less than one-quarter
of the $37,200 median net wealth of those in the second-lowest quintile. At
$141,500, the median net wealth of the second-highest quintile was more than
eighteen times greater than the median net wealth of the bottom quintile. At the
extreme, the median net wealth of households in the top 10 percent of the
income distribution was more than 100 times greater than that of the bottom
quintile.

Equally troubling, only 30 percent of all households in the bottom quintile
reported having saved anything in 2001. For those in the second-lowest quintile, a larger 53 percent had saved, and among those in the top 10 percent of the
income, distribution fully 84 percent had saved in 2001. Not only was the share
of households that had saved much lower in the bottom-income quintile, it was
the only quintile to register a decline in that share between 1992 and 2001
(Aizcorbe, Kennickell, and Moore, 2003). The median value of transaction
accounts among those in the lowest-income quintile was only $900 in 2001.
Among renters in the same quintile, the median amount saved was an even
lower $500. Fully 17 percent of households in the bottom-income quintile and
11 percent of households in the second-lowest-income quintile reported savings
of $200 or less. At such low levels, it is very hard for households to weather even
modest disruptions in incomes or budget shocks.

It is best to evaluate elderly and nonelderly households separately when
examining household asset ownership by income because they have distinctly
different propensities to own assets and carry debts. While further subdividing
by age results in very small sample sizes, it is clear that ownership of all assets is
lower for younger adults in the bottom-income quintile than for middle-aged
households (see table 2-1).

Minorities in the lowest-income quintile have much lower rates of asset ownership than whites in the same quintile. For example, among all minority households
in the lowest-income quintile in 2001, only 55 percent had transaction accounts,
21 percent owned homes, and 8 percent had retirement accounts. Among whites
in the lowest-income quintile, 80 percent had transaction accounts, 53 percent
owned homes, and 15 percent had retirement accounts. Ownership rates of stocks,
savings bonds, and mutual funds among minorities in 2001 were half that of

Table 2-1. Ownership of Nonfinancial Assets

Percent of households holding the asset

Household type	Vehicles		Primary residence		Other residential property		Equity in nonresidential property		Business equity		Other		Any nonfinancial asset		Any asset	
	1989	2001	1989	2001	1989	2001	1989	2001	1989	2001	1989	2001	1989	2001	1989	2001
Households aged less than 66																
Quintile 1	53.13	55.67	22.07	27.79	3.4	2.22	2.5	2.1	3.34	3.5	5.5	3.47	60.01	63.57	72.04	79.87
Quintile 2	79.71	87.18	40.89	54.6	4.93	3.29	5.87	5.1	10.31	8.45	6.51	5.58	82.05	91.2	92.3	97.62
Quintile 3	94.96	91.4	59.76	61.09	7.38	5.89	8.56	4.78	9.42	9.11	12.19	4.39	97.1	95.21	99.93	99.9
Quintile 4	96.37	95.22	74.72	79.94	14.3	12.77	12.3	6.09	12.67	12.25	15.4	8.08	97.51	97.58	99.4	100
Quintile 5	96.01	94.37	90.1	92.06	25.98	24.26	22.12	16.88	25.08	27.83	19.21	12.14	99.08	99.48	99.99	100
Households aged more than 65																
Quintile 1	47.19	56.27	53.28	60.74	4.62	4.88	1.98	4.24	0.37	0.45	4.42	1.32	72.97	72.75	90.49	93
Quintile 2	83.08	83.61	79.1	86	9.55	10.72	11.1	9.92	3.27	3.47	10.69	5.98	96.55	95.63	99.65	99.54
Quintile 3	93.68	89.08	90.1	84.4	29.5	14.8	15.04	14.26	8.54	7.35	7.93	8.7	97.83	95.91	100	99
Quintile 4	81.85	92.51	86.33	94.47	27.28	22.96	20.39	10.46	10.81	9.03	16	13.46	94.89	99.05	100	100
Quintile 5	97.93	90.48	87.76	93	47.51	40.53	31.82	25.27	31.94	32.46	29.07	20.98	99.35	98.69	100	100
Whites																
Quintile 1	61.83	66.25	41.77	52.39	5.54	4.94	2.66	3.89	4.03	2.96	7.35	4.23	75.77	80.22	91.16	93.8
Quintile 2	85.88	90.37	60.72	62.12	6.97	6.5	8.64	7.9	8.27	9.11	9.77	6.61	92.2	95.24	97.78	99.28
Quintile 3	95.63	92.43	66.57	69.27	11.78	8.57	10.93	7.3	9.59	10.05	13.55	5.98	97.53	95.96	100	100
Quintile 4	94.71	94.81	77.11	83.63	16.15	14.14	12.9	7.04	13.29	12.54	14.79	9.51	97.6	97.81	99.79	100
Quintile 5	95.99	94.2	90.96	92.92	27.89	26.19	23.15	18.44	27.04	29.67	21.72	14.23	98.99	99.44	99.99	100
Minorities																
Quintile 1	40.57	40.78	23.57	21.04	2.11	0.61	2	1.38	0.66	1.59	2.95	0.46	53.15	47.4	65.55	71.16
Quintile 2	67.4	75.25	37.63	56	5.51	2.66	5.28	2.82	6.53	1.62	3.2	3.33	73.68	85.32	87.16	95.3
Quintile 3	91.33	85.5	59.59	49.55	9.4	3.18	5.05	3.18	8.05	4	3.42	1.98	96.11	92.93	99.73	98.77
Quintile 4	95.59	95.05	70.46	74.15	13.36	14.17	14.27	5.04	8.71	8.59	18.57	5.62	95.59	97.67	97.91	100
Quintile 5	97.89	92.06	81.13	87.07	29.83	25.56	22.52	13.76	15.58	19.54	7.94	5.84	100	99.04	100	100

Source: Joint Center for Housing Studies tabulations of the 1989 and 2001 Surveys of Consumer Finances.

a. Other includes artwork, jewelry, precious metal, antiques, hobby equipment and collectibles.

whites in the same quintile.[6] By contrast, much larger shares of higher-income households own assets of all kinds. Although ownership rates of other financial assets remain low in the second-lowest quintile, they are still multiples higher than those of the lowest quintile. Not surprisingly, middle- and higher-income quintile households have even higher ownership rates of all assets.

Financial Assets

Ownership of financial assets is critical to overall wealth building. Transaction accounts provide a secure place to save, modest returns, and a way to document and make payments. Other financial assets like retirement accounts, stocks, bonds, and mutual funds offer the potential for appreciation on invested capital. In most cases, the risks as well as the achievable returns on such investments are far greater than on savings and money market accounts. But like savings accounts they provide a cushion against income and budget shocks because they can either be liquidated or borrowed against. And, they can help build up enough value to cover the costs of buying a home and reduce the capital costs of ownership by increasing the down payment amount.

A much larger share of low-income households have transaction accounts than any other financial asset. Furthermore, as a result of the expanded use of electronic payments for welfare and other federal benefits programs (Hogarth and O'Donnell, 1999), the share increased from 1989 to 2001 (see table 2-2).

This encouraging growth means that a greater share of lowest-income households has the opportunity to earn interest on their savings and use mainstream methods to make and receive payments.

Mutual fund, stock, bond, and retirement account ownership among all households has increased as well. Direct stock ownership, at 21 percent, surpassed mutual fund ownership in 2001, but was up by only 5 percentage points from 1989. While stock ownership is becoming the norm at the upper end of the income distribution, it remains an anomaly at the bottom. The same holds true for bonds and savings bonds, which are as uncommon as stocks among those in the lowest-income quintile.

Since retirement accounts are often included as an employment benefit, a larger share of households of all incomes holds them than stocks, bonds, and mutual funds.[7] That said, according to Aizcorbe, Kennickell, and Moore (2003), 26 percent of families who were eligible to participate in a job-related defined contribution pension plan failed to do so. Among families in the lowest-income quintile, the failure rate was a significantly higher 46 percent.

6. The higher incidence of asset ownership among whites in the lowest quintile reflects, to a certain extent, their older average age.

7. Retirement accounts include IRA, Keogh, 401k, and 403b. They do not include any employer-sponsored benefit plans that are not portable. Social Security and employer-sponsored defined benefit plans are not included.

Table 2-2. *Ownership of Financial Assets*

Percent of households holding the asset

Household type	Transaction accounts		CD		Savings bonds		Bonds		Stocks		Mutual funds		Retirement accounts		Life insurance		Any financial asset	
	1989	2001	1989	2001	1989	2001	1989	2001	1989	2001	1989	2001	1989	2001	1989	2001	1989	2001
Households aged less than 66																		
Quintile 1	45.2	61.63	4.69	4.66	4.6	3.68	0.05	0.26	2.1	4.06	0.61	2.88	5.08	13.17	10.03	11.86	51.84	67.04
Quintile 2	74.48	85.87	9.39	6.04	13.37	9.78	0.82	0.28	5.66	8.47	1.01	6.11	15.8	33.96	17.23	18.59	82.51	90.38
Quintile 3	91.62	95.17	15.38	10.07	24.01	14.15	2.98	1.04	10.79	13.64	4.99	12.84	40.56	53.67	34.42	24.05	95.43	97.87
Quintile 4	97.21	98.64	17.25	12.95	35.29	24.26	2.68	2.27	15.65	22.91	4.51	18.64	52.27	75.74	48.11	31.35	98.53	99.67
Quintile 5	98.7	99.68	25.76	18.03	42.05	31.33	12.71	7.28	39.43	48.64	17.45	37.62	75.93	88.1	56.08	38.18	99.77	99.72
Households aged more than 65																		
Quintile 1	73.51	84.84	12.05	17.85	4.01	3.79	0.31	0.41	1.26	2.75	1.29	4.63	2.42	11.46	19.26	15.02	77.97	86.37
Quintile 2	95.83	96.92	42.2	38.22	15.04	12.95	4.41	3.06	15.95	16.15	5.36	14.53	15.35	28.38	41.78	39.24	96.83	98.22
Quintile 3	97.36	98.59	53.97	50.72	28.91	12.4	8.07	2.97	19.99	28.35	13.14	29.33	26.04	43.01	34.16	35.51	97.36	98.82
Quintile 4	100	99.17	49.08	35.47	35.97	22.56	30.45	11.16	45.67	44.07	31.92	33.17	48.45	66.31	45.32	59.59	100	99.47
Quintile 5	100	98.02	46.28	34.34	24.4	19.56	50.63	17.59	56.46	48.27	31.25	44.75	57.18	69.95	48.33	54.04	100	100
Whites																		
Quintile 1	74.52	80.27	13.99	13.98	7.58	4.62	0.07	0.42	3.26	4.45	1.61	5.09	5.1	15.6	17.13	13.23	78.91	83.14
Quintile 2	88.06	93.03	26.95	19.32	16.41	13.2	2.83	1.45	12.12	13.4	3.5	10.88	19.23	34.3	30.98	25.58	93.24	96.01
Quintile 3	93.53	97.01	27.06	19.78	26.14	15.85	4.41	1.74	13.99	18.08	7.96	17.67	40.5	52.72	35.74	25.6	96.39	98.85
Quintile 4	98.49	99.43	22.73	17.89	37.62	25.73	6.51	3.93	20.97	26.85	8.95	21.66	55.03	75.98	47.9	36.74	99.47	99.91
Quintile 5	99.08	99.52	29.41	19.92	41.51	31.27	17.74	9.5	43.8	49.76	20.03	41.05	75.65	86.66	55.95	40.89	99.76	99.82
Minorities																		
Quintile 1	35.27	54.96	0.46	2.74	1.26	2.42	0.21	0.15	0.39	2.32	0.08	1.21	3.28	8.13	9.22	12.65	42.68	60.67
Quintile 2	65.84	78.73	5.17	4.88	7.32	4.21	0.12	0.11	1.72	3.65	0	2.46	5.85	27.33	12.4	21.79	72.31	83.91
Quintile 3	89.23	91.02	3.72	7.38	20.07	6.16	1.86	0	6.43	9.14	0.58	8.35	28.49	48.26	29.22	27.83	93.39	94.89
Quintile 4	92.87	95.49	10.5	7.5	24.85	16.44	1.22	1.4	8.58	20.92	0	15.85	37.21	67.69	47.42	28.08	95.04	98.43
Quintile 5	96.8	99.28	14.85	19.64	30.71	21.36	6.21	1.39	19.72	40.74	9.08	20.7	61.57	81.78	50.25	33.84	100	99.28

Source: JCHS tabulations of the 1989 and 2001 Surveys of Consumer Finances.

Note: Any financial asset includes other managed and other.

In sum, apart from transaction accounts, low-income ownership of financial assets is very limited, especially among low-income minorities. Since four in ten lowest-quintile households and nearly half of minorities in that quintile lack even a basic transaction account, there are few opportunities to earn a return on savings or use checks to settle financial transactions.

Credit Utilization

While borrowing money to buy a home is generally seen as necessary and appropriate, the merits of borrowing to finance other forms of consumption are still debated. Some view buying on credit as undisciplined and risky since people often borrow ahead of their capacity to repay debt. Indeed, concern over the rise in personal bankruptcies has led some to conclude that credit is too widely available. According to the American Bankruptcy Institute, personal bankruptcy filings totaled 1.6 million for fiscal year 2003, up 7.8 percent from fiscal year 2002.[8]

However, as Calder (2002) pointed out, taking on debt and making regular monthly payments require discipline. Months or years of regular payments tend to impose a restraint that overrides rampant buy now, pay later consumerism. And, debt can be used to smooth consumption expenditures over one's life cycle, especially during a period of unemployment or to cover an unforeseen expense. Since many households can expect their incomes to grow over time, debt can be a way to begin to build assets earlier in life.

Consumer credit can be a fiscally responsible way to finance consumption but it can also lead to credit problems if the cost of debt overwhelms the ability to repay it. Thus whether individuals borrow, from where they borrow, and whether they are able to make regular payments all influence opportunities to finance subsequent consumption and investment.

Consumer Credit

Disparities in consumer credit use between highest-income and lowest-income quintile households, though large, are not as large as the disparities in their ownership of financial assets. Twice as many highest-quintile households have consumer credit as lowest-quintile households, five times as many of them have retirement accounts, and ten times as many have mutual funds and stocks. Low-income households may have a harder time managing consumer debt due to their lower incomes, but they often need to borrow to purchase goods or meet basic needs. Installment loans and credit cards are each used by about one-third of nonelderly households in the lowest-income quintile (see table

8. See "Personal Bankruptcy Filings Continue to Break Records" (www.abiworld.org/ release/3Q2003.html [November 14, 2003]).

2-3).[9] Unlike asset ownership in which minorities clearly lag whites, credit utilization is modestly higher for minority households. The share of all households in the lowest-income quintile with credit card balances has grown since 1989. The share with outstanding installment loans in the bottom quintile, however, has declined. Similar patterns of rapidly expanding credit card use and modestly declining installment loan use are found among those in the second-lowest-income quintile as well.

A recent study by Demos (Draut and Silva, 2003) found that average credit card debt of families in 2001 was $4,126, up from $2,697 (in 2001 dollars) in 1989. Families earning less than $10,000 a year experienced a 184 percent increase in average credit card debt. Using data from the 1999 Consumer Expenditure Survey, the authors concluded that the rise in debt is not simply a result of overspending. They found that families earning less than $10,000 a year spend, on average, 70 percent of their budget on food and housing, which often means that credit cards are used to cover life basics such as health care costs, transportation, or clothing.[10]

Alternative Credit Providers

The Survey of Consumer Finances does not specifically query respondents about their use of payday lenders, pawnbrokers, or rent-to-own shops. However, other data suggest that these alternative forms of credit are used more often by lower-income households than others and that branches tend to be concentrated in low-income and particularly minority communities (Fishbein and Goldberg, 2003; Richter and Tan, 2002; Carr and Schuetz, 2001). Payday lenders advance credit to borrowers to help bridge the gap between when the borrowers are paid and when their bills come due. Though virtually nonexistent ten years ago, there are now estimated to be as many as 14,000 outlets across the country (Stegman and Faris, 2003). In a typical transaction, the borrower writes the lender a check (or agrees to an automatic debit from an existing account) for the amount to be borrowed plus any fees in exchange for the cash. Next payday, the borrower can either pay cash and redeem the check, allow the check to be cashed, or pay another fee to extend the loan.

The average amount borrowed from payday lenders is around $300, suggesting that consumers use these loans for very short-term credit needs. Caskey (2002a) cited annualized interest rates on payday loans of generally over 100 percent and often as high as 500 percent, while the National Consumer Law

9. In the Survey of Consumer Finances installment loans are defined as consumer loans that typically have fixed payments and terms, such as automobile loans, student loans, and loans for appliances, furniture, and other durable goods.

10. The Demos study showed credit card debt for all families declined between 1998 and 2001, which may be consistent with the finding that families have taken on more home-secured debt through cash-out refinancing and home equity lines of credit.

Table 2-3. *Debt Utilization by Quintile*
Percent of households holding debt

Household type	Home-secured 1989	Home-secured 2001	Other residential property 1989	Other residential property 2001	Installment loans 1989	Installment loans 2001	Credit card balance 1989	Credit card balance 2001	Other lines of credit 1989	Other lines of credit 2001	Other 1989	Other 2001	Any debt 1989	Any debt 2001
Households aged less than 66														
Quintile 1	7.79	14.28	1.17	0.3	42.83	35.44	10.36	33.51	1.07	2	9.08	7.38	52.97	57.04
Quintile 2	26.75	28.93	1.65	1.9	52.45	50.38	32.23	51.8	2.9	2.36	6.34	6.14	71.91	80.36
Quintile 3	41.35	47.74	3.28	2.89	60.38	57.67	54.04	56.98	1.98	1.32	5.15	8.29	85.59	88.35
Quintile 4	59.52	66.29	5.45	5.63	69.16	63.34	61.89	56.49	4.8	1.84	6.26	7.98	92.26	90.86
Quintile 5	77.45	80.55	15.31	12.45	61.01	53.09	54.04	45.63	7.4	2.06	11.53	9.5	94.94	92.56
Households aged more than 65														
Quintile 1	7.23	10.86	0	0.7	13.33	8.43	24.41	22.76	0.52	0	0.1	3.24	35.76	33.59
Quintile 2	15.72	18.59	0.15	1.28	18	22	19.36	25.42	0	0	2.19	4.88	35.73	43.37
Quintile 3	21.46	22.42	4.51	3.86	23.8	17.93	24.17	29.69	0	0.94	3.47	3.69	42.61	46.51
Quintile 4	19.56	32.34	8.01	2.71	10.51	14.9	6.2	24.78	0.34	0.03	3.01	4.31	28.5	50.95
Quintile 5	25.87	40.23	12.25	10.2	15.85	16.35	15.05	16.62	3	0.98	11.3	6.95	52.69	56.77
Whites														
Quintile 1	10.81	14.39	1.57	0.74	32.01	23.67	16.96	29.32	0.6	1.47	5.86	5.46	48.61	46.96
Quintile 2	22.32	26	1.21	1.97	37.68	42.47	28.71	44.21	1.65	2.13	6.19	6.48	56.2	69.68
Quintile 3	36.03	44.1	3.54	3.76	53.59	51.97	45.06	50.2	1.79	1.4	5.34	7.04	74.66	79.8
Quintile 4	54.52	61.41	5.95	5.13	59.72	53.97	55.91	49.98	4.36	1.65	6.11	8.05	83.12	83.79
Quintile 5	72.74	75.88	13.91	12.33	54.85	47.25	48.76	38.81	5.38	1.78	11.21	9.2	90.05	87.72
Minorities														
Quintile 1	4.43	11.09	0	0	33.72	28.72	13.28	30.12	1.16	1.01	6.23	6.51	45.72	51
Quintile 2	24.16	25.85	0.83	1.08	46.92	41.56	24.72	44.24	2.44	0.53	1.24	3.97	66.63	69.83
Quintile 3	44.72	40.18	3.34	0.38	55.22	45.77	62.84	59.8	1.04	0.67	2.98	9.16	90.73	85.57
Quintile 4	59.25	63.02	4.64	5.73	78.53	69.47	56.94	62.2	4.22	1.36	5.04	4.94	97.25	93.02
Quintile 5	69.26	76.49	23.74	11.29	70.12	60.17	61.59	66.14	19.59	3	13.83	9.28	96.44	93.63

Source: Joint Center for Housing Studies tabulations of the Survey of Consumer Finances.

a. Other debt includes loans on insurance policies, loans against pension accounts, borrowing on margin accounts, and a residual category for all loans not explicitly referenced elsewhere.

Center found rates as high as 7,300 percent (Renuart, 2002). Clearly, use of payday loans, especially if not promptly repaid, reduces surplus income and inhibits savings and asset building.

Relatively little is known about the payday lending industry. There are no national studies of the factors driving the use of payday lenders or of where payday-lending establishments are located.[11] However, there have been a few studies that profile payday lending customers, examine the industry, and summarize relevant state laws and regulations (Elliehausen and Lawrence, 2001; Fox, 2003; Stegman and Faris, 2003).

Pawnshops offer short-term loans in exchange for personal items that are held as collateral. Carr and Schuetz (2001) reported that monthly interest rates are subject to state law and range from 1.5 to 25 percent, while annualized rates range from 30 to 300 percent. The authors estimated that pawnshops generate 42 million transactions a year and gross revenues of $3.3 billion. Gaberlavage and Hermanson (2001) reported that the majority of pawnshop loans are for $150 or less and the maturity is generally one to three months, with 80 percent of items eventually redeemed.

Rent-to-own stores extend credit to consumers for durables such as appliances, electronics, or home furnishings. Consumers make weekly or monthly payments that can be put toward ownership. This form of purchasing typically ends up costing the consumer two to three times as much as retail, and failure to pay at any point before the full purchase can result in repossession. Carr and Schuetz (2001) estimated the annual volume of transactions for rent-to-own shops to be about 3 million, with $4.7 billion in gross revenues and $2.4 billion in fees.

Although payday lenders, pawnshops, and rent-to-own stores give credit constrained consumers easy access to cash, consumers pay much higher rates for credit than is typical of institutions that take deposits and credit card companies, and timely payments are typically not reported to one of the credit repositories (Gaberlavage and Hermanson 2001).[12]

Mortgage Credit

Among a representative random sample of home buyers in 2000 and 2001 canvassed by the American Housing Survey of 2001, fully 77 percent of all home buyers and 70 percent of low-income home buyers took out a mortgage to purchase their home.[13] Before the mid-1990s, prime mortgage lenders supplied vir-

---

11. Elliehausen and Lawrence (2001) used a nationally representative sample of customers from nineteen member companies of the Community Financial Services Association. However, no information was provided on the geographic distribution of the companies.

12. Many payday lenders voluntarily report to an alternative credit repository called Teletrack (www.teletrack.com).

13. Low income is defined as an income of 80 percent or less of area median for a family of four, adjusted for household size.

tually all mortgage credit. Over the last decade, however, subprime mortgage originations have increased from around $20 billion in 1993 to $332 billion in 2003. Low-income and minority communities now have much higher shares of subprime, manufactured home, and government-insured loans than higher-income and predominately white communities. Immergluck and Wiles (1999) characterized the tendency for conventional lenders to serve higher-income white areas and other lenders to serve lower-income and minority communities as a "dual mortgage market."

Without question, subprime and alternative lenders have greatly expanded credit to borrowers and neighborhoods that were previously denied. However, the National Community Reinvestment Coalition (2003, p. 4) asserted "that a lack of product choice confronts too many women, minorities, and low- and moderate-income communities across America."

In contrast to studies of basic financial service provision, which have relied primarily on household surveys with relatively small sample sizes, mortgage credit studies can draw on millions of loans reported under the Home Mortgage Disclosure Act (HMDA). Access to HMDA data spawned a host of credit flow studies in the 1980s that suggested that race and income were indeed associated with lower levels of credit than might otherwise be expected given the number of owned homes in the census tract (Bradbury, Case, and Dunham, 1989).[14] With the release of information on the income and minority status of loan applicants in the early 1990s, a second wave of studies to test for discrimination in the mortgage lending process was released, many of which offered compelling evidence of a dual mortgage market (Carr and Megbolugbe, 1993; Immergluck and Wiles, 1999; U.S. Department of the Treasury, 2000; Bradford, 2002).

Debate continues over whether research using HMDA data alone or in combination has conclusively demonstrated that discrimination was or is occurring in mortgage markets, either against individual applicants or whole communities (Turner and Skidmore, 1999). However, attention has shifted away from whether adequate levels of credit are supplied to the prices and terms upon which they are supplied and which financial institutions provide them.

Explaining Disparities in Financial Service Provision

The apparent differences in the types of financial institutions that supply consumer credit in low-income communities, higher costs associated with using alternative credit financial services, and large share of low-income households who are unbanked have spawned a search for explanations. Although there are

14. For a good discussion of the earlier studies see Hula (1991) and Shlay, Goldstein, and Bartlett (1992).

several plausible reasons for the differences, the extent to which one or more reasons plays a defining role has not been determined.

Demand-Side Explanations

Faced with choices of providers and products that are shaped at least in part by where they live, the following are some of the reasons why low-income people may choose to remain unbanked or use alternative providers (namely, check cashers, pawnbrokers, rent-to-own stores, subprime lending specialists, and payday lenders) more extensively.

LOWER COST OF ALTERNATIVE PROVIDERS. If the services available from mainstream institutions (namely, institutions that take deposits, and prime-lending finance and credit card specialists) are more expensive, the cost-minimizing solution for some low-income households with infrequent financial transactions may be to use check cashers and payday lenders (Dunham, 2001; Hogarth and O'Donnell, 1999). Dunham, for example, looked at the cost to the unbanked of cashing checks and found that 52 percent incurred no costs because many supermarkets and issuing banks charge no fee to cash a check. Another 18 percent paid less than $50 a year to cash checks, and the remaining 30 percent paid over $50 annually. Dunham also examined the annual costs of using money orders and found that 12 percent of users had no annual costs, 68 percent paid up to $49, 14 percent spent between $50 and $99, and 4 percent spent over $100. Since banks now charge as much as $35 for a bounced check, households that have trouble managing their budgets may benefit from using money orders to make payments.

ALTERNATIVE PROVIDERS: GREATER ACCESS AND BETTER SERVICE. Consumers may choose higher-cost alternative providers on the basis of service or convenience, or both. Many alternative providers operate outside of regular business hours, simplify loan approval, have multilingual representatives, or create an environment that is welcoming in other respects (Fishbein and Goldberg, 2003; Carr and Schuetz, 2001). Subprime lenders, for example, offer faster and easier loan approvals than many of the loan programs that serve low-income borrowers. In addition, many subprime lenders make widespread use of direct marketing techniques such as mailings and phone solicitations, and even door-to-door sales.

INTEREST IN CONDUCTING ONLY CASH TRANSACTIONS. Some individuals, regardless of income, may prefer not to conduct transactions that are electronically captured by third parties. Some consumers deal primarily or completely with vendors, service providers, or landlords who demand cash as payment, obviating the need for a transaction account. Others may have undocumented income that they want to remain that way. Richter and Tan (2002) pointed out that alternative financial providers have more flexible identification requirements, which appeal to many low-income borrowers, particularly illegal immigrants.

NEGATIVE PAST EXPERIENCE WITH MAINSTREAM PROVIDERS. Some consumers may view mainstream financial service providers with suspicion because of past patterns of discrimination, or in the case of immigrants, experience with banks in their nation of origin (Richter and Tan, 2002). Indeed, the number of families citing "do not like dealing with banks" as the reason they do not hold a checking account in the Survey of Consumer Finances increased from 15 percent in 1992 to 23 percent in 2001 (Aizcorbe, Kennickell, and Moore, 2003).

LOWER CAPACITY TO SAVE. An obvious reason that some low-income customers do not have a bank account is that they have no savings (Caskey, 2002a). Evidence from the Survey of Consumer Finances showed that in 2001, 14 percent of those without a checking account cited "do not have enough money" as the primary reason (Aizcorbe, Kennickell, and Moore, 2003). Low incomes and few incentives to save may lead lower-income households to conclude that they have no use for a bank account. In addition, some cash-strapped homeowners are motivated to tap into their home equity even if it requires working with a subprime lender in a cash-out refinance or second mortgage loan.

LOWER CREDIT SCORES. Although evidence suggests that credit scores are not materially correlated with income, they are correlated with race and ethnicity. And since minorities are overrepresented among low-income individuals, a larger share of low-income households has lower credit scores than higher-income ones. As noted, many banks and thrifts use credit scores to qualify customers for savings and checking accounts. Caskey (2002b) pointed out that households with credit history or past payment problems often have few options for small (up to $500) loans to cover immediate cash needs and consequently turn to check cashers, payday lenders, rent-to-own shops, and pawnbrokers. Lower credit scores also leave some potential home buyers or home equity borrowers without access to a prime conventional loan.

IMPERFECT INFORMATION. Some low-income consumers may not realize that they qualify for lower-cost products. This may result from misinformation, more aggressive marketing by subprime and alternative consumer credit providers, or the failure of mainstream financial institutions to promote the basic products they do offer (Goldstein, 1999; Hogarth and O'Donnell, 1999). Hilgert, Hogarth, and Beverly (2003) found that experience, friends and family, and the media were the main sources for financial knowledge for all households. It can be difficult for even the most financially savvy borrower to compare mortgage products across providers and evaluate the best combination of points and fees. Even more worrisome, there is evidence that some financial servicers intentionally obfuscate fees and costs, or engage in predatory practices such as fraudulent or high-pressure marketing or packing unnecessary fees into loans (Goldstein, 1999; Renuart, 2002). Consumers may be easy prey. A Fannie Mae (2001, p. 12) survey of credit-impaired borrowers found that nearly one-third "of credit-impaired homeowners said that when they were negotiating their mortgage they did not care whether they received the lowest-cost loan for which they were qualified." This suggests that while it may not be rational, getting a yes is often the most important consideration.

Supply-Side Explanations

There are also a variety of reasons why mainstream financial service providers might not serve lower-income customers or communities to the degree that they serve other markets, as explained below.

RESPONSE TO CONSUMER DEMAND. Mainstream service providers may not serve low-income markets as much because demand for their products in these markets is lower. For example, the larger presence of subprime lenders and loans in low-income communities may simply reflect higher concentrations of households with low credit scores. However, few studies have actually tested this theory. After controlling for credit history, demographics, and location of borrowers, Pennington-Cross, Yezer, and Nichols (2000) found that subprime home purchase lending was less concentrated in underserved areas or areas with low-income borrowers. Immergluck and Wiles (1999), however, concluded that the racial disparities in mortgage lending in Chicago were too great to be explained by the difference in the credit quality of the borrowers. Disentangling whether lower levels of mainstream financial service provision in low-income communities merely reflects demand is difficult because providers choose what types of products they offer and where, while consumers are limited to the choices offered. Because supply and demand are simultaneously determined, it is difficult to judge whether providers do not offer certain products because there is insufficient demand, it is simply not profitable, they have imperfect information, or for other reasons.

LOWER PROFITABILITY. Serving low-income markets may not be the highest and best use of capital for institutions that take deposits and prime lenders. Caskey (2002a) pointed out that some banks only operate unprofitable branches in lower-income communities to receive credit from regulators examining banks for compliance with the Community Reinvestment Act. The smaller size of transactions and account balances of lower-income customers may lead mainstream providers to overlook profitable opportunities because higher returns can be earned elsewhere. The fixed costs of attracting and servicing customers may discourage lenders from reaching out to low-income and low-wealth customers who have fewer transactions and fewer relationships (hence opportunities to cross market products) with the bank, thrift, or credit union.

IMPERFECT INFORMATION. Although low-income individuals may be less profitable, it may also be the case that lenders are operating with faulty or incomplete information. Indeed, the basic banking demands of low-income customers and segmentation of the low-income market are poorly understood (Dunham, 2001). Lenders may respond to miscues that, in the absence of good information, cause them to be overly cautious in reaching out to low-income consumers.

COMPETITIVE DISADVANTAGES. If low-income customers are unprofitable for deposit-taking institutions, yet profitable for alternative providers, the question arises as to whether mainstream providers are at some disadvantage relative to alternative providers. Indeed, one reason cited for the recent interest of mainstream financial institutions and their holding companies in alternative products and relationships with alternative providers is that they perceive attractive margins do exist (Fishbein and Goldberg, 2003; Consumer Federation of America and the National Consumer Law Center, 2003). We were unable to identify any literature that seriously evaluates whether alternative providers have some form of competitive advantage.

DISCRIMINATION. Despite theoretical arguments as to whether discrimination should exist in a perfectly competitive market, evidence suggests that it does (Turner and Skidmore, 1999). A recent study of mortgage discrimination by the Urban Institute demonstrated different treatment of white and minority testers (Turner and others, 2002). Many researchers are increasingly concerned with the apparent targeting of low-income, and especially low-income minority, communities by subprime lenders using aggressive and sometimes predatory lending practices (Goldstein, 1999; Gaberlavage and Hermanson, 2001; Renuart, 2002; Fishbein and Goldberg, 2003).

Accurate Explanations Matter

Greater clarity as to which of the above explanations are valid is a precondition for the development of sound public and business policy. Incentives may be required to overcome structural impediments to saving or to serving low-income customers profitably. Other explanations suggest increased regulation is an important part of any solution. If, for example, imperfect information is a problem, regulations to encourage collective action by mainstream financial service providers to improve information make sense. Indeed, this was one of the rationales for the Community Reinvestment Act (Litan and others, 2000). If imperfect information on the part of consumers is a problem, expanded disclosure regulations may be warranted. If competitive disadvantages result from variation in regulation across financial service providers, then greater uniformity of regulation may be a desirable goal. Discrimination and predatory lending suggest expanded enforcement, stiffer penalties, or both may be in order.

Credit Risk Evaluation and Pricing System

Information technology has transformed the credit risk evaluation process. In the 1960s and 1970s, loan underwriters manually reviewed information on loan activity and repayment histories. If any of the information suggested that an applicant's past behavior fell below a lender's standards, the loan was denied. Compensating factors, such as the size of the down payment or stability of employment, were considered at the discretion of individual underwriters.

Today, expanded information on loan activity and repayment history is statistically modeled to predict probabilities and severities of loan losses. Variables on race, ethnicity, religion, gender, and national origin are expressly prohibited from such models. That said, many of the variables in scoring models are correlated with race and ethnicity. Therefore, the application of these models has disparate effects. Loan applicants are assigned credit scores that reflect the predicted risk of delinquencies and defaults. In some cases, the score alone is reason to accept or reject a loan applicant. In other cases, the score is one of several inputs in a statistical model tailored to correlate credit scores with loss probabilities and severities in a particular application, such as mortgage lending. Finally, the scores themselves can be customized to specific loan types or borrower populations so that they reflect what matters most to repayment behavior in specific contexts.

Despite the widespread use of credit scores to evaluate credit card applications, credit scores were rarely used in the mortgage lending industry before 1995. After Fannie Mae and Freddie Mac began requiring their sellers to submit a credit score, the use of credit scores expanded rapidly. As in the credit card industry, access to past credit payment histories on literally millions of individuals allowed mortgage lenders to begin to price for risk rather than simply reject loan applicants that did not meet very high credit standards. Many lenders used the new technology to make more sensitive and statistically informed accept or reject decisions within the traditional prime market of low credit risk borrowers. Other lenders have used the models to specialize in extending subprime credit, others to affiliate with subprime institutions, and others to extend credit across a range of risk grades. The capital markets have also been quick to adopt credit scores. Reliant on the information supplied by lenders, those that bundle and price mortgage pools often use credit scores to set minimum standards for loans they will accept into a pool or to establish concentration guidelines by risk levels.

Now that credit scores influence so many aspects of consumer life, attention to the system by which credit information is collected, reported, scored, and used in underwriting and pricing decisions has increased.

Credit Reporting and Quality

Credit scores are based on information that is reported on a voluntary basis with limited regulatory proscription and oversight. Currently, 190-200 million consumers have credit reports on file at one of the three major repositories: Experian, Equifax, and Trans Union. Reporting is voluntary and many firms, such as small-scale retailers, mortgage and finance companies, and smaller government agencies do not report at all. Nevertheless, both positive and negative credit information is increasingly captured and used to make decisions about creditworthiness. As Fishelson-Holstine points out in chapter 8, in many other countries shared credit data are limited to negative information on past payment problems. Failure to report positive information deprives scoring models of information that can distinguish between borrowers with derogatory information that are more likely to repay loans in the future from those less likely to do so.

In addition to incomplete coverage of firms, the quality, completeness, and timeliness of information supplied to credit bureaus is uneven. In part, this reflects inevitable errors in electronically recording and transferring literally billions of bits of information on hundreds of millions of individuals. But it also may reflect the fact that some lenders have a disincentive to report information that they think gives them a competitive advantage (positive payment histories of individuals with low credit scores for example) and because many errors are impossible to detect unless a consumer challenges them. In chapter 10, Staten and Cate contend that the system nevertheless creates a host of competitive pressures and incentives for accurate, if not fully complete, credit reporting.

Fair Isaac, a developer of credit scores, has acknowledged that the information it receives from credit repositories is deficient in some respects and advocates for better reporting. It also emphasized that it adapts its models to handle conflicting and duplicate information, avoids placing large weights on data known to be unreliable, and tests and retests the scores to improve their predictability (St. John, 2003). Indeed, Avery, Calem, and Canner (2004) found that many of the data quality issues have been recognized and accounted for by scorecard developers. The authors performed several simulations to approximate the effect of correcting the data on their defined "at risk" sample and found little material change in the credit scores. However, examining the failure of some creditors to report credit limits on revolving accounts, the authors found that 55 percent of their sample was affected by their simulations and almost 30 percent would experience a more than 10 point increase of their score.

Credit Scoring and Automated Underwriting

Despite data inaccuracies and incomplete reporting, credit scores have proven highly predictive of loan performance. This has accelerated their diffusion throughout the financial services industry (Feschbach and Schwinn, 1999). While it is entirely possible, and in fact likely, that improved data and better models could make scores even more accurate, they represent a major advance over manual review of credit histories.

Automated mortgage underwriting models use credit scores as just one variable, albeit an important one, in a statistical model of credit risk. Models include information on debt-to-income ratios, loan-to-value ratios, employment histories, and often individual credit bureau lines to allow other variables to offset unfavorable credit scores. And loans that are rejected from automated systems are sometimes referred to manual underwriters as a final check.

The distribution of benefits from the use of credit scores and automated underwriting models, however, is much more complex and uncertain. The introduction of risk-based pricing means that some borrowers who would have received a cross-subsidy under the old system by being pooled with less risky borrowers no longer receive that subsidy.[15] Instead, they are charged a rate that reflects the higher risk category to which they are now assigned. At the same time, prime quality borrowers may inadvertently end up working through a lender that only offers higher cost credit. Finally, building credit scores and prices on past loan performance can lock in past inequities and cause future borrowers to suffer higher costs if lenders underwrote subprime loans poorly in the past.

A major concern related to credit scoring and automated underwriting systems is how their use affects protected classes, especially racial and ethnic minorities (Stanton, 1999). At a minimum automated underwriting results in disparate treatment of minorities. Yet credit scores pass the business necessity test used to judge if disparate treatment constitutes discrimination because they are so closely correlated with observed default behavior and losses. In a system that either accepts or rejects borrowers and does not offer a range of prices, discrimination can only enter into the accept or reject decision. In a risk-based pricing system, lenders can discriminate by offering minority borrowers higher-priced credit than whites with comparable risk profiles. The former practice is relatively easy to detect because it involves treating minority applicants differently than whites. The latter is unfortunately more difficult to detect because

---

15. Amy Crews Cutts and Robert A. Van Order, "On the Economics of Subprime Lending" (www.freddiemac.com/corporate/reports/).

the mortgage industry lacks both transparency and consistency in pricing by risk grade (Stanton, 1999; Ross and Yinger, 2002). For example, a lender that charges a higher interest rate may be intentionally overcharging a borrower or may have better information than other lenders who are not pricing adequately to cover the risk.[16]

The implications of automated underwriting systems for underserved borrowers and areas remain unclear. Gates, Perry, and Zorn (2002) compared accuracy and approval rates of applicants under Freddie Mac's automated underwriting system, Loan Prospector, to those underwritten manually. The authors found that automated systems more accurately predicted default than manual underwriters, which results in higher borrower approval rates, especially for underserved applicants. While they noted that some of the rejected applicants would have been approved under a manual underwriting system, on average more underserved applicants were approved through the automated system.

Although evidence strongly suggests that Loan Prospector has improved access to prime credit among low- and moderate-income borrowers, it is not clear that this is true for all systems. Collins, Harvey, and Nigro (2002), for example, studied loan level data and underwriting decisions of a bank that uses a custom credit score model. They found that since some models neglect factors that are particularly important to approvals of nontraditional borrowers, these scoring systems produce larger disparities than a machine-replicated judgmental system.

Clearly, questions remain regarding the implications of the shift toward automated underwriting, risk-based pricing, and reliance on credit scoring.

Improving Credit for Low-Income Asset Building

Progress in building assets among low-income households was made during the 1990s. In the case of both transaction account and homeownership increases, regulation and technology played a role. In the case of banking, technology lowered the costs to serve small accounts, and in the case of homeownership, it lowered mortgage origination and servicing costs and increased the accuracy of risk assessment. In the case of banking, the Debt Collection Improvement Act passed in 1996 pushed federal payments toward direct deposits. In the case of housing, expanded enforcement and amendments to the Community Reinvestment Act and Home Mortgage Disclosure Act (and continued community activism) stimulated mortgage lending to low-income and minority borrowers and areas. Increasingly aggressive affordable housing goals for Fannie Mae and Freddie Mac also played a role.

16. Indeed, many lenders suffered heavy losses on their subprime lending portfolios in the 1990s because they underpriced their credit.

There are many ways in which the credit needs of low-income and minority communities could be met in a more complete, fair, and cost-effective fashion. Broadly writ, these include interventions to further reduce the number of the unbanked and increase savings rates, improve the accuracy and fairness of credit risk evaluation and pricing systems, improve consumer awareness, and expand the risk mitigation tools available to low-income households.

Reducing the Number of Unbanked, Increasing Incentives to Save

Moving low-income households into the banking sector can expand their opportunities. As Seidman and Tescher note in chapter 13, a bank account allows customers to receive a paycheck quickly and safely, and access funds using checks, automated teller machines, and debit cards. Moreover, establishing a banking relationship can increase financial literacy, create opportunities to establish a credit history, and culminate in access to high-quality credit products.

Providing incentives for low-income households to save can allow them to leverage their savings to buy homes, and help them steer clear of expensive short-term credit and manage repayment risks by providing a cushion against economic hardships. The 1988 Assets for Independence Act, for example, encouraged savings through the creation of individual development accounts (IDAs). IDAs are subsidized savings accounts that allow eligible low-income individuals to make deposits that are matched, usually at a rate of 2:1 or 3:1. With about 40,000 participants, the IDA program has demonstrated that given the right sort of incentives, lower-income households are capable of saving money (Sherraden, Schreiner, and Beverly, 2003).

As an additional way to encourage savings, Orszag and Greenstein (2004) recommended pension reform to help encourage low- and moderate-income households save for retirement and reduce elderly poverty. The authors pointed out that the current system provides disproportionate tax benefits to upper-income households, which are more likely to save anyway. Further, the authors cited evidence that tax preferred savings targeted to low-income households are more likely to generate new savings than those targeted to higher-income households.

Improving the Credit Risk Evaluation and Pricing System

While credit scores appear to be powerful predictors of default risk, several aspects of the current credit risk evaluation and pricing system could clearly be improved. One important step is to try to capture additional measures of willingness to pay. This is important for two reasons. First, a small fraction of Americans appear to have no credit record whatsoever, but a larger fraction has records with thinly populated fields because they have rarely accessed credit, do not have bank accounts, or because they have obtained credit from sources that do not report information to credit bureaus. Second, additional information could improve the accuracy of models even for those with an established credit record.

In response to these concerns, new programs have been designed to broaden the criteria for applicants with minimal or no credit histories. For example, GMAC's Settle America program allows up to 30 percent of an applicant's qualifying income to come from other resident members of the household. Meanwhile, Fannie Mae and Freddie Mac have both introduced mortgage products that reward credit impaired borrowers by lowering their mortgage interest rate by as much as 2 percent after twenty-four months of timely payments.

Another promising effort is Pay Rent, Build Credit, Inc. which enables renters to demonstrate timely payments of rent and of other recurring bill payments to build a credit history.[17] Software allows renters to enter up to thirty-six months of prior rental, utility, insurance, student loan, and other payments to build a historical credit file, provided they have a paper trail such as a signed lease, bills, cancelled checks, money order receipts, or bank statements that can be verified by a third party such as a real estate agent, tax preparation service, or credit counselor.

In chapter 8, Fishelson-Holstine argues that two additional pieces of information—a letter of explanation for past credit problems and information on whether or not the borrower has completed an education or counseling program—could be used to improve the predictive power of credit scores.

There is also room to improve the accuracy and coverage of information that is currently transmitted to credit bureaus under the voluntary reporting system. The Federal Credit Reform Act does not require creditors to report, and if they do report the law requires only that they supply information they know to be accurate. Thus some creditors simply do not engage with the system and others can selectively report so long as it is accurate. Any attempt to introduce additional reporting requirements, however, would go against the grain of more than thirty years of regulations aimed at regulating a voluntary reporting system.

Increased consumer vigilance might help to fix some of the problems with the current system, but it is unlikely that consumers are equipped to detect an error in their credit report or know for certain if they are being unfairly treated by a lender. There is some evidence that consumers frequently underestimate their credit score, which may make it difficult for them to detect a problem (Ards and others, 2003). Recent legislation that provides consumers access to one free credit report a year is an important step, but many consumers are unaware that they have this right or how to exercise it.

With the growing importance of credit scores to so many business decisions, a public debate over whether or not the current regulatory system is fair to consumers and whether it produces satisfactory results is warranted. As Staten and

17. For more information, see www.payrentbuildcredit.com.

Cate report in chapter 10, regulations governing credit reporting have consistently tried to steer clear of mandatory and proscriptive approaches to ensure the quality, completeness, and accuracy of credit information. Instead, regulations have aimed to establish an effective error detection and correction system that is initiated through consumer challenges to faulty credit reports and decisions. The Center for Community Change and Consumer Federation of America have proposed that credit score providers share responsibility for the accuracy of the underlying data, for correcting those data, and for disseminating the correct information if requested by the consumer.

Regulations governing credit decisions also deserve a careful review. While full disclosure about the statistical models would mean little to the general public, at a minimum it seems reasonable to provide borrowers with more information related to their risk. At present lenders and investors have information on the borrower's probability of default, yet the borrower is left in the dark. Even state lotteries generally require the odds of winning to be posted. Lenders therefore could be required to disclose how their model assigns the probability of default, which would allow borrowers to compare their rating across lenders.

Improving Consumer Awareness, Promoting Optimal Credit Selection

Currently, a great deal of the burden for detecting and correcting errors in credit decisions, including pricing decisions, is placed on the consumer. Absent significant changes in the laws that regulate credit reporting and underwriting, consumers must serve as their own watchdogs and remain the principal defense against unfair practices and inadvertent errors. Thus credit and prepurchase counselors must help consumers select appropriate credit products in the first instance and help them to challenge decisions that consumers believe were made in error. Indeed, in chapter 5 Apgar and Fishbein argue that there is clearly a role for community groups to match consumers with the best products for which they qualify.

Counseling is the most logical tool for promoting consumer awareness. The evidence on the success of counseling is mixed, but on balance suggests it has a positive impact on loan performance. Mallach's (2001) extensive review of the prepurchase and postpurchase home buyer education and counseling research unearthed little substantive evidence on the effectiveness of counseling. However, several studies found that counseling both accelerated homeownership and resulted in lower delinquencies and defaults (McCarthy and Quercia, 2000; Mallach, 2001; Hirad and Zorn, 2002). For example, Hirad and Zorn (2002) found that prepurchase counseling resulted in lower delinquencies, all else equal, but only if they were in-depth programs. Indeed, Hilgert, Hogarth and Beverly (2003) have argued that there is an important policy distinction between providing information and providing education. Only the latter is likely to produce a behavioral change.

Expanding and Improving Risk Mitigation Tools for Consumers

Lenders insure themselves against repayment risk through the interest rates and fees they charge, third-party credit enhancements they purchase, and mortgage insurance they demand that the borrower pay. Low-income borrowers pick up the tab for these insurances but are not themselves protected by them. They could therefore benefit from insurance products that protect them rather than the lender.

Asset-building strategies have evolved to include tools designed to help low-income people keep current on their payments. A nascent literature suggests that so-called trigger events, such as unemployment, divorce, unforeseen medical expenses, or a death in the family are usually implicated in loan defaults (Elmer and Seelig, 1999). Low-income households are especially susceptible to trigger events because they have a harder time saving, are more likely to experience job losses and other reductions in income, are less likely to have health insurance, and are more likely to take on credit to cover basic expenses or small discretionary purchases. In addition, they are more likely to buy homes that are in need of significant repairs.

One way to insure against these trigger events is to purchase debt cancellation insurance. Debt protection started with the credit card companies and has spread to consumer loan products, such as home equity loans and auto loans, and is now being tested with mortgages.[18] It is too soon to tell who will purchase mortgage protection and how much adverse selection might occur, making it difficult to price. Typically, debt protection for credit card holders is offered in the form of an addendum to the lender's agreement with the customer. The addendum basically states that if any of these X trigger events should occur, Y payments will be waived. A monthly fee is charged according to the incidence and severity of the covered events. In addition to the standard negative trigger events such as death or accidental death, divorce, unemployment, hospitalization, and disability, many programs now cover positive events such as the birth of a child, wedding expenses, or purchasing a new home.

Another risk to borrowers is that house price declines will wipe out their home equity. Home equity assurance programs were designed to stimulate housing markets and secure real estate investment by protecting homeowners from financial loss in the event of an area-wide house price decline between the time

18. In 2001 Bank of America launched the Borrower's Protection Plan, which offers debt protection for mortgages, credit cards, and other consumer loans. Three major events are covered at different monthly premiums: disability, involuntary unemployment, and accidental death. Similarly, Fannie Mae is piloting a program called Home Stay, which would cancel mortgage payments. Fannie Mae is also piloting Home Manager, which is similar to a home warranty but includes an annual inspection during which the homeowner receives home maintenance information.

of purchase and the time of sale. The first program started in Oak Park, Illinois,[19] in 1977 during an intense period of blockbusting[20] and high racial turnover. Local governments and nonprofit organizations have since initiated other programs, but to date there remain only a handful. Currently, the Neighborhood Reinvestment Corporation is piloting the Home Equity Protection program in Syracuse, New York.[21]

None of the house price programs described above is technically an insurance program. However, Shiller and Weiss (1994) have argued that the risk of house price declines is probably greater than that of fire or other physical disasters routinely covered by insurance. Insurance companies are unwilling to cover borrowers for price declines because of the moral hazards associated with doing so. For example, borrowers could intentionally defer maintenance in areas with higher probabilities of price declines if they did not bear the costs of these declines. These hazards can be tempered but not eliminated by covering only price declines in an entire neighborhood using a home price index such as the Freddie Mac Conventional Home Price Index or the Fiserv Case, Shiller, and Weiss index.

Conclusions

Despite progress in increasing the number of Americans with bank accounts and improving access to credit for asset building in low-income and minority communities, a large share of low-income (and especially low-income minority) individuals remain unbanked, the gaps in asset ownership by income level and race or ethnicity remain wide, and the cost of credit to borrowers in low-income and minority communities is on average higher. Technology has lowered the costs of serving credit impaired borrowers and improved credit risk assessment and pricing. And regulatory pressure to reach out to these markets has come from the Community Reinvestment Act and Home Mortgage Disclosure Act, and the advocacy that has surrounded them. However, the fact remains that a two-tiered system is in place in which lower-income and minority borrowers are often served by different lenders and different products than other borrowers.

What can be done to improve the system? To begin, more research is needed and more original data need to be collected and analyzed. The financial services

---

19. Illinois is the only state with a law (Home Equity Assurance Act of 1988) that outlines how home equity assurance programs operate. Illinois funds programs through a property tax levy. Other places have used gambling revenue, foundation money, or general government funds.

20. Blockbusting occurred through efforts to persuade property owners to sell or rent their property, by making written or oral statements that racial minorities were moving into the neighborhood.

21. See Caplin and others (2003) for a full description.

industry is evolving rapidly as new technologies are refined and new products introduced. The current regulatory and market environment creates many incentives to press for continuous improvements in reaching out to markets alternatively labeled underserved, minority, low-income, or emerging. But potential market failures, new policy challenges, and the existence of unscrupulous lenders in the new risk-based pricing environment all point to the need for new policies. For example, the credit information collected needs to be as complete and accurate as possible and the statistical models as sensitive as possible to the most predictive factors.

Ensuring that all borrowers end up with the lowest-priced credit for which they qualify should be a priority. This can be accomplished through voluntary efforts or regulations that require loan applicants with higher-quality credit to be referred up to lenders that offer lower-cost credit; voluntary efforts or regulations that require or encourage, through an affirmative obligation, transparency and some uniformity in pricing grids by risk grade; and lastly financial literacy campaigns that improve consumer performance under a system that is at present and may remain rooted in *caveat emptor*—let the buyer beware.

Providing incentives and opportunities to save are critical because savings mitigate the risks associated with job loss, family dissolution, income declines, and other budget shocks. In addition, as electronically captured information becomes increasingly important to credit rationing and pricing, it will be even more important for low-income households to have transaction accounts.

Finally, all those involved in extending financial services to low-income households must be cognizant of the practical realities of having a low income and scant savings. Almost by definition, these households are more vulnerable to fluctuations in income and expenses. Budgeting skills and financial literacy can help these households get by without getting into trouble and help them set aside savings as a cushion against economic difficulties. Education can also help them find the lowest price credit for which they qualify. But low-income households also deserve greater incentives to save and better products to help them, not their lenders, mitigate repayment risks. They deserve to benefit from rapidly evolving loan loss mitigation tools that help cure loans, enforcement of antipredatory lending and equal credit opportunity laws, and mainstream financial services providers that compete for their business. To do less will make it harder for low-income households to build assets through homeownership, result in threats to their capacity to sustain their investments and repay their loans, and force some to pay higher credit costs that reduce their wealth accumulation over time. In short, without action on a number of fronts simultaneously, economic insecurity will continue to prevail among low-income households and they will remain at a distinct disadvantage in their wealth-building potential.

References

Aizcorbe, Ana M., Arthur B. Kennickell, and Kevin B. Moore. 2003. "Recent Changes in U.S. Family Finances: Evidence from the 1998 and 2001 Survey of Consumer Finances." *Federal Reserve Bulletin* 89 (January): 1–32.

Ambrose, Brent W., and William N. Goetzmann. 1998. "Risk and Incentives in Underserved Mortgage Markets." *Journal of Housing Economics* 7 (September): 274–85.

Ards, Sheila D., and others. 2003. "The Effect of Bad Credit on Loan Denial Rates." Paper prepared for the Southern Economic Association Meetings, San Antonio, Texas, November 21–23.

Avery, Robert B., Paul S. Calem, and Glenn B. Canner. 2004. "Credit Information Reporting and the Practical Implications of Inaccurate or Missing Information in Underwriting Decisions." Working Paper BABC 04-11. Cambridge, Mass.: Joint Center for Housing Studies.

Belsky, Eric S., and Mark Duda. 2002. "Asset Appreciation, Timing of Purchases and Sales, and Returns to Low-Income Homeownership." In *Low-Income Homeownership: Examining the Unexamined Goal,* edited by Nicolas P. Retsinas and Eric S. Belsky, pp. 208–38. Brookings.

Bradbury, Katherine L., Karl E. Case, and Constance R. Dunham. 1989. "Geographic Patterns of Mortgage Lending in Boston, 1982–87." *New England Economic Review* (September/October): 3–30.

Bradford, Calvin. 2002. *Risk or Race? Racial Disparities and the Subprime Refinance Market.* Washington: Center for Community Change.

Calder, Lendol. 2002. "The Evolution of Consumer Credit in the United States." In *The Impact of Public Policy on Consumer Credit,* edited by Thomas A. Durkin and Michael E. Staten, pp. 23–34. Boston: Kluwer Academic Press.

Caner, Asena, and Edward N. Wolff. 2004. "Asset Poverty in the United States: Its Persistence in an Expansionary Economy." Public Policy Brief 76. Levy Economics Institute of Bard College.

Caplin, Andrew, and others. 2003. "Home Equity Insurance: A Pilot Project." Neighborhood Reinvestment.

Carr, James H., and Isaac F. Megbolugbe. 1993. "Federal Reserve Bank of Boston Study on Mortgage Lending Revisited." *Journal of Housing Research* 4 (2): 277–314.

Carr, James H., and Jenny Schuetz. 2001. *Financial Services in Distressed Communities: Issues and Answers.* Washington: Fannie Mae Foundation.

Case, Karl E., and Maryna Marynchenko. 2002. "Home Price Appreciation in Low- and Moderate-Income Markets." In *Low-Income Homeownership: Examining the Unexamined Goal,* edited by Nicolas P. Retsinas and Eric S. Belsky, pp. 239–56. Brookings.

Caskey, John P. 2002a. *Bringing Unbanked Households into the Banking System.* Brookings.

———. 2002b. *The Economics of Payday Lending.* Swarthmore College.

Collins, M. Cary, Keith D. Harvey, and Peter J. Nigro. 2002. "The Influence of Bureau Scores, Customized Scores, and Judgmental Review on the Bank Underwriting Decision-making Process." *Journal of Real Estate Research* 24 (2): 129–52.

Consumer Federation of America and the National Consumer Law Center. 2003. *Bounce Protection: How Banks Turn Rubber into Gold by Enticing Consumers to Write Bad Checks.*

Draut, Tamara, and Javier Silva. 2003. *Borrowing to Make Ends Meet: The Growth of Credit Card Debt in the '90s.* New York: Demos.

Dunham, Constance R. 2001. "The Role of Banks and Nonbanks in Serving Low- and Moderate-Income Communities." In *Changing Financial Markets and Community Development: A Federal Reserve System Research Conference,* edited by J. L. Blanton, S. L. Rhine, and A. Williams, pp. 31–58. Federal Reserve Bank of Richmond.

Elliehausen, Gregory, and Edward C. Lawrence. 2001. "Payday Advance Credit in America: An Analysis of Customer Demand." Monograph 35. Credit Research Center, Georgetown University.

Elmer, Peter J., and Steven A. Seelig. 1999. "Insolvency, Trigger Events, and Consumer Risk Posture in the Theory of Single-Family Mortgage Default." *Journal of Housing Research* 10 (1): 1–25.

Fannie Mae. 2001. *Examining the Credit Impaired Borrower: 2001 National Housing Survey.*

Feschbach, Dan, and Pat Schwinn. 1999. "A Tactical Approach to Credit Scores." *Mortgage Banking* 59 (5): 46–52.

Fishbein, Allen, and Debby Goldberg. 2003. "Land Sharks Circling: The Changing Financial Services System and Its Implications for Low-Income Families and Communities." Background paper prepared for a meeting of the Annie E. Casey Foundation, June 5–6.

Fox, Jean Ann. 2003. "A Portrait of the Small Loan Consumer." Paper prepared for Woodstock Institute and National Consumer Law Center's Symposium on Market Failures and Predatory Lending, Chicago, May 17–18.

Gaberlavage, George, and Sharon Hermanson. 2001. *The Alternative Financial Services Industry.* Washington: AARP Public Policy Institute.

Gates, Susan Wharton, Vanessa Gail Perry, and Peter M. Zorn. 2002. "Automated Underwriting in Mortgage Lending: Good News for the Underserved?" *Housing Policy Debate* 13 (2): 369–92.

Goetzmann, William N., and Matthew Spiegel. 2002. "Policy Implications of Portfolio Choice in Underserved Mortgage Markets." In *Low-Income Homeownership: Examining the Unexamined Goal,* edited by Nicolas P. Retsinas and Eric S. Belsky, pp. 257–274. Brookings.

Goldstein, Deborah. 1999. "Understanding Predatory Lending: Moving toward a Common Definition and Workable Solutions." Working Paper 99-11. Cambridge, Mass.: Joint Center for Housing Studies and Neighborhood Reinvestment Corporation Emerging Leaders in Community and Economic Development Fellowship.

Haurin, Donald R., Toby L. Parcel, and R. Jean Haurin. 2002. "Impact of Homeownership on Child Outcomes." In *Low-Income Homeownership: Examining the Unexamined Goal,* edited by Nicolas P. Retsinas and Eric S. Belsky, pp. 427–46. Brookings.

Hilgert, Marianne A., Jeanne M. Hogarth, and Sondra G. Beverly. 2003. "Household Financial Management: The Connection between Knowledge and Behavior." *Federal Reserve Bulletin* (July): 309–22.

Hirad, Abdighani, and Peter Zorn. 2002. "Prepurchase Homeonwership Counseling: A Little Knowledge Is a Good Thing." In *Low-Income Homeownership: Examining the Unexamined Goal,* edited by Nicolas P. Retsinas and Eric S. Belsky, pp. 146–74. Brookings.

Hogarth, Jeanne M., and Kevin H. O'Donnell. 1999. "Banking Relationships of Lower-Income Families and the Governmental Trend toward Electronic Payment." *Federal Reserve Bulletin* (July): 459–73.

Hula, Richard C. 1991. "Neighborhood Development and Local Credit Markets." *Urban Affairs Quarterly* 27 (2): 249–67

Hurst, Erik, Ming Ching Luoh, and Frank Stafford. 1998. "Wealth Dynamics of American Families: 1984–94." *Brookings Papers on Economic Activity* 98 (1): 267–338.

Immergluck, Daniel, and Marti Wiles. 1999. *Two Steps Back: The Dual Mortgage Market, Predatory Lending, and the Undoing of Community Development.* Chicago: Woodstock Institute.

Litan, Robert E., and others. 2000. *The Community Reinvestment Act after Financial Modernization: A Baseline Report.* U.S. Department of the Treasury.

Mallach, Allan. 2001. "Home Ownership Education and Counseling: Issues in Research and Definition." Discussion Paper. Federal Reserve Bank of Philadelphia.

McCarthy, George, and Roberto Quercia. 2000. "Bridging the Gap between Supply and Demand: The Evolution of the Homeownership Education and Counseling Industry." Institute Report 00-01. Arlington, Virginia: Research Institute for Housing America.

National Community Reinvestment Coalition. 2003. *America's Best and Worst Lenders: A Consumer's Guide.* Washington.

Orszag, Peter, and Robert Greenstein. 2004. "Progressivity and Government Incentives to Save." Working Paper BABC 04-16. Cambridge, Mass.: Joint Center for Housing Studies.

Pennington-Cross, Anthony, Anthony Yezer, and Joseph Nichols. 2000. *Credit Risk and Mortgage Lending: Who Uses Subprime and Why?* Arlington, Virginia: Research Institute for Housing America.

Renuart, Elizabeth. 2002. *Stop Predatory Lending: A Guide for Legal Advocates.* Boston: National Consumer Law Center.

Retsinas, Nicolas P., and Eric S. Belsky, eds. 2002. *Low-Income Homeownership: Examining the Unexamined Goal.* Brookings.

Richter, Lisa, and Christopher Tan. 2002. *Retail Financial Services Initiative: A Report on Innovative Products and Services for Low-Income and Unbanked Customers.* Chicago: National Community Investment Fund.

Rohe, William M., Shannon Van Zandt, and George McCarthy. 2002. "Social Benefits and Costs of Homeownership." In *Low-Income Homeownership: Examining the Unexamined Goal,* edited by Nicolas P. Retsinas and Eric S. Belsky, pp. 381–406. Brookings.

Ross, Stephen, and John Yinger. 2002. *The Color of Credit.* Cambridge, Mass.: MIT Press.

Shapiro, Thomas M., and Edward N. Wolff, eds. 2001. *Assets for the Poor.* New York: Russell Sage Foundation.

Sherraden, Michael. 1991. *Assets for the Poor: A New American Welfare Policy.* Armonk, N.Y.: M.E. Sharpe.

Sherraden, Michael, Mark Schreiner, and Sondra Beverly. 2003. "Income, Institutions, and Saving Performance in Individual Development Accounts." *Economic Development Quarterly* 17 (1): 95–112.

Shiller, Robert J., and Allan N. Weiss. 1994. "Home Equity Insurance." Working Paper 4830. Cambridge, Mass.: National Bureau of Economic Research.

Shlay, Anne B., Ira Goldstein, and David Bartlett. 1992. "Racial Barriers to Credit: Comment on Hula." *Urban Affairs Quarterly* 28 (1): 126–40.

Stanton, Thomas H. 1999. *Credit Scoring and Loan Scoring: Tools for Improved Management of Federal Credit Programs.* Arlington, Virginia: Price Waterhouse Coopers Endowment for the Business of Government.

Stegman, Michael A., and Robert Faris. 2003. "Payday Lending: A Business Model That Encourages Chronic Borrowing." *Economic Development Quarterly* 17 (1): 8–32.

St. John, Cheri. 2003. "What the CFA Got Right—and Wrong—about Credit Score Accuracy." *Viewpoints* (February) (www.fairisaac.com).

Turner, Margery Austin, and Felicity Skidmore, eds. 1999. *Mortgage Lending Discrimination: A Review of the Existing Evidence.* Washington: Urban Institute.

Turner, Margery Austin, and others. 2002. *All Other Things Being Equal.* Washington: Urban Institute.

U.S. Department of Treasury and U.S. Department of Housing and Urban Development. 2000. *Curbing Predatory Home Lending: A Joint Report*

PART 1

Making Choices

GEORGE MCCARTHY

How poorly does a market need to function before the public sector steps in to correct market imperfections? How would one determine whether a market is functioning?

A main theme of this volume, and the conference that inspired it, is the critical importance of access to a range of financial services to facilitate individual asset building. Using other people's capital to build assets is the historic foundation of most wealth building in capitalist economies: the seemingly ironic use of debt to build assets. For most low- and moderate-income, and minority (LMIM) families in the United States, the only widely available leveraged investment option is the purchase of a home using a mortgage. If homeownership is the way that low-income families leverage debt to build assets, then the terms at which the debt is incurred are a key determinant of the rate at which wealth is built. Thus major concerns for those endeavoring to help LMIM families build assets through homeownership are: the quality of financial services available for LMIM families to manage their incomes and purchase homes; and, then, whether LMIM homeowners choose optimally to manage their debt.

Belsky and Duda (2002) underscore the importance of sound financial decisions. Looking at housing tenure scenarios in U.S. cities, they found that wealth building through homeownership was critically sensitive to: 1) the timing of purchases and sales relative to mark cycles; 2) the terms of the original purchase mortgage; and, 3) whether the owner exercised refinance options when the options were in the money. Bad decisions about when to buy or sell and mortgage terms made at or after purchase negated any of the financial advantages of buying a home. Making optimal decisions, like shopping for the best mortgage at the time of purchase and evaluating refinance options during the course of a mortgage, require significant financial savvy, and access to the right financial products at the right time. It also requires a history of good decisionmaking that is captured in a banking and credit history. However, there is strong evidence that low-income homeowners do not find the best mortgages at purchase. This is suggested by a study done by Mahoney and Zorn (1996), and later corroborated by Fannie Mae, that 35-50 percent of borrowers with subprime mortgages in the Government Sponsored Enterprises (GSEs) portfolios had underwriting characteristics that would have qualified them for prime credit. Further, Van Order and Zorn (2002) show that low-income homeowners exercise the refinance option less frequently than wealthier owners, especially when the option is in the money, and show that the lower propensity to prepay mortgages exhibited by LMIM owners more than offsets their higher default risk.

This volume further scrutinizes the choices made by LMIM families. Because much is known about the context within which housing finance and banking decisions are made, much is revealed about the optimality of choices made by these market agents. Since it is possible to know the optimal choices that consumers should have made, comparing actual choices to optimal choices reveals much about consumers and about the markets themselves. The studies indicate that a significant portion of customers on the demand side of mortgage and banking markets fail to behave optimally. Moreover, LMIM borrowers appear more likely to exhibit suboptimal behavior than wealthier and nonminority borrowers.

This raises one important but rarely asked question: Are LMIM households less rational than other households? After all, borrowers and savers enter into banking arrangements voluntarily and a growing number of studies indicate that suboptimal choices are made in markets in which superior choices were clearly available. While it might be convenient to conclude that some borrowers are just more rational than others, it is important to point out that rationality of all economic agents is the one unyielding assumption upon which market theory is based. Without rational consumers, markets, as one theorizes them, cannot exist because neither individual demand curves nor market demand curves would exist.

Alternately, one might conclude that LMIM households are somehow blocked from acting rationally in banking markets, implying that the inability of market agents to act optimally indicates market failure. Much of the following research presents a vignette into failing markets and a unique way, should one choose to use it, to determine the extent to which a market fails: assessing the optimality of the choices made by individuals transacting in the marketplace.

An essential first step for households expecting to become homeowners is establishing a formal banking relationship. Without a banking relationship, it is almost impossible to get a mortgage to purchase a home, let alone borrow for anything else at reasonable terms. Yet more than 20 percent of LMIM households foreclose homeownership and other wealth-building opportunities by choosing to be unbanked, using informal channels (check cashers, payday lenders, high-cost remittance services) to transact. In chapter 3, Berry shows that families make these choices in response to market imperfections: barriers to entry in the form of minimum balances, identification requirements, and credit histories that screen them out of banking products. Moreover, these consumers, well aware that they incur higher costs using informal banking systems, choose them because they find that banking products and services do not conform to their needs. In most markets, suppliers of goods and services study their markets and develop products that conform to the needs and desires of the demand side of the market. Financial markets, particularly those serving the poor, are one of the only markets that require consumers to conform to the products offered. What form does competition take in a market structured this way? Does the failure to offer products that serve a significant portion of a population indicate a market failure?

In chapter 4, Nothaft and Chang examine financing decisions made by homeowners after purchase regarding decisions to refinance their mortgages. While they find that consumer behavior generally mimics rational responses to market forces, important disparities are evident. Specifically, the authors find that low-income, minority, and less-educated homeowners "experience wealth reductions . . . because of a failure to refinance at opportune times," corroborating the findings of Van Order and Zorn (2002). Moreover, the authors are able to estimate that the failure to behave optimally over a fifteen-year period cost these consumers $22 billion in wealth. What would possess these homeowners to voluntarily forgo billions of dollars of wealth?

While economists might disagree strongly about the appropriate responses to market failure, there remains little argument that well-functioning markets are a desirable public good that must be promoted whenever possible. Any decent first-year economics student can recite the litany of ways that markets can fail: incomplete information; excessive market imperfections (product differentiation, monopoly, monopsony, excessive transaction costs) that provide agents on the demand or supply side power over price; or external economies. An as yet unexplored empirical issue is how one would determine whether a market is failing. What does a failing market look like? When is the failure bad enough to warrant intervention? Read on. While one can argue about whether we need to promote better financial literacy for LMIM families, regulate access to high-quality financial services for all families, and require higher levels of transparency of financial transactions, perhaps, at least, we can agree on one thing:

financial markets are not performing efficiently and something must be done to fix them.

References

Belsky, Eric, and Mark Duda. 2002. "Asset Appreciation, Timing of Purchases and Sales, and Returns to Low-Income Homeownership." In *Low-Income Homeownership: Examining the Unexamined Goal,* edited by Nicolas Retsinas and Eric Belsky, pp. 208–38. Brookings.

Mahoney, Peter E., and Peter M. Zorn. 1996. "The Promise of Automated Underwriting." *Secondary Mortgage Markets* (November): 18–23.

Van Order, Robert, and Peter Zorn. 2002. "Performance of Low-Income and Minority Mortgages." In *Low-Income Homeownership: Examining the Unexamined Goal,* edited by Nicolas Retsinas and Eric Belsky, pp. 322–47. Brookings.

3

To Bank or Not to Bank?
A Survey of Low-Income
Households

CHRISTOPHER BERRY

There has been a recent surge of interest in the market potential for mainstream financial service firms to serve unbanked and marginally banked consumers. The financial services industry is gradually awakening to the message that low-income consumers are a huge, untapped market for financial products and services. Despite the general recognition of unmet demand among lower-income consumers, important gaps in information about this market segment pose obstacles to conventional financial services firms. In particular, while there is an evolving consensus around the description of *who* is unbanked, relatively little is known about *why*. Moreover, many low-income consumers who have bank accounts also conduct business with fringe institutions, straddling both sides of the dual financial service system in ways that are as yet not well understood.

To help banks and other financial service firms learn more about the financial behavior and preferences of low-income consumers, MetroEdge, a business of Shorebank, sponsored a survey of households in the low-income neighborhoods of Washington, Los Angeles, and Chicago. This chapter presents the first analysis of the results from MetroEdge's survey and focuses on two central questions. First, what are the most important reasons why so many low-income households do not hold a checking or savings account? Second, to what extent do households with bank accounts also participate in the fringe financial sector, and in what ways are unbanked households connected to the mainstream financial sector?

47

Literature on the Unbanked

Beginning in the mid-1990s, and inspired in part by the important contribution by Caskey (1994), a cottage industry emerged analyzing data from various national and local surveys to understand the demographics of the unbanked population.[1] A consistent picture of the unbanked has begun to emerge. Specifically, relative to banked households, those without banking relationships are likely to be less educated, lower income, nonwhite, younger, unemployed, and a renter rather than owner of a residence. In addition, the unbanked are more likely to report that they live from paycheck to paycheck with little or no money left for savings.

There is less agreement as to why so many households are unbanked.[2] Common explanations include the scarcity of bank branches in low-income and minority neighborhoods, poor credit ratings that prevent some households from being allowed to have an account, and the availability of lower-cost services provided by nonbanks. It has also been suggested that many unbanked households desire to keep their financial transactions off the books, banks present language or cultural barriers for immigrants, and unsophisticated consumers chose fringe providers because they do not fully appreciate—or are intentionally misled about—costs. There is almost certainly some truth in each of these explanations. But there have been few systematic attempts to sort through the competing explanations and identify the relative importance of each.

Survey Design

The design of MetroEdge's survey of households living in low- and moderate-income (LMI) census tracts in Chicago, Los Angeles, and Washington[3] was loosely modeled on the Survey of Financial Activities and Attitudes, which was conducted by the Office of the Comptroller of the Currency in 1998–99. The MetroEdge survey uses a similar multistage, stratified, random sampling design in which census tracts were stratified by city, race and ethnicity, and income. Survey households were drawn from sixty-two LMI tracts, twenty-one tracts in each of the three cities. Approximately 500 households were surveyed in each city, for a total of 1,532 interviews. About two-thirds of the interviews were conducted by telephone and one-third in person. All respondents were offered

1. See Caskey (1994, 1997a, 1997b, 2001); Hogarth, Anguelov, and Lee (2003); Hogarth and O'Donnell (1998, 1999, 2000); Hungerford (2000); Rhine and others (2001); Dove Associates (1999); Dunham (2001); Kennickell, Starr-McCluer, and Surette (2000); U.S. Department of the Treasury (1997).
2. For a comprehensive review of the literature, see chapter 2 in this volume.
3. Following convention, LMI tracts were defined as those having less than 80 percent of the median household income of the metropolitan area. Census data and tract boundaries for 2000 were used.

the opportunity to complete the survey in Spanish, and 10 percent chose to do so. In each household, the survey was administered to the person identified as being responsible for most of the financial decisions. The overall response rate for the survey was 48 percent, with a higher response rate for in-person interviews. The survey was conducted from August 2003 to December 2003.

Demographics of the Unbanked

The 1,532 respondents to this survey represent a population of 960,000 households residing in the LMI neighborhoods of Chicago, Los Angeles, and Washington. Demographically, the survey population is about 23 percent white, 44 percent black, and 27 percent Hispanic, as well as 6 percent other or multiple race.[4] The median household income of the survey population was approximately $20,000 in 2003. About 26 percent of the survey population were born outside the United States.

Following convention, a household is labeled unbanked if no one in the household has either a checking or savings account. Households in which at least one person holds either type of account are termed banked. We find that 26 percent of the survey population is unbanked, a figure in line with previous surveys.[5] As Caskey (1997) observes, however, estimates of the proportion of the population that is unbanked vary. The Survey of Consumer Finances (SCF), which oversamples wealthy families, finds 13 percent unbanked; the Population Survey of Income Dynamics, which oversamples low-income families, suggests that 22 percent are unbanked. Our estimate is close to the latter number, which is expected (and reassuring) given that we are also focused on the LMI population.[6]

Table 3-1 compares the distribution of banked and unbanked households across a variety of demographic variables. Consistent with several previous studies, we find that the unbanked are disproportionately black and Hispanic, poorer, less educated, younger, more likely to have been born outside the United States, and less likely to own their homes. Perhaps the most striking differences between banked and unbanked households are in income, education, and race. Nearly 70 percent of the unbanked earn less than $15,000, and only about 2

4. Unless otherwise noted, when referring to white and black, we mean non-Hispanic white and non-Hispanic black.

5. The 95 percent confidence interval for the percentage unbanked is 20 to 32 percent.

6. Dunham (2001) estimates that 37 percent of LMI consumers in New York and Los Angeles are unbanked, but she relies on a person-level survey. That is, she samples individuals and codes them based only on their own account holding. We sample households instead. For example, in a husband and wife household, we code the household as banked if either person holds a checking or savings account, whereas Dunham would code the husband as unbanked if he does not have an account, even if his wife does. This difference in the unit of analysis between our survey and Dunham's likely explains why she arrives at a higher estimate of the percentage unbanked than we do, despite otherwise comparable survey methods.

Table 3-1. *Demographic Comparison of Banked and Unbanked Households*

Household type	Banked	Unbanked	Total
Race/ethnicity			
White	30.1	3.7	23.2
Black	40.3	54.1	43.9
Other	5.6	5.7	5.6
Hispanic	24.0	36.5	27.3
Total	100.0	100.0	100.0
Highest education level			
Less than high school	18.6	45.0	25.5
GED	3.0	6.7	4.0
High school	20.1	29.1	22.4
Some college	25.2	13.5	22.1
Community college	4.3	2.1	3.7
Tech school	1.5	1.5	1.5
College grad	17.0	1.9	13.0
Some post-college	1.8	0.0	1.3
Graduate degree	8.6	0.2	6.4
Income			
Less than $10,000	20.2	43.6	26.3
$10,000-14,999	15.1	24.7	17.6
$15,000-24,999	18.0	24.2	19.6
$25,000-34,999	16.5	6.1	13.8
$35,000-49,999	13.0	0.7	9.8
$50,000-74,999	10.5	0.1	7.8
$75,000 and up	6.8	0.7	5.2
Employment			
Unemployed	11.7	14.3	12.4
Multiple workers	49.4	51.5	49.9
Tenure			
Rent	61.3	94.3	69.6
Own	38.7	5.7	30.4
Nativity			
Immigrant	23.3	33.9	26.1
Native born	76.7	66.1	73.9
Marital status			
Single	67.1	83.2	71.3
Married	32.9	16.8	28.7
Age average	46.14	39.2	44.42
Children, average number	1.0	1.7	1.2

Source: Author's calculations based on data from the MetroEdge survey.

Table 3-2. *Logit Model Results*[a]

Variable	(1) Unbanked=1	(2) Checking=1	(3) Savings=1
Dummy = 1 for single female-	1.281	1.886	0.981
headed household	(0.73)	(1.43)	(0.07)
Dummy = 1 for single male-	2.379	0.820	0.495
headed household	(2.45)*	(0.49)	(2.12)*
Black	5.412	0.260	0.652
	(4.93)**	(4.57)**	(1.69)
Other race	5.889	0.394	1.046
	(2.59)*	(1.56)	(0.09)
Hispanic	5.057	0.366	0.847
	(3.71)**	(2.97)**	(0.61)
Educational attainment	0.489	1.989	1.488
	(6.15)**	(6.41)**	(3.69)**
Respondent age	0.961	1.037	1.020
	(5.04)**	(3.90)**	(2.35)*
Income	0.604	1.782	1.428
	(5.56)**	(6.50)**	(5.28)**
Dummy = 1 if receives welfare	1.380	0.638	1.715
benefits	(0.49)	(0.67)	(1.16)
Dummy = 1 if receives social	0.777	1.270	0.923
security	(0.65)	(1.02)	(0.37)
Dummy = 1 if no one in	2.617	1.338	0.564
household is employed	(3.18)**	(0.77)	(1.38)
Number of children	1.166	0.912	0.837
	(1.65)	(1.07)	(2.25)*
Number of adults in household	0.746	1.276	1.276
	(3.22)**	(1.71)	(4.52)**
Observations[b]	1,281	1,284	1,281

Source: Author's calculations based on data from the MetroEdge survey.

* Significant at 5 percent. ** Significant at 1 percent.

a. Absolute value of *t* statistics in parentheses. Coefficients are reported as odds ratios (that is, in exponentiated form).

b. Observations are weighted by the inverse sampling probability. Standard errors are adjusted for stratification and clustering.

percent have a college degree. Whereas about 30 percent of banked households were white, only about 4 percent of unbanked households were white.

In order to gauge the relative importance of these variables, we estimated a series of logit models, presented in table 3-2. The models estimate the probability of being unbanked, having a checking account, and having a savings account, respectively.[7] Importantly, only three variables emerge as significant predictors in all of the models: education, income, and the number of children.

7. The models are specified comparably to those reported by Washington (2003, table 3-4).

Unsurprisingly, the probability of being banked increases rapidly with income and education, as is evident from the simple tabulations in table 3-1. In addition, the likelihood of holding a checking or savings account increases with age.

Importantly, even after conditioning on the other covariates, race matters. Blacks and Hispanics are about five times more likely to be unbanked than whites. Race appears to matter most for having a checking account. In contrast, neither of the race variables is significant in the savings model, indicating that other variables explain savings behavior.[8]

In summary, there are no surprises here. The results of the models reported in table 3-2 reinforce the accumulated findings of past studies. Income, education, age, and race are the primary variables associated with account holding. It is reassuring that independent studies using disparate data sources have revealed a fairly consistent picture of who is unbanked.

Behind the Correlations

If analyses such as those presented in tables 3-1 and 3-2 reveal the characteristics of the unbanked, they contribute relatively little to explaining why so many households operate outside the mainstream financial sector. While it is important to know, for instance, that black and Hispanic households are far more likely to be unbanked than are comparable white households, we still know relatively little about why this is the case. This chapter sets out to contribute to understanding the financial behavior of low-income households by systematically examining a set of explanations for why so many of them are unbanked.

Income and Cost

To better understand why so many low-income families do not hold a checking or savings account, we began with a direct approach—we simply asked them. Every respondent who reported not having a checking (or savings) account was then asked a follow-up question: What are the main reasons you do not have a checking (or savings) account? These were asked as open-ended questions, and the responses were subsequently categorized and coded. The results are presented in table 3-3 (checking accounts) and table 3-4 (savings accounts). The dominant answers in both cases center around household income and bank fees.

Of those without a checking account, nearly half provide explanations having to do with cost or income, with a plurality saying they "do not have enough money." Others said that fees or minimum balances are too high, or that they

8. The finding of differential effects of race on holding checking and savings accounts is broadly consistent with Vermilyea and Wilcox (2002), who analyze data from the Office of the Comptroller of the Currency (OCC) survey of New York and Los Angeles. They find that blacks and Hispanics are less likely to hold checking accounts, but actually more likely to hold a savings account than are whites. Our findings do not support the latter conclusion, however.

Table 3-3. *Respondents' Main Reasons for Not Having a Checking Account*

Reason	Percent	Standard error (percent)
Income/cost	49.0	
Do not have enough money	38.2	4.4
Minimum balance is too high	6.2	2.4
Service charges are too high	2.4	1.0
Do not write enough checks to make it worthwhile	2.2	0.7
Motivation	12.7	
Do not need/want a checking account	7.1	1.5
Have not gotten around to it	5.6	1.1
Complexity	9.7	
Cannot manage/balance a checking account	5.4	1.2
Not sure how to open an account	2.9	1.2
Fees are too confusing	1.4	1.0
Hard barriers	17.6	
Credit problems	4.1	1.2
Not allowed to have an account	3.1	1.2
Do not have the proper ID/Social Security number	10.4	3.6
Soft barriers	6.1	
Do not like dealing with banks	4.6	1.0
Would not feel welcome or treated with respect	1.4	0.8
Not easy to speak with bank staff in my language	0.1	0.1
Convenience		
No bank has convenient hours or location	1.4	0.7
Other	9.5	
Other	4.1	2.1
Don't know	4.7	1.4
Refused	0.7	0.3

Source: Author's calculations based on data from the MetroEdge survey.

do not write enough checks to make having an account worthwhile.[9] The most common reasons for not having a savings account also revolve around income and cost. Nearly two-thirds of respondents gave such a reason for not having a savings account, with the majority saying either that they have no extra money to save or that they do not have enough extra money to meet the minimum balance requirements for an account. About 3 percent say they do not have a sav-

9. The classification of the responses into these five broad categories is admittedly subjective. For instance, one could interpret "do not write enough checks to make it worthwhile" to mean that it is not worth the expense of having an account (a cost issue), or that it is not worth the hassle of maintaining an account (a complexity issue). Nevertheless, in most cases we believe the coding is fairly straightforward.

Table 3-4. *Respondents' Main Reasons for Not Having a Savings Account*

Reason	Percent	Standard error (percent)
Income/cost	64.2	
Do not have any extra money	35.8	4.5
Do not have the amount of money that banks require to open an account	21.6	4.5
Fees are too high	3.1	1.1
Interest rates are too low	3.7	1.1
Motivation	11.2	
Do not need/want one	9.5	2.3
Prefer to have only checking account	1.7	0.7
Complexity		
Not sure how to open an account	1.1	0.6
Hard barriers	10.4	
Do not have proper ID/Social Security number	7.2	2.8
Bank would not let me open an account (bad credit)	32	0.8
Soft barriers	5.2	
Would not feel welcome or treated with respect	0.4	0.3
Not easy to speak with bank staff in my language	0.1	0.0
Friends/family would borrow savings if I had any	0.1	0.1
Do not trust banks	4.7	1.7
Convenience	1.8	
Banks are not located conveniently	1.3	0.4
Banks are not open when I need to use them	0.5	0.3
Other	12.3	
Other	3.9	1.5
Don't know	7.2	1.6
Refused	1.2	0.5

Source: Author's calculations based on data from the MetroEdge survey.

ings account because fees are too high and, interestingly, 4 percent say the interest rate is too low. In other words, there may be a small segment of consumers who eschew bank savings accounts in favor of more lucrative investment options or do not save at all because the perceived incentives are too small.

By far the most common explanations given for not having a checking or savings account have to do with inadequate income. The relationship between savings and income is obvious. To be able to save, a household must have money left over after paying for basic necessities, and hence we expect a negative relationship between income and savings, all else equal. On the other hand, the relationship between income and checking is more complex. Whereas households with no money to save have no need for a savings account, all households—even those with an income below poverty level—have a need for the

Figure 3-1. *Relationship between Income and Cost of Making and Receiving Payments*

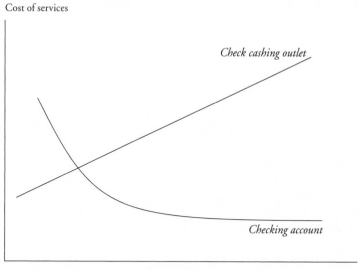

Cost of services

Check cashing outlet

Checking account

Household income

basic services provided by a checking account, that is, making and receiving payments. The choice households face, then, is not whether or not to make and receive payments, but whether to make and receive payments via a checking account or through some other method. So what does it mean when low-income consumers say they do not have enough money for a checking account?

The primary alternative to a checking account for most low-income households to receive income and convert it to cash is to use a check-cashing outlet (CCO) or other nonbank institution for cashing checks, or to cash checks at the issuing bank. The primary alternatives for making payments are to pay by cash or money order. The cost structure of a checking account relative to these alternatives may explain why some low-income households find it more affordable not to have a checking account. Specifically, the cost of maintaining a checking account is decreasing in income, whereas the cost of using CCOs is increasing in income, as illustrated theoretically in figure 3-1.[10] Previous studies show that cashing a check at a CCO costs, on average, approximately 1 to 2 percent of the value of the check (for example, see Washington, 2003). A household earning

10. Of course, the actual costs vary significantly across institutions and also depend on individual consumer behavior. Banks that offer no fee, no minimum balance checking accounts may be able to underprice CCOs even for low-income consumers, although even in this case customers may be willing to pay more at a CCO to avoid having to wait for checks to clear. These qualifications aside, the basic relationship shown in figure 3-1 holds given common pricing structures of banks and CCOs.

$12,000 a year would expect to pay $15 per month, or $180 a year, to cash its paychecks at a CCO charging a 1.5 percent fee. A household earning $120,000 would pay ten times as much, or $1,800 a year, to use a CCO.[11] Moreover, Dunham (2001) shows that many low-income households find even less expensive methods of converting checks to cash—for example, cashing checks at a supermarket that does not charge a fee to customers buying other goods, or cashing checks at the issuing bank for no cost—so that the vast majority of unbanked households in fact pay less than $100 a year in fees for financial services. Consistent with Dunham (2001), we find that only about 40 percent of unbanked households in our survey population actually cash checks at a CCO. In contrast, free or low-cost methods of converting checks to cash are generally not feasible for large checks, and in this sense high-income consumers might just as well be said to make too much money to use a supermarket or CCO for converting income to cash.

The price structure of most checking accounts, in contrast, is such that low-income consumers typically will pay more in fees than will high-income consumers. Many banks charge fees to customers who do not maintain a minimum balance in their checking accounts, and maintaining that minimum balance is especially difficult for low-income households. In addition, banks and merchants charge fees for bounced checks—a distinct possibility for a customer whose account balance dips to zero at some point every month, as Caskey (1994) has emphasized. Moreover, customers with low account balances face nonpecuniary costs, such as the delay waiting for their deposit to clear if they do not have enough money in their account to cover it. On the other hand, customers that maintain a high balance in their checking account can escape most or all fees and even earn interest. Thus when low-income consumers report that they do not have enough money for a checking account, it is likely that they mean that they do not have enough money to make a checking account more affordable than a CCO.

Hard and Soft Barriers

We find that only about 5 percent of unbanked households say the main reason they do not have a checking account is that they simply do not like dealing with banks. Our estimate of the proportion that do not like dealing with banks is substantially lower than that reported from a comparable question in the Survey of Consumer Finances. Between 1992 and 2001, the SCF has shown an increase from 17 to 23 percent of respondents who say their main reason for not having a checking account is that they do not like dealing with banks (Aizcorbe, Ken-

---

11. In fact, most CCOs will not cash checks as large as $10,000 (assuming the household is paid once a month), so this is not even an option for high-income households. We ignore this reality for purposes of illustration.

nickell, and Moore, 2003). We believe one reason we find a smaller proportion giving this answer in our survey is that we ask the question in an open-ended form, allowing for additional responses that were not detected on the SCF question. In particular, the SCF question does not have the option of "do not have proper identification." We find that when the identification option is available more respondents actually chose this than "do not like dealing with banks." Similarly, in explaining not having a savings account, more respondents say that they do not have proper identification (7 percent) than "do not trust banks" (5 percent).[12] The distinction is important because possible policy responses differ. If a large proportion of unbanked households do not like dealing with banks, more research is needed to understand why this is so and what, if anything, banks can do to change this perception. On the other hand, if identification requirements are a major barrier, policy responses are more straightforward, such as allowing the use of matricula cards.

In addition to those without proper identification, approximately 7 percent of the survey population report that they are barred from having a checking account due to credit issues, saying either that they have bad credit or are not allowed to have an account, possibly due to having a record in Chex systems. About 3 percent said they were not allowed to open a savings account due to bad credit. As shown in table 3-5, 15 percent of unbanked households say they have had an application for a bank account denied. Interestingly, 8 percent of banked households also say that they have had an application for a bank account denied. Apparently, they were able to repair their credit rating or to find another bank with less stringent requirements.

Only a small fraction of respondents identified less tangible cultural and language barriers as important reasons for not having a checking or savings account. As mentioned above, 5 percent say they do not have a checking account because they do not like dealing with banks, and 5 percent do not have a savings account because they do not trust banks. Less than two percent of respondents said the main reason they do not have a checking account is either that they do not feel welcome or that bank staff do not speak their language. Less than 1 percent said that respect or language was the reason for not having a savings account. In other words, hard barriers, such as identification requirements and credit ratings, appear to be more important than soft cultural barriers in driving low-income consumers away from banks.

Location and Convenience

The relative scarcity of bank branches in low-income and minority neighborhoods has been commonly suggested as an explanation for why so many house-

---

12. The SCF does not ask a question about why respondents do not have a savings account, so we have no basis for comparison.

Table 3-5. *Banked and Unbanked Respondents' Reasons for Bank Account Denials*
Percent

	Banked	Unbanked	Total
Has a bank ever denied your application for a bank account (not a loan)?			
Yes	8.3	15.2	10.1
No	91.7	84.8	89.9
Total	100	100	100

		Standard error
Why was your application for a bank account denied?		
Bad credit	32.93	
Bad credit history	24.25	7.48
Bounced checks	8.68	3.33
No credit	51.32	
No credit history	16.19	7.12
Insufficient identification	35.13	11.77
Unknown	6.73	
Bank did not tell me why	4.87	2.89
Don't know	1.86	1.07
Other	9.03	4.24

Source: Author's calculations based on data from the MetroEdge survey.

holds in these neighborhoods do not have bank accounts (Juarez, 1997; Lieberman, 1997). Poor and minority households use fringe institutions, the story goes, because they do not have bank branches located nearby. The results shown in tables 3-3 and 3-4 do not support this argument. Less than 2 percent of unbanked households said inconvenient bank locations or operating hours were important reasons for not having a checking or savings account. These figures are consistent with findings from the SCF (for example, Aizcorbe, Kennickell, and Moore, 2003). Although it may well be the case that low-income, and especially minority, neighborhoods have a greater presence of fringe institutions relative to banks than high-income neighborhoods, very few consumers say that the absence of bank branches is an important reason for being unbanked. However, as discussed below, convenient locations do make a difference to consumers in choosing where to cash checks.

Complexity and Motivation

The complexity of opening and managing an account deterred about 10 percent of survey households from having a checking account. These respondents reported an inability to manage an account, uncertainty over how to open an account, or confusion over fees as the main reason for not having a checking account. These households may represent the segment of the unbanked that would benefit most from improved financial education. However, only about 1 percent of the unbanked said that issues related to complexity were important reasons for not having a savings account.

The most opaque reasons for being unbanked were given by those households who said simply that they do not need or want a bank account. About 13 percent of those without a checking account said either that they do not need or want an account, or that they have not gotten around to opening one. Similarly, about 11 percent of those without a savings account say they either do not need or want one, or that they prefer having only a checking account. It is difficult to make inferences about the rationale for being unbanked among this segment of LMI consumers.

Consumer Knowledge and Sophistication

It is possible that the actual reasons why a household is unbanked may differ from the self-reported reasons. In particular, it is often suggested that low-income consumers are financially unsophisticated and do not fully understand the costs associated with fringe banking. In other words, less-sophisticated consumers may perceive the costs of fringe banking to be lower than they actually are, perhaps due to hidden or complex fees. This explanation for the use of nonbank institutions would not appear in self-reports, such as tables 3-3 and 3-4, because respondents themselves would be unaware of their own misperceptions. However, the argument that low-income consumers pay too much for financial services because they are taken advantage of by exploitative fringe institutions is challenged by Dunham (2001), which finds that most low-income consumers without bank accounts actually pay relatively little to make and receive payments. We therefore asked a series of questions in order to understand how low-income consumers gauge the relative costs of bank and nonbank financial services.

We begin by asking those who have cashed a check at a CCO in the preceding twelve months how much they paid. First we asked the amount of the last check the respondent cashed, and then the dollar value of the fee they paid. The median reported fee amounted to 1.75 percent of the face value of the check, which is well within the normal range of CCO fees. In other words, respondents do not report unrealistically low fees. For comparison, we asked those respondents with checking accounts who have never used a CCO to speculate on CCO fees. Specifically, we asked them how much a CCO would charge to cash a $100 check. The median reported estimate was $5, which, although not implausible, is on the high end of industry norms. In other words, it may be that banked consumers actually overestimate the costs of being unbanked.

Of course, CCOs are not the only option for unbanked consumers who need to convert checks to cash. Almost half of unbanked consumers who cash checks have done so at a bank or credit union (22 percent) or a supermarket (22 percent). We then asked why respondents chose a CCO over a bank, or vice versa,

Table 3-6. *Banked and Unbanked Respondents' Reasons for Cashing Checks at Banks and CCOs*

Percent

	Banked	Unbanked	Total
Why do you prefer cashing checks at a bank rather than CCO?			
Cheaper	48.7	73.2	50.1
More convenient	35.2	21.2	34.4
Faster, lines are shorter	7.0	2.3	6.7
More convenient location	21.2	17.5	21.0
More convenient hours	3.3	1.4	3.2
Can take care of other business at the same time	3.7	0.0	3.5
Safety/privacy	18.2	4.1	17.4
It is safer	16.6	4.1	15.9
There is more privacy	1.6	0.0	1.5
Relationship with bank	10.0	1.5	9.6
Direct deposit	1.8	0.0	1.7
Habit/accustomed to bank	1.6	1.5	1.6
Have a relationship/account with the bank	6.6	0.0	6.3
Other	1.8	1.5	1.8
Don't know	1.8	0.0	1.7
Why do you prefer cashing checks at a CCO rather than bank?			
Cheaper	6.2	14.3	11.3
More convenient	76.7	64.8	69.2
Faster, lines are shorter	19.5	8.7	12.7
More convenient location	46.3	46.3	46.3
More convenient hours	9.8	6.2	7.5
Can take care of other business at the same time	1.1	3.6	2.7
Safety/privacy	4.0	3.8	3.9
It is safer	4.0	3.6	3.7
There is more privacy	0.0	0.2	0.1
Relationship with bank	9.5	18.5	15.2
Do not have a bank (checking) account	5.8	15.2	11.7
Cannot/do not want to use a bank	3.7	3.3	3.5
Other	5.3	8.1	7.1
Don't know	1.3	2.9	2.3

Source: Author's calculations based on data from the MetroEdge survey.

for cashing their checks, as shown in table 3-6. The most common reason for cashing checks at a bank rather than a CCO is that it is less expensive, presumably because the unbanked were cashing checks at the bank of issue.[13] In contrast, a relatively small proportion of unbanked consumers said they cashed their

13. Indeed, of the unbanked consumers who cashed their checks at a bank, only 25 percent reported having to pay any fee.

checks at a CCO because it was cheaper than a bank. Rather, nearly two-thirds of unbanked consumers who cashed a check at a CCO said they did so for convenience. A more convenient location was the top reason for choosing a CCO over a bank for check cashing. Interestingly, a significant proportion of consumers with checking accounts has also cashed checks at a CCO (19 percent) or supermarket (8 percent). Three-quarters of consumers with bank accounts who cash their check at a CCO say they did so because the location or hours were more convenient or the lines were shorter. In short, banked and unbanked households exhibit a similar motivation for cashing checks at a CCO: convenience.

If unbanked consumers seem to have a fairly clear understanding of the costs of using a CCO, perhaps they overestimate the barriers to obtaining a checking account. We asked respondents without a checking account to estimate the minimum balance needed to maintain a no-fee checking account. The range of responses was wide, with a median of $100 and mean of $270. Although minimum balance requirements vary from one bank to another, these estimates are within the range of industry norms, although clearly there is a segment of the unbanked that dramatically overestimates the barriers to banking—the highest estimated minimum balance was $5,000. We then followed up by asking whether the respondents believed they could maintain their estimated minimum balance: 75 percent said yes. In other words, most unbanked respondents believe that they could maintain a no-fee checking account but chose not to do so.

The picture that emerges here is not one of uninformed consumers being exploited by predatory fringe financial institutions, although surely that does occur. Rather, unbanked consumers are generally well informed about the relative costs of CCOs and banks. Those that chose to cash checks at CCOs appear to be motivated primarily by convenience, while those that cash checks at banks are motivated by lower costs. In other words, for many LMI households, being unbanked is the result of an informed choice rather than involuntary exclusion from the mainstream financial sector. This is not to say that LMI consumers find themselves in the best of all possible worlds. Rather, for the most part, they make the best of the limited options available to them given their income. Nevertheless, the vast majority of households in our survey population appear satisfied with the financial institutions they have chosen. When asked to rate their level of satisfaction with their financial institution, 91 percent of banked customers said they were satisfied or very satisfied, and so did 85 percent of the unbanked.

Network Externalities

Within an economic network, each member's use of a checking account increases the value to others of holding an account by increasing the opportunities to make payments by check, the sort of benefits that economists refer to as network externalities. Thus another possible barrier to checking account holding among low-income consumers is that personal checks may not be as widely accepted as forms of payment in low-income neighborhoods. In this respect, we were surprised to find that households with checking accounts nevertheless report buying an average of two money orders per month, compared with an average of 2.5 for households without a checking account. When asked why someone with a checking account buys money orders, the most common reasons, shown in table 3-7, are that the person or business to receive the money does not accept checks. Moreover, half of households with a bank account nevertheless pay their rent by cash or money order (table 3-7).[14] About one in five households, banked and unbanked, report that their landlord will not accept a check for rent (table 3-7). We also find evidence that unbanked households are more likely to belong to social networks including other unbanked households. For example, about 47 percent of unbanked households report than none or only a few of their closest friends and relatives have a bank account. Only 22 percent of banked households said that most or all of their friends and relatives were unbanked.

To Bank or Not to Bank? Is This the Right Question?

Our discussion so far has proceeded as if low-income consumers fit neatly into two mutually exclusive categories, the banked and unbanked. The banked, it would seem, are fully integrated into the mainstream financial sector by virtue or having a checking or savings account, whereas the unbanked are on the fringe, completely excluded from traditional financial networks. The reality is that most low-income households rely on a patchwork of financial services provided by both bank and nonbank institutions. If there is indeed a dual financial sector, many consumers find themselves on both sides. As Dunham (2001) has emphasized, engagement in the mainstream and fringe sectors by low-income households therefore should be thought of as a continuum rather than a simple dichotomy of banked and unbanked. This chapter now briefly explores some of the ways in which low-income households have developed overlapping relationships with both banks and fringe service providers.

Perhaps the most direct relationship that most unbanked consumers have had with the formal financial sector is through their own past holding of bank accounts. As seen in table 3-8, half of the currently unbanked in our survey population actually held a checking or savings account in the past, and therefore might be more aptly termed *formerly banked*. The most common reason for closing the account was a change in personal finances that made it impossible to maintain the minimum balance. In addition, about 12 percent said they closed their accounts because bank fees were too high. Nearly a quarter of households

14. Among households with a checking account specifically, 37 percent still pay rent by cash or money order.

Table 3-7. *Acceptance of Checks Written by Banked and Unbanked Respondents*
Percent

	Banked	Unbanked	Total
How do you pay your rent?			
Cash	20.4	35.0	25.4
Check	48.9	4.3	33.8
Money order	29.6	58.7	39.5
Other	1.0	2.0	1.4
Total	100	100	100
Does your landlord take checks for rent payment?			
Yes	73.0	56.4	64.8
No	17.5	21.7	19.5
Don't know	9.5	21.9	15.7
Total	100	100	100

		Standard error
Person with checking account: Why do you buy money orders?		
Person I wanted to give money to does not have a checking account	8.4	2.2
Person I wanted to make payment to does not have a checking account	22.1	3.7
Business I wanted to make payment to does not accept checks	11.3	2.4
I ran out of checks	4.6	1.2
Easier/more convenient	16.1	4.8
Not enough funds/will not bounce	9.4	2.5
Does not have to clear	3.4	1.1
Widely accepted	1.6	0.6
Receipt/proof of payment	2.6	1.0
Preference	6.6	2.4
Other	13.9	2.4

	Banked	Unbanked	Total
Of the friends and family members closest to you, how many do you think have checking accounts?			
None	3.5	8.2	4.7
Only a few	18.4	38.8	23.7
Most	30.9	30.5	30.8
All	43.3	14.5	35.8
Don't know	4.0	7.9	5.0
Total	100	100	100

Table 3-8. *Past Banking Experience of the Unbanked*
Percent

	Percent who said yes	Standard error
If Unbanked: Have you ever had		
A checking account	43.4	5.7
A savings account	35.7	4.3
Any other kind of account at a bank	4.3	1.9
Percent with some previous account	48.9	5.2
		Standard error
If yes, why did you close your most recent bank account?		
Cost	46.7	
Change in personal finances meant no longer could afford minimum balance	31.0	6.6
Increase in minimum balance or fees meant no longer could afford account	3.3	1.4
Fees too high	12.3	4.6
Account management	22.7	
Bouncing too many checks	13.0	3.7
Problem with the bank/unauthorized withdrawls	4.5	1.7
Someone stole checks from me/used my account	5.1	2.7
Location	8.6	
Bank branch closed	1.3	0.8
I moved	7.3	1.7
Other		
Found it easier to use other financial institution	1.9	1.1
Other	13.1	4.2
Don't know	4.0	1.6
Refused	5.6	1.7

who used to be banked closed their accounts for reasons related to account management, with the most common reason being that they bounced too many checks. Finally, 9 percent closed their bank account either when they moved or their local bank branch was closed.

Aside from past account ownership, the most common banking relationship among the unbanked comes through using banks to cash checks. About 20 percent of unbanked households who receive income by check say they cash a check at a bank each month, and 4 percent cash checks at a credit union, as shown in table 3-9. Of those who cash their check at a bank or credit union, only 25 percent pay any fee, which suggests that most cash their check at the bank of issue for no charge. Beyond check cashing, banks and credit unions attract about 4 percent of the unbanked who buy money orders and about 11 percent of the unbanked who send money outside the country. In addition, about 10 percent of the unbanked report having a major credit card, which rep-

Table 3-9. *Use of Fringe and Mainstream Financial Institutions by Banked and Unbanked Households*

Percent

	Banked	Unbanked	Total
Did you receive any income by			
Check	75.8	67.2	73.5
Cash	22.0	26.0	23.1
Direct deposit/EFT	61.0	17.3	49.6
If received income by check: Did you ever cash your check at			
Bank	80.4	18.5	63.9
Credit union	13.5	3.6	10.9
Check cashing outlet (CCO)	19.5	68.2	32.4
Supermarket	8.0	22.3	11.8
Other	0.9	0.7	0.8
Have you purchased a money order in the last twelve months?			
Percent yes	51.0	74.8	57.2
Did you ever buy a money order at			
Post office	39.6	18.5	32.4
Check cashing outlet	41.3	63.5	48.9
Supermarket/convenience store	33.6	30.5	32.5
Workplace	1.9	0.5	1.4
Bank or credit union	23.9	4.3	17.2
Western Union	10.6	5.7	8.9
Liquor store	4.1	3.4	3.9
Have you sent money outside the United States in the last twelve months?			
Percent who said yes	15.5	21.2	17.0
Did you ever send money from			
Bank or credit union	18.0	11.1	15.7
CCO or currency exchange	17.9	23.9	19.9
Western Union	48.6	29.4	42.3
Other stand-alone wire service	16.9	43.9	25.7
Mail/express mail	8.3	10.8	9.1
Some other establishment	8.1	4.6	7.0
Borrowing			
Have a major credit card	60.9	9.5	47.5
Have any outstanding loans or other debt	49.0	31.8	44.5
Payday loan	4.6	3.4	4.3
Pawned anything	3.0	10.1	4.8
Rent-to-own	2.3	5.9	3.2

resents a connection to the mainstream financial sector, if not necessarily to a local bank or credit union. In total, about 34 percent of unbanked households have at least one relationship with the formal financial sector through check cashing, money order purchases, sending money outside the United States, or holding a credit card.

Interestingly, table 3-9 also demonstrates that many households with bank accounts also have ties to the so-called fringe financial sector. About 20 percent of banked households who receive income by check chose to cash a check at a CCO in the past month, and 8 percent cashed a check at a supermarket. Half of banked households purchased money orders in the past year, and of these households only 24 percent bought their money orders at a bank or credit union. About 40 percent bought money orders at a post office, 41 percent at a CCO, and 34 percent at a supermarket or convenience store. Other banked households that bought money orders did so at a Western Union (11 percent) or liquor store (4 percent). In addition, 15 percent of banked households sent money outside the United States during the past year, although only 18 percent of them sent the money through a bank. Western Union and other stand-alone wire services still dominate this market and were used by two-thirds of banked customers who send money internationally. Neither banked nor unbanked households were widespread users of fringe institutions for borrowing. Less than 5 percent of banked households had received a payday loan, pawned their possessions, or bought on rent-to-own terms in the past year. All told, 52 percent of banked households obtained at least one of these financial services from a non-bank institution: check cashing, money orders, international money transfers, payday loans, rent-to-own financing, or pawnbroking.

Summary

The main findings of the analysis may be summarized as follows:

—By far the most common reasons respondents gave for not having a bank account related to income and costs. Nearly half of those without a checking account and over 70 percent without a savings account said that they did not have enough money or that minimum balance requirements are too high. Under current pricing structures, there appears to be a sizable segment of LMI consumers for whom fringe institutions represent a lower-cost alternative to traditional bank accounts.

—By and large, LMI consumers are not ill-informed about the relative costs of banks and CCOs. Unbanked consumers, on average, give plausible estimates of the costs of using a CCO and minimum checking account balances. The majority of unbanked consumers believe they could afford the minimum balance if they wanted a checking account.

—Explicit barriers to account holding, such as lack of required identification and bad credit history, appear to be more important in keeping LMI consumers from having bank accounts than softer barriers, such as feeling unwelcome or not speaking English.

—Scarcity of bank branches in LMI neighborhoods does not appear to be a major barrier to account holding. Only a trivial fraction of respondents said they did not have a bank account because banks were not conveniently located.

—However, location does influence where consumers conduct their check-cashing business. In fact, two distinct segments are evident among those who regularly cash checks: a convenience-oriented group, which primarily patronizes CCOs, and a cost-oriented group, which patronizes banks.

—The complexity of opening and managing an account is an important barrier for about 12 percent of those without a checking account, but complexity is almost never an important reason for not having a savings account.

—A seldom-recognized deterrent to holding a checking account in LMI neighborhoods is that checks may be less widely accepted as a form of payment. For instance, about 20 percent of the survey population say their landlord will not accept a check for rent.

—The dichotomy between the banked and unbanked, which has framed much recent discourse about LMI consumers, is too rigid. Among those currently without a bank account, about half had an account in the past, and 34 percent have some ongoing relationship with a bank. In addition, about half of those with a bank account nevertheless conduct some financial business with a nonbank. In short, it is common for households to straddle both sides of the dual financial system.

—The vast majority of both banked and unbanked households say they are satisfied with the financial institutions they use.

Opportunities for Banks in the LMI Marketplace

The sheer volume of financial activity in LMI neighborhoods should cause mainstream financial institutions to sit up and take notice. Generalizing from our survey to the total population of LMI neighborhoods in Chicago, Los Angeles, and Washington, we estimate that there are 585,000 households with checking accounts and 480,000 households with savings accounts. Another 250,000 households are unbanked. Together, households in these LMI neighborhoods buy 1.25 million money orders each month and cash 1.7 million checks. Moreover, 165,000 households sent money internationally last year, many doing so on multiple occasions. With so much activity in these three cities alone, the total size of the urban LMI market nationally is simply too great for any financial institution to ignore.

With over 25 percent of LMI households unbanked, and half of banked households conducting at least some of their financial business with nonbank institutions, there is plenty of opportunity for banks to acquire new customers and expand their share-of-wallet with existing customers. However, banks seeking to expand in the LMI market face challenges. First, nonbank institutions are highly competitive, even on price. If exploitative fringe institutions charging supracompetitive prices dominated the LMI marketplace, as some critics suggest, then it would be relatively easy for banks to compete on price. However, findings from the MetroEdge survey reinforce the point originally made by Dunham (2001) that most LMI consumers pay relatively little in fees for financial services. For example, many consumers without bank accounts are able to cash checks for free at banks or retail stores; and those that patronize CCOs pay on average less than 2 percent of face value to cash a check. Banks considering expanding their business in LMI markets, therefore, must carefully consider whether they will be able to compete on price and still make a profit. Banks that cannot compete on price for basic services may nevertheless be able to compete on value by offering products and services for which consumers are willing to pay a premium. It is clear from this analysis that even very low-income consumers often are willing to pay a premium for convenience, and so banks might focus on improving the convenience of their offerings, possibly exploiting their ATM networks.

Second, low-income consumers are a heterogeneous group, and a one-size-fits-all strategy in marketing and product development for LMI consumers runs the risk of appealing to no one in particular. In addition to the remarkable demographic diversity in the LMI market, we have also seen that there is substantial diversity in attitudes, preferences, and experience. For example, half of unbanked households have had a bank account in the past, and winning back old customers is a fundamentally different marketing challenge from attracting new ones. In addition, customers who find managing a checking account difficult and confusing may require a different set of products and services than customers who write only one or two checks each month. Of course, any particular bank will probably want to focus on a few market segments that are suited to the bank's areas of competitive advantage. Responding to the diversity within urban neighborhoods will be a challenge for mainstream financial institutions, many of which look upon LMI consumers as already a fairly specialized market niche. In this respect, the industry is in need of better information about the distinct segments of the LMI market, comparable to the segmentation models of affluent consumers that are widely available.

An obvious starting point for any bank is to focus on capturing additional business from existing customers. We estimate that half of bank customers do business with at least one nonbank institution. Thus there is a significant opportunity for many banks to expand their market share in products they may already offer, such as money orders or wire transfers, with customers they already have. Convincing unbanked customers to open a bank account may be more difficult. Here, the low-hanging fruit may be the sizable portion of unbanked consumers who currently cash checks at a bank or credit union. Banks interested in tapping this segment may find it easier to identify and win over customers who are already doing business in their branches regularly.

References

Aizcorbe, Ana M., Arthur B. Kennickell, and Kevin B. Moore. 2003. "Recent Changes in U.S. Family Finances: Evidence from the 1998 and 2001 Survey of Consumer Finances." *Federal Reserve Bulletin* (January): 1–32.

Caskey, John P. 1994. *Fringe Banking: Check-Cashing Outlets, Pawnshops, and the Poor.* New York: Russell Sage Foundation.

———. 1997a. "Defining the Market. Financial Access in the 21st Century." Proceedings of a forum, Office of the Comptroller of the Currency, Washington, February 11.

———. 1997b. *Lower-Income Americans, Higher-Cost Financial Services.* University of Wisconsin at Madison: Center for Credit Union Research.

———. 2001. "Reaching Out to the Unbanked." In *Changing Financial Markets and Community Development: A Federal Reserve System Research Conference,* edited by Jackson L. Blanton, Sherrie L. Rhine, and Alicia Williams, pp. 81–92. Federal Reserve Bank of Richmond.

Dove Associates. 1999. *Survey of Non-Bank Financial Institutions for the Department of the Treasury.* Boston.

Dunham, Constance R. 2001. "The Role of Banks and Nonbanks in Serving Low- and Moderate-Income Communities." In *Changing Financial Markets and Community Development: A Federal Reserve System Research Conference,* edited by Jackson L. Blanton, Sherrie L. Rhine, and Alicia Williams, pp. 31–58. Federal Reserve Bank of Richmond.

Hogarth, Jeanne M., Chris Anguelov, and Jinkook Lee. 2003. "Why Households Don't Have Checking Accounts." *Economic Development Quarterly* 17 (1): 75–94.

Hogarth, Jeanne, and Kevin O'Donnell. 1998. "Bank Account Ownership and Use of Financial Institutions: Helping the 'Unbanked' Become 'Banked.'" Proceedings of the Eastern Family Economics and Resource Management Annual Conference, pp. 15–28.

———. 1999. "Banking Relationships of Lower-Income Families and the Governmental Trend toward Electronic Payment." *Federal Reserve Bulletin* 85: 459–73.

———. 2000. "If You Build It, Will They Come? A Simulation of Financial Product Holdings among Low- to Moderate-Income Households." *Journal of Consumer Policy* 23: 409–44.

Hungerford, Thomas. 2000. "Who Doesn't Have a Bank Account?" *Challenge* 43 (6): 65–75.

Juarez, Richard. 1997. "Financial Access in the 21st Century." Proceedings of a forum, Office of the Comptroller of the Currency, Washington, February 11.

Kennickell, Arthur, Martha Starr-McCluer, and Brian Surette. 2000. "Recent Changes in U.S. Family Finances: Results from the 1998 Survey of Consumer Finances." *Federal Reserve Bulletin* 86: 1–29.

Lieberman, Martin. 1997. "Financial Access in the 21st Century." Proceedings of a forum, Office of the Comptroller of the Currency, Washington, February 11.

Rhine, Sherrie L.W., and others. 2001. "The Role of Alternate Financial Service Providers in Serving LMI Neighborhoods." Research Study CCA-2001-1. Consumer Issues Research Series, Federal Reserve Bank of Chicago.

U.S. Department of the Treasury. 1997. "Mandatory EFT Demographic Study." OMB 15100-00-68. Washington: Financial Management Service.

Vermilyea, Todd, and James A. Wilcox. 2002. "Who is Unbanked and Why: Results from a Large, New Survey of Low- and Moderate-Income Adults." Unpublished paper prepared for the Federal Reserve Board of Chicago Conference on Bank Structure and Competition, May 8–10.

Washington, Ebonya. 2003. "Does Regulation of Banking and Fringe Banking Markets Impact Upon the Number of Unbanked Americans?" Massachusetts Institute of Technology, Department of Economics.

4

Refinance and the Accumulation of Home Equity Wealth

FRANK E. NOTHAFT AND YAN CHANG

In aggregate across the United States, home equity totaled $9.6 trillion by the end of 2004, an increase of $3.7 trillion in just five years.[1] According to the 2001 Survey of Consumer Finances, home equity (the difference between the home value and amount of mortgage debt on the property) accounted for at least 50 percent of net wealth for one-half of all households. Home equity is not only the single largest component of net wealth for most families, but is also held by a broader cross section of families when compared with other assets. For example, the U.S. homeownership rate was 69 percent in 2004, while only 52 percent of American families held stock either directly or indirectly.[2] Thus an increase in real home equity (that is, adjusting for general inflation) is the most significant component to overall wealth building.

This is particularly true for lower-income households, who tend to have more limited access to and investment in other forms of wealth. The homeownership rate for families with income below the median was 52 percent in 2004, while only 28 percent held stock market assets. Poterba (2000) reported that in 1998 the top 1 percent of stock equity investors held about one-half of total

---

1. Federal Reserve Board, "Flow of Funds, Release Z.1," table B.100. Home equity was $5.9 trillion as of December 31, 1999.

2. Homeownership data were from www.census.gov. Stock holdings were reported in Aizcorbe, Kennickell, and Moore (2003, table 6) and reflect 2001 data.

Figure 4-1. *Home Equity and Stock Holdings by Income Group Decile*

A. Home equity

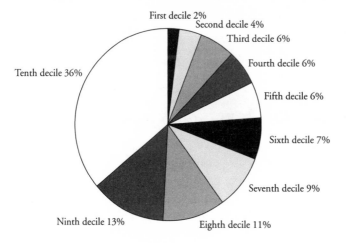

B. Stock holdings

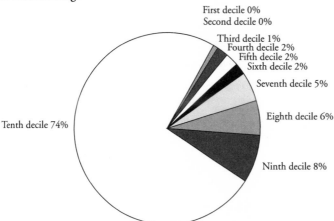

Source: Survey of Consumer Finances, 2001.

stock market wealth, while the 1 percent of households with the greatest holdings of real estate owned only 15 percent of all real estate. In fact, about three-
quarters of all stock-market wealth is held by the highest decile of income earners in the United States and almost none is held by families whose earnings fall
in the lowest third of the income distribution, whereas home equity wealth has a
more equal distribution across income groups, as shown in figure 4-1. Because
home equity wealth is more evenly distributed, lower-, middle-, and higher-
income families all benefit from a general rise in home equity.

Figure 4-2. *Lorenz Curves for Stocks and Home Equity*

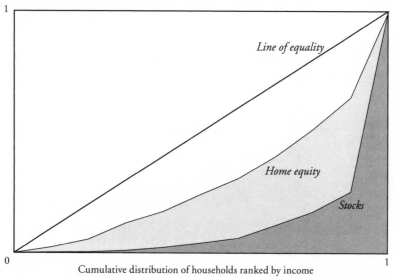

Cumulative distribution of asset

Line of equality

Home equity

Stocks

Cumulative distribution of households ranked by income

Source: Survey of Consumer Finances, 2001.

Calculation of Gini ratios confirms the more equitable distribution of home equity wealth across the American population. The Gini ratio has a value between zero and one, with zero designating the financial item under analysis is evenly distributed across income groups, and one indicating the highest-income household exclusively holds it. Using the 2001 Survey of Consumer Finances, the Gini ratio was 0.40 for home equity, 0.62 for net wealth, and 0.76 for stock market assets. Thus home equity is more evenly distributed across families than total wealth or stock market holdings.

Figure 4-2 shows the Lorenz curves for home equity and stock market assets, with the home equity curve closer to the straight line that indicates equal distribution across all families. The Lorenz curve is used in economics to describe inequality in wealth. The Lorenz curve is a function of the cumulative proportion of ordered individuals mapped onto the corresponding cumulative proportion of their wealth. Given a sample of n ordered individuals with x_i' the wealth of individual i and $x_1' < x_2' < \ldots < x_n'$, then the sample Lorenz curve is the polygon joining the points $(h/n, L_h/L_n)$, where

$$h = 0, 1, 2, \ldots, n,$$

$$L_0 = 0,$$

$$L_h = \sum_{i=1}^{h} x_i'.$$

If all individuals have the same wealth, the Lorenz curve is a straight diagonal line, called the line of equality. If there is any inequality in wealth, then the Lorenz curve falls below the line of equality. The total amount of inequality can be summarized by the Gini ratio, which is the ratio between the area enclosed by the line of equality and the Lorenz curve, and the total triangular area under the line of equality. For data ordered by increasing wealth of individuals, the Gini ratio is calculated by

$$G = \frac{\sum_{i=1}^{n}(2i - n - 1)x_i'}{n^2\mu} ,$$

where μ is the mean wealth of the individuals. In our calculation, we used $n = 10$, for the ten deciles of the population income distribution.

This chapter investigates the effect on home equity accumulation of different factors such as income, education, racial characteristics, and location. The analysis finds, after controlling for other variables, that racial and income differences continue to play important roles in determining a family's home equity level.

Accumulation of home equity wealth is important for providing a financial cushion to support household consumption when the head of the household is retired and for enabling a household to transfer wealth to a successive generation (for example, from parents to children). Moreover, home equity has also been shown to provide an important stimulus to current consumption. An increase in home equity has been found to have a more powerful wealth effect on consumption than an equivalent increase in stock market assets. This occurs because of the more equal holdings of home equity wealth across families and because of the lesser volatility of home values compared to stock market values, which translates into home equity wealth gains being viewed as more permanent than the seemingly transitory gains in the stock market. Home equity growth is more stable largely because home values are far less volatile than stock prices. Since 1970, the quarterly growth rate of home values has averaged 6.1 percent (at an annual rate) with a standard deviation of 4.9 percent, while the market value of corporate equities has gained 15.3 percent on average with a standard deviation of 42.6 percent. Clearly, stock values have been far more volatile than house prices. As a consequence, aggregate home equity in the United States has grown 8.6 percent per quarter (annualized) with a standard deviation of 7.8 percent, far less variable than stock market gains.[3]

3. Home value growth was measured by Freddie Mac's Conventional Mortgage Home Price Index (www.freddiemac.com). The market value of corporate equities and aggregate value of home equity were from the Flow of Funds data released by the Board of Governors of the Federal Reserve System (www.federalreserve.gov). The period of analysis was first quarter of 1970 to fourth quarter of 2003.

Case, Quigley, and Shiller (2001) as well as Bayoumi and Edison (2002) use a cross section of nations to separate the home equity and stock equity effects on overall consumption and find that the housing wealth effect is stronger. Based on estimates for 1984–2000 for the United States, Bayoumi and Edison (2002) found that each $1 increase in housing wealth led to a 7 cent increase in consumption, whereas a $1 increase in stock wealth caused a 4.5 cent increase. Research staff at the Federal Reserve Board have also found stronger marginal propensities to consume out of housing wealth, as reported by Federal Reserve Board Chairman Alan Greenspan (2001). Greenspan placed the effect on personal consumption expenditures generated from realized capital gains on home sales to be about 10 to 15 cents on the dollar, compared with a general wealth effect of 3 to 5 cents incorporating all components of household wealth. The International Monetary Fund (2003) also reported larger wealth effects from home value changes than from comparable stock equity movements. Skinner (1996) found that increases in housing wealth result in increased consumption spending by younger households, but not by older households.

The growth in home equity has not only stimulated aggregate consumption through a wealth effect, but it has provided an opportunity for families to convert some of this equity into cash by placing second mortgage loans (such as with home equity lines of credit) or cashing out equity as part of a refinance of an existing first mortgage.[4] Greenspan (2001) speculated that families offset declines in spending from falling stock prices by increased spending from real estate wealth. Thus an increase in home leverage helps smooth and stabilize household consumption. The secondary market activity of Freddie Mac and Fannie Mae has played an important role in ensuring a steady flow of credit to primary market lenders to meet the mortgage credit needs of U.S. families, as noted by Greenspan (2002):

> Especially important in the United States have been the flexibility and the size of the secondary mortgage market. Since early 2000, this market has facilitated the large debt-financed extraction of home equity that, in turn, has been so critical in supporting consumer outlays in the United States throughout the recent period of stress.

A second part of this chapter's empirical analysis addresses the determinants of leverage of a home, including the demographic characteristics of households.

---

4. "Households have been able to extract home equity by drawing on home equity loan lines, by realizing capital gains through the sale of existing homes, and by extracting cash as part of the refinancing of existing mortgages, so-called cash outs. Although all three of these vehicles have been employed extensively by homeowners in recent years, home turnover has accounted for most equity extraction. . . . Indeed, of the estimated net increase of $1.1 trillion in home mortgage debt during the past year and a half, approximately half resulted from existing home turnover." Greenspan (2003).

Refinance stimulates family consumption and investment in two ways. First, families benefit by paying lower mortgage rates, which saves about $10 billion a year in total mortgage interest costs. Second, families have engaged in a record level of cash-out refinance, which serves as a cash infusion to a family's balance sheet. Based on calculations made by Freddie Mac, during 2002 and 2003 families converted more than $250 billion of home equity into cash at the time of their conventional mortgage refinance, which they have plowed back into the economy.[5] A survey conducted by the Board of Governors of the Federal Reserve System (2002) of senior loan officers at commercial banks found that the median amount cashed out equaled about 10 to 15 percent of the balance of the loan that was paid off. Canner, Dynan, and Passmore (2002) found that 61 percent of the monies obtained in 2001 and early 2002 went toward home improvements and the repayment of other debts; the use of the remaining funds was approximately split between consumer expenditures and various financial or business investments. The recent senior loan officer survey also confirms this pattern: the two most common uses were home improvements and debt consolidation, with consumer expenditures and investments following.

Variations in the propensity to refinance and the type of refinance—cash out versus rate-and-term (that is, to obtain a lower interest rate or better loan term, with no cash out)—can vary substantially by demographic characteristic of the family and affect the ability of lower-income or minority families to accumulate wealth in the long run. Archer, Ling, and McGill (2002) found little difference between low- or moderate-income families and high-income families in mortgage prepayment activities. Van Order and Zorn (2002) found that low-income and minority households are significantly less likely to refinance when interest rates drop. Susin (2003) reported that blacks pay a higher interest on their mortgages than whites, and concluded that this is partially due to the lower propensity of blacks to refinance, and the lower likelihood of reducing their interest rate when they do refinance. Susin's study linked the mortgage interest rate to the refinance propensity by ethnic and racial groups, yet his study was based on one-year's survey data and his focus was on household mortgage rates in a particular survey rather than the refinance decision made by households. Boehm, Thistle, and Schlottmann (2003) observed that black borrowers pay a significantly higher annual percentage rate than white borrowers for both purchases and refinancing loans, and pricing differences largely explain the rate dif-

5. To identify the amount of mortgage rate reduction and volume of cash-out activity, we identified refinance loans that Freddie Mac purchased and which paid off a first mortgage loan in Freddie Mac's portfolio. This enabled us to directly measure the average rate reduction, as well as the amount of increase in loan balance for a cash-out refinance. During the refinance boom 2002–03, the average family reduced its mortgage rate by 1.125 percentage points. Based on the average loan size purchased by Freddie Mac in 2002 (about $130,000-$140,000), the average family shaved $100 per month off its mortgage payment, or an estimated $10 billion a year across all families in the United States.

ferential for refinance loans, indicating that black borrowers are experiencing negative impact in the refinance market. Instead of looking at individual household decisions in a defined period of time, their study offered an overview of all the refinance loans in the period of 1989 to 2001.

This chapter uses the national American Housing Survey (AHS), available for odd-numbered years from 1985 to 2001, to explore home equity accumulation, aggregate leverage, and refinance behavior among households of different ethnic and socioeconomic characteristics, especially the difference between old and young households, white and minority households, and high- and low-income households. The longitudinal perspective is particularly important to investigate the factors affecting the refinance decision, including the propensity to refinance, the likelihood of cashing out equity, and the consequences after a household refinances. The regression analysis shows that significant differences exist between these groups; in particular, minority and low-income groups have lower home equity, higher home leverage, and are less likely to take advantage of refinance opportunities. The lower refinance propensity implies a financial loss over time, as the family does not benefit from having the lowest possible mortgage interest rate.

Home Equity Study

Home equity is the foundation of household wealth accumulation and provides the basis for cash-out refinancing. The patterns of home equity accumulation by different age, racial, income-level groups are particularly of interest to us as the results have important social policy implications.

Data and Methodology

We used the biennial American Housing Survey for 1985–01, yielding nine national data waves. The AHS is ideal for our study since it provides detailed information concerning a homeowner's demographic, housing, and mortgage characteristics.

We limited our sample to homeowners aged 25 to 74 as these are the primary ages of ownership and mortgage use and because sample sizes became very small for younger and older households. We then grouped individual data by two years of age to form twenty-five separate age groups per AHS wave, from the 25–26 age group to the 73–74 age group. Within each group, sample size runs from 295 to 1,541 people, with an average of 973 per group.

For geographic location, we grouped data by the four census regions: Northeast, West, South, and Midwest. Data were also grouped by three metropolitan-area classifications: location within the primary central city of a metropolitan statistical area (MSA), outside the central city but within the MSA, and outside an MSA.

From the demographic information of the head of the household, we formed:

—three groups according to race and ethnicity: white non-Hispanic, African American, and other minorities;

—three groups according to marital status: married, single male, and single female;

—four groups according to education level: no high-school diploma, high-school graduate, some college, and bachelor's degree.[6]

For income level, we compared each household's income with its MSA median income, or consolidated MSA (CMSA) median income if the MSA code was absent. In the case that both the MSA and CMSA codes were missing, we used the median income of the same region and central city or metropolitan status as the basis for comparison. We then divided the population into five income categories—those with income:

—less than or equal to 80 percent of the area median income;

—above 80 percent but less than or equal to 120 percent of the area median;

—above 120 percent but at or below 160 percent of the area median;

—between 160 and 200 percent of the area median;

—and above twice the area median.

Based on housing characteristics, we formed two groups based on whether the dwelling was a condominium or cooperative, or not. We also divided the data into two groups according to whether the owner had a mortgage or home equity loan outstanding on the property or owned it free and clear.

Home equity value was calculated as the difference between home value and the balance of all the mortgages and home equity loans outstanding. In the case that the homeowner indicated the existence of a mortgage in the survey yet the debt balance was missing, we used the regional mean value to replace the missing value. All home values and mortgage balances were translated into 2001 dollars using the national Consumer Price Index (urban consumers) published by the Bureau of Labor Statistics (BLS).

Trends in Home Equity Accumulation

We study both the cross-sectional pattern between years and the longitudinal trend of certain age cohorts. While the former provides a collage of snapshots to compare groups within and across years, the latter focuses on particular cohorts and follows their equity changes through time.

---

6. The wording of the educational attainment item changed beginning with the 1995 AHS. Before1995, the question was "what is the highest grade or year of regular school . . . has ever completed?" Beginning in 1995, the question became "what is the highest level of school . . . has completed or the highest degree (he/she) has received?" Since 1995, the education field permits a distinction between attending twelfth grade (but not graduating) and being a high-school graduate, as well as attending four years of college versus receiving a bachelor's degree.

Figure 4-3. *Average Home Equity Grouped by Age of Household Head, 1985, 1993, 2001*

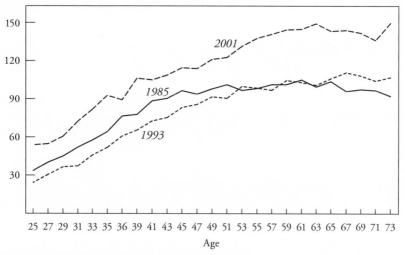

Home equity value (thousands of 2001 dollars)

Age

Source: American Housing Survey, 1985, 1993, 2001.

CROSS-SECTIONAL AND TEMPORAL DIFFERENCES IN HOME EQUITY WEALTH. Figure 4-3 shows average home equity for homeowners in the 1985, 1993, and 2001 AHS, grouped by the age of the household head. All three years show that home equity increases with age and peaks between the ages of 60 to 70, and this increase is more apparent in 2001 than in 1985 or 1993. Home equity gain from 1985 to 2001 is widespread for all age levels.

Figure 4-4 shows average home equity for homeowners in 2001 grouped by age and income (a similar pattern occurs for other AHS years). Homeowners with income above the median have substantially more real home equity, on average, than homeowners with income at or below the median. The home equity wealth gap widens with the age of the household head, from almost zero at the youngest age to about $40,000–$50,000 for age groups over sixty years. This likely reflects the fact that higher-income families generally will own higher-valued homes. For a given rate of appreciation, more expensive homes will create more home equity in dollar terms. Higher income families may also be more likely to pay down their mortgage debt more readily.

There are also significant mean home equity differences by location and other demographic characteristics, as shown in table 4-1. For example, homeowners who live in the West and Northeast have substantially more home equity than those who live in the South and Midwest, likely reflecting the higher value of homes in the former. By race and ethnicity, non-Hispanic white homeowners have more equity, on average, than minorities, while African Americans have

Table 4-1. *Average Home Equity in Real Dollars, 1985–2001*

Parameter	1985	1987	1989	1991	1993	1995	1997	1999	2001
Region									
West	108,083	105,135	130,843	118,184	103,971	110,646	102,368	131,684	171,542
Midwest	65,991	67,970	69,575	64,655	64,688	73,839	77,389	87,481	91,981
South	71,234	70,861	73,008	65,970	63,740	65,813	72,853	76,042	90,351
Northeast	112,982	142,264	147,071	119,786	109,032	106,111	97,032	109,193	140,560
Race/ethnicity									
Black	49,487	53,040	61,882	49,517	45,520	52,879	59,485	64,686	77,907
White, non-Hispanic	88,051	93,706	100,426	88,084	83,294	87,876	87,796	100,627	119,900
Other	85,244	90,122	107,054	96,198	85,252	86,374	73,415	92,436	116,826
Income group[a]									
≤80	67,863	73,484	79,420	72,039	71,897	76,505	76,195	86,448	96,011
>80 and ≤120	75,880	81,395	86,822	74,681	73,129	76,482	74,018	77,830	90,680
>120 and ≤160	79,055	85,690	88,465	76,935	71,616	77,639	76,157	82,772	101,103
>160 and ≤200	85,055	90,282	96,417	82,903	75,704	77,978	80,022	86,678	104,900
>200	112,081	117,457	129,448	113,014	100,104	102,139	103,121	126,090	157,332
Education									
No high school diploma	65,462	69,723	74,441	63,868	61,201	69,142	68,406	74,577	84,244
High-school graduate	77,394	82,474	85,717	74,743	70,985	76,235	78,450	81,192	91,254
Some college	85,246	90,031	96,629	84,685	77,612	81,815	78,925	88,972	103,703
College graduate	114,186	121,057	131,460	115,986	104,770	105,517	102,751	127,832	162,808
Marital status									
Married	89,155	94,870	102,774	90,079	85,030	88,946	89,299	102,930	125,825
Single male	70,102	77,016	84,527	72,792	63,959	71,180	68,947	80,935	97,236
Single female	76,206	81,930	88,075	78,378	75,016	79,106	76,636	85,512	95,634
MSA or non-MSA[b]									
Central city	83,683	90,031	95,814	83,960	75,647	79,285	75,501	91,368	115,377
MSA (noncentral city)	98,694	107,736	117,135	102,337	94,212	96,210	90,560	103,656	124,968
Non-MSA	58,961	60,300	59,159	56,228	56,194	63,183	74,387	77,281	86,263

Source: American Housing Survey, 1985–2001.
a. Family income measured as a percentage of area median family income.
b. MSA = metropolitan statistical area.

Figure 4-4. *Average Home Equity by Age of Household Head and Income, 2001*

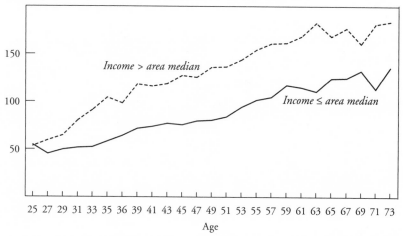

Home equity value (thousands of 2001 dollars)

Income > area median

Income ≤ area median

25 27 29 31 33 35 36 39 41 43 45 47 49 51 53 55 57 59 61 63 65 67 69 71 73

Age

Source: American Housing Survey, 2001.

less mean equity than other minorities. Married couples, who have the financial resources and greater spatial needs than single-person households, also have higher amounts of home equity. Home equity also rises steadily with educational attainment. Although not shown in the table, we found that the disparity between each of these groups was larger for older-age households.

Table 4-1 also illustrates how home equity wealth has varied over time. There was a pronounced dip in home equity in the 1991–93 period, especially in the Northeast and West regions. This coincided with the economic recession of 1990–91, which hit those two regions particularly hard, as described in Dzialo, Shank, and Smith (1993). Likewise, home equity increased sharply after 1997, especially in the Northeast and West, reflecting the acceleration in home value appreciation. Over the sixteen-year period, the West gained the most home equity in both absolute and relative dollars, with a 59 percent increase in real equity. Regional home value trends play an important role in affecting home equity increases for various demographic groups.

AGE COHORT HOME EQUITY WEALTH ACCUMULATION. Figure 4-5 summarizes the trends in home equity accumulation by cohort, by age in 1985. The lowest curve shows the mean home equity values for homeowners who were aged 25–26 in 1985, the curve immediately above gives home equity values for owners who were 35–36 in 1985, and so on. Within a year, the data show the same cross-sectional pattern as in figure 4-3, that is, that home equity rises with age. This was also generally true over time, as each age cohort had a rise in real home equity over the observation period. In general, younger cohorts have

Figure 4-5. *Home Equity Value by Age Cohorts, by Age in 1985*

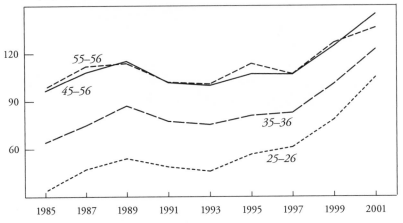

Home equity value (thousands of 2001 dollars)

Source: American Housing Survey, 1985–2001.

enjoyed more growth in home equity in both absolute and relative terms than older cohorts. The youngest group, 25–26 in 1985, had a growth of more than $70,000 through 2001, or a 213 percent increase. The cohort aged 35–36 in 1985 experienced a 91 percent increase in mean home equity, while the cohorts aged 45–46 gained 50 percent, and 55–56 gained 38 percent.[7]

Regression Estimation Using Grouped Observations

Given the large number of observations and aggregate nature of the data set, we decided to apply weighted generalized least squares (WGLS) to grouped data rather than household-level data. A simple explanation of this method is as follows: in the two-regressor case in which the data have already been grouped according to the size of one of the regressors, the method requires recombining the ungrouped data according to the value of the other explanatory variable; the two sets of grouped data are then pooled to form a regression equation. Since our sample data are cross-classified by our explanatory variables, we used the group regression method proposed by Haitovsky (1967) that corrects for the heteroscedasticity associated with grouped data. The regression results presented in tables 4-2 and 4-4 show both the number of ungrouped observations and number of groups formed from these observations that are used in our regressions.

---

7. A full set of appendix tables can be viewed at www.freddiemac.com/news/pdf/refinance_040604.pdf. At this website, appendix table 1 shows the equity growth paths for age cohorts. The average growth per age group is $55,000 in the sixteen-year span.

Table 4-2. *Home Equity Value Regression Results*

Parameter	Model 1			Model 2	
	Estimate	p-value		Estimate	p-value
Age	1,590	0.000		1,595	0.000
Region					
Northeast	37,894	0.000		37,800	0.000
South	−1,847	0.414		−2,111	0.267
West	41,367	0.000		41,219	0.000
Metro					
Central city	19,015	0.000		19,037	0.000
Noncentral city	32,925	0.000		32,838	0.000
Race					
Black	−16,333	0.000		−16,309	0.000
Other	781	0.818		755	0.792
Marital Status					
Single male	−10,540	0.000		−10,517	0.000
Single female	−8,566	0.001		−8,579	0.000
Income					
80+	10,644	0.000		10,459	0.000
120+	16,669	0.000		16,514	0.000
160+	21,306	0.000		21,257	0.000
200+	44,691	0.000		44,679	0.000
Education					
High school	15,598	0.000		16,011	0.000
Some college	24,531	0.000		24,957	0.000
Bachelor	50,117	0.000		50,451	0.000
No mortgage on house	41,755	0.000		41,717	0.000
Condo or co-op	−13,994	0.001		−13,696	0.000
Constant term	−132,176	0.000		−82,084	0.000
Year (1985–2001)	579	0.001			
Year					
1987 dummy				5,443	0.085
1989 dummy				11,027	0.001
1991 dummy				−176	0.956
1993 dummy				−6,672	0.040
1995 dummy				−3,608	0.255
1997 dummy				−6,302	0.054
1999 dummy				5,567	0.078
2001 dummy				26,045	0.000
R^2	0.974	0.982			
Number of groups	387	387			
Number of observations	218,816	218,816			

Source: American Housing Survey, 1985–2001.

Deterministic Factors of Home Equity Level

Applying WGLS on grouped observations, we examined the effects of multiple factors on determining the level of home equity for each year and for all. The factors in consideration include age, region, metropolitan group, race, marital status and gender, income level, and education level. We also controlled for whether the property was classified as a condominium or co-operative, or not, and whether it had a mortgage or home equity loan on it or not. The results of our regression on the pooled sample are in table 4-2. The single-year regressions gave very similar results; noteworthy results by single year are discussed below.[8]

Homeowner age contributes significantly to increasing home equity values. Each year increase in age brings $1,600 more in home equity according to the pooled regression results. For individual years, the increase is between $1,400 in 1985 and $1,900 in 2001.

Racial and ethnic differences are captured using African American and other minority binary variables. Coefficients represent differences between the respective race and ethnic group and non-Hispanic whites. Home equity for the African American group is significantly lower than the white group for all the years examined. The other race group (primarily a mixture of Hispanic, Asian, and Native Americans) is not significantly different from the white group. Everything else equal, an African American family has $16,000 less in home equity than a white non-Hispanic family.

Income also makes a large contribution to home equity differences. Real home equity varies directly with household income as measured relative to the local-area median income. For example, households with income more than twice the median have $45,000 more in home equity than low-income households (those with income at or below 80 percent of the median), holding other factors constant.

Home equity also increases directly with educational attainment. Significantly higher home-equity levels are observed for groups with a bachelor's degree or higher, some college education, and a high-school diploma than those with less than high-school education. For example, household heads with a bachelor's degree had $50,000 more home equity wealth, on average, than high-school dropouts.[9]

Married couples have higher home equity wealth than their single counterparts. Single males had $11,000 less home equity compared to married couples, and single females had $9,000 less than married couples. Our single-wave regressions show a consistent difference over time, with statistically significant gaps in eight of nine waves for single males, and seven of nine waves for single females.

---

8. The single-year models are shown in appendix table 3 at the website.

9. As shown in appendix table 3 at the website the coefficient for bachelor's degree was much larger in 2001 than in previous years.

Regional differences in home equity level were observed for each year and for the pooled sample. The West and Northeast consistently show higher home equity levels than the Midwest. Reflected in the overall regression, Northeast homeowners have $38,000 more home equity wealth than Midwest owners, and households in the West region have $41,000 more home equity than those in the Midwest. The amount of the regional difference differed by year, reflecting asynchronous housing cycles. To illustrate, home equity in the West declined relative to other regions in the 1991–93 period, but grew substantially larger in 2001, reflecting the severe recession of the early 1990s and the housing boom of the last few years.

The central city or suburban status of the property affects home equity value as well. The regression for all the years shows that families who reside in metropolitan areas have larger home equity wealth. Homeowners in a central city average more equity than those in nonmetropolitan areas, but less than those who live in suburbs, holding other factors constant. The homeowner in a suburban portion of an MSA had $33,000 more home equity than those living in a nonmetropolitan area, and households in a central city had $19,000 more home equity.

The year dummies show large home equity increases in 1989 and 2001, in part reflecting periods of relatively rapid real home-value appreciation. In those two years, real home equity was, on average, $11,000 and $26,000 greater than in 1985, holding various other factors constant. Likewise, in 1993 home equity values were $7,000 lower than those in 1985, reflecting weak home-value growth during the immediately preceding years.[10]

Aggregate Leverage Study

Using the nine waves of the AHS, we applied the same trend analysis and group regression methods to study aggregate leverage as we had for home equity. Aggregate leverage was calculated as the ratio of total mortgage balance in a group over total home value in the same group. The mortgage balance was given the value of zero for those who owned their home without mortgages or home equity loans.

Trends in Aggregate Leverage

Both the aggregate leverage by age groups and the leverage for age cohorts show a continuous decline through the years. The speed and pattern of the reduction in leverage differ, however, across various groups.

---

10. Real home-value appreciation, measured by deflating Freddie Mac's Conventional Mortgage Home Price Index by the Bureau of Labor Statistics' Consumer Price Index, showed negative change each year from 1990 to 1993. Real price growth was especially strong in the latter part of the 1980s as well as since 1998.

Figure 4-6. *Aggregate Leverage by Age of Household Head, 1985, 1993, 2001*

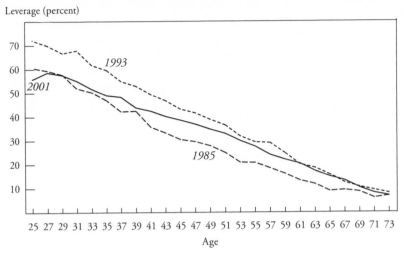

Source: American Housing Survey, 1985, 1993, 2001.

CROSS-SECTIONAL AND TEMPORAL DIFFERENCES IN LEVERAGE. Aggregate leverage declines steadily with age, as shown in the age-leverage profiles for 1985, 1993, and 2001 in figure 4-6. Reflecting the weakness in home values during the early 1990s, the 1993 profile shows higher leverage ratios across nearly all age groups than for the other two years. The leverage ratio and dollar amount of home equity are inversely related for any given homeowner; all else the same, a larger amount of equity implies a lower leverage. This pattern is also generally borne out in the aggregate data, as 1993 age groups usually had the lowest amount of real home equity of these three years, as was observed in figure 4-3.

Within each age group, leverage ratios appear higher for higher-income families. Using 2001 data, figure 4-7 shows two age-leverage profiles that differ only by homeowner income: those above the area median and those at or below. Those with income above area median have higher leverage in every age group than those with income at or below area median. However, figure 4-7 does not control for other factors that are correlated with income that may determine aggregate leverage ratios.

Cross-sectional analysis on leverage reveals that, from 1985 to 2001, all the groups we observed experienced growth in their aggregate leverage. The results are listed in table 4-3. By region, homeowners in the Northeast had lower leverage values than those in other regions, while owners in the West had the highest leverage ratios. White non-Hispanic owners had the lowest leverage compared with African American and other minority groups. Leverage appears to increase as income increases: homeowners with income at or below 80 percent of area median

Figure 4-7. *Aggregate Leverage by Age of Household Head and Income, 2001*

Leverage (percent)

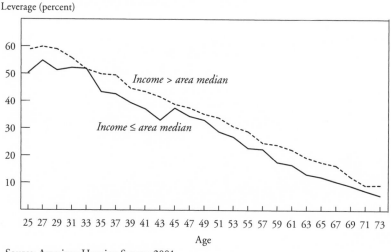

Age

Source: American Housing Survey, 2001.

had the lowest leverage, and leverage rises with income up to homeowners with income twice the area median, above which the leverage ratio begins to decline. This is consistent with Merry's (2002) findings using 1989, 1993, and 1998 SCF data. Leverage also generally rises with educational attainment: owners with less than a high-school education had the lowest leverage while those with a college degree and above were typically the most highly leveraged. Single males tended to be more highly leveraged than married couples or single females, and single females had the lowest leverage. Homeowners in central cities were the most highly leveraged, and those living in a non-MSA area were the least leveraged.

AGE COHORT LEVERAGE TRENDS. Figure 4-8 shows the time series of aggregate leverage for four age cohorts, by age in 1985. The highest curve reflects the average leverage over time of those homeowners that were aged 25-26 in 1985, the curve immediately below it shows aggregate leverage of those aged 35-36 in 1985, and so on. Compared with the amount of leverage they had in 1985, each age cohort had reduced their aggregate leverage ratio by 2001, with an average reduction across all age cohorts of 14 percentage points. The declines were more pronounced for younger cohorts, with a drop of 19 percentage points for the youngest cohorts versus about 12 percentage points for the oldest. Nonetheless, additional analysis shows that each age cohort in 2001 had higher leverage than its counterpart in 1985. That is, the cohort aged 41–42 in 2001 (who had been aged 25–26 in 1985) had higher leverage than the 41–42-year-olds in 1985. Overall the increase was 6 percentage points across all the age cohorts, with a

Table 4-3. *Aggregate Leverage, 1985–2001*

Percent

Parameter	1985	1987	1989	1991	1993	1995	1997	1999	2001
Region									
West	34.7	38.1	34.7	39.5	44.7	42.5	41.5	40.0	34.7
Midwest	30.6	30.5	32.2	35.1	38.1	37.4	33.7	36.0	35.5
South	31.3	33.3	34.3	36.5	39.4	38.8	34.5	37.7	35.2
Northeast	21.2	21.4	24.4	29.1	32.6	32.4	33.3	34.3	30.0
Race/ethnicity									
Black	37.2	38.4	36.0	42.9	47.4	40.9	35.4	38.1	36.3
White, non-Hispanic	28.6	29.5	30.4	34.1	37.7	37.0	34.8	36.3	33.1
Other	37.4	39.2	37.3	41.7	45.4	45.0	45.5	43.5	38.9
Income group[a]									
≤80	20.1	19.9	20.2	22.6	26.0	23.9	20.8	21.9	22.2
>80 and ≤120	27.5	27.4	28.6	32.2	35.2	32.3	32.0	35.6	33.1
>120 and ≤160	31.8	32.6	33.6	38.2	40.8	38.7	37.6	39.8	37.3
>160 and ≤200	32.8	34.1	35.5	39.1	43.1	42.3	40.8	43.8	39.6
>200	32.7	34.8	35.0	39.6	44.4	44.5	42.1	41.5	36.5
Education									
No high school diploma	20.1	20.0	20.8	24.1	27.6	26.1	22.3	26.5	25.6
High-school graduate	26.7	27.0	28.2	31.6	34.5	31.8	28.4	32.0	30.3
Some college	33.5	34.8	34.1	38.4	41.6	39.7	38.0	39.4	36.8
College graduate	34.0	35.3	35.4	39.1	43.2	44.0	42.3	40.7	35.6
Marital status									
Married	30.2	31.2	32.1	36.0	39.8	39.6	37.2	38.7	34.9
Single male	33.9	34.4	34.2	38.9	44.0	39.4	36.4	36.6	32.9
Single female	23.4	24.0	24.9	27.9	30.8	29.4	28.9	30.8	30.7
MSA or non-MSA[b]									
Central city	31.9	32.9	33.3	37.7	41.7	40.1	38.9	38.7	34.4
MSA (noncentral city)	29.0	30.2	30.7	35.0	39.1	39.3	37.0	38.3	35.1
Non-MSA	27.4	28.3	30.0	31.9	33.6	29.3	24.7	27.7	26.9

Source: American Housing Survey, 1985–2001.

a. Family income measured as a percentage of area median family income.

b. MSA = metropolitan statistical area.

Figure 4-8. *Aggregate Leverage by Age Cohorts, by Age in 1985*

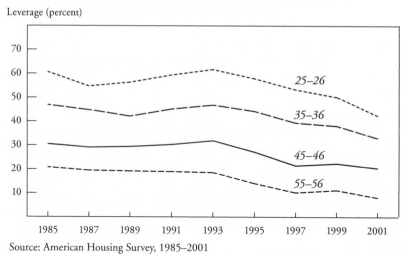

Leverage (percent)

Source: American Housing Survey, 1985–2001

larger increase among younger cohorts.[11] The mean increase for the homeowners aged 25–40 in 1985 was 8 percentage points, double the mean increase of 4 percentage points for those aged 41–58 in 1985. This confirms the findings of Nothaft (2000) comparing 1989 and 1999 AHS data, and suggests that younger cohorts may be more willing to take on mortgage debt than older cohorts.

Deterministic Factors of Leverage

We applied the same regression method on grouped data as in our home equity analysis to identify significant determinants of aggregate leverage. Including both homeowners with a mortgage on their home at the time of interview and those owning free and clear, we found that most of the factors that affect home equity accumulation also determine aggregate leverage. Table 4-4 presents the regression results for the pooled sample. The single-year models gave similar results, and interesting findings are noted in the following discussion.[12]

The regression analysis confirms the pattern in figure 4-6: Leverage decreases with age. One year's advance in age brings a 0.7 percentage point drop in leverage. In the annual regressions, the effect remains consistently between 0.6 and 0.8 percentage points over the 1985–2001 period, despite the substantial increase in cash-out activity during the past decade. Aggregate home equity extraction as part of a prime, conventional refinance has been estimated to have

11. A table with leverage ratios by year and age cohort is presented in appendix table 2 at the website.

12. Regression estimates for each of the nine AHS years are in appendix table 6 at the website.

Table 4-4. *Aggregate Leverage Regression Results*

Parameter	Model 1		Model 2	
	Estimate	*p-value*	*Estimate*	*p-value*
Age	−0.006	0.000	−0.007	0.000
Region				
Northeast	−0.046	0.000	−0.046	0.000
South	0.025	0.000	0.026	0.000
West	0.015	0.073	0.015	0.043
Metro				
Central city	−0.022	0.007	−0.021	0.004
Noncentral city	−0.039	0.000	−0.037	0.000
Race				
Black	0.022	0.031	0.023	0.016
Other	−0.009	0.368	−0.009	0.331
Marital status				
Single male	0.010	0.224	0.010	0.187
Single female	−0.013	0.094	−0.013	0.063
Income[a]				
>80 and ≤120	−0.081	0.000	−0.081	0.000
>120 and ≤160	−0.090	0.000	−0.089	0.000
>160 and ≤200	−0.091	0.000	−0.090	0.000
>200	−0.097	0.000	−0.097	0.000
Education				
High school	−0.121	0.000	−0.123	0.000
Some college	−0.123	0.000	−0.124	0.000
Bachelor	−0.127	0.000	−0.129	0.000
No mortgage on house	−0.504	0.000	−0.504	0.000
Condo or co-op	0.046	0.001	0.045	0.000
Constant term	0.774	0.000	0.991	0.000
Year (1985–2001)	0.003	0.000		
Year				
1987 dummy			0.016	0.106
1989 dummy			0.021	0.046
1991 dummy			0.053	0.000
1993 dummy			0.084	0.000
1995 dummy			0.068	0.000
1997 dummy			0.063	0.000
1999 dummy			0.066	0.000
2001 dummy			0.025	0.018
R^2	0.987		0.990	
Number of groups	387		387	
Number of observations	218,816		218,816	

Source: American Housing Survey, 1985–2001.

a. Family income measured as a percentage of area median family income.

grown from $20 billion during the 1993 refinance boom year, to $40 billion during the 1998 refinance boom, to more than $80 billion during 2001.[13]

African American homeowners had a significantly higher leverage ratio, estimated at 2 percentage points above that of white non-Hispanic homeowners. Other minorities had a leverage rate that was insignificantly different from that of white non-Hispanic owners.

In contrast to the pattern in figure 4-7, higher income is associated with lower aggregate leverage once other factors are controlled for in the regression. Homeowners with income above 80 percent but no more than 120 percent of area median income had leverage that was 8 percentage points lower than those with income less than or equal to 80 percent of area median income; those with income above 120 percent of area median income and no greater than twice area median income had leverage that was 9 percentage points less; and those with income more than double area median had 10 percentage points less. In the annual models, this difference between the highest- and lowest-income groups increased between 1985 and 1991, where the largest difference was observed at 12 percentage points, and gradually decreased to 2001, where the lowest difference was measured at less than 8 percentage points.

Educational attainment was also inversely related to leverage. High-school graduates and homeowners with some college education had 12 percentage points lower leverage than high-school dropouts. Homeowners with a college degree and higher had leverage that was 13 percentage points less. This distinction between education groups increased from 1985 to 1993, peaking with an 18 percentage point difference between highest- and lowest-education groups, and declined to 2001, where the difference was less than 10 percentage points. Marital status had little effect on aggregate leverage, after controlling for other factors.

We observed significant leverage differences by census region and central city MSA location. Homeowners in the Northeast had 5 percentage points less leverage than Midwest owners. Families in the South had 3 percentage points more leverage, and in the West had 2 percentage points more leverage, than those in the Midwest. Homeowners in metropolitan areas generally had lower leverage ratios than those who lived outside of MSAs. Central city families had 2 percentage points less leverage than non-MSA families. Families in an MSA but outside the central city had 4 percentage points less leverage than non-MSA families.

The goodness of fit is higher in the model that allows for separate year effects. Aggregate leverage ratios reached 8 percentage points above the 1985 level by 1993, reflecting the relatively slow pace of home-value growth in the

---

13. Freddie Mac's estimates of the amount of home equity cashed out rose to about $140 billion during 2003. See www.freddiemac.com/news/finance/refi_archives.htm.

early 1990s related to the economic recession. The pickup in appreciation after 1993 gradually reduces the difference to 3 percentage points by 2001.

Comparison of Home Equity and Leverage Models

The first two empirical portions of this chapter have examined the determinants of home equity both in absolute dollar terms and also relative to home value (for any given homeowner, the leverage ratio equals one less the ratio of home equity to home value). The two sets of analyses lead to similar conclusions. For example, home equity increases and leverage decreases as age increases. In other words, homeowners increase their home equity in real dollars and also relative to their home value as they age. The duality also flows to comparisons by race and ethnicity, income, and other variables. Compared with white non-Hispanic homeowners, African Americans have lower average home equity and higher average leverage. Compared with the highest-income group (homeowners with income double the area median), the lowest-income group had less home equity wealth and also a higher leverage ratio.

The year dummies show that aggregate leverage is always higher than in 1985. This result is different from the pattern in the home equity model, which had some years in which real equity was below the 1985 level, and some years above. Over the entire 1985–2001 sample period, the average home equity value increased about $600 a year, and the average leverage increased about 0.3 percentage points per year. The main reason that both real home equity wealth and aggregate leverage increased over the sample period is because home values appreciated more than the Consumer Price Index (CPI). Between 1985 and 2001, home values increased 4.8 percent per year (from 91.0 to 193.5), as measured by Freddie Mac's Conventional Mortgage Home Price Index, while the CPI-urban consumers increased by 3.2 percent per year (from 107.6 to 177.1). Thus real home value growth allowed both real home equity and the leverage ratio to increase over the sample period.

Refinance Study

The difference in propensity to refinance is not merely a random household decision. Taken as a group, those who miss the opportunities to reduce interest payments through refinance trail significantly in wealth accumulation.

Data and Methodology

Our refinance study focuses on the decision made by the homeowner to refinance, take cash out, or place additional second mortgages. The AHS is well suited for this task because it goes back to the same dwelling unit every survey and one knows whether the same homeowner is still in the home. By comparing the mortgage information provided at each survey, we determined whether homeowners had chosen to refinance, place an additional mortgage, or leave their mortgage unchanged in the two-year period the two surveys bookend. We used logit regressions to identify the effect of household characteristics and mortgage-related variables on the likelihood of a household's decision. There were four major refinance booms during our sample period: 1986, 1992–93, 1998, and 2001–02, so we studied the following consecutive surveys that correspond: 1985–87, 1991–93, 1997–99, and 1999–2001.

We identified the same household in consecutive survey years by longitudinally matching the control numbers and keeping those reported as "same household" and "same unit." We also required that the reported move-in year and month were the same in both years' surveys. Additional restrictions we imposed on our sample were: mortgage characteristic values were not assigned; the year of obtaining the first mortgage had to be nonmissing; and the year of obtaining the first mortgage provided in the latter survey cannot predate the year provided in the former survey.

We study three kinds of choices made by homeowners that affect their mortgage loan profile. The first one is refinance. This is identified by a change in the origination year of the first mortgage loan in the subsequent survey, or, in the case that the same mortgage initiation year is reported in the two surveys, a change in loan amount or fixed-rate mortgage interest rate.[14] The second kind of decision is whether to cash out some home equity. This includes an increase in the unpaid loan balance reported in the subsequent survey, or a second mortgage is present in the subsequent survey where there was not one in the previous survey.[15] The third kind of finance decision we explore is the placement of a second mortgage. Households may elect to cash out home equity by placing a second mortgage or increasing their second-mortgage indebtedness (for example, by paying off a second mortgage and placing another with a larger balance). We identified households in this category by comparing the second-mortgage characteristics reported in consecutive surveys to determine whether they had placed a new second mortgage or reported an increase in the unpaid loan balance of the second mortgage in the subsequent survey.

14. In the case where the same origination year and loan amount is reported in the two surveys, we exclude ARMs and define refinance only if the fixed-rate interest rate has changed; ARMs are otherwise included in the analysis if the origination years or the loan amounts differ. As a robustness check when the origination years were the same, we defined a loan amount change several ways: loan amounts unequal; differ by more than $5,000; differ by more than $10,000; differ by 5 percent; differ by 10 percent. Likewise, we considered two cases for fixed-rate change: interest rates unequal and interest rates differ by more than 0.4 percentage points. The resulting logit estimates did not vary substantively with the alternative cuts. Table 4-5 results use a loan amount change of more than $5,000 and a fixed interest rate change of more than 0.4 percentage points.

15. We conducted sensitivity analysis by specifying several alternative definitions of loan balance increase: loan balance greater; greater by $5,000; greater by $10,000; greater by 5 percent; and greater by 10 percent. The estimates were not sensitive to the definition used. Table 4-5 results use a loan balance increase of more than $10,000.

Deterministic Factors of Refinance Probability

We used logit regression techniques to separately model the probability of refinance, cash out, and second mortgage placement, where a binary dependent variable indicates whether the homeowner had refinanced, cashed out equity, or placed a second mortgage, respectively. For each probability, we estimated the model for an overall sample pooled across the four refinance booms (1985–87, 1991–93, 1997–99, 1999–2001).[16] The results for the pooled regressions are presented in table 4-5.[17]

To capture the incentive to refinance, we put in a binary variable that indicates whether the real house value had increased over the two-year period between surveys (that is, that home value had increased by more than CPI inflation), and another binary variable that showed whether the mortgage interest rate (or if there was a second lien, the average interest rate on both mortgages, weighted by unpaid balance) had declined over the same period. We found that both the value increase and interest rate reduction variables were positively related to the refinance probability, indicating that refinance is a rational decision by households in reaction to market changes. Both of these variables were also positively related to the cash-out likelihood and additional second mortgage likelihood, which means that they are not actions solely driven by a need for cash, but actions driven by economic incentives as well.

Our two racial indicators, black and other minorities, were both negative and significant, indicating minorities have a smaller likelihood of refinancing. This is consistent with the findings of Susin (2003), though Archer, Ling, and McGill (2002) find no significant difference in the pretermination risk of loans for blacks and Hispanics. Furthermore, when they do refinance, the average rate reduction is lower than those whose head of household is white. The average rate reduction experienced by a household headed by African Americans is 0.39 percentage points, compared to a rate reduction of 1.33 percentage points on average for white households.

Our income variable had five values to match the five relative income groupings used in our home equity and leverage regressions (1 for income at or below 80 percent of the area median, 2 for income greater than 80 percent but no more than 120 percent of area median, and so on). The coefficient on income

16. Pooling may introduce serial correlation because the same homeowner may appear in successive refinance periods. For simplicity, we chose to ignore this effect. To ascertain whether that would alter our conclusions, we also reestimated the model eliminating duplicate records from the same homeowner, thus eliminating serial correlation caused by multiple homeowner records. We reestimated the model keeping only the first homeowner record, and then keeping only the last homeowner record. The parameter estimates in these models did not differ in any substantive fashion from those reported in table 4-5.

17. Logit models for each of the four periods were also estimated separately and are shown in appendix table 5 at the website.

Table 4-5. *Refinance Probability Regression Results*

Parameter	Refinance		Cash-out		Take out additional second mortgage	
	Estimate	p-value	Estimate	p-value	Estimate	p-value
Age	−0.019	0.000	−0.020	0.000	−0.020	0.000
Region						
Northeast	−0.173	0.006	0.095	0.192	0.022	0.824
South	−0.364	0.000	−0.193	0.009	−0.170	0.082
West	0.001	0.993	0.363	0.000	−0.194	0.065
Metro						
Central city	0.010	0.892	−0.018	0.836	0.105	0.414
Noncentral city	0.155	0.018	0.065	0.408	0.277	0.015
Race						
Black	−0.669	0.000	−0.013	0.924	0.523	0.001
Other	−0.160	0.066	−0.251	0.015	−0.133	0.394
Marital status						
Single male	−0.056	0.437	0.087	0.298	0.195	0.093
Single female	0.015	0.838	−0.139	0.129	−0.158	0.241
Income level	0.074	0.000	0.131	0.000	0.122	0.000
Education level	0.072	0.003	0.049	0.082	−0.010	0.799
First-time homebuyer	−0.156	0.001	−0.307	0.000	−0.362	0.000
Condo or co-op	−0.175	0.074	−0.372	0.007	−0.813	0.001
House value increase?	0.063	0.160	0.412	0.000	0.288	0.000
Interest rate reduced?	2.131	0.000	1.093	0.000	0.394	0.000
Loan-to-value	−0.026	0.474	−2.332	0.000	−1.994	0.000
Log (loan size)	0.346	0.000	0.257	0.000	0.312	0.000
At top code?	0.217	0.056	0.129	0.232	−0.236	0.168
Payment-to-income	0.003	0.184	0.002	0.447	−0.006	0.137
Year						
2001 dummy	0.512	0.091	1.004	0.001	0.644	0.078
1999 dummy	0.349	0.228	0.529	0.105	−0.991	0.182
1993 dummy	0.687	0.000	0.275	0.000	−0.223	0.003
Constant term	−5.866	0.000	−4.510	0.000	−4.977	0.000
R^2	0.3557		0.1283		0.0560	
Number of observations	13,152		15,201		15,201	

Source: American Housing Survey, 1993, 1999, 2001.

was positive and significant. While the estimation controlled for loan size, education level, ratio of payment to income, and age, income may also proxy for financial sophistication and wealth of the household. Higher-income applicants generally have higher loan origination rates, as shown in Canner and Gabriel (1992). Giliberto and Thibodeau (1989) and Dickinson and Heuson (1993) find that income contributes directly to the likelihood of interest rate-driven mortgage terminations.

Homeowner's age was negatively related to the refinance probability. This may show a difference in attitude toward refinancing: younger homeowners are more willing to try refinance. Younger owners were also more prone to take out cash through refinance or placing an additional second mortgage.

Our first-time homebuyer indicator was negative and significant in all three models: refinance, cash out, and placing an additional second mortgage. This is in line with the results of Archer, Ling, and McGill (2002), which showed that first-time homebuyers who obtained their first mortgage less than five years earlier were less likely to prepay their mortgage.

Our educational attainment variable had four values, representing the four education groups used in our home equity and leverage models (1 for high-school dropouts, 2 for high-school graduates, and so on). As a proxy for financial sophistication, our education level variable was positive and significant in the refinance regression, meaning that higher educational attainment increased the likelihood to refinance. This finding agrees with that of Archer, Ling, and McGill (2002) and Quigley (1987).

We included four variables that show the financial condition of the families in the earlier year of the matched survey, or for those who refinanced, their financial conditions before their refinance decision:

—a loan size variable, which is the natural log of the unpaid principal balance of the mortgage in the first year of the matched surveys, proxies for the strength of the incentive to refinance;

—the ratio of loan to value in the earlier year, proxies for collateral and liquidity constraints;

—a binary top-code variable is included, which equals one whenever the home value or loan size is at the AHS top code (maximum value released by the Census Bureau) for that survey year, to capture the effects of a truncated value distribution;

—and the ratio of payment to income, the ratio of monthly payments to household income. We found that higher loan-to-value reduced the likelihood of refinance in some years, and significantly reduced the chances of taking cash out or placing new second mortgages for all the years. Archer, Ling, and McGill (1996, 2002) point out that increased collateral constraints reduce the probability of prepayment. We find evidence that high loan-to-value also reduces the odds of cashing out equity or placing second mortgages. Homeowners with larger loan sizes were more prone to refinance, cash out equity, or obtain second mortgages. Controlling for other factors, this shows that a larger loan balance provides more incentive for a homeowner to reduce monthly payments through refinance motivated by interest-rate reduction, or that a homeowner with larger wealth had more opportunity to refinance or cash out equity. The payment-to-income ratio in the prior year of the matched surveys had insignificant effects.

Implications of Regression Results

Our refinance study indicates that minorities, especially blacks, and lower-income homeowners were less likely to take advantage of refinance opportunities to reduce the interest rates on their mortgages, even after adjusting for other demographic, loan, and property characteristics. A cause of such findings, of course, may be one or more omitted variables. For example, the AHS lacks credit score or self-employment data; Avery and others (2000) have shown that median credit scores among homeowners with a mortgage are lower in ZIP code areas with higher minority composition, suggesting a correlation of score with race that could account for our finding. Likewise, self-employed workers generally have more volatile income, which may reduce their loan acceptance rates for prime loans or lead them to apply for so-called alt-A or A-minus loans, which carry higher interest rates than prime loans.[18] Another explanation for our findings is that minority and lower-income homeowners are less knowledgeable of the refinance process and have less access to information on current mortgage rates. Some of this may reflect language barriers and cultural differences (especially for immigrants), lack of access to the Internet and personal computers, and a generally lower level of financial literacy.

A refinance boom driven by low interest rates allows homeowners to reduce their mortgage interest payments, freeing income to meet other expenses or increase savings, or use the funds taken out from home equity extraction to pay off high-rate consumer debts such as credit card and automobile loans. Missed refinance opportunities have a negative effect on household finances in many ways, and represent a sizable loss in wealth over time.

We illustrate the cost of this missed-opportunity effect to a black homeowner through a simulation summarized in table 4-6. Assuming two homeowners with exactly the same characteristics except one is an African American household head and the other a white non-Hispanic household head, we calculated the probability of refinance for each based on the coefficients from our refinance regression. The characteristics we choose were: married, aged 35–36, income between 1.2 and 1.6 times the area median, living in the Northeast, college

18. The AHS had no self-employment information before 1997. Beginning that year, there is a question that refers to the number of self-employed hours worked in the week before the survey, but no information is available regarding the past year or whether the previous week was a typical workweek.

Table 4-6. *Cost of Missed Opportunity to Refinance*

	Black	Low income	Black and low income
Lower refinance probability	–0.165	–0.069	–0.236
Loan size	$100,000	$100,000	$100,000
Interest rate reduction through refinance (percent)	–1.327	–1.361	–1.381
Current interest rate (post-refinance) (percent)	7.944	7.792	7.786
Monthly payment difference	$94.33	$96.34	$97.77
Simple aggregate overpaid interest[a]	$33,960	$34,682	$35,196
Present value of forgone benefit over life of loan	$12,394	$12,657	$12,845
Future value of opportunity cost at retirement	$653,095	$666,982	$676,862
Number of homeowners with mortgages (2001 AHS)	3,938,515	9,145,090	1,230,859
Group wealth loss[b] (billions of dollars)	$22.0	$21.9	$10.2

Source: American Housing Survey, 2001.

a. Simple aggregate overpaid interest = monthly payment difference * 360 months.

b. Group wealth loss = number of homeowners with mortgages * simple aggregate overpaid interest * lower refinance probability.

degree or above, owning a house (not a condo or co-op) with an 80 percent loan-to-value ratio and 18 percent payment-to-income ratio. The African American household would have a 16.5 percent lower refinance probability than their white non-Hispanic counterpart. Over our sample, the average interest rate was 7.944 percent for white homeowners who refinanced, and the average rate reduction they achieve through refinance is 1.327 percent. Assuming a loan balance of $100,000, we calculated the value of the benefit of refinance, or the value lost for the black household that does not refinance, assuming a thirty-year fixed-rate mortgage. The simple aggregate interest overpaid is $33,960 over the life of the mortgage. Taking the number of African American families with a mortgage from the 2001 AHS and the lowered propensity to refinance, the group as a whole overpays $22.0 billion in mortgage interest over thirty years because of missed refinance opportunities; alternatively, this is the amount of forgone wealth. Discounted at 8.39 percent, the average yield on the thirty-year constant-maturity Treasury from 1977 to 2002, the overpayment by those who missed the refinance opportunity equals $12,394 in present value; alternatively, these homeowners are paying interest sufficient to borrow $112,394, even though they have borrowed only $100,000. (The present value of overpayments averaged across all black homeowners, not solely the estimated 16.5 percent who missed refinancing, is ($12,394)*(0.165) = $2,045 per homeowner.)

Furthermore, there is an opportunity cost to the forgone monthly savings that would have accrued if the black homeowners had refinanced at the same rate as white homeowners. For example, the monies could have been invested in interest-generating securities or mutual funds. Recent studies have shown an average annualized return of 15.2–17.8 percent on pension funds (Ferson and Khang, 2002), 16.9 percent on equity mutual funds, 15.4 percent on S&P 500 (Wermers, 2000), 11.0–17.8 percent on stock returns (Fama and French, 2002), and 18.7 percent on household stock holdings (Barber and Odean, 2000). Assuming an investment return at 15 percent compounded monthly (based on the monthly payment savings of $94.33 shown in table 4-6), this additional income could generate a total value of $653,095 thirty years later, per homeowner who had missed refinancing.

We also simulated the case of lowest-income class (those at or below 80 percent of area median income) versus highest-income class (those above twice area median income) using our refinance regression coefficients. We made identical assumptions as for the first row of table 4-6, but chose white non-Hispanic homeowners. Holding these characteristics constant, a low-income family was 6.9 percent less likely to refinance. This translates into a loss of $34,682 in aggregate interests over the life of the loan, or a $21.9 billion loss for the group as a whole. The present value equals $12,657, which may also be viewed as an increase of $12,657 in loan amount today. Assuming the families could make an investment that generates a return of 15 percent, the opportunity cost is $666,982 in thirty years.

In the case of a low-income African American family compared to a high-income white non-Hispanic family, the difference in refinance probability becomes greater. Based on our calculation, a low-income family whose head of household is African American is 23.6 percent less likely to refinance than a high-income white non-Hispanic family. The forgone benefit is $35,196 over the life of the loan, or $12,845 in present value, and the reduction in wealth from the lost opportunity is $10.2 billion for the group as a whole. The opportunity cost of forgone investment returns is $676,862 in thirty years.

The losses calculated above only take into account the direct cost of higher mortgage payments as a result of not refinancing to a lower rate. These estimates may be high or low, but at least provide a reference point for quantifying the magnitude of the forgone wealth. As noted earlier, there have been studies that suggest that African American and lower-income borrowers, even when they refinance, may not receive the lowest possible interest rate that they could have received. We ignore this phenomenon, so our estimates of wealth loss may be too low as a result. Further, we ignore the benefits that could accrue from more optimal cash-out refinancing, and the consolidation of high-cost consumer loans within the cheaper mortgage loan. However, to the extent that African Americans and lower-income families have worse credit histories on average, then the average interest rate reduction obtained through refinance would not be as large as we have assumed, and our estimates of wealth loss may be too high. A complete calculation of the loss to the family should include losses in these areas as well. Nonetheless, the cumulative loss in wealth over time is sizable.

Summary

This chapter analyzed the growth in home equity and its determinants. From our cohort and cross-sectional study, we found that the home equity increase from 1985 to 2001 was widely experienced by every age, geographic, and demographic group.

Through the period we studied, an increase in leverage was observed for the same age groups. Our cohort study found that the increase in leverage by age cohort in 2001 over their counterpart in 1985 was bigger for younger cohorts than for older cohorts. In other words, today's younger generation is more leveraged today than their predecessors. They also were more likely to refinance, cash out home equity, or take a second mortgage. This may reflect a shift in attitude toward more current-period consumption as well as a greater acceptance of having mortgage debt by younger generations.

We also found that the decision of the household to choose a rate-and-term refinance, cash-out refinance, or extract home equity through a second mortgage was related to the amount of the interest rate reduction and to real house value increases, and therefore was a rational response to market forces.

Disparities exist between income, education, and racial groups as to the home equity value in a particular year and the extent of growth through the years. This was also confirmed by our regression results that isolate the contribution of each factor to equity values. Minority, especially black, and low-income are both negatively related to the home equity level. Furthermore, our aggregate leverage regression showed that, holding everything else equal, household heads with lower educational attainment, lower income, or who are African American have higher leverage. Our refinance study further showed that lower-income and African American families experience significant wealth reductions over time because of a failure to refinance at opportune moments. Because of these missed opportunities, these homeowners pay about $34,000–$35,000 in additional interest payments over a thirty-year horizon. As a group, African American homeowners forgo $22 billion in wealth thirty years hence because of missed refinance opportunities; lower-income homeowners are estimated to also experience a $22 billion loss over thirty years.

References

Aizcorbe, Ana M., Arthur B. Kennickell, and Kevin B. Moore. 2003. "Recent Changes in U.S. Family Finances: Evidence from the 1998 and 2001 Survey of Consumer Finances." *Federal Reserve Bulletin* (January): 1–32.

Archer, Wayne R., David C. Ling, and Gary A. McGill. 1996. "The Effect of Income and Collateral Constraints on Residential Mortgage Terminations." *Regional Science and Urban Economics* 26 (3–4): 235–61.

———. 2002. "Prepayment Risk and Lower-Income Mortgage Borrowers." In *Low-Income Homeownership: Examining the Unexamined Goal,* edited by Nicolas Retsinas and Eric Belsky, pp. 279–321. Brookings.

Avery, Robert B., and others. 2000. "Credit Scoring: Statistical Issues and Evidence from Credit-Bureau Files." *Real Estate Economics* 28 (3): 523–47.

Barber, Brad M., and Terrance Odean. 2000. "Trading is Hazardous to Your Wealth: The Common Stock Investment Performance of Individual Investors." *Journal of Finance* 55 (2): 773–806.

Bayoumi, T., and H. Edison. 2002. "Is Wealth Increasingly Driving Consumption?" Mimeo. International Monetary Fund Research Department (October).

Board of Governors of the Federal Reserve System. 2002. Senior Loan Officer Opinion Survey on Bank Lending Practices (October) (www.federalreserve.gov).

———. 2003. Monetary Policy Report submitted to Congress on July 15 (Section 1) (www.federalreserve.gov).

Boehm, Thomas P., Paul D. Thistle, and Alan Schlottmann. 2003. "Rates and Race: An Analysis of Racial Disparities in Mortgage Rates." Paper presented at the 2003 Fannie Mae Foundation monthly research seminar, Washington, November 21.

Canner, G., K. Dynan, and W. Passmore. 2002. "Mortgage Refinancing in 2001 and Early 2002." *Federal Reserve Bulletin* (December): 469–81.

Canner, Glenn B., and Stuart A. Gabriel. 1992. "Market Segmentation and Lender Specialization in the Primary and Secondary Mortgage Markets." *Housing Policy Debate* 3 (2): 241–329.

Case, Karl, John Quigley, and Robert Shiller. 2001. "Comparing Wealth Effects: The Stock Market versus the Housing Market." Working Paper 8606. Cambridge, Mass.: National Bureau of Economic Research.

Dickinson, Amy, and Andrea J. Heuson. 1993. "Explaining Refinancing Decisions Using Microdata." *Journal of the American Real Estate and Urban Economics Association* 21 (3): 293–311.

Dzialo, Mary C., Susan E. Shank, and David C. Smith. 1993. "Atlantic and Pacific Coasts' Labor Market Hit Hard in Early 1990s." *Monthly Labor Review* (February): 32–39.

Fama, Eugene F., and Kenneth R. French. 2002. "The Equity Premium." *Journal of Finance* 57 (2): 637–59.

Ferson, Wayne, and Kenneth Khang. 2002. "Conditional Performance Measurement Using Portfolio Weights: Evidence from Pension Funds." *Journal of Financial Economics* 65: 249–82.

Giliberto, S. M., and T. G. Thibodeau. 1989. "Modeling Conventional Mortgage Refinancings." *Journal of Real Estate Finance and Economics* 2 (4): 285–99.

Greenspan, Alan. 2001. Remarks at a symposium sponsored by the Federal Reserve Bank of Kansas City. Jackson Hole, Wyoming, August 31.

———. 2002. Remarks before the Council on Foreign Relations. Washington. November 19.

———. 2003. Testimony before the Committee on Financial Services, U.S. House of Representatives. July 15.

Haitovsky, Yoel. 1967. *Regression Estimation from Grouped Observations.* Cambridge, Mass.: National Bureau of Economic Research.

International Monetary Fund. 2003. *World Economic Outlook.* Washington.

Merry, Ellen. 2002. "Who Moved the LTV? Examining the Increase in Home Leverage."
    Paper presented at the 2003 American Real Estate and Urban Economics Association
    Annual Meeting, Washington, January 3-5.

Nothaft, Frank E. 2000. "Trends in Homeownership and Home Equity." Report to the Con-
    sumer Federation of America's National Forum to Promote Lower-Income Household Sav-
    ings. November 16.

Poterba, James. 2000. "Stock Market Wealth and Consumption." *Journal of Economic Perspec-
    tives* 14: 99–118.

Quigley, John M. 1987. "Interest Rate Variations, Mortgage Prepayments, and Household
    Mobility." *Review of Economics and Statistics* 69 (9): 636–43.

Skinner, Jonathan. 1996. "Is Housing Wealth a Sideshow?" In *Papers in the Economics of
    Aging*. University of Chicago Press and National Bureau of Economic Research.

Susin, Scott. 2003. "Mortgage Interest Rates and Refinancing: Racial and Ethnic Patterns."
    Paper presented at the 2003 American Real Estate and Urban Economics Association, mid-
    year meeting, Washington, May 27-28.

Van Order, Robert, and Peter Zorn. 2002. "Performance of Low-Income and Minority Mort-
    gages." In *Low-Income Homeownership: Examining the Unexamined Goal,* edited by Nicolas
    Retsinas and Eric Belsky, pp. 322–347. Brookings.

Wermers, Russ. 2000. "Mutual Fund Performance: An Empirical Decomposition into Stock-
    Picking Talent, Style, Transaction Costs, and Expenses." *Journal of Finance* 55 (4):
    1655–95.

2

Beyond Prime

EDWARD GOLDING

Technology has driven two changes in the mortgage market, consolidation in the industry and use of automated underwriting to assess quickly and at low cost the risk of borrower default. For many borrowers, the changes have been unambiguously good. Low-cost mortgages are available with little hassle. These borrowers, who are likely to be proficient in dealing with financial institutions and have good credit, are considered in the prime market. For others with less financial sophistication or blemished credit, the changes in the mortgage market raise important policy issues. There are roles for both government action and community-based organizations in addressing these policy issues. The chapters in Part 2, by William Apgar and Allen Fishbein, and by Michael Collins, Eric Belsky, and Karl Case, provide important insight into these policy issues.

The development and widespread adoption of automated underwriting during the 1990s has transformed the mortgage finance industry. By automating a previously manual loan evaluation process, automated underwriting created scale economies and other efficiencies that reduced mortgage costs. By enabling lenders to measure better the likelihood of default, automated underwriting expanded access to mortgage credit. With better tools to measure risk, lenders reduced down-payment requirements and expanded credit availability, which, along with a strong economy, has been a key contributor to America's increased homeownership rate. By making underwriting guidelines easier to implement, automated underwriting facilitated the proliferation of mortgage brokers and third-party originators that, in turn, has lowered costs and increased consumer choice among mortgage products and providers.

In the conventional prime market, most mortgage applications are evaluated using automated underwriting systems. The following chapters explore the challenges posed and the opportunities presented by expanding automated underwriting more fully into nonprime, nonconventional markets. Over 50 percent of borrowers in the subprime market and 70 percent of Federal Housing Administration (FHA) and manufactured housing borrowers have incomes below the area median family income.[1] While these markets may be meeting the needs of certain borrowers, there is empirical evidence that borrowers in these markets could benefit from additional choice and the lower costs of the prime market. Therefore, the opportunities for expanding access to mortgage credit in nonprime markets are substantial and disproportionately can benefit lower-income families.

Against these benefits, automated underwriting in nonprime markets poses challenges and raises thorny public policy questions. Foremost is the question of whether the move toward credit scoring and risk-based pricing in nonprime markets would result in a more equitable and socially desirable allocation of mortgage credit. Other policy issues arise out of concern that some borrowers and organizations that thrived under manual underwriting may be disadvantaged by the growing role of automated underwriting.

Apgar and Fishbein describe the organizational changes that have taken place in the mortgage industry during the last several decades—regulatory change and ensuing consolidation in the banking industry, growth of the secondary market, widespread adoption of automated underwriting, and the proliferation of third-party originators and brokers—and how these changes have affected the delivery of mortgage credit to lower-income families. They call attention to a bifurcation in the mortgage market, where lower-income families disproportionately receive mortgages from nonprime lenders. They worry that uninformed and choice-constrained borrowers with good credit may inappropriately be put in high-cost mortgages or otherwise be subjected to abusive lending practices.

Historically, community-based organizations (CBOs) have played an important role helping lower-income and other traditionally underserved borrowers to prepare for and negotiate the home purchase and refinancing process, and to avoid undesirable lending practices. However, many of the services provided by CBOs tend to be labor intensive, and their customers tend not to meet traditional underwriting standards, instead requiring specialized or individualized attention from lenders that partner with CBOs. As a consequence, CBOs increasingly find themselves squeezed by the individualized needs of their cus-

---

1. In the conventional prime market, less than 40 percent of borrowers have below-median incomes. Source: 2002 HMDA data and Federal Reserve Board's 2002 HMDA lender file.

tomers, and the lenders' need for low-cost, standardized, or automated application processing. The authors worry that the aggressive tactics among some subprime lenders take business from CBOs. This reflects a version of Gresham's law in which quality underwriting, including time-consuming counseling and home buyer education, is driven out of the market by easy lending standards among some subprime participants.

Caught in the middle, innovative CBOs are beginning to turn to information technology automation to improve their services and deliver them more efficiently. CBOs are beginning to use automated underwriting themselves to evaluate applications. Credit counselors now have access to automated underwriting technology to help borrowers understand their credit and the set of mortgage products likely available to them. Automated servicing helps CBOs catch (and hopefully to fix) delinquencies early.

Collins, Belsky, and Case explore the welfare implications of credit scoring, perhaps the most important feature of automated underwriting. Credit scoring is the evaluation of loans according to statistical models that correlate borrower and mortgage characteristics and the likelihood of default. By quantifying more precisely the probability of default, credit scoring enables lenders to more accurately price borrower risk and lend to borrowers previously deemed too risky. Credit scoring further enables lenders to automate substantial portions of the application evaluation and origination process, reducing the time and ultimately the expense involved in underwriting and servicing mortgages.

By enabling lenders to more accurately link the price of mortgage credit to the likelihood of default, credit scoring further expands the mortgage market. On the other hand, although credit scoring may enable lenders to predict and price default risk, the chapter highlights several areas where policymakers and industry leaders need to consider the broader welfare implications of the technology.

More information about risks makes it more difficult for competitive, unregulated markets to insure the high risk. With little information about risk, insurers end up cross-subsidizing the high risk in what is known as a pooling equilibrium, where high- and low-risk individuals purchase the same contract. Better information eliminates the possibility for cross-subsidization in competitive markets because some firms will only target low-risk individuals. We have seen this phenomenon to some extent in the mortgage market where those with high credit scores have ample choices for low-cost mortgages. The result is a greater segmentation of the market with those perceived as higher risk paying higher mortgage rates. Automobile insurance regulators address this issue by mandating assigned risk policies. The authors raise the question of whether the mortgage market has adequately addressed the question of segmentation by risk.

Lastly, the chapter raises issues related to the role of housing in wealth accumulation. The vast majority of wealth for low- and moderate-income families is held in the form of housing wealth. Certain mortgage products such as the long-term, fully amortizing mortgage with no prepayment penalties aid in the accumulation of wealth. Other products that are more prevalent in the sub-prime market strip equity and reduce wealth. As the chapter points out, these products have deleterious effects to neighborhoods as they often lead to foreclo-sures which can further depress housing prices and destroy wealth.

Part II advances our understanding of the potential benefits of automated underwriting, as well as how some borrowers may be disadvantaged by recent changes in the mortgage industry. Even with these two excellent chapters, the question remains what is the right collection of industry, government, and com-munity-based actions to improve the mortgage market and bring the benefits of technology to more families. This will have to be the subject of future papers.

5

Changing Industrial Organization of Housing Finance and Changing Role of Community-Based Organizations

WILLIAM C. APGAR AND ALLEN J. FISHBEIN

B uilding on the recent revolution in computer technology and telecommunications, today's mortgage market bears little resemblance to the one that
existed just a few decades ago. While new approaches to mortgage marketing,
underwriting, and servicing have prompted a surge in lending in lower-income
and minority neighborhoods, this growth is linked to the emergence of a dual
mortgage delivery system characterized by a noticeable absence of conventional
prime mortgages in these same areas. Instead, low-income and minority borrowers and communities are disproportionately served by government-backed, subprime, or manufactured home lending, and exposed to new threats linked to rising rates of mortgage delinquency and default and a noticeable uptick in abusive
lending practices.

As the dual market has expanded access to capital to families that historically
have been shut out of the mortgage market, it has prompted some CBOs[1] to
rethink their role in the marketplace. Following a discussion of the changing
structure of the mortgage industry, this chapter examines how a few CBOs have
responded to change by restructuring existing operations and initiating new

1. Community-Based Organizations (CBOs) are broadly defined as nonprofit providers of
housing services, home buyer counseling, and mortgage finance, as well as nonprofit housing advocacy organizations. As used here, CBOs range from relatively small Neighborhood Housing Services organizations operating in a single neighborhood, to larger Community Development Financial Institutions (CDFIs) that may operate on a regional or even national basis.

programs and activities. In particular, some CBOs have altered their advocacy efforts to expand access to mortgage capital by lower-income people and communities. Others have restructured their community lending programs by partnering with private sector mortgage companies to establish new, automated mortgage-lending or loan-servicing operations, or by creating their own state-of-the-art mortgage-lending and loan-servicing systems. Still other approaches just now in the early stage of development—including efforts to combat abusive lending practices, increase the effectiveness of homeownership counseling, and expand foreclosure avoidance initiatives—also hold much promise.

Unfortunately, many community groups have not adapted their activities to reflect the changes in the mortgage banking industry. For example, even as private lenders are increasingly selling off servicing rights to a handful of mortgage-servicing giants, only a relatively few CBOs now outsource their loan servicing operations. This not only prevents small-scale CBOs from gaining access to state-of-the-art servicing technology, but also diverts resources and management capacity away from activities where a CBO's presence in the community gives it a strong comparative advantage over its private sector counterparts.

This chapter builds on previous Joint Center for Housing Studies research and uses the Joint Center Enhanced Home Mortgage Disclosure Act (HMDA) database (Joint Center for Housing Studies, 2002, 2004). This database combines HMDA data on borrower and loan characteristics with Federal Reserve Board data on lender characteristics, as well as 1990 and 2000 census tract information on the neighborhoods where loans were made. In addition to quantitative analysis, this chapter draws on qualitative information gathered from 150 community leaders and mortgage industry experts during in-depth telephone and in-person interviews and discussion groups held in Atlanta; Baltimore; Birmingham, Alabama; Boston; Chicago; Los Angeles; New York; and San Francisco.

Mortgage Banking Industry's Changing Structure

The mortgage industry today bears little resemblance to the mortgage industry of even a decade ago. Key changes include:
  —use of automated underwriting, credit scoring, and risk-based pricing;
  —rise of mortgage brokers and new mortgage banking organizations;
  —unwinding of regulations limiting the geographic expansion of branch activity;
  —growth of secondary mortgage markets; and
  —associated decline in the share of mortgages funded by bank deposits.

In combination, these changes fostered dramatic increases in lending to low-income people and communities. They also gave rise to what appears to be a dual market in mortgage finance in which low-income and often minority bor-

Table 5-1. *Top Twenty-Five Mortgage Originators' Market Share, 1989–2003*

Year	Total (billions of dollars)	Total for top twenty-five originators (billions of dollars)	Share for top twenty-five originators (percent)
1989	453	118	26.1
1990	458	130	28.4
1991	562	151	26.8
1992	894	272	30.5
1993	1,020	373	36.6
1994	773	259	33.4
1995	636	252	39.6
1996	785	317	40.4
1997	859	384	44.6
1998	1,430	780	54.5
1999	1,275	732	57.4
2000	1,048	637	60.8
2001	2,058	1,458	70.8
2002	2,680	1,971	73.5
2003	3,760	2,880	76.6

Source: *The 2004 Mortgage Market Statistical Annual.*

rowers are served by different lending organizations using a different mix of loan products than is found in the mainstream market (Joint Center for Housing Studies, 2004). A summary of these trends and assessment of their implications for the evolution of mortgage markets follow.

Consolidation Reshapes the Banking and Mortgage Banking Industries

Consolidation continues to be one of the most striking aspects of industry change. The largest twenty-five lending organizations accounted for 76.6 percent of the $3.8 trillion in home purchase and refinance mortgage loans originated in 2003 (table 5-1). As recently as 1990 the top twenty-five originators accounted for only $130 billion (or 28.4 percent) of the industry.

Structural shifts in the industry were largely driven by the declining importance of bank deposits as a source of funds for mortgage lending. Historically, deposit-taking institutions (thrifts and commercial banks) originated the bulk of all home mortgages. In 1980, nearly half of all home mortgages were originated by thousands of thrift institutions, while another 22 percent were originated by commercial banks (U.S. Department of Housing and Urban Development, 1997). Over the past two decades, the ability to package and sell loans to the secondary market reduced the need to hold deposits (or other sources of cash) to fund mortgage loans (Kendall and Fishman, 2000). New technology and marketing approaches enabled lenders to reach customers via mass media and interact with them via phone, fax, and now the Internet. Enhanced telecommunications also allowed lenders to consolidate back office functions needed to originate, underwrite, and service loans. Lacking the economies of scale to compete in this increasingly automated business, many smaller banks and thrifts abandoned their mortgage origination activities entirely. At the same time, several large independent mortgage and finance companies continued to compete head to head with banking organizations in mortgage markets across the country.

Regulatory changes also supported this consolidation (Joint Center for Housing Studies, 2002). At the federal level, interstate banking became a reality in the 1990s. Banks could expand beyond boundaries that had been in place since the Depression, and larger organizations increased the scale and scope of their operations through mergers and acquisitions. Many large banking operations took advantage of the changing regulatory environment and consolidated retail banking operations within and across individual metropolitan market areas. Growth of both regional and national banking operations reflected a desire of larger banks to capitalize on potential scale economies and name recognition, as well as reduce risk by diversifying across numerous spatially distinct market segments (Avery and others, 1999).

The rise of mortgage securitization has been a particularly important feature of the rapidly expanding subprime lending industry. According to one widely used mortgage industry source, subprime loan originations increased from $35 billion in 1994 to $332 billion in 2003, with the twenty-five largest subprime lenders accounting for 93.4 percent of the total (Inside Mortgage Finance, 2004). Before the 1990s, subprime mortgages were chiefly provided by large finance companies that funded them with secured and unsecured debt. As recently as 1994, less than one-third of total subprime volume was securitized. By 2003, the securitization of subprime loans totaled $195 billion, or 59 percent of total subprime originations.

New Origination System Facilitates Industry Growth

Growth in mortgage lending was aided by the creation of a highly automated origination system. Today, loans are originated through one of three channels: retail, correspondent, or broker. Retail activity is most akin to traditional lending, where employees of a mortgage banking organization reach out to potential customers, take a mortgage application, and underwrite and fund loans for those who meet the underwriting standards. Many retail mortgage lenders conduct business from branch operations, though increasingly the marketing (and even closing) of loans is being done via fax or the Internet. Once funded, these loans may be held in portfolio, sold to another lender, or packaged and sold to the secondary market.

Two decades ago, retail lending dominated the business. Since then, wholesale activity (the combination of correspondent and broker channels) has grown rapidly, as has the number of firms engaged in these activities. Correspondents are typically smaller mortgage brokers, thrifts, or community banks. Similar to the retail channel, correspondents reach out to borrowers, take mortgage applications, and underwrite and fund mortgages. While loans are funded in the name of the correspondent, they are then sold to a larger wholesale lender under prearranged pricing and loan delivery terms, and in compliance with established underwriting standards. In contrast to correspondent lenders, mortgage brokers do not fund loans with their own money and only serve to identify potential customers, process the paper work, and submit the loan application to a wholesale lender, who underwrites and funds the mortgage.

A dramatic rise in the number of mortgage brokers and correspondent lenders facilitated the rise in wholesale lending. In 2002, there were an estimated 44,000 firms (with 240,000 employees) engaged in mortgage brokerage and correspondent lending activities, almost double the number of firms operating in 1995, and up markedly from the estimated 7,000 firms operating in 1987 (Wholesale Access Mortgage Research and Consulting, 2003). These third-party originators, especially mortgage brokers, are particularly important in the subprime arena. In 2002, 44.7 percent of all subprime originations flowed through a mortgage broker channel, compared with only 29.5 percent for prime mortgages (Inside Mortgage Finance, 2004).

The changing mortgage industry structure—and particularly enhanced risk-evaluation tools—enabled lenders to offer mortgages with lower down payment requirements to creditworthy borrowers, or to make higher-priced loans to borrowers with less than perfect credit.[2] As a result, HMDA data indicate that home purchase loans to low-income borrowers and low-income communities increased by 80.4 percent between 1993 to 2001, well in excess of overall market growth of 48 percent. Growth in lending to minorities was equally strong.[3] From 1993 to 2001, HMDA data show that the number of home purchase loans made to African American borrowers increased by 93 percent, to Hispanic borrowers by 159 percent, and to Asian and other minority borrowers by 93 percent. In contrast, home purchase lending to white borrowers increased 29 percent over the same period.

Emergence of a Dual Market in Mortgage Lending

The growth of lower-income and minority lending is closely linked to the emergence of a dual mortgage delivery system. In particular, there is a noticeable

2. Throughout this chapter, low-income borrowers are defined as having incomes less than 80 percent of metropolitan area median, and low-income communities are census tracts with 1990 median family income that was less than 80 percent of their metropolitan area median.

3. Over the period 1993–2001, the number of home purchase loans originated without gathering information on the race of the borrower increased by nearly 400,000 to 458,000. For home refinance loans, the increase was from 189,000 to 1.06 million. In 2001, no information on borrower race was present in the HMDA files for some 12.1 percent of all home purchase loans, and 18.6 percent of all home refinance loans.

shortage of prime loans in lower-income and minority markets. Typically, products targeted to lower-income and credit-impaired borrowers have higher interest rates and less favorable terms than the conventional prime loans that serve the larger mainstream market. This has led many housing advocates to question whether households in these areas are gaining access to financing on the best terms for which they qualify. In addition, many of the newer and rapidly growing organizations that provide alternative mortgage products fall outside of the existing federal regulatory framework that remains largely focused on deposit-taking banking organizations. Lack of federal regulation may help explain the rise in predatory lending in recent years and the associated increase in defaults and foreclosures in low-income neighborhoods across the country.

Using HMDA data it is possible to assess trends in conventional prime lending, as well as subprime, government-backed, and manufactured lending by borrower type.[4] All of these three types of lending are alternatives to conventional prime lending in that they typically entail different pricing and terms than conventional prime mortgages, which remain the standard. These alternative-financing types figured prominently in the growth of lending to the lower-income segment of the market. Here, conventional prime loans accounted for only about 40 percent of all growth in home purchase lending (figure 5-1). These numbers contrast significantly with higher-income areas, where conventional prime lending accounted for almost 80 percent of all 1993–2001 home purchase lending growth.

While there were significant increases in government-backed and manufactured lending since 1993, there was a dramatic eightfold increase in the number of home purchase loans reported by subprime lending specialists. By 2001, subprime lending specialists accounted for over 6 percent of all home purchase lending, up from just 1 percent in 1993. For lower-income households living in lower-income communities, the subprime share topped 10 percent.

Subprime lending was also a growing share of the more volatile home refinance market. By 2001, the share of refinance lending captured by firms specializing in subprime loans was 10.4 percent, up from only 2 percent in 1993. For households living in lower-income communities, subprime represented a striking 27.5 percent of home refinancing loans in 2001, a more than fourfold increase in market share since 1993. In predominately African American, lower-income areas, the subprime share of home refinancing stood at 45.2 percent in 2001.[5]

---

4. While HMDA does not label the loan type directly, the U.S. Department of Housing and Urban Development (HUD) supplies a list of each lender's specialization in prime, subprime, or manufactured home lending. Government-backed loans are reported in HMDA, and are defined here as loans made by prime lending specialists that are insured or guaranteed by the Federal Housing Administration (FHA), the USDA's Rural Housing Service, or the Veterans Administration. For a brief description of the HUD methodology, see Scheessele (2002).

5. Here, a census tract where African Americans constitute more than 50 percent of the population is classified as being "predominately African American," while as before, lower-income areas

Figure 5-1. *Share of Growth in Home Purchase Lending by Lender Type, 1993–2001*

A. Lower-income borrowers in lower-income neighborhoods

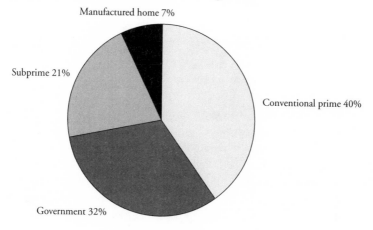

Manufactured home 7%

Subprime 21%

Conventional prime 40%

Government 32%

B. Higher-income borrowers in higher-income neighborhoods

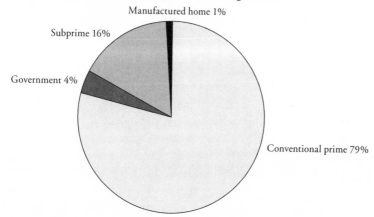

Manufactured home 1%

Subprime 16%

Government 4%

Conventional prime 79%

Source: Joint Center for Housing Studies of Harvard University (2002).

a. Lower (higher) income borrowers have income of less than (at least) 80 percent of area median in that year. Lower (higher) income neighborhoods have income of less than (at least) 80 percent of area median as of 1990.

The tendency for subprime lenders to focus on lower-income and minority markets is well documented. For example, Fishbein and Bunce (2002) concluded that a lack of competition from prime lenders enabled subprime lenders to gain a growing share of mortgage lending activity in these markets. Bradford (2002), who examined subprime lending patterns in 331 metropolitan areas and

are census tracts where median household income is less than 80 percent of the metropolitan area median.

found that racial disparities in access to prime loans existed in all regions and cities of all sizes, reached a similar conclusion.

Mortgage Industry Structure Perpetuates Dual Market

An efficient market will allocate mortgage capital according to the ability and willingness of potential borrowers to pay for mortgage credit. Despite the potential for substantial competition on the supply side of the marketplace, a dual market persists. In this dual market, some individuals pay more for their mortgage credit, receive less favorable treatment than other similarly situated and equally creditworthy borrowers, or both. As a result, well-informed borrowers benefit significantly from the range of product choices and the speed and efficiency of the current mortgage delivery system. At the same time, less-informed borrowers—especially those who have lower credit quality, are attempting to purchase homes in riskier neighborhoods, or both—remain vulnerable and may not receive the best terms for which they would qualify.

Central to the emergence and persistence of this allocational inefficiency is a market failure linked to so-called principal-agent risk that arises from the growing importance of mortgage brokers and correspondent lenders in the market. Brokers and loan correspondents, also called third-party originators, have different incentives in the market than participants in retail lending operations. In seeking to maximize their compensation for identifying a borrower, third-party originators do not necessarily act in the best interest of either the borrower or the investor in the mortgage transaction. Subject to whatever regulatory constraints are effectively operating in the market, the incentive of a third-party originator is to charge the highest combination of fees and mortgage interest rates the market will bear.

A mortgage delivery system where brokers and correspondents are compensated for making loans, but have no long-term interest in loan performance is subject to principal-agent risk. For example, in broker-originated loans, there is a lack of alignment of interest between the lender/investor (the principal) and the mortgage broker (the agent). In such a situation, the broker has little incentive to worry about whether the information presented in the mortgage application is accurate, so long as the information gathered is sufficient to cause the mortgage banker to fund the loan and trigger the payment of the broker's fees. Lacking a long-term interest in the performance of the loan, the broker is immune from many of the adverse consequences of failing to match the borrower with the best available mortgage or providing accurate data needed for loan underwriting to assess the probability that the loan will default or otherwise prepay faster than anticipated.

At the same time, the broker has substantial incentive to provide less-than-accurate information. This could result in the broker failing to verify the accuracy of information presented on the loan application or attempting to falsify income, creditworthiness, or the value of the mortgaged property. Armed with inaccurate information, the lender (and the ultimate investor) may not fully understand the default risk associated with a particular loan.

Borrowers Have Limited Capacity to Shop for Mortgages

In a market where people have the ability to comparison shop, brokers risk losing business if they push costs too high. Unfortunately, given the bewildering array of mortgage products available, many potential borrowers lack the information needed to shop for the best mortgage product available in the market. This in turn encourages some brokers to seek out naïve individuals who lack the experience to correctly evaluate the terms being offered.

Available data suggest that all too many borrowers succumb to the sales pitch of aggressive brokers, in effect becoming unwitting accomplices in the dual mortgage market (Kim-Sung and Hermanson, 2003). For example, an AARP (2003) survey of individuals who refinanced their homes in 1999 and 2000 found that in many instances refinance loans were "sold, not sought" in that they resulted from extensive and often unsolicited outreach by brokers. Consistent with this view, some 56 percent of borrowers with broker-originated loans reported that brokers initiated contact with them, compared with only 24 percent of borrowers with loans originated by retail lenders. Since they did not initiate the search activity, it is not surprising that a larger share of borrowers with broker-originated loans (70 versus 52 percent) "counted on lenders or brokers to find the best mortgage" (AARP, 2003). Even so, a greater share of borrowers with broker-originated loans believed that they did not get a loan that was "best for them" (21 versus 9 percent), received a loan with rates and terms that were not "fair" (23 versus 8 percent), and did not receive "accurate and honest information" (19 versus 7 percent).

Courchane, Surette, and Zorn (2004) echoed the AARP findings. Using a survey of prime and subprime borrowers, this study examined whether borrowers are inappropriately channeled into the subprime segment. The survey data suggested that subprime borrowers are less knowledgeable about the mortgage process, less likely to search for the best mortgage rates, and less likely to be offered a choice among alternative mortgage terms and instruments.

Though the allocation of higher-priced subprime loans obviously reflects differences in the risk profile of borrowers, Courchane, Surette, and Zorn (2004) concluded that it also depended in part on the borrower's search behavior and knowledge of the marketplace, as well as the mortgage delivery channel, that is, whether the loan was a retail- or broker-originated loan. As a result, the paper supported the notion that the current mortgage delivery does not efficiently and fairly allocate mortgage credit in that households of similar economic, demographic, and credit risk characteristics do not pay the same price for mortgage credit in today's marketplace.

Studies Confirm Mortgage Pricing Disparities

The findings outlined above are reinforced by a series of econometric studies that demonstrate how principal-agent risk associated with third-party originations can result in borrowers with similar characteristics obtaining different pricing depending on the process or channel through which they receive their loan (Joint Center for Housing Studies, 2004). Building on an earlier study by LaCour-Little and Chun (1999), Alexander and others (2002) demonstrated that broker-originated loans are not only likely to prepay faster, they are also more likely to default than loans originated through a retail channel, even after controlling for credit and ability-to-pay factors. Alexander and others (2002) further demonstrated that before 1997 the different default characteristics of broker-originated loans were not recognized in the marketplace and therefore were not priced. They argued that as a result of growing capital market awareness of the principal-agent risk associated with brokered loans, borrowers receiving their funding via the broker channel are now charged a premium to compensate lenders for the higher default and prepayment risk associated with these loans.

This discussion is a reminder that investors care primarily about being compensated for the risks they bear. The fact that a pool of mortgages includes individual mortgages with excessive fees or rates, or contains some inaccurate information is not important so long as the investor is able to assess the prepayment and foreclosure rates associated with these transactions. Recognizing that misrepresentation and mispricing still exists, some lenders/investors simply protect their interests by buying loans from less-reliable brokers at a discount.

Of course, lenders/investors do care deeply about receiving misleading information from brokers, particularly about the appraised value of the mortgage property or the capacity of the borrower to repay the loan. As result, there is now aggressive and technologically sophisticated monitoring of brokers by lenders/investors designed to root out fraud (Inside Mortgage Technology, July 2003). However, these systems are costly to acquire and not universally implemented.

A careful review of financial disclosure documents prepared for investors by issuers of subprime mortgage-backed securities further confirms that investors focus on whether the risk-adjusted rate of return is sufficient to cover any expected losses, including losses linked to the fact that more than one in ten subprime loans will result in foreclosure (Mansfield, 2003). But despite the fact that such high foreclosure rates, if realized, would have potentially devastating consequences for individual borrowers and communities, the documents simply note that the pools were priced to compensate investors for bearing these risks.

Since returns depend on the details of the underlying mortgage assets and the performance of the mortgage pool, mortgage investors are faced with the problem of deciding how to manage the risk. Of course, the investor could present relatively strict rules governing the process of loan originations, and through a system of representations and warranties hold the mortgage banker accountable for any deviation from these terms. Mortgage bankers in turn would have incentives to hold their brokers accountable to these standards, and in effect push this risk back downstream. Since there are reputational risk considerations associated with loans that go into foreclosure, such actions should pressure brokers to more closely align their practices to general industry standards. Undoubtedly, some of this is happening, but Alexander and others (2002) demonstrated that the tendency for subprime mortgage brokers to charge excessive fees or present misleading information is not corrected, but rather priced in the market. As a result, some buyers pay more, the broker earns a premium return, and investors are compensated.

Banking Industry Changes Challenge Community-Based Organizations

The U.S. mortgage market has evolved into one of the world's most efficient capital markets. Even so, the emergence of a dual mortgage market structure has limited the ability of unsophisticated borrowers to gain access to the best mortgages for which they qualify, and is associated with rising defaults and foreclosures in the subprime marketplace. These trends not only threaten to undermine the work of CBOs in revitalizing distressed neighborhoods, but also call into question the effectiveness of many CBO activities, including direct lending and home buyer education operations.

Community-Based Organizations' Historical Role

CBOs have long been central to efforts to expand access to mortgage capital to low-income people and communities. Seeking to rally public support against redlining (the systematic denial of mortgage credit to neighborhoods and groups in less-prosperous sections of American metropolitan areas), grassroots organizations began in the 1960s and 1970s to mobilize residents of economically distressed neighborhoods. Banks were one logical target of this activism. Indeed, much of the effort that led to the passage of the Community Reinvestment Act (CRA) in 1977 was built on the simple proposition that federally insured and regulated commercial banks and thrift institutions had an affirmative obligation to lend in areas where they maintained deposit-taking operations or were otherwise chartered to serve.

The combination of community-based activism and legislative efforts in the 1970s and 1980s put significant pressure on banks to expand the reach of their lending and banking activities. Dubbed "regulation from below," community groups, armed with HMDA data and backed by the legislative mandate of CRA, pressured federally regulated banking organizations to increase the number of loans made to minority and low-income borrowers (Fishbein, 1992). The relationship that evolved between community groups and banks involved both collaboration and confrontation (Schwartz, 1999). Negotiations between community groups and local banks focused on residential mortgage and small business lending, as well as provision of banking services in low-income areas. Forced to take a closer look, some banks found these markets held some potential borrowers that could be served through existing loan products.

Of course, many CRA-eligible customers presented additional lending risks that banks were reluctant to tackle. One common approach was for CBOs to work to restore the market by developing an array of lending programs that relied on both public and foundation monies, as well as grants and below market rate capital from the banking industry to write down mortgage interest rates, help borrowers to make the required down payment, or otherwise expand access to mortgage capital to borrowers unable to qualify for a market rate loan.

A recent case study of the Neighborhood Housing Services of Chicago (NHSC) documented the forces that prompted the growth of one of the largest community-based direct lending operations (Husock, 2002). NHSC began its revolving loan fund in 1984 by making small home improvement loans targeted to borrowers unable to secure a bank loan. At first, the effort was supported by foundation grants as well as state and federal funding. In 1995, a pledge of $41 million in below-market-rate loan capital from Continental Bank (later part of Bank of America) pushed the program into high gear, and enabled NHSC to expand its loan operations to include home purchase loans and second mortgages to help meet closing costs, down payment requirements, or fund needed home rehabilitation.

In addition to expanding access to capital in underserved communities, these programs became a significant revenue source for the sponsoring CBOs. For example, in making a Chicago Family Fund loan in the mid-1990s, the NHSC typically received a 3 percentage point origination fee paid by the borrower, a fee of $200 per loan charged to participating banks, and a loan servicing fee of 50 basis points a year per loan. Reflecting the views of many CBOs engaged in the direct lending activities, NHSC director Bruce Gottschall observed that you have to "figure out how you actually get paid for what you're doing" (Husock, 2002).

The NHSC lending initiatives received a significant boost from CRA requirements that encouraged banks to reach out to community organizations. As was the case in Chicago, when faced with activism that could delay planned mergers, damage their reputation in the market, or both, bankers in cities across the country reluctantly entered into negotiations with community groups and began to aggressively expand their outreach to low-income and minority neighborhoods. While most early commitments were limited in scope, the emergence of interstate banking dramatically increased the number and scale of CRA commitments. According to the National Community Reinvestment Coalition, since 1977 banks and CBOs have entered into some 400 commitments to provide over $1 trillion in loans, investments, and services to minority and low-income households.

In addition to the creation of local lending programs, another common approach was for community groups and banks to join forces to promote home buyer education. Homeownership counseling, along with related efforts to promote financial literacy, is particularly important for low-income and minority home seekers, two groups that lenders have had difficulty serving. Over time the efforts of counseling and financial literacy networks operated by the Neighborhood Reinvestment Corporation, the National Community Reinvestment Coalition, ACORN, and others have enabled thousands of potential buyers to realize their dreams of homeownership. Home buyer education and counseling programs have also emerged as an important revenue source for CBOs. What started out as opportunities for lenders and CBOs to work together has grown to a nationwide network of community-based home buying counseling and education groups, and has become good business for both banks and community groups.

Changing Nature of CBO Negotiating Power

Though CRA, HMDA, and related fair-lending legislation continue to play a significant role in expanding access to credit to underserved communities, the ability of CBOs to use this nearly 25-year-old regulatory framework to extract concessions from the banking industry is waning. Several bankers conceded that as they have grown in scale and their lending operations have became more sophisticated, there was less need to work with community groups. Community groups used to help banks identify good borrowers with limited or no credit history living in distressed neighborhoods. Now, advocates and lenders alike acknowledge that with today's automated systems, banks now possess so much data about potential borrowers that their need for assistance in marketing and outreach is steadily eroding.

Furthermore, over the years the legislative and regulatory framework has failed to keep pace with the marketplace, especially with respect to the lower-income and minority segments. Even as Congress, through the Gramm-Leach-Bliley Act of 1999, focused on financial services modernization, little was done to bring CRA into conformance with the rapidly evolving world of mortgage banking and financial services (Apgar and Duda, 2003). CRA mandated intensive review of lending in assessment areas, defined as areas where banks maintain deposit-taking branches. Yet over the past decade, an increasingly large share of all loans are not subject to intense CRA scrutiny, as mortgage banking organizations not covered by CRA regulations together with banking organizations operating outside of their CRA assessment areas now represent the fastest-growing segment of the residential mortgage market. Indeed, by 2001 only 28.4 percent of all home purchase loans were made by CRA-regulated institutions lending in their assessment areas, down from the 36.0 percent share recorded in 1993, and the more than 80 percent share recorded in the early 1980s.

This changing regulatory and market environment has had a noticeable impact on the ability of CBOs to extract concessions from lenders in support of their mission. One manifestation of this phenomenon is the decline of locally specific lending agreements negotiated between banking institutions and CBOs. Once the bread and butter of community organizing efforts, these bilateral agreements are increasingly being replaced by highly visible unilateral commitments made by larger regional and national scale lenders.

The decline of bilateral agreements also has implications for the ability of community groups to secure funding and technical assistance from the new breed of larger, more sophisticated mortgage banking organizations. For example, the executive director of one Baltimore-based CBO watched financial support for his organization dwindle as a direct result of industry consolidation due to the acquisition of a local bank by a national financial services giant. For twenty years, the locally based bank had been a major financial supporter of this community organization, but also directly helped to craft new program initiatives. While funding from the new national organization continued (at reduced levels), this executive director perceived that his area also suffered from losing the close personal relationships, and the various forms of technical assistance, support, and guidance exchanged between the locally based lending organization and the group (Apgar and Duda, 2003).

Many CBOs believe that they have no choice but to continue to work with the locally based CRA-regulated entities that remain. When asked to name a mortgage lending organization with an outstanding record of meeting local neighborhood credit needs, one Boston-area advocate identified a small local bank that made fewer than fifty loans each year. This institution does have a solid record, but they are a relatively minor player in the market. When pressed to discuss the activities of others, this advocate admitted that he had limited interaction with, or knowledge of, the largest mortgage lenders operating in their area.

At the same time, recent actions demonstrate that CBOs' experiences in negotiating CRA agreements can be adapted and successfully applied to the changing business behavior of non-CRA-regulated financial institutions. For example, in the absence of adequate consumer protection laws, CBOs and their national networks have worked to persuade individual subprime lenders to discontinue certain abusive mortgage practices, such as the sale of single-premium credit life insurance (SPCI). SPCI is a low-value product financed completely up front into the loan and is considered by advocates to be a particularly egregious example of predatory lending. CRA does not extend to most lenders that were offering SPCI, so CBO activism took other forms. They convinced Fannie

Mae and Freddie Mac not to purchase loans containing this product, and encouraged the Federal Reserve Board of Governors to make changes to existing Home Ownership and Equity Protection Act (HOEPA) regulations to require lenders offering this product to abide by additional consumer protections for high-cost mortgages. The major subprime lenders eventually got the message and agreed to stop offering the SPCI.

Impact on Community Loan Programs

As private entities expanded their capacity, many communities once constrained by a lack of mortgage lending were now awash with lenders seeking to provide capital. CBOs face new competition that challenges both the need for their presence in the market and the efficiency of their operations. Table 5-2 depicts the number of loans and lenders, and the top twenty-five largest national lending organizations operating in census tracts of varying income and racial characteristics. In 1993 there were 32.6 home purchase loans made on average in predominately minority, lower-income census tracts. These loans were made by an average number of 11.9 lenders, including an average of 2.9 of the nation's top twenty-five lenders for 1993. From 1993 to 2001, the number of loans made in predominately minority lower-income census tracts almost doubled, as did the number of total lenders and top twenty-five lenders active in these areas. While there remains a tendency for lenders (including the top twenty-five lenders) to focus on higher-income and largely white areas, the growth in the number of lenders serving lower-income areas has nevertheless been impressive. By 2001, top twenty-five lenders accounted for close to half of all loans made in predominately minority, lower-income areas, a figure that reflects the growing presence of these mortgage giants in neighborhoods across the country.

The arrival of well-capitalized lenders, aided by the outreach efforts of literally thousands of mortgage brokers and loan correspondents posed several challenges to community-based lending operations. First, in this increasingly competitive lending environment, banks that were once active partners in locally crafted lending initiatives either abandoned their mortgage lending operations entirely, or now serve as a loan correspondent to a larger national lender. Second, even banks with a strong commitment to CRA activities confirmed that the increasing competition among banks for CRA-eligible loans made it difficult to deal with special cases.

As a result, several advocates interviewed expressed concern at how automated underwriting and computer-based loan processing made it more difficult to establish programs tailored to meet local needs. One neighborhood advocate from Chicago observed that many banks no longer had the time or interest to sit down with community group representatives and go through specific loan files.

Together these trends challenge the effectiveness of community-based lending programs. Even highly successful organizations such as the NHSC found

Table 5-2. Mortgage Lending in Neighborhoods of Varying Income and Racial Composition, 1993 versus 2001[a]

Income and race	Number of home purchase loans per census tract		Number of lenders per census tract		Number of top twenty-five lenders per census tract		Share of loans by top twenty-five lenders (percent)	
	1993	2001	1993	2001	1993	2001	1993	2001
Income < 80 percent AMI								
Predominantly white	32.6	52.2	11.9	19.7	2.9	7.4	25.4	46.8
Predominantly minority	15.7	30.3	8.4	15.1	2.4	5.9	32.3	49.7
Income 80–120 percent AMI								
Predominantly white	60.9	90.1	19.4	28.5	4.9	10.4	26.2	47.8
Predominantly minority	42.0	72.5	17.9	26.2	5.0	9.8	33.3	51.7
Income > 120 percent AMI								
Predominantly white	90.8	117.3	26.0	32.2	7.0	12.1	30.0	51.3
Predominantly minority	64.9	106.5	21.8	28.5	5.6	10.3	32.8	54.9

Source: Joint Center for Housing Studies enhanced HMDA Database.

a. Predominantly white neighborhoods have less than 10 percent minority population, while predominantly minority neighborhoods have more than 50 percent minority population.

themselves losing borrowers to aggressive subprime lenders and their network of highly motivated brokers. Despite its lower interest rates (as much as 900 basis points lower than prominent subprime lenders such as Household Finance Corporation), NHSC still lost business to for-profit competitors. In part their inability to compete reflected their commitment to quality lending, including a requirement that borrowers complete rigorous, and often time-consuming, home buyer education. In contrast, most subprime lenders had no such requirements, but instead offered fast decisions that appealed to families anxious to purchase a home of their own.

The NHSC faced other challenges related to their relatively small-scale operations. Subprime lenders could use their marketing savvy and state-of-the-art mortgage origination technology to reach a broad segment of the NHSC target markets in a cost-effective manner. Although well known in the Chicago area, the NHSC was no match for the sophisticated use of direct mail, billboard, radio, and television advertising. Nor could they match the speed (and low costs) at which the well-capitalized subprime lenders using state-of-the-art technology originate loans. As a result, many potential home buyers in Chicago-area neighborhoods ended up securing more costly subprime loans, even though they might have qualified for a less expensive NHSC loan. Worse still, the NHSC found that its counselors spent weeks advising some families on the intricacies of home mortgage finance, only to lose these potential customers and associated fee income to a subprime lender.

Unfortunately, the Chicago situation has been repeated around the country. ACORN reported that many members of its national network were now experiencing difficulty in placing their loans. Participants in Neighborhood Reinvestment's Campaign for Homeownership also noted the increased competition. Indeed, in establishing their goals for 2003–07, the campaign noted that today "almost anyone can get a mortgage," but often at "higher rates and more restrictive terms." As a result, to better address the new competition in the market, the campaign's new strategy has added a renewed focus on the "pricing of credit," and more extensive monitoring of the "rates special populations actually receive."[6]

Complex Mortgages Challenge CBO Advocacy and Education Efforts

The changing industry structure challenges the ability of CBOs to ensure that borrowers are treated fairly in the mortgage market. A decade ago, HMDA data on the presence or absence of loans in particular neighborhoods was sufficient to mount a persuasive antiredlining campaign. With mortgage lending growing rapidly in lower-income and minority neighborhoods, today community advocacy must focus less on whether lending is taking place at all, and more on

6. For further description of the effort, see Neighborhood Reinvestment, www.nw.org.

whether the lending that is taking place is being done at the best rates and terms for which borrowers would qualify. As of January 2004, lenders are required to report the mortgage interest rate for higher-cost mortgages. While this will enable advocates to better identify the presence or absence of subprime loans in the marketplace, regulators have been reluctant to require lenders to report data on credit scores or other factors needed to assess whether this higher rate is appropriate given the creditworthiness of the borrower.

The growing complexity of mortgage products also presents new challenges to home buyer education programs. The national focus on home buyer education builds on the fundamental proposition that consumer education should enhance the fairness and effectiveness of the mortgage market. A recent study suggests that the impact of counseling depends on the details of the counseling effort (Hirad and Zorn, 2002). The study found that less-expensive forms of counseling (including telephone sessions and shorter, one-day group counseling sessions) had limited impact, at least when compared with more extensive (and expensive) one-on-one counseling efforts. This finding raises serious questions about the effectiveness of current counseling operations. Groups interviewed for this study reported that all too often even counseled borrowers were victimized by misleading mortgage marketing pitches of subprime lenders. The head of a Boston-based counseling group noted that in the past, most of their counseled borrowers were able to obtain "good loans" through one of the area's community loan programs, but today that was often not the case.

While general mortgage counseling may help, borrowers must have access to the type of loan-specific and trusted advice currently available to higher-income borrowers—advice that helps borrowers to evaluate any current loan offer against the best terms available in the market. While in principle, the "let the buyer beware" approach could limit abusive pricing in the market, the complexity of current mortgage instruments suggests that consumer education alone will not address the problem.

Enhancing Efficiency and Effectiveness of CBO Lending Initiatives

The concerns about predatory lending, rising foreclosures, and persistent disparity in access to conventional prime loans have led some CBOs to reevaluate their role in expanding access to capital. Some CBOs are partnering with private sector mortgage companies to establish new automated mortgage lending or loan servicing operations, while others are developing their own state-of-the-art mortgage lending and servicing systems. This section examines the potential for community groups and national nonprofit financial intermediaries to make better use of emerging technologies to enhance the operations of their community lending, mortgage counseling, and foreclosure avoidance initiatives.

Automated Lending Tools: Widening the Reach of Community Loan Programs

Historically, hundreds of local groups have engaged in what at best can be described as low volume and relatively inefficient home lending operations that have failed to take full advantage of the best available technology. Despite having access to subsidized money and better pricing, many community-based lending operations find it difficult to compete with the extensive marketing tactics and fast turnaround times of the more sophisticated and technologically proficient subprime players.

Even so, there are a number of remarkably successful lending initiatives that apply state-of-the-art program design and operations to reach credit-impaired, low-wealth, and low-income borrowers. The Community Advantage Program of the Self-Help Credit Union is one leading example. Banks around the country deploy best available technology to originate loans to high-risk borrowers according to flexible lending guidelines developed in partnership with Self-Help. Banks in turn sell these loans to Self-Help, which assumes the default risk. Using grant funds provided by the Ford Foundation, Self-Help retains a portion of the default risk sufficient to enable them to sell the loans into the secondary market through Fannie Mae. In turn, the participating banks are required to use the proceeds of these loan sales to fund new loans to low-wealth families, and the process starts all over again. As of 2002, Self-Help had provided $1.5 billion in financing to 22,000 low- and moderate-income buyers in forty-six states and the District of Columbia.

Though few programs can match the scale of the Community Advantage Program, there are other programs that demonstrate equally sophisticated use of best available technology and program design. For example, Chattanooga Neighborhood Enterprises (CNE) first deployed automated underwriting technology nearly a decade ago. The efficiency gains not only enhanced the quality and speed of its underwriting decisions, they also lowered the cost of loan origination and have turned into a stable source of revenue for the organization.

Despite the success of these ventures, many CBOs resist use of automated underwriting and other technologically advanced systems. Many CBO leaders interviewed for this study argued that the use of automated underwriting systems would limit their ability to tailor loan products to meet the needs of their customers. Fearing that these systems placed undue weight on inaccurate or incomplete credit bureau reports on credit histories, one of these respondents disparagingly described the use of automated systems as "technological redlining" (Apgar and Duda, 2003).

These concerns have some merit. Noting the significant discrepancy in credit scores as reported by the three major credit repositories—Equifax, Experian, and Trans Union—a recent study conducted by the Consumer Federation of America and the National Credit Reporting Association concluded that one in five consumers is at risk of being misclassified into the subprime market due to inaccurate information in credit reports. Common reporting errors include the failure to report a revolving charge account that was in good standing or a mortgage account that had never experienced a late payment (Consumer Federation of America, 2002).

While acknowledging the limitations of the underlying credit reporting data, proponents of automated underwriting systems argue that well-designed systems not only improve the ability to correctly evaluate and price mortgage risk, they enable many lenders to reach out and extend credit to borrowers with less than perfect credit records, limited capacity to make a down payment, or other characteristics that previously have limited access to credit. Moreover, the best automated underwriting systems seek to offset the limitations of credit reporting by combining data generated by all three of the major credit repositories, and by including in their evaluations not only aggregate credit scores, but other specific measures of consumer behavior (such as a recent bankruptcy) likely to be more accurately estimated.

While many CBOs argue that some lenders have used automated underwriting systems as an excuse to deny loans to creditworthy borrowers, these concerns need not apply to the use of these systems by knowledgeable CBOs. For example, one official at CNE noted that automated underwriting enables them to quickly fund the "easy cases" and allows them to devote additional staff time and effort to serving those borrowers with more substantial credit blemishes, or those with thin or inaccurately reported credit histories. In short, CBOs can develop automated underwriting systems that reflect the underwriting criteria and the values and norms of their organization, while at the same time substantially improving operational efficiency.

Undoubtedly, more could be done to properly evaluate the credit quality of low-income people living in low-income communities. For example, work remains to ensure that steady payment of rent and utilities is accurately included as a factor in credit scoring. As technology improves, there will be further improvement in the ability of credit bureaus to gather needed data and translate those data into meaningful mortgage evaluation tools. The result is likely to be a growth in the ability of CBOs to tailor automated underwriting systems to better serve nontraditional borrowers and meet local needs, while at the same time capturing the operational efficiencies associated with risk-based pricing, automated underwriting, and state-of-the-art mortgage servicing.

Contracting Out: Make or Buy Decision

In deciding how best to structure their operations, CBOs face what public finance experts term a "make or buy decision." Neighborhood Housing Services of Chicago (NHSC) once again provides a useful example. Even as one of the nation's largest community-based loan programs, the NHSC lacked the internal organizational capacity to take advantage of the latest loan origination and servicing technology, and was unable to sell loans into the secondary market in a cost-effective manner. As result, some share of the subsidy present in its below-market capital pools was increasingly being diverted to cover the costs of program operations.

To address these issues, the NHSC recently decided to outsource its loan servicing operations to MB Bank Corporation, a move that both improved the quality and lowered the costs of its mortgage servicing operations. Similarly, working in partnership with Chicago area banks, the NHSC created a $100 million loan facility that enables it to sell loan pools to Chicago area banks. This arrangement not only allows the NHSC to replenish funds available to make new loans, it dramatically reduces the interest rate, and credit and collateral risk associated with originating and holding loans in portfolio. This outsourcing should improve program operations and help place NHSC's programs on a more sound financial footing.

While the NHSC opted to buy access to technology through its partnership with MB Bank, other groups choose to make (or create) their own in-house mortgage lending and servicing capacity. This tendency to keep functions in house reflects a legacy of conditions that prevailed when these programs first appeared on the scene. Until recently, many CBOs were the only entities willing to lend in distressed inner-city communities. Absent the availability of other potential partners, they had little choice but to "go it alone."

Yet the world today presents CBOs with a richer set of options. There has been a rapid growth in private sector lending in most low-income and minority areas, and equally substantial growth in the number of organizations—especially well-capitalized, large financial services organizations—making loans in these areas. Recognizing the expanded array of potential new partners, the "buy approach" enables smaller community groups to tap into state-of-the-art loan origination, servicing, and packaging by outsourcing these functions to an existing mortgage lender. The premise is that the larger players in the mortgage industry have considerable economies of scale and the ability to update their technology regularly. In addition, by outsourcing some or all aspects of mortgage lending, a CBO can focus its attention on activities that take advantage of its presence in the neighborhood, such as home buying counseling, neighborhood outreach, and foreclosure avoidance.

Some CBOs interviewed for this project expressed fear that partnering with private sector entities would not be cost effective, would leave them with little or no control over their mortgage-lending operations, or both. This need not be the case. For example, one Boston-area CBO is considering hiring a large mortgage lender to originate and service a loan product that the CBO would design and fund with low-cost money obtained from foundation grants. The CBO would continue to provide home counseling and engage in foreclosure avoidance efforts when needed—two areas where the CBO perceives its presence in the community adds value. At the same time, the CBO recognizes it may be able to achieve greater efficiency in its overall lending operations by outsourcing some mortgage origination and servicing functions to a private sector partner.

Contracting obviously requires identification of a willing and able partner. For example, based on its successful assumption of servicing activity for the NHSC, MB Bank is exploring the possibility of providing similar services to other CBOs, while the Boston-based group discussed earlier solicited the advice of a leading financial services expert to identify a list of qualified potential partners. Intervention by a national network of community loan programs or major national foundation could accelerate outsourcing possibilities by developing a prescreened list of potential qualified partners or by assisting local CBOs with the often difficult task of conducting the due diligence required to select a suitable outsourcing partner.

Creating New Sources of Fee Income

Many CBOs have grown to rely on their direct lending efforts as a source of fee income. Yet lacking the scale economies of larger, well-capitalized players, this is a difficult business proposition. Even so, many small CBOs still attempt to earn a profit from originating and servicing a handful of mortgages. Some claim to actually make money, but frequently these statements are more a product of their failure to accurately account for the total costs of their operations than a carefully honed estimate. In too many instances, this situation diverts subsidy dollars that should go to reduced mortgage rates to compensate for inefficient lending operations.

One way to address problems associated with operating small-scale lending programs is for a CBO to expand the scale of its operations. Today, there exist a limited number of CBOs that have the capacity to run a state-of-the-art mortgage banking operation. Chattanooga Neighborhood Enterprises (CNE) is a standout example. Offering a variety of mortgage products, CNE has developed in-house systems and expertise to turn a small profit from its mortgage operations. CNE is now considering offering its services to other CBOs in the region, groups that would benefit from contracting for more cost-effective loan origination or loan-servicing tools, but are reluctant to secure these services in the open marketplace.

Similarly, the Phoenix NHS is looking to translate its success at servicing its own loan portfolio into new business opportunities. Though its loan portfolio is far smaller than CNE's, the Phoenix NHS already has contracts in place to service loans for several local government-funded revolving loan funds, as well as the loan portfolio of several local Habitat for Humanity groups. Having mastered the intricacies of adapting an off-the-shelf loan servicing software package to meet its own mortgage servicing needs, the Phoenix NHS is able to service additional loans at a relatively low marginal cost, and earn a small profit in doing so.

Many smaller CBOs currently lack the scale and capacity to take advantage of these new technologically driven business opportunities. For these entities, it will be important to identify those aspects of the home buying process where they have a strong competitive advantage. For example, several CBOs have identified real estate brokerage as a potential source of revenue. The NHS of the Inland Empire, a group serving the Central Valley of California, now has several real estate brokers on staff to handle the marketing and sale of homes that it builds and rehabs. The Santa Fe NHS is planning to extend this process, by building a full-service company that provides real estate brokerage, as well as mortgage origination and servicing. It hopes to capture some fee income from graduates of its home buyer counseling programs, as well as earn additional fees from the sale and financing of its single-family construction programs.

Though these examples differ in many details, they share the common thread of the search by CBOs for fee income to support overall program operations. While this can be a worthy goal, care must be exercised to carefully select business ventures suitable for small-scale operations that take advantage of having a visible and trusted presence in their community. Yet name recognition and community savvy is no guarantee that a small-scale organization will ever be able to efficiently service a small loan portfolio, or package and sell loans into the secondary market—two tasks that exhibit substantial scale economies often lacking in all but the largest of CBO programs.

The ability of smaller CBOs to adapt to the changing lending environment has important ramifications not only for individual CBOs, but also the future of the organizational structure of the nonprofit housing industry. If scale economies enable a few nonprofit organizations to expand the scale and scope of their loan origination and servicing operations, the nonprofit housing industry will face the challenge of maintaining the strong community ties that are a critical element of their ability to serve diverse neighborhoods. Fortunately, there are important roles that smaller CBOs can play—including providing home buyer education and counseling and participating in foreclosure avoidance efforts that benefit from their extensive knowledge of local market conditions and the trust they have engendered as a result of years of neighborhood service.

Helping Home Buyers Get the Best Mortgage Available

In a world where many brokers have incentives to "sell" mortgages, the task of ensuring fair pricing in the marketplace falls to regulators and consumers themselves. Unfortunately, many consumers are not up to this task. Many do not shop for mortgages and instead rely on brokers for information, believing incorrectly that brokers have an incentive to get them the best terms available.

Indeed, some consumers falsely believe that approval of their mortgage application is an indication that they can handle the mortgage payments.

Of course, the complexity of pricing of the current array of mortgage products can pose challenges to even the most knowledgeable borrower. Yet for many borrowers, the consequences of this knowledge gap may be less severe than others. For example, many higher-income borrowers have access to financial or legal advisers to guide them through the intricacies of the borrowing process and to help them evaluate whether they are obtaining credit on the best terms available. In communities where homeownership is the norm, other borrowers obtain useful advice from family and friends.

In contrast, in the current system less sophisticated borrowers are more likely to suffer the adverse consequences of being overcharged for their mortgages. And in many instances they have little knowledge of the pitfalls associated with specific mortgage transactions. For example, at the time of closing, the broker, lender, and investor may have good information about the likelihood that the borrower has an above-average probability of defaulting on the loan and losing his or her home to foreclosure, but each of these parties has limited incentive to reveal whether the loan is being made on the best terms available. Lacking this knowledge, many less financially sophisticated borrowers willingly enter into transactions that may require them to pay too much for their mortgage or expose them to relatively high risk of future foreclosure, and in doing so enter into a transaction that may impose serious financial and emotional costs on themselves and their neighbors.

The creation of a system of buyer's brokers could help potential borrowers identify the best loans for them. Unlike mortgage brokers, these buyer's brokers would work on behalf of the borrower. Like the trusted advisers available to many higher-income borrowers, a buyer's broker would provide lower-income and less-knowledgeable borrowers access to information on available mortgage terms and pricing.

There is a growing awareness of the importance of providing better pricing information to potential borrowers. In their strategic plan for the 2003–07 period, the Campaign for Homeownership underscored the importance of assisting borrowers to obtain better information on terms and prices. This will not be an easy task. One approach is to expand the capacity of CBOs to work with buyers individually to search for the best mortgages. Some CBOs are already gearing up to develop a mortgage brokerage business with the explicit goal of using their good standing in the neighborhood to become a buyer's broker, while at the same time earning a small fee for offering this service.

To do this efficiently, CBOs will need automated tools to evaluate the risk profile of individual borrowers, and develop capacity to identify the best products available in the market. Again, this is possible, but difficult. Today, mortgage pricing and terms are largely determined by credit history, income, and a limited number of other factors. Indeed, most brokers receive daily rate sheets that specify the monthly payments or terms required to compensate lenders for risk associated with a particular set of borrower and loan characteristics. Using software similar to that developed by large-scale mortgage originators or secondary market players, CBOs could help cut through the current complexity that now works to the detriment of many borrowers.

There are other ways that CBOs can help borrowers search for better mortgages. Borrowing from the blue books of the automobile industry, CBOs could periodically make rate sheets available to recent graduates of its home buying courses or fairs. Armed with knowledge of their credit score, income, and other characteristics, these rate sheets could help borrowers shop for the best terms in the market.

Of course, to provide this service, CBOs must keep abreast of market trends for credit and be recognized by potential borrowers as a trusted source of information. CBOs have to be mindful of the actual or even perceived conflict of interests inherent in assuming the role of buyer's broker. For example, to the extent that a particular CBO receives funding from a particular lending institution, they may be pressured to recommend this institution's products even in situations where more advantageous products exist in the marketplace. A CBO's failure to provide proper safeguards to avoid either a perceived or actual conflict of interest would quickly erode the trust that community residents have placed in their organization.

Expanding Outreach to Potential Home Buyers

To enhance their capacity to move to a buyer's broker approach, CBOs must expand their capacity to reach out and help buyers review the terms of an imminent mortgage transaction. Yet today, many CBOs struggle to maintain their visibility in the marketplace. Historically, real estate brokers referred credit-impaired customers to CBOs in hopes that they would be able to identify an appropriate loan product. While many real estate brokers continue to make these referrals, they can now refer potential customers to any one of a number of mortgage brokers operating in their area. Several respondents noted that referrals by real estate brokers had "dried up."

Recognizing the need to reach out and help borrowers obtain useful information to guide them through the mortgage application process, many local CBOs are ramping up their outreach to potential borrowers. In one common approach, a CBO will host a home buyer fair and invite a prescreened group of mortgage brokers and lenders to participate. While falling short of a full-scale referral or buyer's broker service, these home buyer fairs not only seek to educate prospective buyers, but also help them identify specific mortgage products and providers that are best suited to meet their needs.

Other organizations have mounted campaigns to challenge the activities of lenders operating in what they perceive to be a particularly abusive manner. For example, a Des Moines, Iowa, CBO reviewed court house records to identify households facing foreclosure in their target areas and found that one lender in particular was responsible for making loans at inflated terms. Through skillful use of the media, this CBO obtained restitution for the borrowers who paid too much for their credit, and encouraged others to avoid this particular lender. In addition, by involving the Iowa attorney general's office, the CBO was able to get the lender to pledge to fund more appropriately priced loans in the future.

While efforts to distribute pricing information could help, there is also a need to review and strengthen existing regulations in the mortgage lending arena. As long as brokers are able to use the current complex array of available mortgage products to conceal the true extent of fees associated with any given mortgage, borrowers can be easily misled. Further work needs to be done on how best to arm borrowers with the information required to improve their capacity to shop for good loan terms. Absent detailed advice on best available terms and rates in the market, the dual mortgage structure is not likely to disappear soon.

New Focus on Foreclosure Avoidance

Whatever factors sustain the dual mortgage market, there can be little doubt that foreclosures are on the rise in many neighborhoods across the country. The National Training and Information Center (NTIC) estimated that the foreclosure rate in Chicago stood at 4.7 percent in 2001—over ten times the national average foreclosure rate for prime conventional loans. In the nine low-income neighborhoods served by Neighborhood Housing Services of Chicago (NHSC), the foreclosure rate reached 7.7 percent. Overall, some 40 percent of all completed foreclosures in Chicago were in these nine targeted neighborhoods. Yet, these communities represented only 5 percent of all mortgage originations in 2001 and account for just 18 percent of the city's population (NHSC, 2004).

Unfortunately, high foreclosure rates are found in many low-income communities across the country. The recent surge in foreclosures appears to stem in large measure from the growing presence of subprime lending in these communities, and in particular the extension of loans to borrowers with limited capacity to repay, or at above-market rates. As reported by the HUD/Treasury Task Force on Predatory Lending, from January 1998 through September 1999 delinquency rates (total loans past due for at least thirty days) in the subprime market averaged 13.5 percent and foreclosure rates averaged 2.6 percent. Over the same period, delinquency rates for prime mortgages averaged 2.8 percent and foreclosure rates averaged 0.24 percent (U.S. Department of Treasury and Housing and Urban Development, 2000).

To date there have been more than ten separate studies of foreclosure activity in specific metropolitan areas. Though they differ in terms of the quality and extent of available data, they paint a remarkably consistent picture of the rising incidence of foreclosure, especially in lower-income and minority neighbor-hoods (see, for example, Abt, 2000, and Gruenstein and Herbert, 2000). Clearly, the extension of loans to borrowers with limited capacity to repay has contributed to the rise in foreclosures. This imposes hardships on individual families, but also threatens to limit home sales, dampen home price apprecia-tion, and destabilize communities. Recognizing this, some CBOs that once only offered prepurchase counseling are expanding their operations to better serve the many thousands of households who have fallen behind on their mortgage payments and are facing foreclosure. Advocacy groups are pressuring lenders to fund loan products that help delinquent borrowers remain in their homes.

Rising foreclosures are also of concern to the mortgage industry, particularly large servicers that handle mortgages in default that they did not originate. Over the past five years, servicers have developed sophisticated models to sort borrowers by the likelihood that loss mitigation efforts will generate a favorable outcome. Despite the fact that such efforts could benefit the lender/investor and borrower, servicers report that they often have trouble reaching lower-income borrowers in a timely fashion. This can be problematic where the decision to fund a broker-initiated loan was based on limited, false, or misleading documentation.

Aware of both the financial and reputation costs of foreclosures, many large lender/servicers are partnering with CBOs to develop more effective foreclosure avoidance efforts. In general, these partnerships seek to take advantage of the CBO's relationship with the borrower and CBOs' ability to offer credit counsel-ing or in other ways assist the borrower and avoid the costly foreclosure process. The Home Ownership Preservation Initiative (HOPI) of the NHSC represents one such partnership. Working with the Mayor's Office and Federal Reserve Board officials, HOPI is challenging large servicers to create new foreclosure avoidance tools. Concerned about their ability to conduct business in the city, as well as the reputational risk of being associated with Chicago's growing foreclo-sure problem, representatives of several large mortgage servicers are now work-ing with the HOPI initiative to see if they can create mutually beneficial alter-natives to current foreclosure practices (NHSC, 2004).

Though just in its early stages, the HOPI initiative is already bearing fruit. Most large-scale mortgage servicers have at their disposal a wide array of loan modification and other loan loss mitigation tools designed to help borrowers avoid foreclosure. Moreover, as is true in many cities, the City of Chicago sup-ports a variety of community-based programs to help finance workouts for bor-rowers in the early stages of default. For example, Chicago is now considering augmenting its nonemergency 311 call system to provide information to bor-rowers in risk of default. The city hopes to help borrowers obtain assistance in handling past-due mortgage debt, including referring these borrowers to a spe-cial help desk created to link borrowers with available foreclosure avoidance resources (NHSC, 2004).

New Approaches to Industry Outreach and Advocacy

The changing mortgage structure poses difficult challenges for low- and moderate-income communities. CBOs working in this area must confront a series of complex considerations related to industry trends, the limitations of the existing regulatory framework and marketplace, and the preferences and choices of individual consumers. This is leading some community leaders to take a hard look at the effectiveness of their organization's current activities and to consider ways of adapting to the new lending environment. As a result, new paths of work are emerging.

One approach recognizes that the growing concentration of mortgage lending necessitates changes in the way CBOs relate to these mega-institutions. The response by CBOs to the explosion in predatory lending in their communities reveals how they are adapting to this new concentrated lending environment. Working through their support organizations and networks, CBOs have joined forces with banks and the secondary mortgage market entities to fund financial education and counseling efforts managed by a single community partner that serves as a conduit for numerous smaller participating groups. Such arrangements can be particularly important in those areas lacking a significant community-based capacity. For example, as an outgrowth of a regionwide planning effort, Region 2020, a Birmingham, Alabama-based nonprofit, is working to form a Community Development Financial Institution (or CDFI) that could serve as a conduit for the charitable contributions and CRA-related investments of locally based banks.

CBOs are also aware that bank support for their work may be declining and therefore have mounted campaigns to diversify their funding bases. Consequently, some CBOs are turning to other private sector institutions and trying to get corporate leaders from the health care, manufacturing, service, and other sectors to get more involved with neighborhood issues and learn firsthand what effective CBO approaches can accomplish.

Another emerging approach seeks to refocus CBO advocacy toward finding new ways to improve the regulatory framework. Despite a challenging federal policy environment, many CBOs continue their efforts to adapt or modernize CRA so that it covers a greater share of mortgage lending activities. These advocates seek to convince banking regulators to update the present geographically based assessment area definitions for CRA reviews so that examiners can take into account the growing share of bank lending that occurs outside of these areas. They also are looking for ways to apply CRA rules to subprime affiliates of banks to prevent these institutions from engaging in predatory and other exploitative lending practices.

Similarly, following recent allegations that several companies have engaged in abusive subprime mortgage servicing practices, advocates are now encouraging federal regulators to take a hard look as this important industry segment. While awaiting the release of new FTC guidelines on what constitutes fair approaches to mortgage servicing, Ameriquest (one of the nation's largest subprime issuers and servicers) was first to release a comprehensive set of best practices for subprime mortgage servicing. Under the leadership of the Mortgage Bankers Association, other subprime mortgage servicers are now working to create their own set of best practices in mortgage servicing. To the extent that advocates can pressure both regulators and industry participants alike to weed out predatory practices in subprime servicing, the result will enhance ongoing CBO efforts at foreclosure avoidance.

Advocates are also forging coalitions with the capacity to prompt regulatory changes at the state and local level. In Massachusetts, CBO advocates have already won passage of a CRA-like regulation for mortgage companies and a community reinvestment requirement for insurance companies. Elsewhere, CBOs and their allies have pushed for the passage of tough new state antipredatory lending standards and have succeeded in a number of states including North Carolina, New Jersey, New York, New Mexico, and Georgia. Even in Alabama, with its relatively weak nonprofit infrastructure, local CDCs have created a statewide coalition to share experiences and advocate about issues of common concern.

Others are seeking to expand advocacy beyond mortgage lending, and have begun to develop a variety of community-based responses to the problems created by the two-tiered financial system that imposes unreasonably high costs for consumers without access to mainstream banking services. Further, one welfare rights organization challenged a major national banking operation to offer direct deposit accounts for families participating in a welfare-to-work program. In Birmingham, a church-based group worked in partnership with local banks to fund a financial literacy campaign in a local housing development that included efforts to teach young adults how to manage credit card debt and start to save for future needs.

Conclusion

The initiatives discussed in this chapter suggest that CBOs are beginning to respond to the challenges posed by the new lending and financial services environment. In the process, they are undertaking new programmatic activities. Some are using new lending tools available to them to widen the reach of community loan programs. Others are partnering with larger entities, exploring new ways that they can assist home buyers in obtaining suitable mortgage products, or providing foreclosure avoidance services. CBO advocacy and outreach is also taking new forms.

These efforts suggest a series of important questions that community groups, national nonprofit support and intermediary organizations, and funders who support their work must address:

—What is the optimum scale of operations and structure for CBOs taking on these new challenges? The strength of the nonprofit community organization sector traditionally has been its ties and connections to the communities in which they operate. Achieving larger economies of scale for CBOs has proven difficult. Does the increasing concentration of the mortgage lending industry dictate a similar need for CBOs and their support systems to ramp up and consolidate their operations?

—What new institutional infrastructure and technological innovations are needed to enable more CBOs to undertake these new responsibilities?

—What will it take for local community groups to connect better with other local and national organizations to provide the additional capacity they will need to relate to national financial institutions?

—What is the appropriate public policy agenda for CBO advocacy that addresses market abuses and the need for better regulatory oversight, while not interfering with what can be accomplished through marketplace innovation?

Adapting to the dramatic shifts that are transforming the mortgage and financial services industry is clearly the central challenge facing many CBOs today. The answers to these questions will go a long way in determining how well these organizations are able to adapt to the changing mortgage banking industry.

References

AARP. 2003. *The 2003 Consumer Experience Survey: Insights on Consumer Credit Behavior, Fraud, and Financial Planning.* Washington.

Abt Associates Inc. 2000. *Analyzing Trends in Subprime Originations and Foreclosures: A Case Study of the Atlanta Metropolitan Area* (February).

Alexander, William P., and others. "Some Loans Are More Equal than Others: Third-Party Originations and Defaults in the Subprime Mortgage Industry." *Real Estate Economics* 30: 667–97.

Apgar, William C., and Mark Duda, 2003. "The 25th Anniversary of CRA." *Economic Policy Review* (June): 169–91.

Avery, Robert W., and others. 1999. "Changes in the Distribution of Banking Offices." *Federal Reserve Bulletin* 85: 81–102.

Bradford, Calvin. 2002. "Risk or Race? Racial Disparities and the Subprime Refinance Market." Paper prepared for the Center for Community Change, May.

Consumer Federation of America and National Credit Reporting Association. 2002. *Credit Score Accuracy and Implications for Consumers.* Washington.

Courchane, Marsha J., Brian J. Surette, and Peter M. Zorn. 2004. "Subprime Borrowers: Mortgage Transitions and Outcomes." *Journal of Real Estate Finance and Economics* 29 (4): 365–92.

Fishbein, Allen. 1992. "The Ongoing Experiment with Regulations from Below: Expanded Reporting Requirements for HMDA and CRA." *Housing Policy Debate* 3 (2): 601–36.

Fishbein, Allen, and Harold Bunce. 2000. "Subprime Market Growth and Predatory Lending." In *Housing Policy in the New Millennium*, edited by Susan M. Wachter and R. Leo Penne, pp. 275–90. Department of Housing and Urban Development.

Gruenstein, Debbie, and Christopher E. Herbert. 2000. "Analyzing Trends in Subprime Originations: A Case Study of the Boston Metro Area." Paper prepared for the Neighborhood Reinvestment Corporation.

Hirad, Abdighani, and Peter Zorn. 2002. "Purchase Homeownership Counseling: A Little Knowledge Is a Good Thing." In *Low-Income Homeownership: Examining the Unexamined Goal*, edited by Nicolas P. Retsinas and Eric S. Belsky, pp. 146–74. Brookings.

Husock, Howard. 2002. "Seeking Sustainability: Neighborhood Housing Services of Chicago Faces Financial Challenge." Case C16-02-1658.0. Kennedy School of Government, Harvard University (August.)

Inside Mortgage Finance. 2004. *The 2004 Mortgage Market Statistical Annual.*

Inside Mortgage Technology. 2003. July.

Joint Center for Housing Studies of Harvard University. 2002. *The 25th Anniversary of the Community Reinvestment Act: Access to Capital in an Evolving Financial Services System.* Report prepared for the Ford Foundation (March).

Joint Center for Housing Studies of Harvard University. 2004. *Credit Capital and Communities: The Implications of the Changing Mortgage Banking Industry for Community Based Organizations.* Report prepared for the Ford Foundation (March).

Kendall, Leon, and Michael J. Fishman. 2000. "The Origins of Securitization, Sources of Its Growth, and Its Future Potential." In *A Primer on Securitization*, pp. 17–30. MIT Press.

Kim-Sung, Kellie K., and Sharon Hermanson. 2003. "Experience of Older Refinance Mortgage Loan Borrowers: Broker- and Lender-Originated Loans." AARP Public Policy Institute, Data Digest.

LaCour-Little, Michael, and Gregory Chun. 1999. "Third-Party Originators and Mortgage Prepayment Risk: An Agency Problem?" *Journal of Real Estate Research* 17 (1/2): 5–70.

Mansfield, Cathy Lesser. 2003. "Predatory Lending: The Failure of Consumer Choice as a Regulatory Model in the United States." Paper prepared for the Ninth International Consumer Law Conference, Athens, April 10–12.

National Mortgage News. 2002. Mortgage Industry Directory.

Neighborhood Housing Services of Chicago. 2004. "Preserving Homeownership: The Community-Development Implications of the New Mortgage Market." (March).

Scheessele, Randall M. 2002. "1998 HMDA Highlights." Housing Finance Working Paper 9. Washington: Office of Policy Development and Research, U.S. Department of Housing and Urban Development.

Schwartz, Alexander. 1999. "From Confrontation to Collaboration: Banks, Community Groups, and the Implementation of Community Reinvestment Act Agreements." *Housing Policy Debate* 9 (3): 631–62.

U.S. Department of Housing and Urban Development. 1997. "Survey of Mortgage Lending Activities."

U.S. Department of the Treasury and U.S. Department of Housing and Urban Development. 2000. *Curbing Predatory Home Lending: A Joint Report.*

Wholesale Access Mortgage Research and Consulting. 2003. "Mortgage Brokers 2002."

6

Exploring the Welfare Effects of Risk-Based Pricing in the Subprime Mortgage Market

J. MICHAEL COLLINS, ERIC S. BELSKY, AND KARL E. CASE

Over the last ten years, subprime mortgage lending has evolved from a small niche in home equity lending to a market valued at over $200 billion annually, or roughly 10 percent of the overall single-family residential mortgage market (Cutts and Van Order, 2005). The term *subprime*, which covers a wide-ranging set of mortgage products and practices, is also called *nonprime*. In simplest terms, it is mortgage lending where the cost of credit is higher than that offered by prime and FHA lending specialists. In most cases, the higher cost reflects the lower credit quality of approved applicants as measured by their credit scores. This chapter presents a stylized overview of the economic benefits that could be derived from the emergence of risk-based pricing in mortgage lending. It explores outcomes that are conditional on retail and wholesale practices in the marketplace as the mortgage industry matures, as well as policy and business implications of this shift.

Shift to Risk-Based Subprime Lending

Lenders evaluating loan applicants attempt to predict the default risks associated with a given loan. Loss of income, divorce, and severe illness are comparatively random events that could fall upon any class of borrowers to create a loan default. Other events are systematically related to the borrower and property characteristics and can be predicted based on the loan applicant's past behavior. Lenders have developed more refined tools to predict systematic risks in the last decade, allowing risk-based pricing to achieve increasing degrees of granularity.

A decade ago lenders manually examined payment ratios, loan-to-value ratios, employment histories, assessments of the value of the collateral, and credit histories of loan applicants to evaluate if a loan should be approved. Each was compared to relatively rigid standards established by decades of past industry practice. Stiglitz and Weiss (1981) argued that rationing by qualification standards in this way is the result of imperfect information about the uncertainty surrounding the systematic credit risks of a loan application. Since originators cannot observe the credit risk profiles of borrowers with certainty, they resort to rigid rationing systems. Chinloy and Macdonald (2004) build on this model of credit allocation, adding a secondary step of lenders sorting approved loans by loan-to-value (LTV) ratio and then pricing into two general categories based on collateral risk. Loans above 75, then 80 (and later higher) LTV ratios require the added cost of mortgage insurance, either at the loan closing in the form of an upfront premium or an increase in monthly debt service payments to cover premiums. These models ration credit to prime quality borrowers with a simple pricing structure. While these models prevailed, subprime borrowers were denied access to credit at any price.

Chinloy and Macdonald (2004) suggest the advent of subprime lending has expanded credit allocation by a new dimension—credit quality. The lender now can accept most loan applications, but pricing becomes more complex, effectively expanding from two price levels into hundreds of risk-priced categories. True risk-based pricing implies each borrower's unique observable systematic credit risk characteristics would be assessed and priced along a continuum of mortgage prices. In practice, most lenders continue to censor the riskiest corner of the credit pricing grid—sorting out the most risky applicants and rationing them out of the market. Lenders also use other mechanisms to govern the risk and revenue related to loans. For example, riskier loans have more restrictive terms than prime loans, including prepayment penalties, origination fees, and other features (Pennington-Cross, Yezer, and Nichols 2000).

In practice, subprime loans are priced based on past loan payment behavior and credit scoring metrics. Temkin, Johnson, and Levy (2002) suggest the following categories of borrowers:

— A, or prime, borrowers, generally have Fair Issac Company (FICO) scores above 660, have never missed a mortgage payment, and missed only one revolving debt payment in the last twenty-four months;

— A-minus borrowers have scores above 620, and have missed no more than one mortgage payment or two credit-card payments;

—B borrowers have missed several payments, one of which was at least sixty days late;

—C borrowers have had a serious delinquency in the last two years, that is, a payment over ninety days delinquent (technically in default for a mortgage loan);

—D borrowers are typically emerging from bankruptcy.

—Finally, related to these categories are "Alt-A" borrowers, who generally have prime quality credit scores, but whose loans have reduced documentation regarding income or assets, or have unusual collateral characteristics.

A review of a rate sheet provided by a major subprime lender is helpful in understanding the industry's pricing structure. As of October 2003, an 80 percent LTV loan for a borrower with a 560 FICO is priced at a premium of 270 basis points over a borrower with a 680 FICO score[1] (Option One Mortgage, October 1, 2003). The pricing sheet also demonstrates how lenders trade off credit risk for collateral risk—at the lowest FICO scores, lenders will not make loans with LTV ratios over 90 percent. Also, lowered standards for income verification and documentation require an interest rate premium of 75 basis points over full documentation loans regardless of other charges associated with FICO score or loan-to-value ratios. Ratios of debt to income are allowable up to 55 percent of income, and even up to 60 percent if the loan-to-value ratio is low. Borrowers can pay a 1.5–3.0 point premium on the loan at origination to waive prepayment penalties for refinancing within the first three years. Because low-balance loans cost relatively more to administer and incur high loss severity in the case of a foreclosure, loans below $130,000 require a premium of 50 basis points, and loans below $30,000 as much as 100 basis points. While not a widespread practice, the price sheet shows the same borrower characteristics might require a pricing premium if the state in which the property is located in represents added collateral risks due to fluctuations in regional home values or state and local regulations.

Potential Benefits of Risk-Based Subprime Lending

Risk-based pricing could, under the right circumstances, produce a more efficient allocation of resources. But whether risk-based pricing achieves greater efficiency is an empirical question, and is conditional on business practices, consumer behavior, and if the structure and analysis of information accurately captures underlying risk. Efficiency gains are only realized if the industry is able to measure, predict, and price for systematic credit risks.

Innovations in information technology for measuring risk have already had significant repercussions on the operation of the mortgage market. In the prime market, the development of automated underwriting systems and the extensive use of credit scores have expanded the pool of applicants approved for home mortgage loans. Although not all automated systems and credit scores have

---

1. Option One Mortgage Rates and Guidelines (www.oomc.com/broker/broker_rateguide.asp [October 1, 2003]).

proven equally as reliable in predicting loss rates and severities, the systems used on Wall Street and by the government-sponsored agencies have so far predicted risks well. However, this has occurred during an unusually favorable period of home price appreciation that reduces collateral risk and the likelihood that loan defaults will culminate in foreclosures.

Meanwhile, the subprime market has developed rapidly as a result of capital market appetite for the equivalent of corporate junk bonds that are secured by real estate instead of claims against a company's cash flows. As in the prime market, information technology is being used to model and price credit risk. However, success in the use of these new technologies has been uneven. Some subprime lenders have incurred higher-than-expected losses while others may have earned economic rents by being able to charge borrowers more than it takes to earn a competitive rate of return (Capozza and Thomson, 2002).

Clearly, the move from the old rationing regime to the new subprime credit pricing system is still a work in progress. During this transitional stage, it is not clear whether efficiency gains are being realized. This chapter discusses the benefits that could flow from the emergence of risk-based pricing as it is evolving in the subprime lending market, as well as how practices in reality may diminish these benefits. Three primary benefits could result: 1) completion of a truncated market; 2) increased allocative efficiency; and 3) increased positive externalities. Of these three, the only one that has been clearly realized is the completion of a truncated market. Simply put, a market for loans to credit-impaired borrowers has been established, whereas one did not exist in any meaningful way before the 1990s. However, this new market is itself subject to failures that can cause allocative inefficiencies and negative externalities within the new market.

COMPLETING THE MORTGAGE CAPITAL MARKET. The flow of capital to subprime credits has created a market where one previously did not exist. The nonexistence of markets for goods and services that consumers demand and suppliers can satisfy while earning a competitive return constitutes an important market failure. In fact, the relatively rapid emergence of the subprime market can be seen as a response to the failure of the rule-based credit rationing regime to serve borrowers with blemished credit or no credit history (Chinloy and Macdonald, 2004).

This new credit marketplace could result in additional efficiencies. First, subprime mortgage lending allows consumers to substitute lower cost, long-term mortgage loans for higher interest rate credit card and other consumer debt. Debt-consolidation loans existed in the pre-subprime regime as well, but borrowers could not secure these loans with their properties if they had blemished credit and liquidity constraints. Second, the cost of mortgage capital is often lower than the cost of comparable credit that is unsecured by a primary residence. There are three reasons for this—interest on mortgages is deductible from income taxes, mortgage loans are secured by an asset that may be worth nearly as much or more than the debt, and people require shelter and are therefore more apt to default on other loans rather than risk losing their homes. Not only is capital often cheaper, but tapping home equity to finance consumption may be the only option for otherwise liquidity constrained borrowers with especially low credit scores. The consumer sector's assets and overall cost of debt service may decrease as the mortgage market is completed, permitting that savings to be more efficiently invested or consumed than through other mechanisms.

Before the advent of risk-based pricing in the subprime market, mortgage credit was rationed based on imperfect information. This system resulted in adverse selection—riskier borrowers pushed out less risky ones (also known as the "lemons problem," as described by Akerlof, 1970). Because lenders were previously unable to observe loan applicants' systematic credit risk accurately, some truly high-risk borrowers were able take out loans. These borrowers increased losses in loan pools and, as a result, lenders charged higher rates for all borrowers in the market. Because high-risk loans are underpriced in this system and low-risk loans are overpriced, high-risk borrowers are encouraged to enter the mortgage market and low-risk borrowers are discouraged from entry. This adverse selection effect results in increased average costs of credit in the mortgage market. Under the new subprime pricing system, the market has moved from rationing credit to large heterogeneous classes of borrowers with good credit, to providing expanded approval for mortgages to more homogeneous categories of borrowers, each with a loan rate more closely related to the relative risk involved. Adverse selection, which drove out better credits in the former system, is reduced due to improved (less imperfect) information and the market performs more efficiently overall.

INCREASED POSITIVE EXTERNALITIES. Renters still building credit ratings and financial assets may find they can become homeowners sooner due to the existence of subprime loans. Goodman and Nichols (1997) suggest FHA plays such a role—accelerating homeownership for first-time buyers. Recent research suggests there are significant private benefits to homeownership, the most notable of which is asset accumulation and better educational outcomes for children (Haurin, Dietz, and Weinberg, 2003).

However, at least three-quarters of subprime loans are used to refinance an existing loan, as opposed to being used for home purchase (Temkin, Johnson, and Levy, 2002). In fact, the entire subprime industry evolved as part of the home equity second mortgage lending industry in the 1990s, not from the purchase mortgage industry.[2] Yet even as capital for refinancing, subprime loans

---

2. Even today, subprime loans are referred to as home equities among Wall Street investment bankers and issuers.

may prolong homeownership for existing owners. Some may use a subprime refinance loan to avoid having to sell their home in a financial crisis, while others may use loan proceeds to make critical repairs to their homes, making continuing ownership in a property viable.

For the last twenty-five years, community reinvestment regulations have focused on the negative externalities associated with denying credit to certain communities and categories of borrowers. The subprime lending system inevitably results in more credit flowing to predominantly minority and low-income communities than in the prior credit rationing system. Analysis of Home Mortgage Disclosure Act (HMDA) data shows a much larger market share for minority and low-income borrowers in the subprime than prime market (Joint Center for Housing Studies, 2003). Constrictions on credit flows to particular neighborhoods in the past meant that potential buyers of housing could not be converted into effective demand, constraining residential property transactions and values. Opening these markets to mortgage approvals may overcome the negative externalities of credit rationing.

Several studies suggest homeownership is associated with positive externalities for communities (Haurin, Parcel, and Haurin, 2002; Haurin, Dietz, and Weinberg, 2003). The new subprime regime may result in gains for distressed neighborhoods and local jurisdictions if expanded or prolonged owner-occupied properties have such positive impacts.

Potential Market Failures in the Completed Market

As the truncated market broadens out, market completion carries risks of other market failures. While less dramatic than the absence of a market where willing buyers would purchase credit if it had been made available to them at a mutually acceptable price, the new market can fall victim to other market failures that are nevertheless material. In the context of the rapidly evolving subprime market place, four market failures are of special concern:

—underestimating risk (mispricing and misallocation of risk due to incorrect measurement of systematic risk);

—principal-agent problems (misalignment of incentives and asymmetric information between principals in a transaction and the agents acting on their behalf);

—asymmetric information (unequal bargaining power due to information advantages of one party over another); and

—negative externalities (costs not internalized by the entities that create them).

UNDERESTIMATING RISK AT THE MACRO LEVEL. The extent of the benefits associated with completing the market depends importantly on the quality and accuracy of the risk measures and pricing mechanisms in use. If lenders and investors have misjudged credit risk, collateral risks, and loss severity, the market will face a correction. Indeed, just such a correction occurred in 1997 and 1998 because several lenders suffered such significant loss and many declared bankruptcy in the following years. The collapse of the manufactured housing lending industry in the late 1990s is also illustrative. Lax underwriting resulted in heavier than expected loss severities and many lenders exited the market.

Indeed, when default rates and losses are greater than anticipated, investors and lenders face significant losses. Households in foreclosure are forced to pay high transaction costs, have their credit ratings ruined, and lose homeownership as a tenure choice for at least several years. Some borrowers, depending on their ownership period and default status, may be worse off than they would have been if they had been denied credit. Higher than anticipated losses reduce the rate of return to capital and result in misallocation of resources in the economy.

Whether the rise of the subprime market and risk-based pricing in general enhances market efficiency and fairness depends upon whether lenders in fact are better able to evaluate risk on a loan-by-loan basis or, at minimum, are better able to evaluate risk by finer and finer categories. Those who argue for moving ahead to a fuller risk-based pricing model believe that analytical advances in the form of better default and loss models and the availability of better data, such as widespread credit scoring, have indeed enhanced the ability to measure risks. Critics, however, caution that most credit and default models are estimated with data from the last twelve years, which include the longest and strongest expansion in U.S. history (1991–2001), and an incredibly robust housing market that has kept the American economy out of a double dip recession since 2001. Since real losses occur primarily when collateral values fall, the small standard errors estimated in recent default and loss models may reflect the strong housing market and not a better ability to fragment risk. Subprime lending has never been tested by a severe downturn in house prices and the economic cycle. This lack of testing under stressed conditions presents an empirical question beyond the scope of this chapter, but because the potential social welfare losses are significant, this issue deserves further inquiry.

PRINCIPAL-AGENT ISSUES. A number of principal-agent problems exist in the mortgage market and they may be exacerbated by the expansion of the subprime market. Most subprime loans are sold into the secondary market by originators who pass the risk of default on to the ultimate holder of the mortgage. Clearly, originators have an incentive to keep origination volumes as high as possible, which involves taking as much risk as the secondary market will absorb. While in cases of fraud, losses can be put back onto the originator, the originator has the incentive to make the application look as good as possible.

Similarly, the largest holders of mortgage debt, the government sponsored enterprises (GSE's), have an incentive to accept risks that they would otherwise decline because of the existence of private mortgage insurance, which covers a substantial portion of default risk for loans with greater than 80 percent loan-to-value ratios. Because of competitive pressure, the mortgage insurers have tended to accept GSE underwriting standards as a result of the widespread and convenient use of *Desktop Underwriter* and *Loan Prospector*, the GSE's automated underwriting systems. The underwriting standards built into those systems assume that the insurers stand in front of the GSEs in case of default.

In both cases, the decisionmaker does not bear the full cost of a default and decisions are likely to lead to more risk than would otherwise be efficient.

ASYMMETRIC INFORMATION. In order for markets to be efficient, buyers and sellers must have complete information on both product quality and available pricing. As products become more complex, the asymmetry of information between well-informed buyers and sellers and less well-informed buyers and sellers increases, and the potential for unfair, discriminatory, and inefficient transactions grows.

Clearly, the rise of the subprime market has led to very complex pricing structures that are difficult for even the most financially literate borrowers to fully understand and evaluate. Most subprime borrowers are ill-equipped for the rigors of financial analysis. Brokers and other originators know these pricing algorithms well, and the potential for abuse is high. Even in the absence of abuse, borrowers who end up with loans that are more expensive than the minimum they could qualify for are allocated credit inefficiently. Of course, these are not new issues. The Real Estate Settlement Procedures Act, Truth In Lending Act, and Homeowners Equity Protection Act were each a response to the issue.

NEGATIVE EXTERNALITIES. Loan defaults that lead to foreclosures can lead to negative externalities that have welfare implications for both lenders and neighbors of foreclosed properties. While subprime loans as a pool experience higher serious delinquencies, subprime loans were only about 10 percent of the overall market in 2002–03. Since the market is still relatively small, the absolute number of foreclosures that began as subprime loans is dwarfed compared to foreclosures from prime and government-backed loans nationally.

However, subprime lending is spatially concentrated in low-income—and especially low-income minority—communities. Using HMDA data, merged with a designation of lenders that specialize in subprime lending, researchers have documented patterns of loan origination by lender type (Scheessele, 2002; Calem, Gillen, and Wachter, 2004). These studies consistently find subprime loans tend to be disproportionately located in low-income and minority census tracts, as well as with low-income and minority borrowers. Pennington-Cross (2003) finds race, even controlling for other factors, explains much of the variation in what type of loan a borrower receives. African American borrowers in particular are more likely to take out subprime instead of prime loans.

If risks are concentrated in a spatial area, potentially a contagion effect of foreclosures might result if property values deteriorate. Foreclosures might also bring on other negative externalities to local real estate markets, such as vacant properties, abandonment, underinvestment, and crime. Anecdotal evidence suggests concentrations of homes in foreclosure are associated with neighborhoods with high concentrations of subprime loans (Collins, 2003). Both lenders to other properties in neighborhoods and neighbors experience welfare losses if foreclosures are concentrated enough to reduce surrounding property values in a community. Hence the lenders who made the foreclosed subprime loans and borrowers who accepted them create costs for others.

Equity Effects of Risk-Based Subprime Lending

Improved information and a movement from rationed credit to subprime pricing may result in improvements in efficiency in the mortgage marketplace. Whether lenders in fact are better able to evaluate risk on a loan by loan basis is clearly an important question, but equity issues remain thorny and will remain so regardless of the quality of risk modeling and pricing.

ELIMINATED CROSS SUBSIDIES. Due to the finer granularity and reduced adverse selection in the new risk-based subprime lending regime, the system is more efficient overall. However, some borrowers are penalized relative to the old system as they move into the new system. Under the old regime, each borrower pays the average price for the class based on the average risk in the class. Borrowers with poorer credit relative to others in the approved category benefit from being included in the class, while the rest of the class pays more than their average risk. The discontinuous nature of more finely grained risk segments with very similar borrowers in each category allows lenders to better price risk than two broad heterogeneous categories. The more the number of risk grades, the smaller the likely variance around the means. Some consumers with marginally more risk would have been approved for credit under the previous regime, but now face increased credit prices. From the perspective of individual consumers who benefited from the coarser grading of credit, the transition to risk-based pricing and their subsequent downgrading represents a welfare loss. The reduction of cross-subsidies is more efficient, however, from a marketwide perspective. Whether the equity of credit pricing within these groups is a matter of importance for society is questionable. However, it is important to recognize how this shift will negatively affect borrowers with marginally prime credit.

INCREASED DEFAULTS. Households gaining access to mortgage credit also assume risk. Some will be made better off by assuming the risk (their assets will

Table 6-1. *Serious Delinquency Rate by Risk Category of Subprime Borrower*[a]
Percent

Borrower credit segment	Share of subprime market	Serious delinquency rate
A	6	8
Alt A	41	17
A–	24	23
B	11	33
C	8	40
CC	11	44

Source: Crews Cutts, Van Order, and Zorn (2002, table 1).
a. Serious delinquency is a payment more than ninety days delinquent.

appreciate or they will build equity over time through forced savings). Others will be made worse off (their assets will depreciate, they will be unable to repay their loan and lose their home, or they will move too quickly to cover the steep costs of buying and selling a home). But to the extent most subprime borrowers successfully use debt to buy or remain in their home, and can repay their loans, it potentially benefits a great many households more than it harms. Some sub-set, though, are placed at greater risk as a result of subprime transaction.[3]

Subprime loans are much more likely to become seriously delinquent, that is, more than ninety days past due, than prime loans (Cutts and Van Order, 2005; Temkin, Johnson, and Levy, 2002; Chinloy and Macdonald, 2004). Table 6-1 shows serious delinquencies for each risk category of subprime borrower, including the share of each type in the overall subprime market. Not all subprime loans are of the highest risk for delinquency, but under the subprime regime borrowers with very spotty credit records, at the B and C levels, are given an opportunity to borrow. At this level, one-third to one-half of borrowers may struggle to keep up with their mortgage payments. Lenders and investors can, assuming accurate information, price for this level of default, and with precision model the severity of losses. But, as many as one out of two of these loans is likely to run into trouble. An expansion of subprime lending equates to an increase in defaulted loans. Even if gains of access to credit benefit nine out of ten borrowers, the harm to the one who defaults may be significant.

In the extreme, lenders could make very high-cost loans to borrowers with very little probability of repaying their loan. It is unlikely regulators and public opinion would permit such lending, however. At some point the risk of foreclosures will become too much for lenders, borrowers, or society to absorb. Regula-

3. Edward Gramlich, Federal Reserve governor, spoke in October 2003 about the "double-edged sword of subprime lending," suggesting it helps to expand housing opportunities, but brings riskier borrowers into the system, increasing foreclosures. Governor Gramlich also noted the problem is exacerbated if unscrupulous tactics are used to attract the borrower and originate the loan (www.federalreserve.gov/BoardDocs/Speeches/2003/20031009/default.htm).

tors have intervened in other types of product markets when the risk level of a particular good or service became perceived as too risky for the public's own good. Loan products are not considered in this way currently, but if concentrated defaults occur, the consumer safety approach could become applicable in the mortgage market.

EXACERBATED INEQUALITY OF WEALTH. The advent of risk-based subprime lending may adversely affect those consumers most at risk of spending their assets in the present and leaving little for the future. As many as half of minority households in low-income neighborhoods may use subprime refinance loans, ten times the share of white refinance borrowers in upper-income areas (Joint Center for Housing Studies, 2003). Given the important role of home equity as a wealth-building device, this may have negative implications for individuals as well as the social systems supporting low-income seniors. Prepayment penalties, in the best cases affirmatively selected by consumers in exchange for a lower interest rate, in the worst included in loan contracts without the borrower's understanding, also might limit equity accumulation. Even if subprime refinance loan products are efficiently priced and useful for borrowers, the imposition of loan terms, which could reduce the wealth-building capacity of subprime borrowers relative to prime borrowers, may introduce inequities.

Hurst and Stafford (2005) suggest some consumers may be better off if high transaction costs prevent them from refinancing consumer debt into a home equity loan. Borrowers however, may have intertemporal discount rates that favor such borrowing, including unobserved expectations about future income, assets, or endowments. Intertemporal discount rates, which cause borrowers to convert assets to consumption, are not well understood.

Implications for Policy and Regulation

There are four primary failures in the subprime market that policymakers and regulators can address in addition to equity concerns. First are problems of inaccurate pricing models untested under stressed market conditions. Regulators might want to expand oversight to cover riskier lending pools, enhancing safety and soundness parameters, and ensuring investors fully understand credit and collateral risks of expanded mortgage approvals. While the safety and soundness of the mortgage market overall is not at risk as long as subprime lending is a small segment, the concentration of foreclosures and any contagion effects are important to monitor.

Second are issues related to information asymmetry. This suggests an expanded public sector role to increase financial literacy, increase disclosure and reporting requirements, and other means of helping consumers understand their options. Because loan pricing is not transparent and the market displays more heterogeneity, it is more confusing. Policymakers might also consider requiring lenders to offer borrowers the lowest-priced product for which they qualify. If unclear systems and boundaries create an opportunity for lenders, borrowers, and brokers to game the system, then regulators might work to increase standardization in this market. One example cited by many lenders is simply requiring all borrowers within a certain threshold to establish escrows for taxes and insurance, a common practice in prime markets but rare in subprime.

Third are principal-agent problems. While in-house retail loan officers are not immune from borrower or lender deception, third-party originators are often accused of the worst practices. The effective outsourcing of loan applicant recruitment, loan document preparation, and underwriting to brokers is not a temporary phenomenon. Regulators therefore might want to have their oversight extend to the affiliates supporting a financial institution. Lawmakers may want to more closely regulate or even license third-party mortgage brokers. Increased disclosures might help obviate principal-agent problems, including efforts by lenders to push loan products on consumers (so-called sold not sought loans). Regulators might also want to consider additional ways of increasing accountability for managing the quality of the origination process, rather than simply pricing for flaws in practice. Best practices in the industry in loan auditing might become required procedures.

Finally, while it requires difficult value judgments, policymakers should carefully consider the impacts on social equity related to the rise of subprime lending. The lowest quality subprime loans will have default rates six to eight times the rate of prime loans. The use of subprime loans as a temporary tool to smooth income shocks or provide emergency funds needs more study. It could be that subprime lending is an important tool, but if its use becomes the only source of credit for low-income and minority households, social welfare could be diminished. More analysis is also needed to assess impacts of the special terms under which expanded access to credit is occurring, including prepayment penalties and other terms that may alter behavior or limit consumer welfare. Policymakers also should explore how to measure and price for the negative public externalities created by practices in mortgage markets. Foreclosures due to stochastic risks are inevitable, no matter how much the credit screen is refined. It is important that borrowers have adequate information and training, as well as access to financial counseling and a higher standard of care when falling behind on their financial obligations.

Conclusion

The potential for efficiency gains from subprime lending and risk-based pricing is real. If risk can be more accurately measured, the benefits to low-income and low credit score households and to society as a whole are great. Consumer choice is enhanced, risk is more efficiently priced, capital is increasingly allocated to highest and best use, while numerous households that would have been denied credit find access to the ownership market. A major source of asymmetric information and adverse selection may be reduced as we gather increasingly accurate and reliable predictors of default. Other households are given the incentive to generate positive neighborhood externalities.

On the other hand, if the risks of subprime lending are underestimated, the result may be very costly and inefficient. Spatial concentration of foreclosures can also generate negative externalities and potentially lead to neighborhood decline. More borrowers will default, creating significant future credit and social problems for individual households. Because subprime loans make it possible for credit/liquidity constrained borrowers to convert equity into current consumption, already low-wealth households could have lower levels of savings in the form of home equity in the future.

Overall, the emergence of risk-based subprime lending should produce positive social welfare effects. However, the industry is growing rapidly. Policymakers and regulators need to closely watch this field, while lenders should work to overcome failures in current practices.

References

Akerlof, George A. 1970. "The Market of Lemons: Qualitative Uncertainty and the Market Mechanism." *Quarterly Journal of Economics* 84 (3): 488–500.

Alexander, William P., and others. 2002. "Some Loans Are More Equal than Others: Third-Party Originations and Defaults in the Subprime Mortgage Industry." *Real Estate Economics* 30 (4): 667–98.

Board of Governors of the Federal Reserve System and others. 1999. "Interagency Guidance on Subprime Lending" SR Letter 99-06. Board of Governors of the Federal Reserve System, Federal Deposit Insurance Corporation, Office of the Comptroller of the Currency, Office of Thrift Supervision, March 1, 1999 (www.federalreserve.gov/boarddocs/srletters/1999/sr9906.htm).

Calem, Paul, Kevin Gillen, and Susan Wachter. 2004. "The Neighborhood Distribution of Subprime Mortgage Lending." *Journal of Real Estate Finance and Economics* 29 (4): 393–410.

Capozza, Dennis R., and Thomas A. Thomson. 2002. "Losses on Subprime Mortgages: Research Study." University Financial Associates (www.ufanet.com/Studies_std6.pdf).

Chinloy, Peter, and Nancy Macdonald. 2004. "Subprime Lenders and Mortgage Market Completion." *Journal of Real Estate Finance and Economics* 30 (2): 153–65.

Collins, J. Michael. 2003. "Chicago's Homeownership Preservation Challenge: Foreclosures in NHS Neighborhoods." Neighborhood Reinvestment Corporation presentation at Federal Reserve Bank of Chicago, February 19.

Courchane, Marsha J., Brian J. Surette, and Peter M. Zorn, 2004. "Subprime Borrowers: Mortgage Transitions and Outcomes." *Journal of Real Estate Finance and Economics* 29 (4): 365–92.

Cutts, Amy Crews, and Robert Van Order. 2005. "On the Economics of Subprime Lending." *Journal of Real Estate Finance and Economics* 30 (2): 167–97.

Getter, Darryl E. 2002. "Are Rejected Households Credit-Constrained or Simply Less Credit-worthy?" Working Paper HF-016. Washington: Department of Housing and Urban Development, Office of Policy Development and Research.

Goodman, John L., Jr., and Joseph Nichols. 1997. "Does FHA Increase Homeownership or Just Accelerate It?" *Journal of Housing Economics* 6 (2): 184–202.

Haurin, Donald R., Robert Dietz, and B. Weinberg. 2003. "The Impact of Neighborhood Homeownership Rates: A Review of the Theoretical and Empirical Literature." *Journal of Housing Research* 13 (2): 119–52.

Haurin, Donald R., Toby L. Parcel, and R. Jean Haurin. 2002. "Impact of Homeownership on Child Outcomes." In *Low-Income Homeownership: Examining the Unexamined Goal,* edited by Nicolas P. Retsinas and Eric S. Belsky, pp. 427–46. Brookings.

Hurst, Erik, and Frank Stafford. 2005. "Home Is Where the Equity Is: Liquidity Constraints, Refinancing, and Consumption." *Journal of Money, Credit, and Banking* 37 (1): 985–1015.

Joint Center for Housing Studies. 2003. *The State of the Nation's Housing.* Harvard University.

Laderman, Elizabeth. 2001. "Subprime Mortgage Lending and the Capital Markets." *FRBSF Economic Letter.* December 28.

Nichols, Joseph, Anthony Pennington-Cross, and Anthony Yezer. 2004. "Borrower Self-Selection, Underwriting Costs, and Subprime Mortgage Credit Supply." *Journal of Real Estate Finance and Economics* 30 (2): 197–219.

Pennington-Cross, Anthony. 2003. "Performance of Prime and Nonprime Mortgages." *Journal of Real Estate Finance and Economics* 27 (3): 279–301.

Pennington-Cross, Anthony, Anthony Yezer, and Joseph Nichols. 2000. "Credit Risk and Mortgage Lending: Who Uses Subprime and Why?" Working Paper 00-03. Washington: Research Institute for Housing America.

Scheessele, Randall M. 2002. "Black and White Disparities in Subprime Mortgage Refinance Lending." Housing Finance Working Paper HF-014. U.S. Department of Housing and Urban Development, Office of Policy Development and Research.

Stiglitz, Joseph E., and Andew Weiss. 1981. "A Credit Rationing in Markets with Imperfect Information." *American Economic Review* 71 (3): 393–410.

Temkin, Kenneth, Jennifer E. H. Johnson, and Diane Levy. 2002. "Subprime Markets, the Role of GSEs, and Risk-Based Pricing." Report for the U.S. Department of Housing and Urban Development, Office of Policy Development and Research, Washington.

PART 3

Keeping Score

STEPHEN BROBECK

The use of credit scores to assess consumer financial risk has grown rapidly. Increasingly, utilities, landlords, and even employers are using these scores to predict not just payment risk but also, more broadly, financially prudent and responsible behavior. Consumer lenders, first to demand credit scores, continue to use them most extensively, with mortgage lenders leading score demand and use.

The use of credit scores by mortgage lenders has had a significant impact on homeownership rates and sustainability. In addressing issues related to credit scores and risks, the chapters of part 3 provide new research on the question of whether the growing use of credit scores encourages or discourages homeownership, and at what price. New information about the accuracy and fairness of credit scores is also presented.

Bostic, Calem, and Wachter's chapter examines whether the increasing influence of credit scores in mortgage lender decisions has made it more difficult for renters to purchase a home at an affordable price. They find a significant decline over the past decade in estimated credit scores for renters, especially those who are young, low income, or black. Because during the same period mortgage lenders were relying more on credit scores (and less on other risk-related information, such as income and assets), the deterioration of renters' scores itself tended to limit the opportunities of these renters to purchase homes at conventional mortgage rates. Declining scores may also help explain the growing purchase of subprime mortgages.

Fishelson-Holstine's chapter suggests a different reason for the expansion of subprime mortgages. The author argues that credit scoring has enabled lenders to predict credit risk more accurately—and thus extend mortgage credit more quickly—to a larger number of high-risk borrowers. This rising knowledge of consumer credit risk would appear to have greatly facilitated the expansion of subprime mortgage markets.

While acknowledging incompleteness and inconsistencies in the data used to compute credit scores, Fishelson-Holstine also maintains that these scores represent the most precise way to measure credit risk, are relatively accurate measures of this risk, and are becoming even more accurate. Many of these improvements are being made by Fair Isaac, Fishelson-Holstine's employer.

Both papers emphasize the importance of lenders supplying more complete information and consumers more carefully checking this information's completeness and accuracy. In 2003, the achievement of both goals was facilitated by congressional approval of amendments to the Fair Credit Reporting Act. Credit bureaus are now required to provide to consumers once a year, upon request, a free copy of their credit report. In addition, mortgage lenders are required to supply an applicant's credit score used as the basis for the lender's response to the application. If used, both new consumer rights could dramatically increase consumer monitoring and knowledge of credit reports and scores.

7

Hitting the Wall: Credit as an Impediment to Homeownership

RAPHAEL W. BOSTIC, PAUL S. CALEM, AND SUSAN M. WACHTER

Representing the American Dream, homeownership has long held a special place in the United States. A significant fraction of the typical American household's wealth is wrapped up in its primary residence, which makes homeownership a vital investment tool (Kennickell, Starr-McCluer, and Surette, 2000). Moreover, homeownership has been found to have ancillary benefits, such as better health outcomes for members of a homeowner's family and a lower incidence of neighborhood challenges such as crime and blight (Aaronson, 2000; DiPasquale and Glaeser, 1999; Rohe, McCarthy, and van Zandt, 2000; Haurin, Dietz, and Weinberg, 2002). These perceived benefits have been the motivation for the many homeownership incentives extended by all levels of government, including the mortgage interest deduction for federal income tax calculations and the Bush administration's American Dream Down Payment Initiative, whose goal is to dramatically increase homeownership rates among lower-income households.

Given the important role that homeownership plays for households and communities, overcoming barriers to homeownership is an important social and public policy goal. This is especially true in the case of minority and lower-income communities, many of which have struggled to build and maintain the wealth and stability that homeownership has been shown to confer. Identifying how changing credit quality—poor credit quality being one of the major financial barriers to homeownership that households must overcome (Rosenthal,

2002; Barakova and others, 2003)—may be affecting access to homeownership across demographic groups is a key step to informing policies to overcome these barriers.

Important changes in consumer credit markets occurred between 1989 and 2001, including expanded access to bank revolving credit, the emergence of a subprime market, larger debt burdens among some segments of the population, and increased bankruptcy rates. These changes all have implications for the distribution of credit quality across the population. This chapter examines how credit quality has evolved during this period. The focus is on the incidence of poor credit quality, with an eye toward identifying those segments of the population that have seen significant improvements or setbacks over the past decade. The results of the analysis are considered in the context of home-ownership and the success of policy initiatives designed to increase the home-ownership rate. Given areas of current policy focus, a central issue is the experience of minority and lower-income individuals and their prospects looking forward.

Background

Many researchers have studied the extent to which households have been unable to become homeowners due to borrowing constraints, which include income, wealth, and credit quality limitations. Most of this work has centered on the importance of income and wealth constraints and has found that insufficient wealth is the biggest barrier for households contemplating homeownership (Rosenthal, 2002; Stiglitz and Weiss, 1981; Linneman and Wachter, 1989; Zorn, 1989; Haurin, Hendershott, and Wachter, 1997; Quercia, McCarthy, and Wachter, 2003). Two additional recent studies explicitly quantify the importance of poor credit quality as a barrier to homeownership, and provide evidence that credit quality is becoming an increasingly important barrier to homeownership.

Rosenthal (2002) finds that credit quality is indeed a barrier to homeownership for households, as bankruptcy and a history of delinquent loan repayment are positively related to the likelihood of being credit constrained but unrelated to the probability of wanting to own a home. The key finding is that the removal of credit constraints, as defined by Rosenthal, would increase the homeownership rate by about 4 percentage points (or about 6 percent).

Barakova and others (2003), like Rosenthal (2002), incorporates credit quality into the analysis of terminal outcomes. But, in addition, this research distinguishes among the effects of constraints based on income, wealth, and credit, and tracks how the impact of each type of constraint has evolved during the 1990s. Barakova and others find that in 1998 the homeownership rate among recent movers would increase by 10 percent if those households with poor credit quality had had unblemished credit records.[1] This compares to a 6 percent increase for a comparable thought experiment in 1989. Thus for this population, the importance of credit quality constraints nearly doubled during the 1990s, reflecting an increase in the proportion of households with poor credit quality.

At the same time, Barakova and others find that wealth constraints, while continuing to be the predominant barrier to homeownership, have become less so. Indeed, the mortgage industry has expended a substantial effort to provide affordable lending products in recent years. The increased prevalence of these products, which are designed to be more accessible to households with relatively limited means in terms of income and wealth, has coincided with declines in the importance of income and wealth constraints as documented by Barakova and others.

This evidence of a decline in the importance of financial constraints is consistent with evidence that homeownership rates improved during the 1990s. According to the U.S. Census, homeownership rates surged during the decade, from 64 percent in 1990 to over 68 percent today.

Several researchers have examined how borrowing constraints have affected minority and lower-income households in particular. Wachter and others (1996) and Quercia, McCarthy, and Wachter (2003) demonstrate that income, and in particular wealth, constraints are a significant impediment to homeownership for underserved groups in the population, including younger families, low-income individuals, and especially minority households. Similarly, Rosenthal (2002) finds that the effects of borrowing constraints are most pronounced among Hispanic and lower-income households. However, these papers do not separately identify the influence of credit quality and thus cannot estimate the impact of changing credit quality across subgroups over time. In addition, while Barakova and others (2003) do separately identify how credit quality acts as a constraint in the homeownership decision for recent movers, it does not examine the distribution of credit quality for the U.S. population and how it has evolved over time.

This chapter uses the Survey of Consumer Finances' (SCF) representative sample of the U.S. population to measure how credit problems are distributed across population subgroups and how they have changed over time.[2] The study

---

1. Barakova and others (2003) define recent movers as those households that have moved in the last two years. These households represent a sample that recently faced the choice of whether to rent or buy a home.

2. We also choose to focus on changes in credit quality over time rather than on wealth or income constraints. While the evidence is that wealth constraints remain important in access to homeownership, the ability to overcome this barrier depends on savings that are linked to the use of credit. The ability to pay credit in a timely way and the ability to repay credit allows growth of savings. Thus a measure of credit quality is likely to be linked to the ability to overcome the wealth constraint as well.

assesses trends in credit quality across segments of the population stratified by demographic characteristics, and quantifies the extent to which credit quality constraints are likely to be a significant factor for households as they consider homeownership and other purchases that require some degree of indebtedness. If trends indicate that historically disadvantaged groups, such as minority and lower-income populations, have fallen further behind, then public policy might seek to address this and improve the standing of the disadvantaged populations.

Indeed, given the broad consensus regarding the benefits of homeownership and the myriad policies whose objective is to increase the homeownership rate, it is important to understand how changes in credit quality are affecting the likelihood of achieving these goals. The analysis therefore places particular attention on the degree to which credit problems are concentrated among the renter population, from which the new homeowners must originate.

Credit Quality: What Are the Trends?

For this portion of the analysis, we use the SCF, which provides detailed information on U.S. families' assets and liabilities, use of financial services, income, and housing and demographic characteristics.[3] Household balance sheet and financial variables used in this study include liquid plus semiliquid financial assets.[4] Housing-related variables employed include whether the household rents or owns. Demographic variables employed include age, years of education, marital status and number of dependents, and racial and ethnic classification. The SCF is a triennial survey, and our analysis uses data from the 1989, 1995, 1998, and 2001 surveys.[5]

We identify an individual's credit quality using a procedure analogous to the credit scoring statistical methodology used by most credit-granting institutions

3. The SCF is a triennial survey of U.S. households sponsored by the Board of Governors of the Federal Reserve System in cooperation with the U.S. Department of the Treasury, and conducted by the Survey Research Center at the University of Michigan.

4. Liquid and semiliquid financial assets as defined by the SCF include all financial assets other than long-term savings instruments (such as pension plans) that cannot be borrowed against.

5. The SCF employs a dual-frame sample design that overlays a standard geographically based random sample with a special sample of relatively wealthy households (Kennickell, 2000). Weights are provided for combining observations from the two samples to make estimates for the full population. We estimate regression models without weights, but use sample weights when calculating summary statistics and predictions based on the estimated equations in order to generate summary statistics and predictions representative of the United States. Beginning with the 1989 survey, missing data in the SCF have been imputed using a multiple imputation model, as described in Kennickell (1991, 1998). Each missing value in the survey is imputed five times, resulting in five replicate data sets, referred to as implicates. Here, we pool the five implicates and adjust regression standard error estimates for the multiple imputation, following the procedure described in Kennickell (2000). The 1989 and 2001 pooled samples contained 15,675 and 22,210 observations, respectively.

(Avery and others, 1996). Specifically, we rely on a special sample of credit records to develop a model for assigning credit scores to SCF households. This nationally representative sample was obtained by the Federal Reserve System's Board of Governors and contains credit scores of about 200,000 individuals, along with their full credit records exclusive of any personal identifying information.[6] We develop an empirical model of a credit score by regressing the reported credit score in the sample on various individual characteristics chosen to match those available from the SCF survey in all four survey years. Because the data are proprietary, we are restricted on the extent to which we can report details of the specification or estimation results.[7]

Given the model, each household in the SCF receives a predicted credit score by calculating Zb, where Z consists of the values of the variables included in the regression model for the household, and b is the vector of estimated parameters from the credit score model. Credit-constrained individuals are defined as those whose credit score falls below some minimum threshold level below which credit is unlikely to be extended. The mortgage industry generally views individuals with credit scores in about the bottom 20 percent of the national credit score distribution as not of good credit quality, and those in about the twentieth to twenty-fifth percentile range as requiring extra attention. These ranges correspond to individuals with FICO scores below 620 and those with FICO scores between 620 and 660.[8] Along similar lines, the mortgage industry generally views individuals with credit scores exceeding 660 as being creditworthy and not requiring more time-consuming file reviews.

A significant limitation of the SCF is that information on the status of credit accounts is limited to accounts that are open and active.[9] Households that have obtained credit in the past but whose accounts are closed and paid out are indistinguishable from those who never had any credit accounts. Our quantitative analysis treated these households as though they had no open and active credit accounts and no credit blemishes but did have credit histories, and thus assigned scores to these individuals based on such characteristics and their age. As such,

6. Scores range from 480 at the first percentile to 820 at the ninety-ninth percentile, with a median of 716 and mean of 696, and with a lower score indicating greater credit risk (lower probability of repayment). The sample contains credit records and scores as of June 1999.

7. Some of the key predictive variables in the credit score model are indicators for thirty-day delinquency and sixty-day or longer delinquency within the past year; aggregate balance and utilization rate on bank credit cards; and age of the individual. No housing-related variables (such as whether the individual has a mortgage) were included in the regression equation. The R^2 for the imputation regression equation is .70; predicted scores range from 561 at the first percentile to 818 at the ninety-ninth percentile, with a median of 738 and a mean of 724.

8. See www.ficoguide.com.

9. Another limitation in attempting to predict scores and the main source of unexplained variation in scores in the imputation equation are lack of information in the SCF on episodes of delinquency more than one year old, accounts in collection, and derogatory public records (other than bankruptcy). Moreover, even delinquencies within the past year may be underreported in the SCF.

only relatively young households within this cohort were classified as credit constrained.

Households with no reported credit accounts in the SCF account for about 23 percent of the sample in 2001 and a comparable amount in 1989. Excluding them was found to have little impact on the results for 2001, but resulted in a larger proportion of the population measured to be credit constrained for 1989, reflecting the fact that older households were less likely to have open and active credit accounts in 1989 compared to 2001. We believe that excluding these households would yield misleading results regarding trends in credit quality between 1989 and 2001, since older individuals indeed do tend to be of higher credit quality. We acknowledge, however, that the presence of these individuals in the sample is a potential source of measurement error.

Our discussion focuses on the 660 threshold (the twenty-fifth percentile of the score distribution in our credit records database) as the cutoff for identifying a credit-constrained individual.[10] In other words, we use this cutoff to measure the percentage of the population likely to be subject to more extensive reviews, which could serve as a deterrent for those considering becoming homeowners.[11]

The credit scoring procedure was applied to each observation in both the 1989 and 2001 surveys, using the same scoring model for both surveys. Thus in addition to identifying the cross-sectional distribution of credit quality, we can also identify how this distribution has shifted over the past twelve years.

Results

The estimates provide a variety of insights regarding the general state of credit quality in the United States and how it has changed over the past decade (table 7-1). The first key observation is that among households with open and active credit accounts, most are estimated to have good credit quality, as the median credit score for this subpopulation is well above the 660 threshold that is typically the trigger for extensive reviews of mortgage applications. Moreover, the median credit score for this subpopulation has been stable over time.

However, credit quality, as measured by the percentage of the population estimated to be credit constrained, deteriorated substantially between 1989 and 2001. The percentage estimated to be credit constrained was more than 25 percent higher in 2001 than in 1989. This trend is consistent with trends in consumer bankruptcy and credit delinquency, important determinants of measured

10. About 20 percent of the full SCF sample for 1998 had imputed scores in this range, suggesting that the proportion of SCF respondents with low credit quality is reasonably close to the proportion of such individuals in the general population.

11. The more restrictive definition of credit constrained, the twentieth percentile (FICO score below 620), yields cross-sectional distributions and trends over time that are similar to those observed using the 660 threshold. However, point estimates of the percent constrained within various demographic groupings may be less reliable under this definition, due to relatively small numbers of households with estimated credit scores below 620.

Table 7-1. *Selected Credit Score Characteristics, 1989 and 2001*

Characteristic	Median score		Percent constrained at 660	
	1989	*2001*	*1989*	*2001*
Total	721.3	730.1	19.3	24.5
Income quintile				
Bottom	702.5	688.3	21.0	38.7
2	716.1	704.9	20.1	28.7
3	728.7	725.5	20.4	19.3
4	739.3	743.3	16.2	10.0
Top	729.0	753.5	7.7	2.8
Race				
White	727.0	737.7	17.0	18.8
Black	693.0	676.0	27.1	41.7
Hispanic	695.0	670.0	25.4	48.5
Other	710.9	725.5	25.3	32.9
Location				
Central city	724.1	727.3	19.7	27.4
Suburb	714.8	725.2	19.4	22.2
Rural	724.6	734.9	18.9	22.2
Education				
Less than high school	709.1	701.6	18.1	33.2
High-school diploma	715.3	712.4	23.8	30.0
Some college	726.9	719.7	18.7	25.8
College degree	730.5	742.8	19.2	14.7
Graduate school	734.4	750.6	11.2	10.0

Source: Author's calculations using the Survey of Consumer Finances.

credit quality. For example, consumer bankruptcy filings, which significantly reduce estimates of household credit quality, doubled between 1989 and 2001.[12]

The mild increase in the population's median estimated credit quality masks considerable variation in the experiences of subgroups in the population. For instance, we observe divergent trends by ethnicity, as the median estimated credit quality for whites increased through the 1990s while the median credit quality for minorities (blacks and Hispanics) declined. Likewise, among minorities the percent estimated to be credit constrained grew significantly, while among whites it increased only slightly. Divergent trends also are observed when the population is stratified by income. Median estimated credit quality for lower-income individuals fell, while median quality for upper-income individuals, which was already quite high in 1989, was even higher by 2001. The per-

12. American Bankruptcy Institute, U.S. Bankruptcy Filings, 1980–02 (www.abiworld.org/stats/1980annual.html).

cent estimated to be credit constrained for lower- versus upper-income populations also moved in opposite directions.

Similarly, the less educated saw their credit quality fall, while those with
much more education had credit quality improvements. This divergence is especially evident in the estimates of percentage of credit-constrained households.
Among households headed by an individual with less than a high school degree,
the percentage estimated to be credit constrained (660 threshold) almost doubled, while the corresponding percentage among households headed by an individual with a college diploma fell by one-fourth.

Credit Trends and Tenure

While the overall trends are illuminating from a general credit policy perspective, for the purposes of housing policy and the issue of increasing homeownership rates it is more useful to evaluate the trends separately among renters and
homeowners. This breakout provides initial evidence regarding the extent to
which poor credit quality is likely to impede efforts to further increase homeownership. Further, to gain additional insights as to how trends vary across the
population, we also generate pairwise statistics for subgroups defined by interactions among the categories identified in table 7-1.[13]

At the outset, we should emphasize that our analysis is meant to be suggestive
of underlying patterns and should be interpreted in the context of additional
information. We recognize that credit quality trends are not purely exogenous
within each housing tenure category, but that the trends within a category may
in part reflect correlation between credit quality and likelihood of becoming a
renter or owner. Thus, for instance, credit quality among homeowners might
increase not because credit quality is improving among existing homeowners,
but because ownership rates are increasing among households with good credit
quality and declining among households with poor credit quality.

The first set of results, pertaining to partitions of the samples by income and
race along with ownership status, are shown in table 7-2. The results reveal
starkly different experiences among renters and homeowners. During the 1990s,
median estimated credit quality for homeowners as a whole improved, while for
renters it fell. Regarding credit constraints, the percentage of credit-constrained
households among homeowners fell, but the percentage of the renter population
estimated to be credit constrained increased by 75 percent.

The improvement in median credit quality among homeowners occurred
quite consistently across race and income groupings. The decline in percentage

13. Except in the case of cells created using locational information (tables 7-3 and 7-4), cells
with fewer than ten observations were excluded from the analysis. These cells were viewed as containing too few observations to generate reliable statistics. We were provided access only to pairwise
statistics for cells created using locational information, not the size of the cell, due to rules restrict-
ing access to proprietary locational information in the SCF.

Table 7-2. *Credit Trends by Income and Race, 1989 and 2001*

Rent or own home	Race	Income quintile					
		Bottom	2	3	4	Top	All
Panel A. Median Credit Scores							
Renters							
1989	White	699.1	696.5	705.8	725.7	719.5	702.7
	Black	691.9	677.9	655.1	666.0	*	687.2
	Hispanic	685.2	684.0	691.0	x	*	685.2
	All	693.0	692.8	699.9	719.8	719.1	696.0
2001	White	683.0	680.6	702.9	726.7	738.5	694.7
	Black	636.1	633.0	685.6	674.1	*	641.9
	Hispanic	599.2	626.2	692.4	662.4	x	623.7
	All	657.3	669.2	699.4	722.3	736.6	679.5
Homeowners							
1989	White	718.5	728.9	738.8	741.9	729.3	733.6
	Black	698.1	710.0	697.4	720.4	*	704.6
	Hispanic	684.1	701.0	711.3	731.2	*	702.7
	All	716.1	727.2	735.6	740.9	729.5	730.7
2001	White	740.1	740.1	740.7	747.8	754.0	747.5
	Black	712.6	706.0	708.0	729.0	*	709.0
	Hispanic	664.5	718.3	691.5	719.9	745.7	713.5
	All	733.4	735.3	735.8	746.1	753.8	744.5
Panel B. Percent Credit Constrained (660 Threshold)							
Renters							
1989	White	23.9	23.8	28.4	22.0	19.8	24.6
	Black	18.0	34.6	41.6	30.0	*	24.1
	Hispanic	18.6	16.5	37.7	x	*	20.5
	All	22.2	24.1	31.0	24.4	19.6	24.4
2001	White	39.6	40.3	29.2	14.3	0.0	35.4
	Black	56.9	57.3	35.4	32.2	*	54.2
	Hispanic	75.0	55.4	34.1	48.2	x	63.3
	All	50.4	45.2	30.4	17.4	12.0	43.1
Homeowners							
1989	White	11.8	12.3	14.1	14.4	4.8	12.9
	Black	33.7	29.9	32.3	28.7	*	31.5
	Hispanic	41.3	34.1	28.2	21.5	*	32.6
	All	18.8	16.6	16.2	14.9	6.5	15.8
2001	White	16.6	13.9	12.7	7.6	2.2	11.6
	Black	23.7	30.6	30.1	23.7	*	27.1
	Hispanic	44.0	19.1	36.0	0.9	3.2	27.8
	All	20.3	15.7	15.7	9.0	2.3	14.1

Source: Author's calculations using the Survey of Consumer Finances.

* = Omitted due to small number of observations.

x = No observations in the cell.

of homeowners estimated to be credit constrained was most pronounced within the two highest-income quintiles, where it occurred consistently across race categories. In the lowest-income quintile, the percentage of homeowners estimated to be credit constrained increased overall, although it declined for blacks.

Trends for renters also varied somewhat across income categories. For example, the median credit score for renters declined sharply across racial categories in the two lowest-income quintiles. However, it remained relatively unchanged or increased in the higher income groupings. Similarly, the increase in the percentage of renters estimated to be credit constrained was concentrated in the two lowest-income quintiles, where this increase was quite sharp and was consistent across race categories.

In the context of homeownership attainment, minority and lower-income renters appear to be particularly challenged as of 2001, with 55–65 percent of minority renters and almost 50 percent of the lower-income renters estimated to be credit constrained using the 660 threshold. Thus homeownership for these vulnerable groups is less likely from a credit perspective unless their members are willing and able to secure more costly credit in subprime mortgage markets.

Perhaps surprisingly, even in higher-income quintiles for both owners and renters, blacks and Hispanics exhibit worse credit quality, suggesting that cultural and perhaps other factors play a role in how minorities interact with credit markets. Although it is beyond the scope of the current study, this issue merits additional attention by researchers.

Table 7-3 repeats this exercise with interactions of the income quintile and urban location variables. Here again, the homeowner/renter dynamic observed in table 7-2 generally holds sway. For owners, as an example, median credit quality increased within almost all income and location groupings. For renters, median credit quality declined sharply in all three location categories and within the two lowest-income quintiles. Interestingly, the suburban homeowners exhibited trends that were somewhat distinct from those observed among central city and rural homeowners. For example, within the lowest-income quintile, the estimated percent of credit-constrained homeowners increased in the suburbs but declined in central city and rural areas.

The data also show that central city and suburban minority renters have had their median credit quality plummet from well above 660 to far below 660 between 1989 and 2001 (table 7-4). In addition, as of 2001, a substantial majority of the households in each of these categories were credit-constrained based on the 660 threshold. Regarding education, the deterioration in credit quality among renters between 1989 and 2001 was most pronounced for households headed by a person with relatively little education (not shown in tables). Declines were largest among renter households headed by less-educated people that were also either lower-income or minority. As of 2001, one-half to two-

Table 7-3. *Credit Trends by Income and Urban Location, 1989 and 2001*

Rent or own home	Location	Income quintile					
		Bottom	2	3	4	Top	All
		Panel A. Median Credit Scores					
Renters							
1989	Central city	688.7	694.1	705.8	702.7	717.7	695.0
	Suburb	700.9	683.9	699.1	718.0	715.6	700.0
	Rural	691.3	693.0	696.6	736.2	723.3	696.0
	All	693.0	692.8	699.9	719.8	719.1	696.0
2001	Central city	649.3	663.2	701.6	718.5	732.1	678.6
	Suburb	676.8	671.9	705.3	765.9	738.5	687.3
	Rural	656.9	672.1	694.3	711.5	738.8	677.7
	All	657.3	669.2	699.4	722.3	736.6	679.5
Homeowners							
1989	Central city	717.0	729.6	744.2	740.9	729.2	733.5
	Suburb	714.1	722.2	727.3	734.6	731.8	720.0
	Rural	716.7	728.6	735.6	741.9	729.5	733.2
	All	716.1	727.2	735.6	740.9	729.5	730.7
2001	Central city	732.5	742.1	736.3	746.1	752.9	745.2
	Suburb	730.0	728.1	729.0	736.7	759.4	734.6
	Rural	734.6	734.4	737.8	746.6	754.4	746.1
	All	733.4	735.3	735.8	746.1	753.8	744.5
		Panel B. Percent Credit Constrained (660 Threshold)					
Renters							
1989	Central city	28.1	16.0	25.9	37.2	15.3	23.6
	Suburb	24.3	39.3	34.3	12.8	31.1	29.3
	Rural	16.5	24.8	34.7	24.1	23.9	22.8
	All	22.2	24.1	31.0	24.4	19.6	24.4
2001	Central city	52.3	47.1	28.5	20.2	18.1	44.6
	Suburb	42.1	43.1	20.6	0.0	0.0	37.3
	Rural	51.2	43.2	25.4	17.2	0.0	43.1
	All	50.4	45.2	30.4	17.4	12.0	43.1
Homeowners							
1989	Central city	23.8	21.0	12.9	15.6	8.5	16.9
	Suburb	10.2	15.4	18.3	7.6	1.6	13.3
	Rural	24.0	13.3	17.8	16.7	5.5	16.3
	All	18.8	16.6	16.2	14.9	6.5	15.8
2001	Central city	20.5	16.1	17.5	10.8	1.7	15.0
	Suburb	20.5	19.2	13.1	6.2	1.2	15.6
	Rural	19.9	13.7	14.9	8.1	3.1	12.6
	All	20.3	15.7	15.7	9.0	2.3	14.1

Source: Author's calculations using the Survey of Consumer Finances.

Table 7-4. *Credit Trends by Race and Urban Location, 1989 and 2001*

Rent or own home	Location	Race			
		White	Black	Hispanic	All
		Panel A. Median Credit Scores			
Renters					
1989	Central city	702.7	693.3	681.3	695.0
	Suburb	706.3	678.1	703.1	700.0
	Rural	702.7	685.2	689.3	696.0
	All	702.7	687.2	685.2	696.0
2001	Central city	696.4	638.5	624.7	678.6
	Suburb	698.5	618.4	599.2	687.3
	Rural	693.0	664.0	624.0	677.7
	All	694.7	641.9	623.7	679.5
Homeowners					
1989	Central city	737.1	713.2	700.4	733.5
	Suburb	723.6	698.9	700.9	720.0
	Rural	734.4	704.9	719.7	733.2
	All	733.6	704.6	702.7	730.7
2001	Central city	749.5	709.3	708.9	745.2
	Suburb	736.7	698.6	734.1	734.6
	Rural	748.4	715.1	714.0	746.1
	All	747.5	709.0	713.5	744.5
		Panel B. Percent Credit Constrained (660 Threshold)			
Renters					
1989	Central city	22.1	23.0	27.1	23.6
	Suburb	27.7	35.3	29.6	29.3
	Rural	24.8	21.2	6.7	22.8
	All	24.6	24.1	20.5	24.4
2001	Central city	34.8	55.6	63.1	44.6
	Suburb	32.8	66.5	73.3	37.3
	Rural	37.6	48.7	62.2	43.1
	All	35.4	54.2	63.3	43.1
Homeowners					
1989	Central city	11.8	31.4	39.2	16.9
	Suburb	11.1	22.7	0.0	13.3
	Rural	14.5	36.1	15.1	16.3
	All	12.9	31.5	32.6	15.8
2001	Central city	10.8	28.8	36.7	15.0
	Suburb	14.9	28.3	0.0	15.6
	Rural	10.8	24.7	19.4	12.6
	All	11.6	27.1	27.8	14.1

Source: Author's calculations using the Survey of Consumer Finances.

thirds of minority households headed by a person with no more than a high-school education were credit constrained.

Additional analysis (also not shown in tables) revealed that younger minority renters show the largest quality deterioration.[14] Unlike other cases, minority deterioration occurs through virtually the entire age distribution; only minority senior citizen renters have increases in average credit quality. As before, this result raises questions as to the origins of poor minority credit performance, as it suggests that extended experience in credit markets may not translate into improved performance for many minority individuals.

In these results, there is one notable exception to the overall homeowner/renter credit quality dynamic that prevailed during the 1990s. Renters with a graduate school education did not show deterioration in credit quality. Median credit quality for this group rose and the incidence of being credit-constrained fell. It thus seems that this group is qualitatively different from other renter groups. Perhaps these individuals more often than other renters either prefer renting as opposed to owning or have more limited options due to wealth or credit constraints.[15]

Validation of the Trends: Regression Estimates

To account for correlation among income, race, education, location, and other individual characteristics, regressions of our measures of credit quality on individual characteristics were estimated. The results of these estimates, which are shown in table 7-5, corroborate the earlier findings. In each sample year, lower-income individuals, people with less education, ethnic minorities, and younger people had significantly lower estimated credit scores and were more likely to be credit constrained.[16]

The first two columns of the table also document what appears to be a general deterioration in credit quality among the disadvantaged or vulnerable groups during the analytical period. The average credit score was almost identical in 1989 and 2001. However, the estimated regression coefficients for income, race, and age are generally significantly larger in 2001 than in 1989, indicating that the magnitude of the effect—in this case, a reduction in credit quality—is larger

14. The regression equation employed to create a credit score for SCF respondents included age as an explanatory variable to proxy for excluded credit-related variables, so that the estimated credit score by construction is strongly related to age. However, there is little reason to believe that changes over time in the distribution of estimated credit score by age would not be indicative of underlying changes in credit quality.

15. The other renter category that showed no deterioration in credit quality was senior citizens (not shown). Like highly educated renters, this population might be more like homeowners save a preference for renting.

16. While the biggest effects are associated with age, with the very young being severely disadvantaged compared to senior citizens, in part this may be due to the fact, noted above, that age was included as an explanatory variable in the regression model employed to predict credit scores.

Table 7-5. Estimates for Regressions on Individual Credit Score

| | Individual credit score | | | | Percent credit constrained (660) | | | |
| | 1989 SCF sample | | 2001 SCF sample | | 1989 SCF sample | | 2001 SCF sample | |
Parameter[a]	Estimate	S. E.	Estimate	S. E.	Estimate	S. E.	Estimate	S. E.
Intercept	731.49	7.35	737.25***	6.31	0.003	0.053	0.132**	0.046
Income quintile (top omitted)								
Bottom	−7.54	4.35	−20.03***	3.46	0.042	0.031	0.156***	0.025
2	−2.16	3.77	−11.36***	3.09	0.073**	0.027	0.090***	0.022
3	6.47	3.32	−3.35	2.78	0.073**	0.025	0.024	0.020
4	9.72**	3.01	2.18	2.55	0.049*	0.022	−0.012	0.019
Education (less than high school omitted)								
Graduate school	18.83***	3.42	18.88***	3.04	−0.083***	0.025	−0.071**	0.022
College degree	10.77**	3.38	17.30***	2.90	−0.038	0.025	−0.068**	0.021
Some college	16.63***	3.17	10.83***	2.80	−0.068**	0.024	−0.039	0.020
High school diploma	7.52**	2.73	6.12*	2.60	−0.008	0.020	0.004	0.019
Race (white omitted)								
Other	−4.12	4.61	−8.31	4.55	0.020	0.034	0.064	0.033
Latino	−12.78**	4.30	−18.47***	3.25	0.023	0.031	0.119***	0.024
Black	−18.92***	3.18	−22.64***	2.64	0.084***	0.023	0.112***	0.019
Age (65+ omitted)								
< 25	−69.09***	5.73	−84.31***	4.18	0.304***	0.041	0.341***	0.031
25–34	−56.50***	3.41	−75.82***	2.87	0.222***	0.024	0.270***	0.021
35–54	−36.25***	2.74	−49.16***	2.25	0.158***	0.020	0.162***	0.017
55–64	−20.60***	2.82	−34.72***	2.45	0.085***	0.020	0.144***	0.018
Location (suburb omitted)								
Rural	1.20	2.09	0.59	1.59	0.004	0.015	−0.002	0.012
Central city	−4.44	2.44	0.50	2.31	0.019	0.017	−0.012	0.017
Homeowner	9.74***	2.72	24.81***	1.95	−0.034*	0.016	−0.143***	0.014
Dependent variable mean	703.3		703.5		.153		.204	
Number of observations	15,675		22,210		15,675		22,210	
R^2	.230		.410		.097		.256	

Source: Author's calculations using the Survey of Consumer Finances.   *** $p < .001$.   ** $p < .01$.   * $p < .05$.

a. Other controls include gender, self-employment, marital status, health condition, and regional dummy variables, as well as a variable for the number of children for which the individual has responsibility.

in 2001. Interestingly, the differences for the education coefficients, particularly at the extremes, are not significantly different in the two years. This suggests that the education effect observed in the cross tabs is simply an artifact of the correlation between level of education and race and income characteristics.

The last two columns of table 7-5, which show the results for the likelihood of being credit constrained, tell the same story. Regardless of the credit score threshold used, being an individual in a disadvantaged group was associated with a higher likelihood of being credit constrained, sometimes a considerably higher likelihood. For example, in 2001, a household in the lowest-income quintile was about 16 percentage points more likely to be credit constrained than one in the top quintile. In addition, the deterioration in credit quality observed in earlier tables for disadvantaged groups also is present in the likelihood of being credit constrained estimates: the marginal effect of being a minority, lower-income, or young on the probability of being credit constrained was greater in 2001 than in 1989.

The regression coefficients on a dummy variable identifying whether a household is homeowner or renter also corroborate earlier findings. Renter credit quality is worse than homeowner credit quality, whether measured by credit score or the probability of being credit constrained, holding constant characteristics of the household other than their tenure status. For example, in 1989, a forty-year-old white, college-educated homeowner who is in the fiftieth percentile of the income distribution and lives in the suburbs had a 16.2 percent probability of being credit constrained, while an otherwise identical renter had a probability of 19.6 percent.[17] This gap widened significantly, to 15 percentage points, in 2001. Other simulations of this sort suggest that, on average, renters had a 15 to 20 percent higher probability of being constrained based on the 660 threshold in 1989.

The data also indicate deterioration of credit quality over time for renters relative to homeowners even after holding other household characteristics constant. For example, for the hypothetical homeowner with the characteristics specified above, likelihood of being credit constrained fell from 16.2 to 10.7, while the hypothetical renter's probability of being credit constrained rose from 19.6 percent to 25.0 percent. Consistent with the results in tables 7-2, 7-3, and 7-4, the deterioration of renter credit quality was particularly pronounced among black households and those with less education.

Concluding Thoughts

With homeownership acknowledged as an important goal for ensuring the well being of both individuals and the broader society, understanding barriers to

17. This also assumes that the household has $50,000 in financial assets, lives in the West, has had some health problems in the past three years, and is self-employed.

achieving homeownership is an important first step in designing policies to expand its reach. This chapter traces the recent evolution of credit quality, a key barrier to homeownership. In particular, it describes how an estimated measure of credit quality has changed over time for the general population as well as for various segments of the population. To our knowledge, such an analysis has not been previously conducted by researchers or policymakers.

For the overall population, median credit quality rose modestly, but credit quality as measured by the percentage of the population estimated to be credit constrained deteriorated substantially between 1989 and 2001. The latter trend is consistent with known trends in consumer bankruptcy and credit delinquency, important determinants of measured credit quality.

The key finding is that trends in estimated credit quality vary in important ways by tenure status. Whether measured as median estimated credit score or percentage of households estimated to be credit constrained, credit quality has improved between 1989 and 2001 among homeowners. This finding is broadly consistent across households stratified by race, level of education, income, and urban, suburban, or rural location.

In a striking contrast, credit quality among renters has deteriorated significantly over the same period. Declines are most pronounced among the young, those with lower incomes, and ethnic minorities—populations often referred to as underserved or vulnerable. Importantly, sizable majorities of these subgroups, up to 50-60 percent, would not be eligible for conventional mortgage credit by current mortgage market underwriting standards. Thus the decline in credit quality among members of these groups may serve as a barrier to further expansion of homeownership.

While we identify an important trend, the analysis does not address the question of causation. That is, we do not disentangle the many different factors that could underlie the worsening credit profiles of renters. For instance, it could be that the increase in homeownership during the period studied occurred disproportionately among renter households with good credit quality. In such a case, the patterns we identify would simply be due to a selection process where the best credits leave the renter population, a selection process that has become more accurate and pervasive over time. Such a skimming effect would be benign from a policy perspective, as it would be consistent with the social goal of increased homeownership.

A separate explanation that addresses changing patterns over time is that access to homeownership itself provides conditions that make it easier to improve credit quality over time. This is, after all, what the old forced savings and the new hyperbolic preference literature imply (Phelps and Pollak, 1968; Laibson, 1996, 1997). Alternatively, it is possible that recent immigrants are more likely to be renters than homeowners, all else equal, and that successive waves of immigrants have had larger proportions with credit quality below the critical threshold levels.

Of course, none of these possibilities are mutually exclusive and neither are they exhaustive. For example, race-based discrimination could play a role in these patterns, perhaps in the context of predatory lending. These questions are ripe for future research, the results of which will help provide a considerably deeper and richer understanding of how credit markets operate.

Regardless of the cause, our results indicate that the renter population is currently not in a particularly good position to become homeowners, and that it is in a worse position in this regard than it was five or ten years ago. This has important implications for initiatives with goals to significantly increase the overall homeownership rate and homeownership rate for vulnerable populations. In order to achieve these goals, policymakers will need to focus on strategies to improve renter performance with their existing credit accounts, such as promoting education and financial literacy programs. By improving financial literacy and consequently their credit performance, renters can see their credit quality improve to the point where they are eligible for conventional mortgage credit. They would then avoid the high prices and potential pitfalls of subprime and predatory mortgage markets while still being able to enjoy the full benefits related to wealth, neighborhood, and health that homeownership has been shown to impart.

A final, and important, caveat is that the analysis relies on the assumption that the relationship between individual characteristics and credit quality did not change over the course of the 1990s. We use a single model to estimate an individual's credit score in both 1989 and 2001. If the relationship between an individual's characteristics and the likelihood of repaying a loan evolved over time, though, then we might have inaccurately estimated an individual's credit quality in either 1989 or 2001. If so, then our temporal analysis would be somewhat misleading. However, we have little reason to believe that, even if the relationship has evolved over time, the changes have been sufficiently large to dismiss the general trends we highlight here. If there had been such a change, one might have expected to see some of the models used by the industry over this time perform particularly poorly. To date, we are aware of no such incidences. As a result, we have a degree of confidence that the results we uncover are robust.

References

Aaronson, Daniel. 2000. "A Note on the Benefits of Homeownership." *Journal of Urban Economics* 47: 356–69.

Avery, Robert B., and others. 1996. "Credit Risk, Credit Scoring, and the Performance of Home Mortgages." *Federal Reserve Bulletin* 82 (7): 621–48.

Barakova, Irina, and others. 2003. "Does Credit Quality Matter for Homeownership?" *Journal of Housing Economics* 12 (4): 318–36.

DiPasquale, Denise, and Edward Glaeser. 1999. "Incentives and Social Capital: Are Homeowners Better Citizens?" *Journal of Urban Economics* 45: 354–84.

Haurin, Donald R., Robert D. Dietz, and Bruce A. Weinberg. 2002. "The Impact of Neighborhood Homeownership Rates: A Review of the Theoretical and Empirical Literature." *Journal of Housing Research* 13: 119–51.

Haurin, Donald R., Patric H. Hendershott, and Susan M. Wachter. 1997. "Borrowing Constraints and the Tenure Choice of Young Households." *Journal of Housing Research* 8 (2): 137–54.

Kennickell, Arthur B. 1991. "Imputation of the 1989 Survey of Consumer Finances: Stochastic Relaxation and Multiple Imputation." Washington: Board of Governors of the Federal Reserve System (October).

———. 1998. "Multiple Imputation in the Survey of Consumer Finances." Washington: Board of Governors of the Federal Reserve System (September).

———. 2000. "Wealth Measurement in the Survey of Consumer Finances: Methodology and Directions for Future Research." Washington: Board of Governors of the Federal Reserve System (May).

Kennickell, Arthur B., Martha Starr-McCluer, and Brian J. Surette. 2000. "Recent Changes in U.S. Family Finances: Results from the 1998 Survey of Consumer Finances." *Federal Reserve Bulletin* 86: 1–29.

Laibson, David I. 1996. "Hyperbolic Discount Functions, Undersaving, and Savings Policy." Working Paper W5635. Cambridge, Mass.: National Bureau of Economic Research (June).

———. 1997. "Golden Eggs and Hyperbolic Discounting." *Quarterly Journal of Economics* 65: 443–47.

Linneman, Peter, and Susan M. Wachter. 1989. "The Impacts of Borrowing Constraints on Homeownership." *AREUEA Journal* 17: 389–402.

Quercia, Roberto G., George W. McCarthy, and Susan M. Wachter. 2003. "The Impacts of Affordable Lending Efforts on Homeownership Rates." *Journal of Housing Economics* 12 (1): 29–59.

Phelps, Edmund S., and Robert A. Pollak. 1968. "On Second-Best National Saving and Game-Equilibrium Growth." *Review of Economic Studies* 35: 185–99.

Rohe, William M., George W. McCarthy, and Shannon van Zandt. 2000. "The Social Benefits and Costs of Homeownership: A Critical Assessment of the Research." Working Paper 00-01. Research Institute for Housing America.

Rosenthal, Stuart S. 2002. "Eliminating Credit Barriers: How Far Can We Go?" In *Low-Income Homeownership, Examining the Unexamined Goal,* edited by Nicolas P. Retsinas and Eric S. Belsky, pp. 111–45. Brookings.

Stiglitz, Joseph E., and Andrew Weiss. 1981. "Credit Rationing in Markets with Imperfect Information." *American Economic Review* 71 (3): 393–410.

Wachter, Susan M., and others. 1996. "Implications of Privatization: The Attainment of Social Goals." In *Studies on Privatizing Fannie Mae and Freddie Mac,* pp. 338–77. U.S. Department of Housing and Urban Development.

Zorn, Peter M. 1989. "Mobility-Tenure Decisions and Financial Credit: Do Mortgage Qualification Requirements Constrain Homeownership?" *AREUEA Journal* 17: 1–16.

8

Credit Scoring's Role in Increasing Homeownership for Underserved Populations

HOLLIS FISHELSON-HOLSTINE

C redit scoring grew out of the need to offer more credit more quickly, and without discrimination, to an increasingly mobile population after World War II. It made lending processes faster, fairer, and more accurate and consistent. Loan decisions could be made in minutes, rather than days or weeks. The extension of credit could be based only on factors proven (not assumed) to relate to future repayment. Sophisticated scorecard models precisely weighted and balanced all risk factors, so decisionmakers could apply one consistent measure of risk to all applications. This made credit more accessible and affordable to millions of Americans. Credit scoring such as FICO® scores are accepted, reliable, and trusted to the point that even regulators use them to help ensure the safety and soundness of the financial system.[1]

History, Concepts, and Benefits

Bill Fair and Earl Isaac developed the first commercial scorecard systems in 1958 for St. Louis-based finance company American Investment. Their initial projects successfully demonstrated credit scoring's financial value. Scoring systems reduced delinquencies up to 20–30 percent while maintaining similar volumes of

---

1. Testimony of Cheri St. John to the House Financial Services Subcommittee on the Renewal of FCRA Preemption, Washington. June 4, 2003.

loans, and could also be used to increase lending volume by 20–30 percent at the same level of delinquency then when not using scores. Despite its obvious advantages, scoring was not widely embraced until the early 1970s, when bank credit cards were well established. Fair Isaac successfully developed the first bank scorecard system for Connecticut Bank and Trust. By the end of the 1970s, 60 percent of the nation's largest banks, 70 percent of finance companies, most of the larger national credit card issuers, and all of the travel and entertainment cards employed quantitative credit-scoring systems on one or more types of credit.[2]

Credit Scoring Concepts

The credit decision is a prospective one, that is, it emphasizes borrowers' future behavior, not how they behaved in the past. Past behavior and current status are both useful indicators of a borrower's behavior pattern, and therefore signal possible future fiscal conduct. The credit decision, then, relies on the premise that people will behave in the future, at least in the near term, very much as they have in the recent past. Credit decisions made without scoring rely on credit officers' knowledge of the relationship between past behavior and future performance— and this knowledge, even at its best, is very imprecise. Lenders' rule-based systems for approving or denying credit applications—known as judgmental systems—are often a series of hurdles or so-called knockout criteria. Every credit application must pass all the criteria in order to be approved. Because every factor is considered in isolation, there is no possibility for several strengths in an application to make up for one or more weaknesses. In addition, a person considering a loan application often ends up putting too much weight on different factors that represent essentially the same information. For example, younger borrowers are also less likely to have been at their job a long time or own their own home.

By contrast, a scoring system, or scorecard, performs a very thorough analysis of available data and is based on a rigorous understanding of the relationship between past or present behavior and future performance. A scorecard analyzes all available relevant information to deliver a single score: a number that represents the risk (or odds of positive repayment) for a particular individual. Using scores, a lender can rank borrowers according to the likelihood that they will default on a loan or become seriously delinquent (late in payments). For example, in a system where higher scores mean greater likelihood of repayment, people scoring 200 would be less risky than those scoring 180, but more risky than those scoring 220 (see figure 8-1). Lenders typically establish a cutoff score representing the threshold of acceptable risk. So, a lender might set a cutoff score at a level where, for that lender's portfolio, the odds of repayment are equal to or greater than twenty to one. The lender rejects those applicants scoring below the cutoff, while accepting those who score above it. Cutoffs can also be used to

2. For a survey on the technical development of credit scoring, see Thomas (2000).

Figure 8-1. *Mortgage Delinquency Rates by FICO Score*

Delinquent (percent)

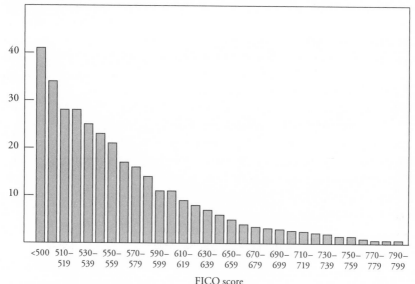

FICO score

Sources: Credit Bureau Score Products, Validation Odds Charts, U.S. Risk Scores, Equifax, BEACON 5.0, Real Estate.

price loans according to the payment risk. Because credit products and lenders' applicant populations differ, the odds of a given score will vary from lender to lender, portfolio to portfolio, and over time. While a given FICO score is not tied to a particular level of risk or odds of repayment, the scores will rank a lender's applicants or customers by risk, making cutoff scores and automated risk-based decisions possible.

In a typical scorecard development, analysts may identify hundreds of factors that have individual predictive value, but only eight to twelve variables are in the final scorecard. Even if each variable has an average of only three possible values, the possible combinations still run to tens of thousands. It would be impossible for a subjective or judgmental decision process to evaluate and weight that much complex information. The distinguishing feature of most credit-scoring models is that they rely on an exhaustive statistical analysis of actual credit experience to determine which factors should be considered in the credit decision, and the weight that each factor should be accorded.[3] By using a consistent set of information, the same decision will be reached by thousands of lenders across an organization.

As noted, scorecards typically utilize only a small fraction of the data available, about eight to twelve variables, because many of the data do not have a

3. For a more detailed treatment of the concepts of credit scoring, see Lewis (1992).

reliable correlation with future payment behavior and those that do are closely correlated with another factor. By analyzing this correlation and selecting the right factors, scorecard developers can avoid using data that are likely to be frequently missing or unreliable, minimizing the impact of poor quality data far more than would be possible using manual underwriting.

Unlike the series of knockout rules common to judgmental systems, scoring produces a balanced picture of an individual's risk. When being assessed, an individual may lose points in one area but gain them in another. The relationship between all the factors is studied, and each factor is weighted to take its relationship with others into account. Scoring and judgmental approaches will not always produce the same decisions with respect to the same applicant. If the individual decisions were always the same, scoring could not produce the reduction in delinquency rates or opportunities to increase volume that lenders typically see. However, the factors analyzed by a scoring system are likely to be very similar to those that would be considered in judgmental decisions. The principal difference is in the weights accorded to each factor, which account for the correlation between factors and the limited number of factors that are included.

FICO Score

Initially, almost all credit-scoring systems were developed on a custom basis for an individual lender. The scoring systems used any data available in a systematized format and were optimized for their particular lending community. One limitation of these systems is that a lender would have very few data about any person who was not a current customer—typically, only the application data the prospective borrower supplied, and no data on the individual's past credit performance at all.

Data from the national credit bureaus have the advantage of providing a broad view of consumers' past experience with credit, for example, how long they have used credit, the type of credit available to them, and their past payment performance. Scorecards built using these data enable a lender to accurately assess risk even when the lender has no prior experience with the consumer or when no additional information is available. Score developers began tapping into credit bureau data in the late 1970s, initially to evaluate credit risk in direct mail solicitations. In 1987, Management Decision Systems (now part of Experian) introduced the first mass-marketed generic credit bureau scorecard models, aimed primarily at predicting bankruptcy (Chandler, 1998). Two years later Fair Isaac released the first general credit bureau risk score for use in predicting all types of credit risk throughout the entire customer life cycle, which was quickly dubbed the FICO score.[4]

---

4. These scorecards, commonly known as FICO scorecards, actually have different product names at each of the three major credit bureaus: FICO® Risk Score, Classic at TransUnion (formerly known as Empirica); Beacon® at Equifax; and the Experian/Fair Isaac Risk Model at Experian.

The classic FICO scoring system at each credit bureau contains ten separate scorecards. The wealth of information available from credit files allows development of a much finer segmentation than could be achieved when developing a scorecard from a single lender's data. A key step in the development of multiple scorecard systems is aligning the scorecards so that the resulting scores correspond to the same odds of repayment, regardless of which scorecard was used. Since its introduction in 1989, the FICO score has become the standard measure of consumer credit risk in the United States. FICO scores provide a consistent measure of risk across different kinds of decisions, products, geography, and credit bureaus. Lenders, retailers, telecommunication firms, and other businesses use FICO scores in billions of decisions each year.

By providing a credit risk metric that crosses lenders and credit products, FICO scores facilitated the unprecedented growth in consumer access to credit and a unified market for consumer debt. Initially used for credit marketing as well as account approval and management, in 1995 Fannie Mae and Freddie Mac recommended FICO scores for use in mortgage lending. With that encouragement, mortgage lenders increased their use of credit scoring at a fast and furious pace. FICO scores became the mortgage industry standard because they were widely available through all three major U.S. credit-reporting agencies and thus were accessible to all parties in the lending process—brokers, correspondent lenders, wholesale lenders, mortgage insurance companies, rating agencies, and investors.

Today, Fair Isaac estimates that more than 75 percent of all U.S. mortgage originations involve the FICO score. These scores, used in almost every sector of the nation's economy (mortgages, credit cards, auto loans, retail store accounts, personal loans, cellular phone service), are used not only to evaluate applications, but also to manage the credit needs of existing customers by extending additional credit or by helping consumers avoid overextending themselves. FICO scores are also used by lenders and securities firms to aid securitization of credit portfolios. Securitization, in turn, gives lenders the capital they need to make credit available to more consumers (see box 8-1). Fair Isaac's latest risk score tool, the NextGen FICO score, includes refined segmentation and offers lenders a more advanced alternative to Fair Isaac's classic FICO credit bureau scores.[5]

Consumer Benefits of Credit Scoring

Credit scores have enabled lenders to extend credit quickly while safely managing risk associated with lending to new customers or those turned away by other

---

5. These models are also known as Pinnacle(SM) at Equifax; FICO® Risk Score, NextGen (formerly Precision) at TransUnion; and the Experian/Fair Isaac Advanced Risk Score at Experian. They are currently available at all three credit bureaus.

Box 8-1. *Current Use of FICO Scores*

Risk evaluation.

Accept/reject decisions.

Risk-based pricing.

Solicitation/pre-approval of new customers. Scores determine what to offer (pricing, features) and to whom.

Rating portfolios considered for purchase or sale. Evaluate credit quality and determine price.

Determine which purchases to authorize above open-to-buy.

Identify customers for cross-sell and up-sell promotions.

Credit line increase/decrease.

Timing and type of collection actions.

Customer service. Streamline decisions for good customers.

Securitization.

Regulator exams to ensure fair lending.

Loss forecasting.

Capital allocation.

---

lenders. As a result, credit is more accessible (at lower rates) to a wider group of people, including low-income and minority populations. Scores make credit more affordable by reducing: the cost of acquiring new accounts and managing portfolios; loan losses; marketing costs with prescreening; and the cost of capital with securitization.

Greater Access to Credit

The beginning of the twenty-first century has seen an unprecedented level of consumer credit available in the United States (Cate and others, 2003), particularly compared with other parts of the world. For example, a TowerGroup analyst estimated that European consumers have access to one-third less credit as a percent of gross domestic product than do Americans (Kitchenman, 1999). Credit scoring, based on a rich set of national data, has allowed U.S. lenders to effectively lend to an increasingly mobile population. It has facilitated the development of interstate banking, encouraged competition, and increased liquidity for additional lending through securitization. Interstate banking has increased over the past decades, as has disaggregation, because a consumer can be assessed for credit without having an existing account relationship with the creditor. This

Figure 8-2. *Homeownership Rates, 1983–2001*

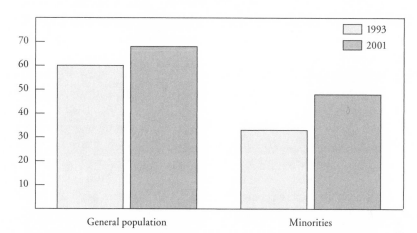

Source: Turner (2003).

makes capital more mobile, allows a consumer to shop for credit at a lower cost, and allows banks to specialize in particular credit products, which improves competition (Kitchenman, 1999).

The increase in mortgage credit available to consumers has played a critical role in increasing the availability of housing. Mortgage credit has increased dramatically in recent decades—the percentage of families with home-secured debt grew from 36 to 45 percent between 1983 and 2001. Over the same period, the percentage of families who owned their homes increased from 60 to 68 percent (Turner, 2003). While homeownership increased in general over this period, it increased most dramatically for minority populations. The use of credit scoring in mortgage underwriting has played a significant role in that increase.

While credit availability has increased overall, it has increased at an accelerated rate for families who have traditionally been underserved. In a 2003 study by the Information Policy Institute, the authors cite an increase in homeownership for minority populations from 34 to 47 percent between 1983 and 2001, an increase of 38 percentage points. This compares to an increase of 13 percentage points for the overall population (figure 8-2). This increase is strongly correlated with the pervasive use of sophisticated risk models and automated underwriting (Turner, 2003).

Federal Reserve Chairman Alan Greenspan also reiterated the positive impact of credit scoring on low-income and minority populations seeking mortgages. Speaking to the Mortgage Bankers Association of America, he said, "this technology [credit scoring] has aided the measurement and pricing of risk on low down payment loans to first-time home buyers, and has accordingly broadened the potential market for homeownership. By tailoring mortgages to the needs of individual borrowers, the mortgage banking industry of tomorrow will be better positioned to serve all corners of the diverse mortgage market."[6]

Studies by both Freddie Mac (Gates, Perry, and Zorn, 2002) and Fair Isaac (Martell and others, 1997) demonstrated that credit scoring is effective for measuring credit risk in underserved populations. Freddie Mac's study analyzed the percentage of lower-income borrowers and minority loans originated in 1993 or 1994, and purchased by Freddie Mac in 1995, as part of its affordable housing initiative with major lenders. The Fair Isaac study evaluated the performance of low- to moderate-income (LMI) loans, as well as those loans in a high minority area (HMA), as defined by zip codes in the U.S. Census. Both the Freddie Mac and Fair Isaac studies indicate that a lender employing credit scoring can accept more underserved applicants without raising its bad rate, because credit scoring is a far more predictive screen for underserved applicants than is judgmental decisionmaking.

The 1997 Fair Isaac study compared acceptance rates for credit scoring versus judgmental underwriting for LMI applicants for a variety of credit portfolios, and assumed a cutoff set to maintain the same delinquency rates. Increases in acceptance rates were in the range of 60 percentage points, and in some portfolios the acceptance rate more than doubled. The study also found that the relative importance of variables that were predictive of risk did not vary between the LMI or HMA population and general populations, and neither did the patterns of risk. For example, variables such as the amount of a past delinquency and how recent it was, were predictive regardless of the population being studied, and increased frequency of delinquency and more recent delinquency were associated with higher risk. Cate and others (2003) noted that the use of credit scoring reduces redlining by providing more precise information on a borrower's own past experience as opposed to relying on geographic or census data. It also reduces redlining by facilitating entry and competition, which stimulates the supply of credit and holds down the price.

Lower Price

Scoring permits credit processes to be automated (financial institutions can automate 70-80 percent of consumer credit decisions), making the credit granting process more efficient and less costly for lenders. Scores make credit more affordable by reducing losses and costs, enabling the systematic use of risk-based pricing, and encouraging competition. These savings are passed along to consumers in the form of lower prices.

Scoring allows lenders to control for risk exposure, and therefore to determine the pricing of loans. Risk-based pricing lowers the price of credit for

6. Remarks by Federal Reserve Chairman Alan Greenspan, Mortgage Bankers Association of America, March 8, 1999 (www.federalreserve.gov/boarddocs/speeches/f1999/199909082.html [December 2003]).

lower-risk consumers, while increasing the price for higher-risk consumers to compensate for the additional losses they generate. This allows lenders to offer credit to a wider segment of the population and has the overall effect of reducing price.

Before using FICO scores, lenders used complex rule-based systems (using debt ratio analysis) to determine pricing. However, score-based systems predict future delinquency significantly better than do these rule-based systems, and thus can be used to more accurately determine the price needed to compensate for the risk. Risk-based pricing has been used for a number of years in the auto industry, where a FICO score is combined with factors such as loan-to-value ratio to determine pricing tiers. It is also used to determine pricing in mortgages. In recent years, scores have been used to drive risk-based pricing in the credit card industry as well.

Alan Greenspan, speaking at an annual meeting of the American Bankers Association in October 1994, praised the concept of using scoring-based risk assessment to "begin pricing properly for the higher-risk borrowers, rather than simply denying credit." Quantifying risk through scoring, he noted, would help banks securitize loans and diversify their loan portfolios.[7]

The Information Policy Institute recently studied the importance of renewing the national uniformity provisions of the Fair Credit Reporting Act, which were set to expire on January 1, 2004. As part of that study, the institute found a significant drop in mortgage costs, which was attributed to increased efficiency in underwriting, more accurate risk assessment and pricing through the use of credit scoring models, and reduced costs of closing loans, which are passed along to consumers. The study explains "if spreads today were at their early 1980s levels, the interest rate on a thirty-year fixed-rate mortgage would be at least 1 percent higher than it is today. This translates into $54 billion in annual savings to consumers" (Turner, 2003).

While use of FICO scores has increased both acceptance rates and homeownership for underserved populations, more can be done to diminish the differential in homeownership between the general and underserved population. Most important, this includes the incorporation of additional data sources, and a focus on financial literacy and homeownership education, issues explored later in this chapter.

Increased Benefits from Added Data and More Predictive Scores

Broad, easily accessible data are essential to the development of scoring models. Since FICO scores have been more widely used by the mortgage and telecom-

---

7. G. Bruce Knecht, "Banks May Be Easing Credit Standards by Too Much, Fed Chairman Suggests," *Wall Street Journal,* October 10, 1994, p. A2.

munication arenas, more data have been shared through the credit bureaus, which in turn has enabled the development of more predictive scores. The availability of positive information has contributed positively to the rise of the robust credit economy in the United States and is an essential component of FICO scores. With increased standardized access to wider sources of positive information, it is easier to assess risk in today's underserved markets for home-ownership.

More predictive scores offer many benefits: they allow for finer gradations in risk assessment and pricing; enable greater, faster access to credit; ensure that credit is granted safely and consumers are not overextended; reduce the cost of credit by lowering the default rate, which the good-paying majority must subsidize; and provide greater operational savings to lenders, which (due to market competition) are passed along to consumers.

Five Categories of FICO Score Information

FICO scorecards consider all information (both positive and negative) available in a credit report. Negative information includes data about past delinquency on credit obligations, public records, judgments, or collection activities. Positive data include how long credit has been used, the type and amount of credit currently being used, search for new credit, as well as payment history where no delinquency has occurred. Positive information generally includes any data that are not the record of previous poor credit payment behavior.

The source of the FICO score's predictive power is a complex analysis of all these factors, both separately and in relation to one another. Because the overall score takes into account the totality of information, it is impossible to precisely describe the importance of any single factor in determining a score. However, it is possible to describe the relative value of the types of information available from a credit report.

Performance is predicted by five main categories of information: payment history, financial measures, age of credit file, new credit acquisition, and types of credit in use. Figure 8-3 shows the relative importance of these information categories. Generally, payment history is the strongest (and most obvious). However, this represents only 35 percent of the information, so other data are used to refine decisionmaking. The score optimally combines all categories for the most effective risk-assessment tool.

PAYMENT HISTORY. Ratings, delinquency trends, payment patterns on a credit account, or the presence of public records are all evidence of payment history. Whether the past payment behavior is negative or positive, it is useful in estimating future behavior. Delinquency information, present on only 30-35 percent of all files, is highly predictive of potential risk. Delinquency payment takes into consideration:

Figure 8-3. *Relative Importance of FICO Information Categories*

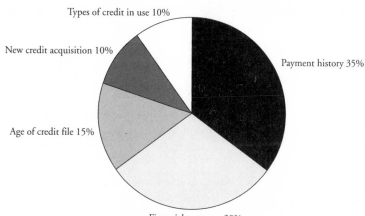

Types of credit in use 10%

New credit acquisition 10%

Payment history 35%

Age of credit file 15%

Financial measures 30%

Source: www.myfico.com/CreditEducation/WhatsInYourScore.aspx.

—severity (degree of delinquency, for example ninety days late is a higher risk than thirty days late);

—age of delinquency (for example, recently reported is worse than a severe delinquency several years old);

—frequency (the number of delinquent accounts present, for example delinquency on a single account is better than delinquency on multiple accounts).

These factors need to be considered together. A consumer who missed a couple of payments within the last two months, for example, may be a higher risk than someone with a much older but more severe delinquency.

If past problems were severe enough to initiate judgments, foreclosures, or bankruptcy, these will be represented by public records and collections. While the presence of these items is very significant, they are considered within the context of the entire file. In the United States, most public records and delinquency information is retained for seven years on reports (Chapter 11 bankruptcies are retained for ten years). Although such occurrences imply serious credit performance problems, a six-year-old item may not indicate high risk if everything else is paid as agreed.

FINANCIAL MEASURES. Financial measures provide a reflection of the amount of credit in use. In general, those who use a lot of credit are riskier than those who use less. For example, one extremely predictive piece of information is the proportion of credit actually in use, relative to the available credit. Someone using all of his or her available credit is a strong indicator of risk. The frequency of accounts with a balance and amount of outstanding balance are also good risk predictors. The amount of an installment loan still owed compared with the original loan amount is also important. Paying down installment loan debt is a good sign that someone is able and willing to manage and repay debt.

NEW CREDIT ACQUISITION. This category, which considers whether someone is actively seeking additional credit (and to what degree), includes: the number of new accounts, time since new accounts were opened, and presence of good recent credit history following past payment problems. If there are many inquiries but few new accounts, the consumer is riskier than someone without any inquiries. If someone has a record of credit for twenty years without many outstanding balances, several inquiries or one or two newly opened accounts would not represent inordinate risk. However, if the history is short (for example, two to three years) and the file contains a group of recently opened new accounts, it would be a reason for lenders to be cautious, particularly if balances are building up quickly or there are early indications of mild delinquency.

AGE OF CREDIT FILE. How long an individual has had credit established is used to determine the importance of other information. Older, more established reports generally indicate lower risk. For instance, credit histories with accounts open for ten or more years with few outstanding balances and one or two newly opened accounts would not be considered a high risk, but a shorter credit history with one or two newly opened accounts would represent a higher risk level.

TYPES OF CREDIT IN USE. These include obligations that a consumer has sought and acquired in the past. As an example, a file with a breadth of credit in use—revolving as well as installment—will score higher than one without. A file will also score higher if there is more than one bank card account (versus none), although not too many. While this category is generally secondary to the others, it may be used as a tiebreaker.[8]

Value of Positive Information

In many countries shared credit information is limited to negative information, that is, past payment problems. However, a number of studies have demonstrated the beneficial impact of positive information on the predictiveness of credit scoring systems and the subsequent influence on credit availability and pricing. Barron and Staten (2000), who compare U.S. credit reports with Australian credit reports, estimate the following impacts if data were restricted to only negative information: consumer credit would be less available, credit rates would escalate, and competition would be reduced. The study also notes that reduced information would give rise to alternative measures for assessing the

---

8. For more detailed information, see "Understanding Your Credit Score," www.myfico.com/Offers/RequestOffer.asp.

likelihood of repayment, measures which could be more invasive and less objective than factual payment history.

In 1996, as part of an effort to evaluate the importance of positive information at the credit bureaus, Fair Isaac created two subpopulations (based on data provided by Trans Union) with an overall bad rate of 12.8 percent where bad equals an account that resulted in ninety-plus days' delinquent payment, charge-off, default, bankruptcy, or judgment within the two years following when it was scored. The first subpopulation was clean (no previous delinquency when scored, overall bad rate of 4.4 percent) and the second was derogatory (previous delinquency on file when scored, overall bad rate of 49 percent, or eleven times riskier than the clean population) (Fair Isaac, 1996).

A scorecard was developed using only positive information (ignoring information on delinquencies). Fair Isaac used this score to rank the clean subpopulation into deciles that ranged from 0.5 to 20 percent probability of going bad (see figure 8-4). In other words, the riskiest segment in the clean population was forty times riskier than the best segment—a distinction available only through the use of positive information. This scorecard was also used to segment the derogatory subpopulation more finely into deciles, with the probability of going bad ranging from 5.7 to 92.9 percent—a factor of sixteen times. Significantly, without the use of positive information the derogatory population would be presumed to pose greater risk than the clean population, because people in the first group had exhibited at least one instance of poor credit payment in the past. But by using positive information, Fair Isaac could sharpen its focus on risk. In fact, the lowest two deciles of the clean subpopulation performed worse than the best decile of the derogatory subpopulation. This has critical importance for segments of the population with damaged credit, since the positive information can be used to mitigate past credit problems. Without positive information, the existence of any negative information would be used as a knockout rule for declining credit applications.

More Predictive FICO Score

The increased information in credit bureau files, along with innovations in scoring model development, allowed Fair Isaac to develop a more predictive set of credit bureau scores, the NextGen FICO scores. Although based on the same credit reports that FICO scores evaluate, NextGen FICO scores provide a stronger risk assessment across the entire risk spectrum, allowing for better, more accurate risk-pricing decisions.

While the new generation of scores provides value to all industries, there is significant predictive lift for consumers with prior derogatory credit references. This consumer segment is of particular interest to those seeking to widen the availability of consumer credit and thus increase homeownership. NextGen FICO scores' increased focus on the population with previous delinquency

Figure 8-4. *Fair Isaac Population Risk by Score*

A. Clean population

Probability of going "bad" (percent)

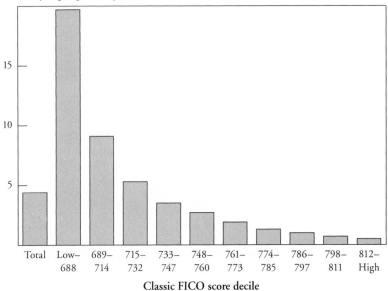

Classic FICO score decile

B. Derogatory population

Probability of going "bad" (percent)

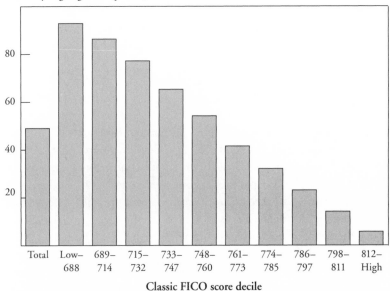

Classic FICO score decile

Source: Fair Isaac (1996).

allows the score to better separate those with less serious past-payment problems from consumers with collections, charge-offs, or prior bankruptcies on their credit reports. Fair Isaac was also able to draw greater distinctions between consumers with respect to file age or thickness of the file, and to consider new factors such as credit usage as the basis for subpopulations.

The NextGen FICO model has eighteen scorecards (the classic FICO scoring systems has ten). This enhanced segmentation isolates important subgroups of accounts, with scorecards focusing on populations such as consumers with a prior bankruptcy, a delinquency on new accounts (called the Rocky Start segment), and limited use of credit or limited reported credit.

In classic FICO scores, good or bad performance is based on the worst delinquency or derogatory status on any obligation over two years. NextGen FICO is more tiered, classified by the degree of positive or negative performance across all credit obligations. So a consumer who is delinquent on two out of ten open accounts will represent a different level of unsatisfactory outcome than someone who is delinquent on all ten accounts. This new system benefits consumers who have had some difficulty in the past but have successfully paid down existing credit obligations.

Segmented scoring systems offer users qualitative and strategic benefits as well as refined risk prediction. For example, when reviewing accounts with prior delinquency, if one were using a single overall scorecard, the account would be evaluated as high risk. A special scorecard for that segment can determine who is most likely to become seriously delinquent again rather than stay in good standing. Thus one can find the hidden low-risk accounts that might not have been identified by a single scorecard.

For example, in a derogatory subpopulation the timing, severity, and persistence of past payment behavior is dominant, while other factors are somewhat less important. On the other hand, in a nonderogatory subpopulation, credit account, financial information and history, inquiries, and the mix of credit are proportionately more important (see figure 8-5). These differences are reflected in the variables used in the models and the magnitude of the scorecard weights, and will have a direct bearing on the precision of the scorecards.

NextGen FICO scores are also able to refine the importance of file age or thickness and consider new factors, such as credit usage, as the basis for subpopulations. For example, two situations provide a limited amount of information available for analysis—consumers who have used credit for only a short time but have varying numbers of accounts (short time in file) and consumers who have very little credit (only one or two accounts), but may have used credit for a long period of time (limited credit). Consumers in each case are widely recognized as having profiles quite different from consumers with well-established credit, but they are also quite distinct from each other (see figure 8-6).

Figure 8-5. *Derogatory and Nonderogatory Subpopulation Score Cards*

A. Subpopulations with no prior delinquency

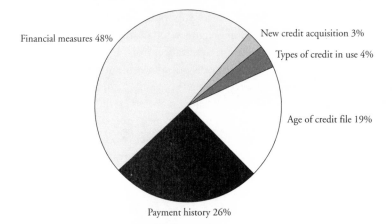

B. Subpopulations with prior delinquency

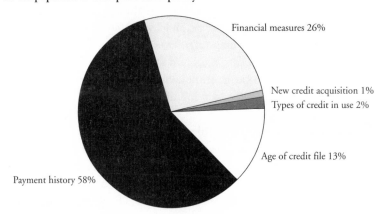

Source: Fair Isaac (1992).

For limited credit files, for example, the time that credit has been in use is an important predictor, while the types of credit used are relatively meaningless given the small number of accounts available. On the other hand, for the short time in file populations, the time that credit has been in use is not predictive since it was only recently established, but variables that measure the account balance are more powerful than for either limited credit or well-established accounts.

In the most recent redevelopment of NextGen FICO scores, Fair Isaac made additional modifications to enhance the availability of credit. The portion of the population for which a score can be calculated was expanded by approximately

Figure 8-6. *Refining Subpopulation Score Cards*

A. Limited credit

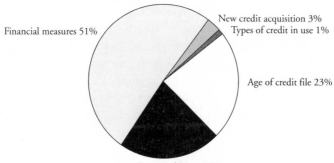

Financial measures 51%

New credit acquisition 3%
Types of credit in use 1%

Age of credit file 23%

Payment history 22%

B. Short time in file

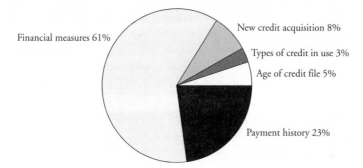

Financial measures 61%

New credit acquisition 8%

Types of credit in use 3%

Age of credit file 5%

Payment history 23%

C. Well-established credit

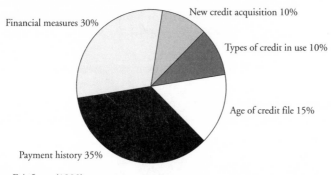

Financial measures 30%

New credit acquisition 10%

Types of credit in use 10%

Age of credit file 15%

Payment history 35%

Source: Fair Isaac (1993).

2 percent, which particularly benefits the underserved markets that have little credit experience.

Fair Isaac also removed variables that caused concerns for consumers in the past. For example, the greater predictive power of NextGen FICO allowed Fair Isaac to exclude from the model the variable "number of finance company credit accounts." It had been a source of concern because specific cultural groups have demonstrated a higher tendency to use this form of financing in the past. This change is consistent with the findings of the Federal Reserve Board, which found that the differences between risk segmentation by banks and finance companies with regard to the personal loan market had disappeared by the end of the twentieth century, and the risk profiles of these two groups were far more overlapping (Durkin and Elliehausen, 2000).

Additional Data Sources Could Improve Prediction

Fair Isaac expects FICO scores' predictive power will continue to increase through the addition of new credit file data as well as continued technological innovation. However, the best way to increase predictive power is through the addition of new sources of data. As an example, most special programs for non-traditional mortgage applications include other methodology to assess credit-worthiness, such as requiring twelve months of on-time rent, utility (electricity, gas, cable, telephone), insurance (car and life), or health care payments. This type of information can potentially overlap a number of data categories used in the current FICO scores, but is most relevant to the category of payment history, since a complete record of payments on these obligations would mimic the payment history currently present at the credit bureau. At a minimum, negative information about missed payments would be predictive. Ideally, this would include not only that a payment was missed, but how recently, how often, and to what degree of severity (number of days or months). This information would be far more valuable, however, if it also included the positive information about payments made on time.

Positive information would also contribute to the category of (or measure of) age of credit. This is particularly important for those segments of the population who have been averse to using credit from banks and other financial institutions, preferring to rely on family members for loans. When these individuals apply for a mortgage they have no previous credit history at the credit bureau, so it is impossible to calculate a FICO score and the applicants have difficulty obtaining a mortgage. However, a FICO score enhanced by information about these other payments offers a more complete reflection of the time any type of credit has been in use. Should all of these categories of information be available—rental, utility, insurance, health care, telecommunication, and so on—the breadth of credit being used could also be assessed and contribute to the category of types of credit in use.

Two segments of the population would benefit from additional data sources: those with previously damaged credit and those with little credit experience. Clearly, there is value for those with little credit experience, since this additional information could supplement the data currently available at the credit bureau. For those with previously damaged credit, additional positive information could be used to offset the past credit problems.

Two other sources of information may prove to be predictive. First is the provision of a letter of explanation for past credit problems. While there have been qualitative indications from consumer advocacy groups that this can be predictive, this information would need to be available in a quantitative format that includes subsequent performance in order to assess its real value. Second is the completion of a counseling and education program, particularly on mortgages. A recent study by the Credit Research Center demonstrated that the successful completion of such programs lowers risk of default (Staten, Elliehausen, and Lundquist, 2002). This conclusion has also been supported by conversations between Fair Isaac and mortgage lenders. Again, the successful completion of approved programs would need to be accessible in a consistent manner for it to be included in a scorecard.

Lenders who want to take advantage of this predictive information ask the consumer to collect the data manually and return it to the lender. In most instances, when faced with this request the consumer never returns to the bank. Even if consumer advocacy groups are involved and help the consumer obtain the necessary data, the lender must undertake a slow and costly manual process to evaluate the information provided.

Unfortunately, there is no systematic way to access this type of information, and the cooperation and format vary considerably across the agencies that supply it. While a number of efforts are under way to try to access rental information (for example, PRBC), existing rental information is scattered and inconsistent. Likewise, utility information is difficult to obtain. In some instances, states may actually prohibit access to these data. For lenders to capitalize on the value of this information, it must be available in a consistent format from a small number of repositories, and must then be summarized in a score to successfully integrate with today's automated underwriting systems. Finally, it is essential that such a score be one that aligns seamlessly with today's FICO score to achieve its full potential benefits for mortgage lending.

As a step in this direction, in 2004 Fair Isaac announced the launch of the FICO® Expansion™ score to help lenders expand their presence in markets that are underserved in terms of credit. This FICO score can tap nontraditional sources of credit data to assess the credit risk of individuals who have minimal or no credit history on file with the major credit-reporting agencies. Predictive information considered in the formulation of this score includes performance data on financial activities such as deposit accounts and product purchase payment plans.

Threats to the Availability and Quality of Credit Scoring Data

Complete, consistent data make scorecards smarter (or more predictive), which benefits both consumers and lenders. Removing information from credit reports, or even varying reported information from state to state, would make the process of obtaining credit difficult for consumers to understand and take charge of their credit health. While credit-reporting agency data quality has increased considerably over the past decade, credit risk assessment (and the concomitant increase in available credit) could be further enhanced by continuing to improve the accuracy of information used in credit scoring systems.

The most recent threat to the availability of data for credit scoring occurred in 2003, when the so-called national uniformity provisions of the Fair Credit Reporting Act (FCRA) were nearing a sunset date of January 2004. In December 2003, President George W. Bush signed into law the Fair and Accurate Credit Transactions (FACT) Act, which amended the FCRA and made permanent seven existing FCRA provisions that, in part, preempt states from making laws that govern the content and use of credit files.

If national uniformity provisions had been allowed to expire, states could have imposed their own restrictions on credit scoring, including reducing the length of time that negative information may be included on credit reports. This and other changes could have driven some financial institutions to provide only partial information or completely stop reporting information to the credit bureaus completely. While the passage of FACT removed these threats, it is worth considering the impact that even well-meaning legislation may have when it reduces the data available to credit scoring. Some of the research presented while Congress debated the FCRA amendment demonstrates this impact.

Constraining Data

The Information Policy Institute's 2003 report examined the impact of four scenarios simulating the changes in available information that could be expected to result from proposed state laws or simply from the expiration of the FCRA preemption provisions. The institute found that acceptance rates would decline or delinquencies would increase under all four scenarios. For example, under the most severe scenario, if delinquency rates were maintained, 30 percent of those consumers currently receiving general-purpose credit cards (41 million people) would be denied credit card access. This percentage would be even higher for minority groups—40 percent for Hispanics and 33 percent for African Americans. Likewise, lower-income and younger consumers would experience larger declines. Indeed, the results obtained for minority, lower-income, and younger borrowers strongly suggest that the removal of, or modifications to, the strengthened preemptions would undermine recent progress in extending credit to underserved segments of the population used (Turner, 2003).

Figure 8-7. *Bad and Bankruptcy Rates by Number of Inquiries in the Past Year*

Bad rate (percent)   Bankruptcy rate (percent)

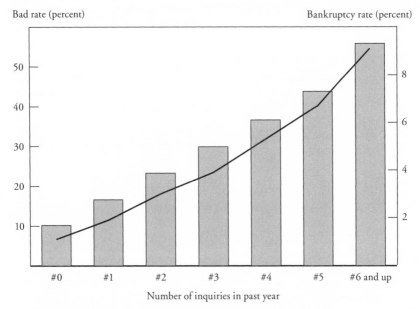

Number of inquiries in past year

Source: Internal Fair Isaac Research. Data supplied by Equifax as of July 1998 observation date.

As another example of how the use of predictive information is threatened, many lawmakers continue to question the predictive value of credit inquiries. As mentioned earlier, new credit acquisition represents approximately 10 percent of the FICO score's value. While this category looks holistically at recent credit, including the opening of new accounts and their performance, an important component is the presence of inquiries for additional credit. By itself, a large number of inquiries are not necessarily negative. As has been explained, the various information categories can compensate for one another. Thus a consumer with a high number of inquiries, who has a well-established file demonstrating successful repayment, will not be negatively affected. Consumers actively seeking new sources of credit with no compensating history can be demonstrated to be higher risk because it generally means that they already are having difficulty handling their existing debt load and are seeking additional credit to compensate. Overall, consumers with six or more inquiries are almost five times as likely to go bad and eight times as likely to go bankrupt than are consumers with no inquiries (see figure 8-7).

Since the number of inquiries as a predictor continues to be a sensitive topic for some observers, and the value of this predictor changes as consumer and lender behavior changes, Fair Isaac continually evaluates the manner in which inquiries are used in credit scores. For instance, certain inquiries are not included, such as inquiries from employers, consumer requests for their own reports, or lender requests for reports to review an account before issuing a preapproved offer of credit. The FICO score also only considers inquiries made within the previous twelve months. Fair Isaac updated its logic for calculating inquiries used in the FICO score in 1995, a time when mortgage and automobile lenders were dramatically increasing their use of scores. In 1998, Fair Isaac further refined the way it handles inquiries, as well as in the later redevelopment of the NextGen FICO score. This approach distinguishes individuals who are shopping for a single large loan from individuals attempting to establish many new sources of credit. The NextGen FICO score treats multiple, mortgage-related, and auto-related inquiries within any forty-five-day period as a single inquiry. Fair Isaac also uses a buffer period such that the score ignores all mortgage and auto-related inquiries made during the thirty days before scoring.

Current Concerns with Data Quality

Consumers and consumer advocacy groups have expressed concerns with the quality of the credit data on which scores are being calculated and decisions are being made. These concerns are reasonable, since scores can influence whether a consumer receives a preapproved offer for credit or a low interest rate for an auto loan or mortgage. A number of recent studies have investigated the quality of data at the three credit-reporting agencies, and hypothesized about its potential impact on scorecard development and score consistency across all three agencies.

In December 2002, the Consumer Federation of America (CFA) and the National Credit Reporting Association issued a report that challenged the accuracy of credit scoring by identifying differences between scores at the three national credit-reporting agencies (Consumer Federation of America, 2002). The CFA report acknowledged that the most important contributor to score differences was the inconsistency in consumer credit data held at the three national credit-reporting agencies.

A recent study by the Federal Reserve Board focused on incomplete or inaccurate data at a single agency, as summarized in box 8-2 (Avery, Calem, and Canner, 2003). The study concluded "overall, research and creditor experience has consistently indicated that credit reporting company information, despite any limitations that it may have, generally provides an effective measure of the relative credit risk posed by prospective borrowers." Although credit-reporting agency data are extensive, they are not complete. It is worth noting that the credit-reporting agencies have a series of protocols to address each of the issues listed in box 8-2.

Significantly, all of the recent studies on credit data agree that consumers need to take a more active role in ensuring the accuracy of their credit reports, checking them periodically and using the dispute process established in the FCRA to correct errors or omissions. Periodic checks are especially important if consumers

---

Box 8-2. *Summary of Data Quality Problems*

Inconsistent data across credit reporting agencies.

Timing of when information is sent to each bureau has an effect on consistency.

Duplication or inconsistency of public records and collection information.

Lack of reporting by smaller lenders.

Credit limits for revolving accounts not always reported.

Occasional failure to notify credit reporting agencies when accounts are closed.

Incomplete or incorrect personal information.

---

are in the market for new credit, they have been denied credit, or a creditor has changed the terms of an account based on credit report information.

The good news is that there is growing consumer awareness of the importance of credit reports. Consumers now have more opportunity than ever to correct information in their credit reports and to understand how the information in their reports affects their scores. Millions of consumers have already used tools available on the Internet to take better control of their credit.[9] In January 2002, Fair Isaac launched the first three-bureau credit report product designed for consumers, which includes the consumer's FICO score, making it easy to review and correct the underlying credit information at all three agencies. The newly passed FACT Act will also make it easier for consumers to review their credit reports and credit scores, and to correct errors in their credit data.

Mitigating Data Quality Concerns When Building Scorecards

Because of its experience with scorecard development, Fair Isaac understands the problems associated with data quality. Analysts building FICO scores routinely downplay or ignore types of data, or fields, that are deemed inconsistent. Inconsistent fields may be those that are not commonly found across all credit reports, or those where the values may represent different things in different reports. Generally, data that are inconsistent are less predictive and do not end up in scorecards. As Fair Isaac described in a written response to the CFA report (Fair Isaac, 2003), FICO scores minimize the impact of data discrepancies because they do not focus on a single piece of data, but evaluate dozens of types of predictive information in combination, a major advantage of scoring systems com-

---

9. See Fair Isaac's consumer website, www.myfico.com.

pared with judgmental review. This also has the result of reducing the impact of errors and omissions in single data elements.

Whenever possible, Fair Isaac also explicitly avoids the use of data that might be incorrect or incomplete. As an example, FICO scores evaluate the date of last activity only in rare cases. Fair Isaac frequently avoids "number of" variables to reduce the impact of data duplications ("presence of" or "time since" tend to be more predictive). It uses a variety of utilization calculations to minimize the impact of missing credit limits, and uses balance information only if recently reported. Fair Isaac has also developed a methodology to handle data issues in the development process, such as fragmented or duplicate files. The company's scorecard developers apply their experience in analyzing credit data to avoid placing weight on unreliable data.

Fair Isaac's first priority is to develop the most predictive scorecard possible. A second priority is to make the scorecards consistent across the credit-reporting agencies. In its development work, Fair Isaac derives the most value from a given agency's unique data strengths. In general, this increases the accuracy of the scorecards for each agency. Identical scoring systems, ignoring data differences and data integrity, would make the scorecards less reliable and would not neces-sarily reduce score differences. As a consequence of increasing scoring accuracy for each agency, the scores are often not exactly alike at each credit-reporting agency for a specific consumer.

Although Fair Isaac has been able to anticipate and mitigate many of the data concerns raised by such studies, it supports all efforts by the credit-reporting industry to improve data quality and consistency, and believes this will improve the quality of the lending process, particularly for individuals of marginal credit-worthiness. Fair Isaac recommends that lenders report complete information on a monthly basis to all three credit-reporting agencies, and encourages lenders to take the time to verify the accuracy of the reporting process. It also endorses the credit-reporting agencies' continued efforts to advance data aggregation processes and improve the integrity of the data they house and share with clients.

Future of Credit Scoring

Consumers today are far more aware of the impact credit scoring has on their ability to gain access to credit. Fair Isaac believes that credit scores will continue to increase in predictiveness and effectiveness to the benefit of all consumers, but especially for underserved populations who have had difficulty in the past gaining access to credit for homeownership. This increase will come as a result of broadly improving consumer education on the importance of properly man-aging credit, creating standardized access to additional sources of data. and con-tinuing innovation in the area of credit decisionmaking. As consumers increase their understanding of responsible credit use, access to credit (and therefore homeownership) will increase and credit rates will decrease as consumers demonstrate lower-risk behavior.

CONSUMER EDUCATION AND EMPOWERMENT. The importance of consumer education on credit management cannot be overemphasized. Consumers are increasingly savvy about credit options and availability, demanding to be evaluated and priced fairly, and requesting information about the role of scores in the lending process. Requests for information are most frequent in the mortgage industry, where brokers sometimes disclose lenders' cutoff scores as well as the consumers' own scores. Typically, consumers not only want to know their score, but what they can do to improve it to gain access to the most favorable pricing.

The high level of consumer interest is evidenced by the more than 1 million visits to Fair Isaac's consumer website, myFico.com, in the first year following the website's March 2001 launch. Through the website, consumers can purchase their own FICO scores and receive copies of their credit reports. In addition, they can receive complementary information to learn more about FICO scores and view tips on how to improve personal credit health.

In its research of consumer attitudes on a broad range of credit and credit scoring topics, Fair Isaac has determined there is a moderate awareness of credit reports, but little knowledge of credit scoring beyond a notion of a credit rating. Most consumers believed they could improve their rating, but often had no knowledge of how to do it, or the consumer had information that was incorrect and could be harmful if acted upon. On its website, Fair Isaac makes a number of specific recommendations to consumers, summarized in box 8-3.

A July 2003 survey of 1,000 adult Americans found that most Americans rate their knowledge of credit reports and credit scores as either fair or poor (50 percent of respondents rated their knowledge fair or poor for credit reports, 61 percent for credit scores). These numbers are even higher for lower-income Americans (those earning less than $35,000 a year; 60 percent for credit reports, 70 percent for credit scores). In surveying actual knowledge about credit reports and credit scores, only 25 percent of respondents (less than 20 percent of lower-income respondents) knew what their credit score was, and 27 percent incorrectly believe credit score mainly measures knowledge of consumer credit, versus creditworthiness (Opinion Research International, 2003).

Education about the importance of credit and basics of sound credit management is an important first step in empowering consumers to take more control of their access to credit. By getting their credit scores and detailed, personalized explanation from experts, consumers can responsibly increase scores by changing credit behavior. To illustrate, a study of 27,000 myfico.com consumers who obtained FICO scores more than once in a six-month period indicates this pop-

Box 8-3. *Tips for Improving Credit Scores*

Do gain access to credit if you have not used it in the past so a FICO
score can be calculated.

Do not open a lot of new accounts too rapidly.

Reestablish credit history by opening new accounts carefully and handling
them responsibly subsequent to credit problems.

Pay your bills on time, every time.

See a legitimate credit counselor if you are having trouble.

Keep balances low on revolving credit accounts and pay off debt versus
moving it between accounts.

Apply for and open new accounts only as needed.

Do your rate shopping for automobiles or mortgages within a thirty-day
period, if possible.

Source: www.myfico.com

ulation improved FICO scores between visits—and did so at a faster rate than
consumers typically migrate to higher scores. The primary reasons for this score
increase include: correcting erroneous information on credit reports, paying
down balances, and limiting new credit to essentials.

While websites such as myfico.com serve an important function, there is a
need for more widespread education, available in a variety of forms and especially targeting underserved populations. This need is made clear by an early
survey of myfico.com users, who were determined to be generally well-educated
homeowners with higher incomes, actively engaged with their lenders. Freddie
Mac's 2002 study on the impact of automated underwriting on minorities
(Gates, Perry, and Zorn, 2002) also cited the need to close the current gap in
financial literacy, specifically suggesting to eliminate the differential in Internet
access across income, racial, and ethnic groups to enable easier access to mortgage and home-buying information. Fair Isaac believes that education should
begin in high school, if not earlier, teaching youngsters of all population groups
how to access and use credit responsibly. A critical component of special CRA
programs is counseling and education, both during the loan process and after
the participants become homeowners. As described earlier, at least one study has
demonstrated that the successful completion of counseling and education programs lowers risk (Staten, Elliehausen, and Lundquist, 2002). Performance of
loans booked through special mortgage programs indicates that these
approaches are successful in identifying applicants of acceptable risk. A Federal

Reserve Board survey found that CRA special mortgage programs performed better (that is, loans extended through them had lower delinquency and net charge-off rates) than overall CRA-related home purchase and refinance lending (Avery, Bostic, and Canner, 2000).

Efforts to educate and empower low-income and minority segments of the population on how to establish credit, use it responsibly, and recover from past problems will result in a significant increase in the ability of these consumers to obtain mortgages. Effective education will also assist consumers by helping to ensure that the data held at the credit-reporting agencies are accurate and complete. All of the studies on data quality agree that consumers need to take a more active role in ensuring the accuracy of their reports.

Need for Additional Standardized Data Sources

The U.S. credit industry, including consumers, must continue to improve the quality of consumer credit data currently being shared for credit lending. The performance of consumer loans made under programs such as the Association of Community Organizations for Reform Now (ACORN) and Project Hope have demonstrated the value of these data for assessing the creditworthiness of the households they serve. Unfortunately, there is no consistency in either the data format or the method for accessing them. To be useful in credit risk scoring, information must be collected in a more complete, accurate, and standardized manner before the benefits they offer can be realized. A number of organizations, such as the Ford Foundation, are trying to create such databases.[10] Unfortunately, it is likely to take some time before these are available in a form convenient for automated credit risk assessment.

More predictive scores are better for consumers, lenders, and the overall economy. Advances in scoring technology will continue to increase the benefits that scoring provides. While details on recent advances in scoring technology are out of the scope of this chapter, they include the ability to summarize and incorporate the preferences of consumers in lending decisions (Fair Isaac, 2002) and the ability to optimize various credit decisions under a set of constrained objectives (Fishelson-Holstine, 2002).

Conclusion

Credit scores enable lenders to extend credit quickly while safely managing the risk of consumers who are new to the lender or who have been turned away by other lenders. This has resulted in more credit being available to consumers at a better price than would otherwise be possible. This has resulted in increased

10. Telephone conversation with Nathan Michael, chief executive officer of Pay Rent, Build Credit, August 27, 2003.

credit availability overall and at an accelerated rate for families who have traditionally been underserved.

Just as credit scoring is more effective than judgmental lending, more predictive credit scores are even more effective at increasing the availability of credit at
a fair price to a wider segment of the population. Increased predictive power
comes from a variety of sources. Those interested in increasing access to homeownership should actively support initiatives that will lead to more predictive
scores. These include the addition of new sources of predictive data in standardized formats, the continuation of efforts to increase the quality of available data,
educating and empowering consumers to use credit responsibly, and defending
the need for unrestricted access to shared data coupled with responsible use of
that information.

Homeownership rates could be increased by standardizing and increasing
the availability of nontraditional data sources used to assess creditworthiness.
For these sources to be used in credit scoring, nontraditional data need to be
collected in a more complete, accurate, and standardized manner. Although
additional information about rental or utility payments can be obtained by
asking consumers to provide this information themselves, this results in a negative customer experience. Most customers are unwilling to supply the additional information and ultimately do not receive the benefit the additional data
could supply.

While the quality of credit-reporting agency data has increased considerably
over the past decade, this improvement (and the concomitant increase in available credit) could be further enhanced by continuing to eliminate sources of
missing or incorrect data. Consumers should be encouraged to take a more
active role in ensuring the accuracy of their credit reports, checking them periodically, and using the dispute process established in the FCRA to correct errors
or omissions, especially if they are in the market for new credit, if they have
been denied credit, or if a creditor has changed the terms of an account based
on credit-reporting agency information.

Consumers are demanding that they be evaluated and priced fairly. They also
are requesting information about the role of credit scores in the lending process.
More types and forms of education are needed in order to reach all parts of the
population, particularly the underserved segments. As consumers increase their
understanding of how to use credit responsibly, access to credit (and therefore
homeownership) will increase and prices will decrease as consumers demonstrate
lower risk behavior.

Complete, consistent data make scorecards more predictive, benefiting both
consumers and lenders. Credit scores have played an essential role in increasing
homeownership for underserved populations. Balanced legislation, broad access
to high-quality data, responsible use of information, and consumer education

and empowerment will increase the benefits that scoring brings to consumers, lenders, and the overall U.S. economy.

References

Avery, Robert B., Raphael W. Bostic, and Glenn B. Canner. 2000. "CRA Special Lending Programs." *Federal Reserve Board Bulletin* (November): 711–31.

Avery, Robert B., Paul S. Calem, and Glenn B. Canner. 2003. "An Overview of Consumer Data and Credit Reporting." *Federal Reserve Board Bulletin* (February): 47–73.

Barron, John M., and Michael Staten. 2000. *The Value of Comprehensive Credit Reports: Lessons from the U.S. Experience.* Washington: World Bank Institute.

Cate, Fred H., and others. 2003. *Financial Privacy, Consumer Prosperity, and the Public Good: Maintaining the Balance.* Washington: American Enterprise Institute-Brookings Joint Center for Regulatory Studies.

Chandler, Gary G. 1998. "Generic and Customized Scoring Models: A Comparison." In *Credit Risk Modeling: Design and Application.* Chicago: Dearborn Publishers.

Consumer Federation of America. 2002. "Credit Score Accuracy and Implications for Consumers."

Durkin, Thomas A., and Gregory Elliehausen. 2000. "Interinstitutional Competition for Consumer Credit at the End of the Twentieth Century." Working Paper 69. Georgetown University, McDonough School of Business.

Fair Isaac. 1992. "Multiple Scorecard Technology Offers Opportunities." *Bureau Scores Today* 2 (1).

———. 1993. "Young, Thin, and Established Files: Targeted Scorecards Optimize Differences." *Bureau Scores Today* 2 (2).

———. 1996. "Value of Positive Credit Bureau Information." *Bureau Scores Today* 5 (3): 8–10.

———. 2002. "Web as 'Lab' Shrinks Credit Card Offer Test Costs." *ViewPoints Newsletter* 26 (1): 5.

———. 2003. "What the CFA Got Right and Wrong about Credit Scoring." *ViewPoints Newsletter* 27 (1): 15–17.

Fishelson-Holstine, Hollis. 2002. "Using Decision Analysis to Improve Strategy Design." *Bank Accounting and Finance* 15 (4): 1–6.

Gates, Susan W., Vanessa G. Perry, and Peter M. Zorn. 2002. "Automated Underwriting in Mortgage Lending: Good News for the Underserved?" *Housing Policy Debate* 13 (2): 369–92.

Kitchenman, Walter F. 1999. "U.S. Credit Reporting: Perceived Benefits Outweigh Privacy Concerns." *Tower Group Report* (January): 1–12.

Lewis, Edward M. 1992. *An Introduction to Credit Scoring.* San Rafael, Calif.: Athena Press.

Martell, Javier, and others. 1997. "Effectiveness of Scoring on Low- to Moderate-Income and High Minority Area Populations." Fair Isaac White Paper.

ORC International. 2003. "Credit Report Survey Prepared for Consumer Federation of America." July 18.

Staten, Michael E., Gregory Elliehausen, and E. Christopher Lundquist. 2002. "The Impact of Credit Counseling on Subsequent Borrower Credit Usage and Payment Behavior." Monograph 36. Credit Research Center, Georgetown University, McDonough School of Business.

Thomas, L. C. 2000. "A Survey of Credit and Behavioral Scoring: Forecasting Financial Risk of Lending to Consumers." *International Journal of Forecasting* (16) 2: 149–72.

Turner, Michael. 2003. "The Fair Credit Reporting Act: Access, Efficiency, and Opportunity. The Economic Importance of Fair Credit Reauthorization." Washington: Information Policy Institute.

4

Role of Regulation

ALLEGRA CALDER

Regulations can help markets operate more efficiently and transparently, or they can protect consumers, or they can accomplish both tasks. It is not easy, however, to strike a balance between efficiency and protection. Prescriptive regulations intended to protect consumers can add to costs and discourage providers from serving certain markets where violations incur stiff penalties. Many of the laws designed to protect consumers' rights and encourage equal access to credit were passed decades ago. Recent market developments raise questions about whether current regulations are up to the task of protecting low-income consumers while providing them with an adequate flow of credit and basic banking services on fair, safe, and reasonably sound terms.

The authors of part 4 approach regulation from different perspectives. Barr examines the breadth of federal laws that have been passed to help low- and moderate-income and minority borrowers overcome credit barriers. Staten and Cate focus exclusively on the Fair Credit Reporting Act (FCRA), the cornerstone of the rules governing collection and use of credit information. Kennedy introduces the idea that there is a "high road" and "low road" in subprime lending, and that the two operate quite differently.

Barr discusses five types of federal laws and evaluates the various laws in the context of their ability to overcome market failure. He points out that it can be difficult to disaggregate the effects of the multiple laws as many of them reinforce each other. Thus he employs a comparative approach and proposes cross-modal strategies to enhance enforcement of the norms underlying the laws. For example, the Equal Credit Opportunity Act (ECOA), an antidiscrimination law, has produced few lawsuits, in all likelihood because of the cost of litigation and the difficulty of gathering proof of discrimination. Yet despite the narrow focus on discrimination in credit markets, the Community Reinvestment Act (CRA), an affirmative obligation, reinforces the ECOA because it addresses broader market failures.

Barr is critical of disclosure laws and maintains that they should not be a substitute for other regulatory approaches. The author makes a distinction between disclosure laws intended to arm the public with information, such as the Home Mortgage Disclosure Act (HMDA), and disclosures designed to enhance borrower information, such as the Truth in Lending Act (TILA). He argues that HMDA, reinforced by the CRA, has helped to improve the mortgage market, but is skeptical that disclosures like those provided by TILA actually alter or inform consumer behavior. Barr states that consumer disclosure frequently provides either too much or too little information and can be expensive for consumers. He commends the CRA since it aims to bring low- and moderate-income and minority borrowers into the financial mainstream and expresses a broad value of inclusion. In addition, the public enforcement aspect of the CRA has led to a dialogue between banks and communities, which Barr argues is one of its chief virtues.

Staten and Cate examine the original intent, outcomes, and debate around the performance of the Fair Credit Reporting Act (FCRA), which was passed in 1970. The authors point out that while accuracy is the stated goal of the FCRA, it is neither well defined nor is there agreement that it should be the ultimate goal of the act. Indeed, many believe that the predictive value of the information in the file is most important because that is the application to which the information is put and because it can be tested. The authors maintain that despite some missing information, American credit files are the most comprehensive in the world and are a good predictor of borrower credit risk.

Staten and Cate conclude that the FCRA has always involved balancing trade-offs since the system relies on voluntary reporting and competitive incentives and regulatory requirements could impose costs that would discourage participation. The authors conclude the voluntary system of credit reporting is beneficial because it is flexible. It does not require regulators to anticipate new businesses and uses for credit information that may emerge. The authors outline two regulatory approaches to promote FCRA accuracy. The preventive approach would have introduced mandatory procedures for submitting, verifying, matching, and reinvestigating credit information. Instead, a remedial approach was selected, which relies on the competitive incentives for accurate reporting and places the responsibility on consumers to detect and correct any erroneous information in their files. The latter approach, the authors note, is analogous to a product warranty that allows consumers to exchange defective merchandise, and lowers production costs and sales prices for the manufacturer. However, the authors emphasize that consumer inspection of reports remains an underutilized tool and facilitating online access and simpler dispute resolution mechanisms would help increase consumer vigilance.

Finally, Kennedy argues that subprime lenders that take the high road minimize default to reduce foreclosure related losses, whereas companies that take the low road opt for a quick and low-cost foreclosure in which they may appropriate some or all of the debtor's equity. Kennedy explores what the effects of a policy of enforced nonwaivable debtor protection might be on options and outcomes to debtors and low road and high road creditors.

The author suggests that in order to pay for debtor protection, the low road (but not the high road) would have to raise prices. He argues that as a result some borrowers would not choose a low road mortgage, which could help put the low roaders out of business. However, he adds that subprime borrowers seem surprisingly unresponsive to price and terms, which might suggest that given the choice they either would not choose protection or uncritically accept higher prices. Kennedy concludes that while it is difficult to predict what all the effects of debtor protections would be, the case for their introduction on efficiency grounds lies somewhere between plausible and highly convincing.

These three chapters examine many of the laws and regulations that govern access to credit, the public purposes they serve and rationale for them, and how well they have kept pace with sweeping changes in the financial services sector. Opinion over the role of regulation will continue to be divided among those that: believe the market, absent intervention, will deliver the desired outcomes; believe regulations are necessary to expand credit to traditionally underserved borrowers and offer protection to consumers; and favor some combination of market incentives and regulation. As Staten and Cate make very clear, balancing the dual goals of efficiency and protection involves trade-offs and often involves costs, which may be passed on to consumers. These chapters make an important contribution through their evaluation of current regulations and the possible outcomes of proposed regulation.

9

Modes of Credit Market Regulation

MICHAEL S. BARR

Despite the depth and breadth of U.S. credit markets, low- and moderate-income communities, as well as minority borrowers, have not enjoyed full access to those markets.[1] Community advocates have long argued that redlining—a practice of not lending to borrowers in neighborhoods with a higher concentration of minority households—has, at least historically, limited the flow of capital from depository institutions for homeownership in minority communities. Enormous progress has been made in expanding access to home mortgage lending, but there is evidence that minority borrowers still face discrimination. Others have argued that low-income communities generally have lower access to capital than they would in a fully functioning market because of market failures, including information externalities and collective action problems. More recently, as capital from subprime[2] lenders has increased in low-income areas, consumer advocates have argued that predatory or abusive lend-

1. This chapter is adapted from Barr (2005) and appears with permission. The chapter focuses on home mortgage lending, which is an important aspect of financial security for low- and moderate-income households, has attracted the greatest attention in the literature, and has different market and regulatory features from other forms of credit. Consumer debt and transactional services are discussed in Barr (2004).

2. Subprime refers to borrowers who pay higher interest rates at least in part because they are thought to have credit histories below the quality of prime borrowers. Subprime lenders specialize in lending to such borrowers.

ing practices are targeted at minorities, the elderly, and other segments of the population.

In response to these and other concerns, Congress has enacted a wide range of federal laws and subsidy programs that affect the provision of credit (see White, 2003). This chapter provides an introduction to five types of federal laws that have been enacted to help overcome barriers to credit. These include laws on:

—disclosure (the Home Mortgage Disclosure Act, HMDA, and Truth in Lending Act, TILA);

—affirmative obligation (the Community Reinvestment Act, CRA);

—negative prohibition (the Equal Credit Opportunity Act, ECOA);

—product regulation (the Homeowner's Equity Protection Act, HOEPA); and

—government subsidies (Federal Housing Administration [FHA] home mortgage insurance and the Government Sponsored Enterprises [GSEs]—Fannie Mae, Freddie Mac, and the Federal Home Loan Bank system).

I first set out a short theoretical framework, then compare these modes of credit market regulation with one another. I also suggest cross-modal strategies to enhance enforcement of the norms underlying these laws. By cross-modal strategies, I mean initiatives undertaken under one regulatory authority to advance norms of another regulation. For example, disclosure can be used to enhance negative prohibitions regarding racial discrimination. Cross-modal strategies hold out the promise of improving how these different modes of credit market regulation can be mutually reinforcing. Given the scope of the topic, this brief treatment is necessarily tentative and suggestive.

Theoretical Foundations

The theoretical support for governmental home mortgage credit market policies derives from three bases. First, market failures from imperfect information, collective action problems, agency costs, and neighborhood externalities are more acute in low-income neighborhoods and for low-income borrowers than in credit markets generally. Second, regulations seek to combat discrimination against minority borrowers and communities, both directly and by overcoming market failures that plague low-income communities, given the significant correlation between race and income, and between the race of homeowners and the racial composition and income of neighborhoods. Third, regulations could help to break down inefficient barriers between the bifurcated prime and subprime credit markets by enhancing competition and by helping to complete the mortgage market.[3]

---

3. Some regulations are pursued in order to foster housing consumption more generally, in the belief that homeownership is good for society, but as this aim is not focused on low- and moderate-income households, I discuss it only in passing.

Market Failures

Credit market imperfections impede lending in low- and moderate-income communities. First, information externalities and asymmetries may lead to credit rationing that excludes creditworthy borrowers and causes banks to overlook profitable loans (Ordover and Weiss, 1981). Information asymmetries can result in credit rationing of creditworthy borrowers (Stiglitz and Weiss, 1981). Information externalities can produce credit constraints in low-income communities because the efficiency of bank lending is in part a function of "market thickness" (Lang and Nakamura, 1993).[4] Second, collective action problems exacerbate information externalities and inhibit entry into these communities (Petersen and Rajan, 1995). CRA and other regulation could help to mitigate these credit constraints by providing "an effective commitment device to coordinate lending" (Zinman, 2002). Third, agency costs make it difficult to align corporate interest in profitable lending with the behavior of loan agents. Lastly, neighborhood externalities provide grounds for governmental intervention (for example, Guttentag and Wachter, 1980; Galster, 1987). Government policies designed to increase access to credit and homeownership can help to turn neighborhoods around, increasing property values for adjacent properties and neighborhoods (Ellen and others, 2001; Schill and others, 2002).

Racial Discrimination

The standard view is that, in the long run, in a perfect market, discrimination will disappear (Becker, 1971). Competition undoubtedly puts pressure on racial and other forms of discrimination. Yet this model assumes that only racial animus is illegal, while statistical discrimination, in which lenders use factors correlated with race as proxies for creditworthiness, in fact violates ECOA (see Federal Financial Institutions Examination Council, 1999). Moreover, credit rationing and segmented markets mean that discrimination in loan denials and price can persist in competitive markets. If credit rationing occurs, identical marginal applicants will be treated differently, and lenders will not charge differential prices to sort borrowers by risk. The single-price model accurately describes the prime credit market dominated by banks and thrifts, while the subprime market differentiates by risk. Since lenders in credit-rationing models do not provide loans to all members of a class of identical loan applicants, they could discriminate without losing profits (absent legal liability under antidiscrimination laws). Statistical discrimination could be profitable if race is correlated with an aspect of creditworthiness that is costly to observe directly. Still, statistical discrimination will be less accurate than a direct measure of creditworthiness. As technological innovation drives down the costs of obtaining such

---

4. Market thickness refers to the amount of economic activity in a market.

measures, one would expect even statistical discrimination to diminish in competitive markets over the long term (Greenbaum, 1996).

The evidence on discrimination in credit markets is hotly contested (Ross and Yinger, 2002). Disparities in the rates at which whites and African Americans are denied home mortgage loans continue to be large. Controlling for creditworthiness and other factors that legitimately affect lending decisions, economists at the Federal Reserve Board of Boston found that African Americans were nearly twice as likely as whites to be denied home mortgage loans (Browne and others, 1992, 1996). The study has come under a barrage of attacks, but rebuttals have affirmed the study's central findings (Ross and Yinger, 2002). Matched pair testing has also found differential treatment (for example, Turner and Skidmore, 1999). These disparities suggest disparate treatment of, or disparate impact on, minorities (Ross and Yinger, 2002, p. 211). In sum, "extensive underwriting discrimination existed in 1990, and there is no more recent evidence to show that this discrimination has gone away" (Ross and Yinger, 2002, pp. 367–68).

In addition to discrimination in loan denials, price discrimination can also occur because of market fragmentation (for example, Ayres, 2002). Prime lenders offer a single price to borrowers who meet their criteria and ration credit among the others. Subprime lenders offer differential pricing of loans based on risk and other factors. Although the growth of risk-based pricing in the subprime market has broadened the eligible pool of borrowers, differentiated pricing may also result in racial discrimination. Using credit scores, creditors can determine the price at which they would be willing to lend to a particular borrower, but the subprime market's fragmented nature prevents all potential borrowers from learning about lenders' pricing schemes. This permits lenders to distinguish among similar borrowers in pricing loans. Creditors price loans based on factors other than risk, including a borrower's willingness to pay. Differential pricing can lead to systematically different prices for minorities than for whites.

Price discrimination occurs in a range of credit markets (for example, Ayres and Siegelman, 1995; Ayres, 2001, 2002; Ross and Yinger, 2002). For home mortgages, studies have focused on overages, the amount by which negotiated loan rates exceed the lender's minimum rates set forth on rate sheets for loan officers. Strikingly, African Americans more often pay overages, and much higher ones, than whites (Ross and Yinger, 2002, pp. 223–27, 307). African Americans fare worse in negotiations with mortgage brokers and loan officers (Buist, Linneman, and Megbolugbe, 1999; Ross and Yinger, 2002, p. 307; Black, Boehm, and DeGennaro, 2003).

Problems in the Subprime Sector

Banks and thrifts have increased their lending to low- and moderate-income borrowers, but subprime lending has grown dramatically at the same time. Subprime lenders specialize in making loans to borrowers with impaired or limited credit history. Most subprime loans are refinance loans. Although refinancing may be used to obtain better rates, subprime refinance loans are usually used for home improvement or consumer purchases, to pay for education expenses, or to consolidate other consumer debt.[5] With new sources of funding available from the secondary market, and advances in information and risk management, subprime lending has grown sevenfold from 1994 to 2002, reaching $241 billion, or 9 percent of the market.[6]

The subprime market is plagued by serious problems. Between 10 and 35 percent of subprime borrowers who could have qualified for loans from prime lenders end up in the subprime market, paying higher rates (Freddie Mac, 2002). While credit risk is a key determinant of receiving a prime or subprime loan, "credit risk alone may not fully explain why borrowers end up in the subprime market" (Courchane, Surette, and Zorn, 2004). For example, borrowers who are older, Hispanic, or search less for interest rates are more likely to end up in the subprime market. Having a subprime loan is predictive of refinancing with a subprime loan, indicating that borrowers get stuck in the subprime market.

In addition, some minority borrowers may have been improperly steered to higher cost lenders. Moreover, studies have documented abusive practices in the sector (U.S. Department of the Treasury and U.S. Department of Housing and Urban Development [Joint Report], 2000; Barr, 2002). These practices have included flipping—repeatedly refinancing a loan in a short period. Loans have been packed with additional products (such as credit life insurance) without informing the borrower that the products were optional or unsuitable. Loans have included disguised fees. Brokers have made home mortgage loans without regard to the borrower's ability to repay. In other cases, "unscrupulous mortgage brokers, lenders, home improvement contractors, appraisers, and combinations thereof" engaged in "outright fraud" as well as "deceptive or high-pressure sales tactics," and often "prey[ed] on . . . the elderly, minorities, and individuals with lower incomes and less education" (Joint Report, 2000, p. 2).

The price that borrowers pay is a function not only of using a subprime lender, but also of negotiating with mortgage brokers, who dominate the subprime market. Brokers are compensated through yield spread premiums for getting borrowers to pay higher rates than those for which the borrower would qualify. In loans with yield spread premiums, there is wide dispersion in fees paid to mortgage brokers. Among borrowers paying yield spread premiums, African Americans paid $474 more, and Hispanics $590 more, than whites (Jackson and Berry, 2003, pp. 125–28; see also Guttentag, 2001). Minority and

5. National Home Equity Mortgage Association, 2004 (www.nhema.org/About/Questions.htm)

6. Remarks by Edward Gramlich at the Texas Association of Bank Counsel, October 9, 2003.

white borrowers tend to go to different lenders, and the subprime lenders that minorities are more likely to use are also more likely to price aggressively (Ross and Yinger, 2002, p. 344).

Moreover, borrowers in the subprime market form a pool whose risk characteristics are worse and more widely dispersed than borrowers in the prime market (Pennington-Cross and Yezer, 2000). Although there is rough risk-based pricing in the subprime market, defaulting borrowers create an externality that raises interest rates on all subprime borrowers. Regulation of the subprime sector is in part a response to the problem of incomplete contracts. Borrowers cannot contract with one another to allocate the costs of the negative externality of default, which raises the cost to all borrowers, and foreclosures concentrated in low-income neighborhoods can also cause negative externalities to neighboring property owners.

Lending by subprime specialists does not replace lending by banks.[7] First, subprime creditors specialize in refinance loans rather than in home purchase originations. Subprime lenders free ride on the information generated by firms engaged in home purchase lending. Second, subprime lenders have failed to report credit scores for sound borrowers in order to capture the informational benefits from their investment. Therefore, the positive externalities from increased lending in low-income areas are not realized. Third, borrowing from a subprime lender signals to prime lenders that a borrower is a bad credit risk. Rather than increasing access to prime lending, subprime borrowing helps to keep borrowers in the subprime market, where borrowers pay more for credit. Fourth, minority households are much more likely to pay higher fees and remain stuck in the subprime market even after accounting for creditworthiness.

Modes of Credit Market Regulation

The presence of market failures is an insufficient determinant of policy. The government may be ill equipped to intervene, and may choose strategies that either make the problems worse or cost more than their benefits. Government agencies might not possess the requisite information to regulate effectively, the agencies may not be able to induce the private sector responses sought, the bureaucracy might not faithfully execute the laws, or the political process might lead Congress or the bureaucracy to create laws that improperly favor the regulated entities or some other preferred groups (for example, Stiglitz, 2000, pp. 8–10). The extent of these problems cannot be assessed in the abstract. One needs to compare systems for redressing market failures.

I classify credit market policies into five types. First, CRA sets forth a broad affirmative obligation on insured depository institutions to lend in their service

---

7. For the remainder of this chapter, the term *bank* refers to banks and thrifts.

areas. Second, negative prohibitions, such as the ECOA,[8] bar discrimination against minority borrowers. Third, disclosure laws may be thought of as having two subtypes. Some laws, such as the HMDA,[9] assist in the enforcement of other legal rules or social norms by requiring public disclosure of lending data. Other disclosure laws, such as the TILA,[10] rely on providing information to consumers to ensure a well-functioning market, backed by enforcement of the disclosure requirement. Fourth, Congress enacted substantive regulation of loan products in the HOEPA.[11] Fifth, government subsidies are pervasive in the housing credit market (White, 2003). I focus here on the GSEs and FHA. Further comparative institutional analysis based on empirical research will be critical to understanding the relative efficiency of these laws.

Affirmative Obligation

The Community Reinvestment Act of 1977 (CRA),[12] enacted in response to concerns about redlining of minority and low-income areas[13] and market failures in low-income communities, encourages federally insured banks and thrifts to meet the credit needs of the entire communities that they serve, including low- and moderate-income areas, consistent with safe and sound banking practices. Federal banking agencies examine banks periodically on their CRA performance and rate the institutions. Regulators consider a bank's CRA record in determining whether to approve that institution's application for a deposit facility, which encompasses mergers with or acquisitions of other depository institutions. Such applications also provide the public with an opportunity to comment on the CRA performance of the institution.

CRA has strengthened over time, particularly during the 1990s, because of both legal and market developments. Legislative changes to CRA enacted in 1989 required regulators to disclose publicly the institution's rating and performance evaluation.[14] Also in 1989, a bank regulator denied for the first time, on

8. 15 U.S.C. 1691–1691f.

9. 12 U.S.C. 2801. The Federal Reserve Board implements HMDA under Regulation C, 12 C.F.R. pt. 230.1.

10. 15 U.S.C. 1601, 1602(aa), 1639(a)–(b). The Federal Reserve Board implements TILA under Regulation Z, 12 C.F.R. pt. 226.1.

11 P.L. 103–325, 151, 108 Stat. 2190 (1994).

12. 29 U.S.C. 2901, 2902, 2903, 2906 (2000); 12 U.S.C. 1831u(b)(3) (2000) (CRA requirement for interstate mergers). See also 12 U.S.C. 1831y (CRA Sunshine Requirements); Id. 1843(l)(2) (2000) (CRA requirement for financial subsidiaries engaging in expanded financial activities).

13. See, for example, 123 Cong. Rec. 17, 604 (1977) (statement of Senator Proxmire) ("[CRA] is intended to eliminate the practice of redlining by lending institutions."). In its structure, CRA focuses on market failures, rather than on discrimination per se, but market failures and discrimination are intertwined.

14. Financial Institutions Reform, Recovery, and Enforcement Act of 1989, P.L. 101–73, 103 Stat. 183 (1989).

CRA grounds, an application for merger.[15] Changes to the regulations implementing CRA issued in 1995[16] focus CRA evaluations on objective performance measures rather than more process-oriented factors that regulators had previously used. These regulations require banks to disclose information about their small business, small farm, and community development lending. Under the 1995 regulations, large banks, small banks, and wholesale or limited-purpose institutions have tailored examinations. Large banks are evaluated on a three-part test of lending, investments, and services. Institutions are rated outstanding, satisfactory, needs to improve, or substantial noncompliance.

These changes occurred during a time of increasingly intense consolidation in the banking industry, providing greater opportunities for community organizations and regulators to evaluate bank performance under CRA in merger applications. With the passage of the Gramm-Leach-Bliley Financial Modernization Act of 1999,[17] CRA was again strengthened. Banks and thrifts must have a satisfactory CRA record if they, or their holding companies, are to engage in newly authorized financial activities, such as certain insurance and securities functions.[18]

CRA has been since its enactment, and remains today, the subject of extensive debate. Legal scholars question vigorously the theoretical and empirical claims that motivated CRA, and many advocate eliminating the policy (for example, Gunther, 2000; Lacker, 1995; Macey and Miller, 1993; White, 1993). These critics argue that CRA is trying to address a nonexistent problem, and that even if intervention is warranted, CRA is the wrong policy to pursue. Critics suggested that CRA was having little, if any, positive effect, and at a high cost (Macey and Miller, 1993). In a related article (Barr, 2005) I systematically rebut prior criticisms of CRA and lay a solid theoretical and empirical foundation for the act. A summary of those findings follows.

EMPIRICAL EVIDENCE THAT CRA IS EFFECTIVE. With impetus from CRA, lenders have:

—formed multibank Community Development Corporations (CDCs) and loan consortia to reduce risk, overcome collective action problems, and share the costs and benefits of developing information about low-income markets;

—invested in locally based Community Development Financial Institutions (CDFIs) to develop specialized market knowledge, share risk, and explore new market opportunities;

—engaged in special marketing programs to targeted communities;

15. Continental Bank Corporation, 75 *Fed. Reserve Bull.* 304 (1989).
16. 12 C.F.R. 228.41 et seq. (2004).
17. P.L. 106–102 (1999).
18. 12 U.S.C. 2903(c) (2000); Id.1843 (l) (2) (2000).

—experimented with more flexible underwriting and specialized servicing techniques to determine if a broader range of applications could be approved without undue risk; and

—funded credit counseling to improve the creditworthiness of potential borrowers.

Many larger institutions have developed specialized units within their organizations that focus on the needs of low- and moderate-income communities. A positive lending cycle has begun in many communities: once lenders know that others will be making loans to a community, they face less liquidity risk, gather and disseminate information more quickly, and produce positive information externalities. Experience suggests that increased lending to low-income communities has occurred, and that such lending has not led to the kind or the extent of unprofitable, excessively risky activity predicted by critics.

Studies have found evidence that CRA improved access to home mortgage credit for low-income borrowers during the 1990s, as CRA enforcement increased (Evanoff and Siegal, 1996; Avery and others, 1999).[19] Brookings–Joint Center on Housing research that I directed at the Treasury Department found that between 1993 and 1999, depository institutions covered by the CRA and their affiliates made nearly $800 billion in home mortgage, small business, and community development loans to low- and moderate-income borrowers and communities (Litan and others, 2000, 2001).[20] The number of CRA-eligible mortgage loans increased by 39 percent between 1993 and 1998, while other loans increased by only 17 percent (Litan and others, 2000, p. ES-3). Even excluding affiliates, banks increased their lending to low- and moderate-income borrowers and areas by 10 percent, compared with no growth at all for these lenders in their other markets (Litan and others, 2000, p. 46). Over this period, the portfolio share of CRA-covered lender and affiliate loans to these borrowers and areas increased from 25 to 28 percent (Litan and others, 2000, p. ES-4).

In the prime market, banks and their affiliates increased their market share of lending to low- and moderate-income borrowers and areas from 66 percent in 1993 to 71 percent in 1998 (Litan and others, 2000, p. ES-7). Yet the dramatic expansion of the subprime refinance market meant that banks lost 2 percentage points in market share overall among low- and moderate-income borrowers and communities (Litan and others, 2000, p. 43). Banks increased their home purchase lending, while others focused on subprime refinance loans.

A series of factors contributed to these gains. First and foremost, strong economic growth during the 1990s led to rapid income growth and lower unemployment rates for minorities and other households. Real interest rates for mort-

---

19. See also Barr and others (2001), Canner and Smith (1991), Avery and others (1996), and LaCour-Little (1998).

20. For further analysis of these reports, see Belsky, Schill, and Yezer (2001).

gages were at low levels during much of this period. Second, innovation helped drive down the costs of assessing creditworthiness, offering mortgage products, effectuating transactions, and funding loans through securitization. Third, consolidation in the financial services sector heightened the importance of CRA on major transactions, and enhanced competition for the delivery of credit in low-income communities. Fourth, CRA, HMDA, ECOA, FHA, and the GSE Affordable Housing Goals all operated in intensified ways during this period.

Controlling for the effects of these factors, however, research found that CRA lenders increased their CRA-eligible home purchase lending faster than those not regulated by CRA from 1993 to 1999 (Litan and others, 2000, p. ES-4). Similarly, analysis of CRA lending across metropolitan areas reinforces the view that CRA helps expand access to home mortgage credit for low- and moderate-income borrowers (Litan and others, 2000, p. 36). Analysis controlling for economic, demographic, and market factors found that CRA increased access to credit (Belsky, Schill, and Yezer, 2001, p. 22). The Joint Center for Housing Studies report concluded:

> CRA-regulated entities still lead the market in the provision of mortgage capital to lower-income people and communities, especially lower-income minorities. Detailed multivariate analysis confirms that CRA-regulated lenders originate a higher proportion of loans to lower-income people and communities than they would if CRA did not exist (2002, p. 135).

Evidence from small business markets reinforces the view that CRA has been effective (Zinman, 2002, p. 2). One study suggests that CRA increases the number of firms that can access credit by 4 to 6 percentage points (Zinman, 2002, p. 20), providing benefits to the real economy—increased payrolls and reduced bankruptcies—without crowding out other financing available to small businesses or adversely affecting bank profitability or loan performance (Zinman, 2002, p. 3).

Changes in the financial services industry may mean that CRA covers less of the financial services world. Banks' and thrifts' share of financial assets has declined dramatically since the end of World War II, from 60 percent to about 25 percent today. Although assets subject to CRA are declining as a share of financial assets, such assets continue to grow in absolute terms. Moreover, as CRA-covered institutions develop new products, train employees, and alter organizational structures to meet the credit needs of low-income communities, such changes influence affiliates. In addition, CRA enforcement through mergers and acquisitions will continue to be important. Consolidation in the banking industry, after a brief respite during the recession of 2001–02, has picked up again, and long-term forecasts suggest that more will likely come (James and others, 1997). Furthermore, the Gramm-Leach-Bliley Act made expansion into new activities contingent on banks' CRA performance. Banking organizations will have to pay attention to their CRA performance for many years to come, as they seek to enter new financial markets. In sum, recent evidence shows that CRA provides important benefits to low-income communities, and these benefits are likely to continue. Other factors undoubtedly contributed to the growth in lending to low-income communities during the 1990s, but careful studies have found support for an independent and important role for CRA.

COSTS OF CRA HAVE BEEN OVERSTATED. A Federal Reserve Board report issued in 2000 found that most institutions responded that CRA lending was profitable or marginally profitable (Board of Governors, 2000, pp. xvii, chart1a; xix, chart 3a; xxi, chart 5a; xxiii, chart 7a.). CRA loans appear not to be overly risky (Board of Governors, 2000, table 3c). Pushing further into low-income markets has not weakened banks' profitability and soundness. In the small special programs serving as banks' laboratories, employing new and innovative strategies, 61 percent of respondents still found CRA special programs to be profitable (Board of Governors, 2000, table 14a). Moreover, most institutions reported low delinquency and charge-off rates; the median charge-off rate on these programs was zero (Board of Governors, 2000, table 14c).

CRA REASONABLY ADDRESSES MARKET FAILURES. CRA helps to overcome market failures in low-income communities. Fostering competition among banks in serving low-income areas leads to larger volumes of lending from diverse sources, adding liquidity to the market, which in turn decreases the riskiness of each bank's loan. CRA has helped banks in developing specialization in serving low-income communities, including innovation in developing products that meet the credit needs of low-income areas with manageable risks, and specialization in serving particular areas through partnerships with community-based organizations and CDFIs. CDFIs demonstrated the possibility of lending in low-income communities, provide local expertise and financial education, and take portions of risk that banks do not want to bear. In turn, banks have invested in CDFIs in record numbers, largely spurred by the CRA investment test. Investments in CDFIs strengthen the ability of banks to serve low-income markets. As banks offer services once only offered by CDFIs, the local institutions move further downstream, reaching lower-income or harder-to-serve borrowers, and developing new approaches that mainstream institutions may later find cost effective.

CRA also provides a precommitment device that helps banks coordinate lending to reduce information costs. Because CRA requires all insured depositories to lend in their communities, it reduces free rider problems. CRA has spurred the development of loan consortia to serve low- and moderate-income communities more effectively. Moreover, banks get CRA consideration for both originating and purchasing eligible loans, creating a trading system. Institutions can rely on the origination expertise of others by purchasing loans. The development of this CRA loan market increases liquidity and reduces loan prices. It also improves transparency in CRA loan pricing, providing valuable information about the performance and profitability of CRA lending.

CRA permits banks to respond to local needs based on their own organization, market assessments, and business plans, without being judged on the basis of national norms. Banks help to shape the content of the standard, not merely through the notice and comment rulemaking process, but also in CRA's application to their local context. CRA also permits greater citizen participation in the application of the rule. This enhances local organizations that in turn improve the performance of loans made in their community. While public involvement adds to the costs of CRA, these benefits of civic engagement, including its expressive benefits (see Anderson and Pildes, 2000), should be weighed also.

The form of CRA's legal directive, as a standard, rather than as a rule, is also desirable for other reasons. CRA's broad standards and public enforcement mechanisms provide for an interplay, a conversation, between banks and communities that is one of CRA's chief virtues. A rule setting forth lending requirements would cut off this dialogue. It would also send a message that banks are to disregard creditworthiness, business strategy, and local context, which is not the goal of CRA. Moreover, CRA's broad standard expresses the value of inclusion in lending. Because interpretation of CRA's standard requires community input, CRA expresses an inclusive ideal of participation in rulemaking that should be counted among the law's benefits.

Negative Prohibition

ECOA prohibits creditors from discriminating in the provision of credit based on "race, color, religion, national origin, sex or marital status, or age."[21] For home mortgage lending, that prohibition is also reinforced by the Fair Housing Act of 1968.[22] Both intentional discrimination (as measured by disparate treatment) and statistical discrimination (as measured by disparate impact) are prohibited by ECOA. ECOA's rule that statistical discrimination is prohibited, as opposed to a rule that subsidized creditors for deciding not to engage in such discrimination, is based on the deeply rooted sense that distinctions based on race, even if rational in the short run, are wrong. Thus the law prohibits the conduct rather than subsidizing adherence to the rule.

Disparate treatment can be proved using direct evidence that the lender considered the race (or other prohibited factor) of the applicant. Disparate treat-

---

21. 15 U.S.C. 1691.
22. 42 U.S.C. 3605. The Fair Housing Act also covers other forms of discrimination in residential real estate transactions beyond fair lending violations.

ment may also be proved using comparative evidence based on statistical inferences of differential treatment on a prohibited basis that cannot be explained by valid factors. Given the complexity and proprietary nature of credit scoring systems, and the difficulty of proving that any two applicants are similarly situated except for their race, disparate treatment proof is hard to make out. Lower courts and commentators have assumed that, as with employment discrimination, credit discrimination may also be proved using disparate impact analysis (Kushner, 1995; Ross and Yinger, 2002, p. 314; Mahoney, 1998). The text, history, structure, and purposes of Title VII and the Fair Housing Act are similar. Moreover, in amending the Fair Housing Act in 1988, Congress discussed the disparate impact standard then well developed under Title VII, and assumed that it would apply to the Fair Housing Act without the need for explicit provisions.

Disparate impact analysis is essential for combating disparate treatment. Disparate impact analysis is also designed (or ought to be designed) to ferret out policies that create unnecessary "headwinds" toward the full inclusion of racial minorities in society.[23] Disparate impact analysis permits regulators to eliminate the use of credit factors that are correlated with race when factors that are less correlated with race but just as predictive of creditworthiness could be used. Unfortunately, current regulatory practice, which focuses on file review and post review regressions, is not designed to address problems of disparate impact (Ross and Yinger, 2002).

ECOA does seem to help increase lending to minorities. For example, the share of bank and thrift lending to low- and moderate-income borrowers and areas that went to minority borrowers increased from 21 percent in 1993 to 28 percent in 1999. Most of the increase occurred during a period of intense Justice Department focus on enforcing fair lending laws, from 1993 to 1995 (Litan and others, 2001, p. 27).[24] HMDA data also show improvements in lending to minority and low-income borrowers, although HMDA data need to be treated with caution (Joint Center for Housing Studies, 2002). From 1993 to 1999, the number of home purchase loans made to Hispanics increased 121.4 percent; to Native Americans, 118.9 percent; to blacks, 91.0 percent; to Asians, 70.1 percent; and to whites, 33.5 percent.[25]

Other laws help to enforce ECOA's norms. For example, CRA may help to remedy some practices with discriminatory effects that both disparate treatment

---

23. See *Griggs* v. *Duke Power*, 401 U.S. 424, 432 (1971).

24. The Justice Department cases resulted in important consent decrees. See Consent Agreement, *United States* v. *Long Beach Mortgage Company*, CV-96-6159 (C.D. Cal., September 5, 1996); Consent Agreement, *United States* v. *First National Bank of Vicksburg*, 5-94-CV-6(B)(N) (S.D. Miss., January 21, 1994); Consent Agreement, *United States* v. *Shawmut National Corporation*, 93-CV-2453 (D. Conn., December. 13, 1993); Consent Agreement, *United States* v. *Decatur Federal Savings and Loan Association*, 1-92-CV-2198-CAM (N.D. Ga., September 17, 1992).

25. HMDA data are available at www.ffiec.gov/hmcrpr/hmda03.pdf.

analysis and disparate impact analysis as they are currently formulated have a hard time detecting or remedying, such as discriminatory overages, or segmented markets in which whites and minorities tend to go to different lenders with significantly different lending practices.[26]

Moreover, relying on ECOA lawsuits alone to advance antidiscrimination norms has limitations. Few ECOA lawsuits have been brought. Developing proof of lending discrimination is costly and difficult. When credit scoring is not the sole basis for a lending decision, lenders have a high degree of discretion, particularly in the case of applicants who are neither highly qualified nor unqualified. Even when credit scoring is the sole basis, disparate treatment might arise when creditors: subjectively evaluate data before entering them into the credit system; provide different levels of assistance to borrowers in completing credit applications; or permit overrides of credit scoring in close cases. Given the complex and proprietary nature of credit scoring systems and the difficulty of proving that any two applicants are similarly situated except for race, disparate treatment is hard to prove. Disparate impact analysis is often no easier. Creditors have essential information about their loan portfolio and proprietary credit evaluation systems and the weights placed on all the variables in their system. Plaintiffs do not have such information, and creditors resist revealing their methodology because of competitive concerns (Ross and Yinger, 2002).

CROSS-MODAL STRATEGIES. ECOA's weaknesses do not necessarily imply that it should be abandoned. ECOA itself sets out important antidiscrimination norms, and should be strengthened. Still, some credit market barriers affecting minority borrowers may be remedied more readily using cross-modal strategies under affirmative obligation, product regulation, and disclosure. Building on the strength of HMDA, Congress could enact a disclosure law requiring creditors to disclose the borrower's credit score and the creditor's rate sheet to help address price discrimination. Brokers could be required to disclose prominently that they represent the creditor, not the buyer. A new law on product regulation could bar the payment of yield spread premiums, which disproportionately fall on minority borrowers, and which consumers are ill-positioned to understand or monitor (Jackson and Berry, 2003).

Furthermore, CRA plays an important role in reinforcing the antidiscrimination principles underlying ECOA and in expanding access to credit for minority borrowers. Minority households are disproportionately represented among low- and moderate-income households and in low- and moderate-income communities. CRA has encouraged banks to increase their lending in such communities,

26. See, generally, Ross and Yinger (2002). But see *Cason v. Nissan*, 3-98-0223 (M.D.T.N. May 25, 2001) (ECOA suit based on discriminatory overages in automobile market leading to settlement order).

and minority households now constitute a larger share of such lending than they did a decade ago. CRA's focus on low-income neighborhoods may address structural inequalities facing African Americans and other minorities more effectively than ECOA's disparate impact standard, which is hemmed in by equal protection jurisprudence and the business necessity defense.[27] Moreover, CRA goes beyond ECOA's focus on credit discrimination to address broader market failures affecting low-income communities.

Disclosure

HMDA requires most home mortgage creditors annually to disclose to the public information about home mortgage loans made or purchased, as well as loan applications denied.[28] Regulations require disclosure of race, ethnicity, sex, and income of borrowers. Unlike TILA,[29] HMDA is not designed to enhance borrower information. Rather, HMDA is designed to increase the ability of the public, regulators, and fair lending enforcement agencies to assess whether lenders are engaged in discriminatory practices and how lenders are meeting their CRA obligations. Because HMDA does not include information on creditworthiness, loan terms, or property characteristics, HMDA data alone provide poor measures of discrimination. However, wide availability of these data has undoubtedly helped to spur changes in creditor practices.

Disclosure laws are perennial favorites in the legal literature (for example, Jolls, Sunstein, and Thaler 1998; Camerer and others, 2003). I agree that disclosure can help to improve the home mortgage credit market. However, I take issue with disclosure advocates on three grounds. First, disclosure serves a broader set of purposes than usually posited. Second, I have a healthier dose of skepticism about the effectiveness of disclosure in helping households than legal scholars have recently espoused.[30] Third, I argue that disclosure is no substitute for CRA or the underlying substantive prohibitions contained in ECOA.

There are two basic types of disclosure: disclosures designed to improve market efficiency by making consumers better shoppers and disclosures designed to

---

27. See, for example, Primus (2003) (lamenting "the growing tendency of equal protection jurisprudence to obscure the dynamics of group hierarchy and to truncate the memory of historical discrimination").

28. 12 U.S.C. 2801, 2803 (2000). HMDA was enhanced significantly in 1989, for example, by requiring data to be not only reported to the regulators, but also disclosed to the public.

29. TILA was designed to help consumers compare the costs of credit offered by requiring the disclosure of the Annual Percentage Rate (APR), the finance charge, the amount financed, and the total of all payments. The theory was that enhanced disclosure would improve price information and thereby enhance competition. See Schwartz and Wilde (1979) arguing for disclosure rather than product regulation. Unfortunately, TILA is extraordinarily complex. See, for example, *Emery v. American General Finance, Inc.*, 71 F. 3d 1343, 1346 (7th Cir. 1995) (Posner, J.) ("So much for the Truth in Lending Act as a protection for borrowers.").

30. See Camerer and others (2003) suggesting that disclosures respond adequately to consumers' need for information about loans.

help regulators enforce other laws and push markets toward compliance with social norms. TILA represents the first type, requiring disclosures to individual consumers regarding the cost of loans that they negotiate, calculated as an APR.[31] This type of disclosure seeks to remedy asymmetric information and improve market competition and efficiency.[32]

HMDA represents the second type of disclosure, requiring information not only for the consumer but also for regulators and the market generally. These broader disclosures reinforce positive social norms, promote market efficiency, and enhance the regulatory effectiveness of other laws.[33] The collection and public disclosure of information is the essential underpinning of CRA, ECOA, and HOEPA in expanding access to credit. Public debate over this performance likely contributed to increased lending to minorities in the 1990s.

The form of the legal directive can enhance compliance because the law helps to create social norms and to reveal instances in which actors transgress those norms. HMDA contains no substantive legal rule, but reveals information about the extent to which creditors may be falling short of meeting the credit needs of minorities or low- and moderate-income communities. Even if no enforcement is taken under ECOA, and even if no mergers are denied under CRA, HMDA data can change creditor behavior. That may be so because the public cares, in general, about the social norm of equal access to credit, and because the creditors care about their reputation with the public. Conversely, the social norm may push behavior beyond what is efficient or fall short of what was intended by the promulgators of the standard.

Although TILA (and HOEPA's disclosure requirements) facilitate comparison shopping by consumers, in some cases too much information is provided for consumers to use, and in other cases too little. Even outside of the subprime market, there is little reason to think that consumers understand most aspects of mortgage transactions (Board of Governors and HUD, 1998; Willis, 2004). Decision theory suggests a need for simplicity: individuals faced with complex problems simplify them to one or two major decisions (Hogarth, 1987; Plous, 1993; Baron, 2000). In addition, mortgage brokers can take advantage of borrowers, who trust mortgage brokers to provide them with full and accurate information and to provide them with the best loan product. Yet it is in the broker's interest to provide the borrower with the highest-rate loan that the broker can convince the borrower to accept. Brokers can earn higher yield spread pre-

31. 12 C.F.R. pr. 226.18(e), 226.4(a).

32. See Congressional Findings and Declaration of Purpose for TILA, 15 U.S.C. 1601; Engel and McCoy (2002); Schwartz and Wilde (1979, p. 635). "Because more consumers will become informed if information acquisition costs are decreased, reducing these costs is thought to be the preferable response to the problem of imperfect information."

33. The Federal Reserve Board amended its HMDA regulations to require lenders to report certain price information about high-cost loans. HMDA reporting could be improved further by requiring information on interest rates and fees.

miums for placing borrowers into more expensive loans than ones for which the borrower could qualify. Unlike retail consumer markets in which commodities are more difficult to price differentially for each consumer (for example, Cheerios in supermarkets), individual transactions for home mortgages present the possibility for price discrimination based on sophistication and willingness and ability to shop for better terms (Jackson and Berry, 2003, p. 63).[34] With credit scoring, creditors know whether borrowers qualify for a less expensive loan, while most borrowers do not.[35]

The efficacy of disclosures is diminished by inadequacies in their nature and timing (Eskridge, 1984; Landers and Rohner, 1979)[36] and consumers' cognitive limitations (Renuart, 2003, pp. 421, 432). In one survey, 75 percent of respondents either agreed somewhat or agreed strongly that TILA statements for credit cards are complicated (Durkin, 2002, pp. 201, 208). This effect is exacerbated for low-income and minority buyers, for whom alternative credit options are more limited (Hogarth and Lee, 1999, 2000). Each of these problems is exacerbated in the subprime market, making disclosure laws even less likely to be effective. Consumers in the subprime market tend to be lower-income, have higher debt-to-income ratios, and lower creditworthiness than borrowers in the prime market. These factors leave them vulnerable as they search for creditors who will approve them for a loan (Zigas and Weech, 2001). Older and minority borrowers are disproportionately represented in the subprime pool and may be more susceptible to aggressive broker practices. Consumers in the subprime market may lack financial literacy and have fewer people in their communities that they can turn to for sound financial advice. Loan price and term dispersion is much higher in the subprime market than in the prime market, making it more difficult for consumers to understand the more varied and complicated loan provisions.

TILA's costs are difficult to measure. Surveys of banks estimate the cost of compliance with TILA at between 1.73 and 2.26 percent of total noninterest expenses, or $13 per loan (see Elliehausen, 1998, p. 15, table 2; p. 18, note 38). The most substantial cost of TILA may be produced by litigation over *de minimis* violations of its technical terms,[37] although consumer rights lawyers con-

---

34. Ayres (2002) has documented similar price discrimination in automobile sales and other markets.

35. FICO scores are now available to borrowers upon request. Empirical research is needed on whether this access has been used.

36. Early disclosure is now required by Regulation Z, 226.19(b), 226.5a, 226.5b.

37. See, for example, *Rodash* v. *AIB Mortgage Co.*, 16 F. 3d 1142 (11th Cir. 1994) (holding that failure to include $22 express delivery charge and $204 intangible tax in finance charge for loan of $102,000 created right of rescission). Congress subsequently amended the act to deny rescission so long as the finance charge omitted from the APR calculation did not exceed $35. See 15 U.S.C. 1635(i)(2); *Reexamining Truth in Lending: Do Borrowers Actually Use Consumer Disclosures*, 52 Consumer Fin. L.Q. 3 (1998) ("Most of the [TILA] lawsuits we see involve technical mistakes with disclosures that have no practical meaning to the consumer." Statement of Robert Cook).

tend that TILA provides them with an opportunity to challenge contracts that ought to be challenged on other grounds but as to which there are significant legal hurdles.

Disclosures can and should undoubtedly be improved.[38] Moreover, financial education can play a role in helping consumers understand disclosures better. The problem is that financial education is notoriously hard to do well. Despite the significant consumer financial education that has been offered over many years, consumers exhibit a wide range of behavior in the extent to which they understand loan terms and shop for a mortgage (Hogarth and Lee, 1999, 2000).[39] Moreover, expenditures for it lead to positive externalities, so it is difficult to induce market participants to offer financial education to the public at the scale it would take to matter.

CROSS-MODAL STRATEGIES. Disclosure laws are no substitute for other regulatory approaches. Relying on HMDA alone to overcome market failures and discrimination in theory could lead to "overenforcement" of antidiscrimination and community investment norms. HMDA information does not contain measures of creditworthiness, loan terms, or property characteristics that influence creditor decisions. Relying on HMDA data alone can lead to dramatic overstatements of lending discrimination. Similarly, HMDA data do not provide any context for understanding creditors' ability to lend in low-income communities, so banks might face undue pressure to make unsound loans. Conversely, relying solely on public disclosure could lead to "underenforcement" of equal protection and community investment norms. Without fair lending laws, HMDA's disclosure might convey less approbation. Without CRA, disclosure under HMDA that a bank did little lending in low-income communities would have little consequence. CRA puts strong incentives on banks, those most able to alter their behavior in response to the problem of information asymmetry and collective action.[40] CRA can enhance competition in fragmented markets where disclosures seem unlikely on their own significantly to affect market structure. CRA also enlists expert agencies to further its goals, rather than rely-

---

38. See, for example, Real Estate Settlement Procedures Act (RESPA); Simplifying and Improving the Process of Obtaining Mortgages to Reduce Settlement Costs to Consumers, 67 Fed. Reg. 49,134 (proposed July 29, 2002, proposing significant simplification). But see Comments of the Staff of the Bureau of Economics, the Bureau of Consumer Protection, and the Office of Policy Planning of the Federal Trade Commission, Before the Department of Housing and Urban Development, in the Matter of Request for Comment on Proposed Amendments to the Regulations Implementing the Real Estate Settlement Procedures Act, Docket No. FR-4727-P-01 (October 28, 2002) (arguing that HUD's proposal would not assist consumers).

39. There are no good data on whether this is because of different preferences as to search costs (see Stigler, 1961) or because consumers do not understand that they can search, or how to search, for lower cost mortgages.

40. Compare, for example, Calabresi (1970) discussing the "cheapest cost avoider."

ing solely on the public to change creditor behavior in response to HMDA data
or TILA disclosures.

Abusive Practice Prohibitions

Congress enacted HOEPA[41] in 1994 to respond to unscrupulous lending practices in the subprime home equity mortgage market. For some high-cost loans,
HOEPA imposes restrictions on certain contract provisions, provides for
enhanced disclosures, and enhances remedies for violations.[42] HOEPA restricts
prepayment penalties, balloon payments, and negative amortization under some
circumstances. Lenders are forbidden from engaging in a pattern or practice of
making high-cost loans without regard to the borrower's ability to repay from
income (rather than from home equity). For any mortgage loan, the Federal
Reserve Board has regulatory authority to prohibit acts or practices that the
board finds to be unfair, deceptive, or designed to evade HOEPA. The board
can also prohibit acts or practices concerning refinance loans that the board
finds to be abusive or not in the interest of the borrower.

In addition to product regulation, HOEPA provides directly and indirectly
for enhanced disclosures for borrowers facing high-cost loans. HOEPA directly
enhances disclosure by requiring creditors to disclose mortgage terms three days
in advance of closing. Indirectly, HOEPA product restrictions tend to drive
more of the cost of the loan into the APR so that consumers can better understand the costs of the loan and comparison shop.

HOEPA's record has been decidedly mixed (Joint Report, 2000). Given the
characteristics of the lower-income consumer credit market—high demand from
a population with imperfect or limited credit history, many lightly regulated
players, and little competition from mainstream lenders—the potential for
abuses is ripe. A Treasury-HUD report that I co-directed proposed a four-part
approach to curbing predatory lending: improve consumer literacy and disclosure; prohibit harmful sales practices; restrict abusive terms and conditions; and
improve overall market structure (Joint Report, 2000; Barr, 2002). None of the
legislative changes have been enacted, but the Federal Reserve Board issued a rule
addressing the harmful sales practices and abusive terms often associated with
high-cost mortgages using its existing authority under HOEPA.[43] This rule takes

41. P.L. 103–325, 151, 108 Stat. 2190 (1994).

42. HOEPA covers mortgage refinancing loans and closed-end home equity loans with annual
percentage rates more than 8 percentage points above the yields on comparable Treasury securities
or loans with certain points and fees that exceed 8 percent of the loan amount or an amount
adjusted for inflation (just under $500 for 2004). The statute sets a default rate of 10 percentage
points above comparable Treasuries, but the Federal Reserve Board has the authority to adjust
downward to 8 percentage points or upward to 12 percentage points. The board adjusted the APR
to 8 percentage points in 2001. Final Rule, Federal Reserve System, 12 C.F.R. Part 226, Truth in
Lending, 66 Fed. Reg. 65604, December 20, 2001.

43. Final Rule, Federal Reserve System, 12 C.F.R. Part 226, Truth in Lending, 66 Fed. Reg.
65,604 (December 20, 2001).

significant steps toward limiting abusive practices, but congressional action would improve matters further.[44] The board's requirement that creditors document and verify a borrower's ability to repay will help deter asset-based lending.[45]

Meanwhile, a number of states have experimented with a variety of different approaches to regulation of high-cost loans. This experimentation is leading to valuable data on how and whether one can use product regulation to deter abusive practices without cutting off access to home mortgage credit.[46] In the midst of these state law changes, the OCC announced that it would preempt state laws regulating home mortgage lending, as they relate to national banks and their operating subsidiaries.[47] State laws as they relate to independent mortgage companies, holding company affiliates, and other banks and thrifts are unaffected.

CROSS-MODAL STRATEGIES. Cross-modal strategies could help to reduce abuses. For example, enhanced disclosures could use public shaming and competition to reduce the scope for problems. Rule changes made in December 2001,[48] under the board's HMDA authority, complement its efforts on predatory lending by requiring disclosure of certain rate spreads and of whether a loan exceeds HOEPA triggers.[49] Requiring automatic disclosure of credit scores (and how they are used in conjunction with other borrower, property, and loan characteristics by the particular lender) and more transparent disclosure of pricing; adopting the TILA and RESPA reforms advocated by the Federal Reserve Board, Treasury, and HUD in earlier reports; and developing a means for track-

44. Congress could bolster the Federal Reserve Board's action in a number of ways, including: banning the financing at or before closing of single premium credit insurance, products often packed into subprime loans; requiring lenders to report the full credit histories of borrowers to the credit bureaus; requiring lenders to offer the borrower a choice of a loan without a prepayment penalty; and including yield spread premiums in the points-and-fees trigger for HOEPA. See U.S. Department of the Treasury Comment on Regulation Z (Truth in Lending Act; Home Ownership and Equity Protection Act) Proposed Rulemaking Docket No. R-1090. Yield spread premiums permit lenders to pass on the cost of a mortgage broker fee to the borrower in the form of a higher interest rate rather than in the form of a cash payment at closing.

45. Stronger requirements might deter asset-based lending even more. See Joint Report (2000) suggesting documentation of ability to repay be signed by broker and acknowledged as received by borrower three days prior to closing.

46. Compare, for example, Litan (2001, 2003) and Elliehausen and Staten (2002), with Quercia, Stegman, and Davis (2002), Stegman, Quercia, and Davis (2003), and Ernst, Farris, and Stein (2002).

47. See Office of Comptroller of the Currency, Notice of Proposed Rulemaking, August 5, 2003, 68 Fed. Reg. 46119; Final rule, Bank Activities and Operations; Real Estate Lending and Appraisals, January 7, 2004, at www.occ.treas.gov/2004-3bPreemptionrule.pdf; OCC Advisory Letter AL 2003-2, Guidelines for National Banks to Guard against Predatory and Abusive Lending Practices, February 21, 2003.

48. Federal Reserve System, Home Mortgage Disclosure; Final and Proposed Rule, 12 C.F.R. Pt. 203, 67 Fed. Reg. 7,221 (February 15, 2002).

49. The rule could be strengthened by requiring disclosure of all rate spreads, points, and fees, as well as other loan characteristics. See U.S. Department of the Treasury Comment on Regulation C (Home Mortgage Disclosure Act) Proposed Rulemaking Docket No. R.-1001.

ing loan characteristics and performance by individual mortgage brokers could help to improve consumer shopping, increase regulatory oversight, shame bad lenders, and thus make it harder for abuses to occur.

Yet the most egregious cases of predatory lending often involve broker fraud, deception, or misrepresentation that is hard to detect. While such broker actions are often illegal under state law, state authorities often lack the resources to police the activities of the thousands of mortgage brokers that may be doing business in their state. Thus greater focus needs to be paid to holding lenders liable for broker abuses through enhanced due diligence requirements. As a further example, product regulation through banning yield spread premiums as the dominant form of broker compensation and replacing it with flat fees disclosed in advance could take some of the sting out of broker abuses.

CRA could play an increasingly important role in reducing abuses. Competition from banks can help to drive out abusive practices and improve price transparency in these markets. Low-income borrowers may be ending up in a bank's subprime unit or affiliate when they could qualify for better terms. Regulators now give CRA consideration for promoting borrowers from the subprime to the prime market. Over the last decade, affiliations between insured depository institutions and nonbank subprime specialists have increased. Thus the effectiveness of this approach will depend on adequate supervision of the relationship between the bank and its affiliates to assess whether borrowers with good credit history are upstreamed from subprime affiliates and offered prime products; whether borrowers with poor credit histories have an opportunity to demonstrate creditworthiness and move into prime products; and whether borrowers are inappropriately steered to higher-cost products or divisions.

As financial institutions increasingly rely on a broad range of affiliations to carry on their businesses, it is both possible and desirable to take account of affiliate activity while respecting the fact that CRA applies only to insured depositories. CRA regulations already provide that evidence of illegal credit practices will affect an institution's CRA rating. The laws governing such credit practices are equally applicable to banks and thrifts as well as nondepository creditors. Illegal credit practices of an affiliate that has been included at the option of the depository institution for purposes of a CRA examination are relevant to its rating, but so too should be the illegal credit practices of affiliates not so included. Given the high cost of examining all affiliates for such practices, enforcement of other credit laws should occur through risk-based examinations of affiliates. The results of such compliance examinations should be taken into account in the performance context under CRA.

Subsidies

Finally, there are a series of subsidies to credit. Most housing subsidies are not aimed at improving access to credit for low- and moderate-income borrowers or redressing housing discrimination. Rather, they mostly subsidize "the American dream" of homeownership for all. Subsidies to home mortgage credit include government insurance through the Federal Housing Administration (FHA) and the Government National Mortgage Association (Ginnie Mae) and government-sponsored enterprises (GSEs),[50] including the Federal National Mortgage Association (Fannie Mae), the Federal Home Loan Mortgage Corporation (Freddie Mac), and the Federal Home Loan Bank (FHLB) system. Tax expenditures and grant programs, including the home mortgage interest and property tax deductions, as well as a wide range of other programs, also affect housing markets. I leave analysis of the housing subsidies in the tax code for others (for example, Glaeser and Shapiro, 2002; Brady, Cronin, and Houser, 2003), and focus on FHA and the GSEs.

During the Great Depression, Congress established FHA, the FHLBs, and Fannie Mae to fill a gap left by the collapse of the private mortgage insurance industry "under the weight of a default rate approaching 50 percent and foreclosures exceeding 1,000 per day" (Pennington-Cross and Yezer, 2000, p. 358). FHA, which operates within HUD, insures home mortgage loans made by private lenders in the event of default. FHA is intended to serve borrowers who cannot qualify for conventional mortgages. Ginnie Mae, also within HUD, provides a credit enhancement to pools of FHA loans and places them for sale on the secondary market. In 2002 alone, FHA insured $150 billion in mortgages for nearly 1.3 million households (HUD, 2003).

The GSEs—Fannie Mae, Freddie Mac, and the FHLBs—were created to "provide liquidity and stability to the home mortgage market" (Crippen, 2001). Fannie Mae and Freddie Mac issue debt to buy and hold mortgages in portfolio, and insure mortgage-backed securities issued to investors. Fannie Mae and Freddie Mac are restricted to the market for conventional, conforming loans,[51] and essentially fund all net new loans meeting those criteria (CBO, 2001, p. 28). The FHLBs were created to provide short-term loans (advances) to thrifts in order to stabilize mortgage lending in local markets. Today, FHLB membership is broad, including the largest commercial banks, and advances can be issued on a variety of collateral and used for any purpose (CBO, 2001, p. 4).

In principle, subsidies should be used "to make marginal private costs equal to marginal social costs, and to make marginal benefits equal to marginal social benefits" (Stiglitz, 2000). In practice, this is hard to do. Substantively, it is difficult to get private market actors to respond to government subsidies unless the

---

50. "In general, GSEs are financial institutions established and chartered by the federal government, as privately owned entities, to facilitate the flow of funds to selected credit markets" (CBO, 2001, p. 1).

51. Conventional loans are those not backed by government insurance. Conforming loans are those that are under the dollar limit set annually for GSE purchases.

subsidies are robust. Politically, it is challenging to prevent the subsidies from becoming too robust.

With respect to Fannie Mae, Freddie Mac, and the FHLBs, the subsidies are large in comparison to the benefits accruing to low-income, moderate-income, and minority borrowers. The GSEs benefit from their relationships with the federal government in a variety of ways. They are exempt from state and local taxation, are exempt from Securities and Exchange Commission (SEC) registration,[52] can borrow from the Treasury, and issue debt that banks and thrifts can hold under capital standards that favor the GSEs over private conduits (CBO, 2001; Treasury, 1996). Unlike privately issued securities, GSE securities are exempt from SEC registration, are treated as government securities under the Exchange Act, and are exempt under the Trust Indenture Act of 1939 and the Investment Company Act of 1940 (MBS Disclosure Report, 2003). Most importantly, the GSEs benefit from the credit enhancement of an implicit guarantee that the federal government will intervene in the event of financial collapse (CBO, 2001; Treasury, 1996). Despite the disclaimer by both the federal government and the GSEs that there is no federal guarantee, there is a general belief by the market to the contrary. That belief may arise because of the GSEs' congressional charters, the indicia of federal support, or the notion that they are "too big to fail." The implicit guarantee permits the GSEs to issue debt at a lower cost, and to hold less capital than similar private firms (Treasury, 1996).

Measuring the subsidy provided to the GSEs is the subject of intense debate. The Congressional Budget Office (CBO) found that the benefits accorded to the GSEs were worth $13.6 billion, of which Fannie Mae received $6.1 billion, Freddie Mac $4.6 billion, and the FHLBs $3.0 billion (CBO, 2001). CBO estimated that a "little more than half ($7.0 billion) of that total subsidy in 2000 passed through" to mortgage borrowers with lower interest rates on conventional, conforming loans (CBO, 2001, p. 1). CBO estimated that Fannie Mae and Freddie Mac retained $3.9 billion (37 percent) of the subsidy for their shareholders or other stakeholders (CBO, 2001, p. 5). As for the FHLBs, CBO estimated that they passed on only $300 million of their $3 billion subsidy to mortgage borrowers, with 90 percent of the subsidy accruing to the benefit of the FHLB member banks or reducing interest rates on other types of loans borrowed from FHLB members (CBO, 2001, p. 5). These estimates are sensitive to assumptions about the funding advantages GSEs receive and about how to model the pass-through to borrowers (for example, Heuson, Passmore, and Sparks, 2000), and the extent of the subsidy is widely debated. For present purposes, the point estimates are not critical. I will assume that the amount of the subsidy is some nontrivial amount above zero.

---

52. Fannie Mae and Freddie Mac agreed in 2002 to begin voluntarily to register their common stock with the SEC.

The GSEs helped to create and sustain a nationally integrated, stable, and liquid mortgage market. Fannie Mae, Freddie Mac, and Ginnie Mae played central roles in creating the secondary market for home mortgage loans (MBS Disclosure Report, 2003, p. 7; Lore and Cowan, 2001). Ginnie Mae guaranteed the first mortgage-backed securities in 1970, and Freddie Mac followed shortly thereafter by issuing mortgage-backed certificates. Fannie Mae followed a decade later (MBS Disclosure Report, 2003, p. 7). As recently as the 1980s, before the rise of a robust secondary market, severe economic dislocations in one region of the country could cause mortgage defaults to increase (Greenspan, 2004). Today, the GSEs likely contribute to the stability and liquidity of national mortgage markets and lower home mortgage rates. To the extent that homeownership externalities might support a general housing policy in favor of the American Dream (for example, Glaeser and Shapiro, 2002), the GSEs contribute to housing consumption.

The GSEs also may contribute to access to home mortgage credit for low- and moderate-income households. Fannie Mae and Freddie Mac have sponsored home counseling programs, trained loan originators, and supported community organizations to increase affordable lending. The GSEs have used more flexible underwriting criteria for loan purchases. Fannie Mae and Freddie Mac's performance has surpassed HUD's affordable housing goals since they were first formally promulgated in 1997,[53] and HUD increased those goals for 2001–04, and again for 2005–08 (HUD, 2004, 2001). However, the share of GSE purchases financing affordable housing under the goals lagged that of the primary market during the 1990s (Treasury, 2000, 1996). In the early 1990s, the GSEs held less of the credit risk associated with lending to low-income or minority borrowers and areas than did FHA, Ginnie Mae, and depository institutions, both as a share of the GSEs' own activities and as a share of the market (Canner and Passmore, 1995, pp. 989, 1000, 1004). In addition to the affordable housing goals, other factors contributed to this activity, such as the GSEs' business strategies and the shift in the primary market toward more lending to low-income borrowers.[54]

The FHLBs also provide modest subsidies for affordable housing and community development through the Affordable Housing Program and Community Investment Program. However, the bank members of the FHLBs enjoy extensive low-cost advances that essentially subsidize the full range of bank activities (CBO, 2001). The FHLBs made $16.9 billion in net advances to members in 2002, with $490 billion outstanding at the end of that year (Board of Governors,

---

53. The GSE definition of low- and moderate-income households, 100 percent of area median income, includes households with higher incomes than as defined for CRA. Under CRA, low- and moderate-income households have incomes less than or equal to 80 percent of area median.

54. The shares of CRA loans sold on the secondary market increased from 54 percent in 1993 to 67 percent in 1998.

2003). In addition, the FHLBs have begun to experiment since the late 1990s with untargeted secondary market operations in the hopes of competing with the other GSEs and now hold in excess of $100 billion in mortgage pools.

The GSEs pose risks and carry high costs. Fannie Mae and Freddie Mac shareholders and FHLB members retain a significant portion of the subsidy, and the portion passed on to consumers is spread diffusely through the market. The GSE duopoly hinders competition in the secondary market for conventional, conforming loans. Taxpayers would face a large, contingent liability in the unlikely event that the GSEs failed. Moreover, the government faces the difficulty of managing risk from an implicit guarantee, rather than an explicit, budgeted one.

In addition to the GSEs, FHA provides mortgage subsidies through insurance. FHA provided $157 billion in insurance on home mortgage loans to 1.3 million households in 2002. FHA's secondary market counterpart, Ginnie Mae, guaranteed $175 billion in mortgage-backed securities that year. FHA specializes in serving borrowers who make "low down payment[s], have high debt-to-income ratios, and/or have tarnished credit." These borrowers tend to be first-time, minority, or low-income and tend to live in low-income or minority-concentrated neighborhoods. A higher share of FHA lending goes to low-income and minority borrowers and areas, as compared to the GSEs.[55] During the 1990s, the share of FHA lending going to low- and moderate-income minority borrowers grew more rapidly than did the share of conventional lending to those borrowers (Joint Report, 2000). FHA also serves a role in regional markets with falling wages, increasing unemployment, and dropping house prices (Pennington-Cross and Yezer, 2000, p. 362). At times, FHA has competed with conventional lenders. A dilemma for FHA is how to reach further into the market while managing risk. As the conventional market serves the more creditworthy portion of FHA's pool of borrowers, adverse selection is leaving FHA with higher risk (Wartell, 2002, pp. 17, 21). That problem is exacerbated because FHA lags the private sector in credit scoring and risk management (Wartell, 2002, p. 16; Stanton, 1999).

In sum, government subsidies generate windfalls for the GSE shareholders and others. A large portion of those whose mortgages are purchased by the GSEs would likely have had access to the credit markets in any event, even if at a higher price. GSE subsidies are not transparent, making it difficult for the public to weigh their costs and benefits, and required levels of capital and regulatory oversight may be insufficient to minimize taxpayer risk. FHA subsidies are more transparent because the cost of the subsidy appears as user fees and as

---

55. See Wartell (2002, p. 11) regarding the profile of the FHA's borrower. The agency's success in serving first-time home buyers may be overstated, since studies suggest that these households would become homeowners anyway at a later age. See Pennington-Cross and Yezer (2000, pp. 362, 367).

an item in the federal budget.[56] The cost of transparency is, however, direct tax-payer liability for the FHA. FHA may not have the management capacity and technical expertise to manage risk as effectively as private market participants.

CROSS-MODAL STRATEGIES. Given the trade-offs involved, the risks and costs of the GSEs ought to be lowered through enhanced supervision by bank-like regulators, significantly improved risk disclosure, and more stringent capital requirements; moreover, the benefits should be increased by raising the afford-able housing goals so that government subsidies are better targeted. In addition, cross-modal strategies using the GSEs might also help to enhance other norms. For example, to the limited extent that the GSEs purchase subprime loans, GSE disclosures of such items as LTVs, points paid at settlement, credit scores, debt-to-income ratios, loan purpose, and identification of the originator, seller, and servicer, which have been recommended to reduce risk (MBS Disclosure Report, 2003, p. 45), might also reinforce norms underlying HOEPA by per-mitting secondary market participants to evaluate the riskiness of loan pools, by permitting regulators to evaluate the extent to which prices track credit risk, and by permitting enforcement officials to track originator behavior regarding high-cost loans. For all loans purchased by the GSEs, such disclosures, coupled with HMDA information on the race of the borrower, could help to evaluate the extent of mortgage lending discrimination. Similarly, HUD could use its super-visory authority over the GSEs for compliance with fair lending laws to review more aggressively GSE underwriting criteria and business practices to ensure that they do not create a disparate impact on minority households, particularly since no agency has supervisory authority over nonbank mortgage originators that sell loans to the GSEs.

Regulation can have important advantages over generalized subsidy approaches. For example, CRA provides no windfall to banks and thrifts. CRA targets all its efforts at expanding access to credit and financial services for low- and moderate-income borrowers and communities, so there is no wasted effort on generalized policies subsidizing housing consumption. Moreover, banks and thrifts have expertise in finding creditworthy borrowers and in using extensive risk-mitigation techniques. If CRA increased risk because of expanded lending to low-income borrowers, that risk would be diffused over the well-diversified port-folios of thousands of depositories, all of which are comprehensively supervised for safety and soundness and required to hold adequate capital. Thus to the extent that generalized subsidies have contributed to concentrating risks in the GSEs, greater attention will need to be paid to further developing appropriate safety and soundness regulations, and creating a strong institution to regulate them.

56. GSE activity is noted in federal budget documents, even though the GSEs are not on budget.

Conclusion

I have briefly introduced and compared five different modes of credit market regulation. Comparing these forms of government intervention reveals hidden strengths and weaknesses of the approaches taken and suggests the important role of comparative institutional analysis in policy reform. Further empirical research should help shed light on the comparative strengths and weaknesses of these regulatory approaches. While deepening our understanding of different modes of credit market regulation, the chapter also suggests innovative, cross-modal techniques for advancing the social norms underlying each mode of regulation. While detailed analysis of these ideas must await another day, these cross-modal strategies could hold important promise in helping to reduce discrimination and overcome market failures affecting underserved communities.

References

Anderson, Elizabeth S., and Richard Pildes. 2000. "Expressive Theories of Law." *University of Pennsylvania Law Review* 148: 1503–74.

Avery, Robert B., and others. 1996. "Credit Risk, Credit Scoring, and the Performance of Home Mortgages." *Federal Reserve Bulletin* 82: 621–48.

———. 1999. "Trends in Home Purchase Lending: Consolidation and the Community Reinvestment Act." *Federal Reserve Bulletin* 85: 81–102.

Ayres, Ian. 2001. Expert Report. *Cason* v. *Nissan*, 3-98-0223 (Middle District of Tennessee, May 25).

———. 2002. *Pervasive Prejudice? Nontraditional Evidence of Race and Gender Discrimination*. University of Chicago Press.

Ayres, Ian, and Peter Siegelman. 1995. "Race and Gender Discrimination in Bargaining for a New Car." *American Economic Review* 85 (3): 304–21.

Baron, Jonathan. 2000. *Thinking and Deciding*. Cambridge University Press.

Barr, Michael S. 2002. "Access to Financial Services in the Twenty-First Century." *Notre Dame Journal of Law and Ethics and Public Policy* 16 (2): 447–73.

———. 2004. "Banking the Poor." *Yale Journal on Regulation* 21 (1): 121–237.

———. 2005. "Credit Where It Counts: The Community Reinvestment Act and Its Critics." *New York University Law Review* 80 (2): 513–652.

Barr, Michael S., and others. 2001. "The Community Reinvestment Act: Its Impact on Lending in Low-Income Communities in the United States." In *Banking and Social Cohesion: Alternative Responses to a Global Market*, edited by Christopher Guene and Edward Mayo, pp. 214–32. Charlbury, Oxon: Jon Carpenter Publishing.

Becker, Gary S. 1971. *The Economics of Discrimination*. University of Chicago Press.

Belsky, Eric S., Michael Schill, and Anthony Yezer. 2001. "The Effects of the Community Reinvestment Act on Bank and Thrift Home Purchase Mortgage Lending." Working Paper CRA01-1. Cambridge, Mass.: Joint Center for Housing Studies.

Black, Harold A., Thomas P. Boehm, and Ramon P. DeGennaro. 2003. "Is There Discrimination in Mortgage Pricing? The Case of Overages." *Journal of Banking and Finance* 27 (6): 1139–65.

Board of Governors. 2000. "The Performance and Profitability of CRA-Related Lending, Report by the Board of Governors of the Federal Reserve System." Submitted to Congress pursuant to section 713 of the Gramm-Leach-Bliley Act of 1999 (July 2000).

————. 2003. "Flow of Funds Accounts of the United States, Flows and Outstandings First Quarter 2003." Federal Reserve Board, Federal Reserve statistical release Z.1. (www.federalreserve.gov/Releases/Z1/Current/zlr-1.pdf [August 10, 2003]).

Board of Governors of the Federal Reserve System and the Department of Housing and Urban Development. 1998. "Joint Study on the Truth in Lending Act and the Real Estate Settlement Procedures Act" (www.federalreserve.gov/boarddocs/RptCongress/tila.pdf).

Brady, Peter, Julie-Anne Cronin, and Scott Houser. 2003. "Regional Differences in the Utilization of the Mortgage Interest Deduction." *Public Finance Review* 31 (4): 327–66.

Browne, Lynne E., and others. 1996. "Mortgage Lending in Boston: Interpreting HMDA Data." *American Economic Review* 86 (1): 25–53.

Browne, Lynne E., Alicia H. Munnell, and Geoffrey M. B. Tootell. 1992. "Mortgage Lending in Boston: Interpreting HMDA Data." Working Paper Series 92-7. Federal Reserve Bank of Boston (October).

Buist, Henry, Peter D. Linneman, and Isaac F. Megbolugbe. 1999. "Residential-Mortgage Lending Discrimination and Lender-Risk-Compensation Policies." *Journal of the American Real Estate and Urban Economics Association* 27 (Winter): 695–717.

Calabresi, Guido. 1970. *The Cost of Accidents*. Yale University Press.

Camerer, Colin, and others. 2003. "Regulation for Conservatives: Behavioral Economics and the Case for Asymmetric Paternalism." *University of Pennsylvania Law Review* 151: 1211–54.

Canner, Glenn B., and Wayne Passmore. 1995. "Credit Risk and the Provision of Mortgages to Lower-Income and Minority Home Buyers." *Federal Reserve Bulletin* 81: 989–1016.

Canner, Glenn B., and Dolores S. Smith. 1991. "Home Mortgage Disclosure Act: Expanded Data on Residential Lending." *Federal Reserve Bulletin* 77: 859–81.

Congressional Budget Office. 1996. "Assessing the Public Costs and Benefits of Fannie Mae and Freddie Mac" (ftp.cbo.gov/0xx/doc13/Fanfred.pdf).

————. 2001. "Federal Subsidies and the Housing GSEs" (ftp.cbo.gov/28xx/doc2841/GSEs.pdf [May 2001]).

Courchane, Marsha J., Brian J. Surette, and Peter M. Zorn. 2004. "Subprime Borrowers: Mortgage Transitions and Outcomes." *Journal of Real Estate Finance and Economics* 29 (4): 365–92.

Crippen, Daniel L. 2001. Statement before the Committee on Financial Services, May 23 (ftp.cbo.gov/28xx/doc2839/GSE-Testimony.pdf).

Durkin, Thomas A. 2002. "Consumers and Credit Disclosures: Credit Cards and Credit Insurance." *Federal Reserve Bulletin* (April): 201–13.

Ellen, Ingrid Gould, and others. 2001. "Building Homes, Reviving Neighborhoods: Spillovers from Subsidized Construction of Owner-Occupied Housing in New York City." *Journal of Housing Research* 12 (2): 185–216.

Elliehausen, Gregory. 1998. "The Cost of Bank Regulation: A Review of the Evidence." Board of Governors of the Federal Reserve System Staff Study (April).

Elliehausen, Gregory, and Michael Staten. 2002. "Regulation of Subprime Mortgage Products: An Analysis of North Carolina's Predatory Lending Law." Working Paper 66. Georgetown University Credit Research Center (October).

Engel, Kathleen C., and Patricia A. McCoy. 2002. "A Tale of Three Markets: The Law and Economics of Predatory Lending." *Texas Law Review* 80 (6): 1257–381.

Ernst, Keith, John Farris, and Eric Stein. 2002. "North Carolina's Subprime Home Loan Market after Predatory Lending Reform" (www.responsiblelending.org/pdfs/HMDA_Study_on_NC_Market.pdf).

Eskridge., William N., Jr. 1984. "One Hundred Years of Ineptitude: The Need for Mortgage Rules Consonant with the Economic and Psychological Dynamics of the Home Sale and Loan Transaction." *Virginia Law Review* 70: 1083–217.

Evanoff, Douglas D., and Lewis M. Siegal. 1996. "CRA and Fair Lending Regulations: Resulting Trends in Mortgage Lending." *Federal Reserve Bank of Chicago Economic Perspectives* 20 (6): 19–46.

Federal Financial Institutions Examination Council. 1999. Interagency Fair Lending Examination Procedures.

Freddie Mac. 1996. "Automated Underwriting: Making Mortgage Lending Simpler and Fairer for America's Families" (www.freddiemac.com/corporate/reports/moseley/ mosehome.htm).

Galster, George C. 1987. *Homeowners and Neighborhood Reinvestment.* Duke University Press.

Glaeser, Edward L., and Jesse M. Shapiro. 2002. "The Benefits of the Home Mortgage Interest Deduction." Discussion Paper 1979. Cambridge: Mass.: Harvard Institute of Economic Research.

Greenbaum, Stuart I. 1996. "Twenty-Five Years of Banking Research." *Financial Management* 25 (2): 86–92.

Greenspan, Alan. 2004. Testimony at a hearing on Government Sponsored Enterprises, Committee on Banking, Housing, and Urban Affairs, U.S. Senate, February 24.

Gunther, Jeffrey W. 2000. "Should CRA Stand for 'Community Redundancy Act'?" *Regulation* 23: 56–60.

Guttentag, Jack. 2001. "Another View of Predatory Lending." Working Paper 01-23-B. Philadelphia: Wharton Financial Institutions Center (August).

Guttentag, Jack M., and Susan M. Wachter. 1980. "Redlining and Public Policy." In *Monograph Series in Finance and Economics*, edited by Edwin Elton and Martin J. Gruber, pp. 1–50. New York University Graduate School of Business, Salomon Brothers Center for the Study of Financial Institutions.

Heuson, Andrea, Wayne S. Passmore, and Roger Sparks. 2000. "Credit Scoring and Mortgage Securitization: Do They Lower Mortgage Rates?" *Federal Reserve Board, Finance and Economics Discussion Series* 2000-44.

Hogarth, Jeanne, and Jinkook Lee. 1999. "The Price of Money: Consumers' Understanding of APRs and Contract Interest Rates." *Journal of Public Policy and Marketing, Special Issue on Pricing and Public Policy* 18 (1): 66–76.

———. 2000. "Consumer Information for Home Mortgages: Who, What, How Much, and What Else?" *Financial Services Review* 9 (3): 277–93.

Hogarth, Robin. *Judgment and Choice.* 2nd ed. New York: John Wiley and Sons. 1987.

Jackson, Howell E., and Jeremy Berry. 2003. "Kickbacks or Compensation: The Case of Yield Spread Premiums." Working paper (www.law.harvard.edu/faculty/hjackson/projects/).

James, Madeleine, and others. 1997. "Playing to the Endgame in Financial Services." *McKinsey Quarterly* (4): 170–2.

Joint Center for Housing Studies. 2002. "The Twenty-Fifth Anniversary of the Community Reinvestment Act: Access to Capital in an Evolving Financial Services System." Report prepared for the Ford Foundation. Harvard University.

Jolls, Christine, Cass R. Sunstein, and Richard H. Thaler. 1998. "A Behavioral Approach to Law and Economics." *Stanford Law Review* 50: 1471–550.

Kushner, James A. *Fair Housing: Discrimination in Real Estate, Community Development, and Revitalization.* 2nd ed. 1995.

Lacker, Jeffrey M. 1995. "Neighborhoods and Banking." *Economic Quarterly* 81 (2): 13–38.

LaCour-Little, Michael. 1998. "Does the Community Reinvestment Act Make Mortgage Credit More Widely Available? Some New Evidence Based on the Performance of CRA Mortgage Credits." Conference paper presented at the Midyear Meeting of the American Real Estate and Urban Economics Association, Washington, May 4.

Landers, Jonathan M., and Ralph J. Rohner. 1979. "A Functional Analysis of Truth in Lending." *UCLA Law Review* 26: 711–52.

Lang, William W., and Leonard I. Nakamura. 1993. "A Model of Redlining." *Journal of Urban Economics* 33 (2): 223–334.

Litan, Robert E. 2001. "A Prudent Approach to Preventing 'Predatory' Lending" (www.aei-brookings.org/admin/authorpdfs/page.php?id=126).

———. 2003. "North Carolina Predatory Lending Law: Still a Problem despite New Study." Regulatory Analysis 03-9. Washington: American Enterprise Institute-Brookings Joint Center for Regulatory Studies.

Litan, Robert E., and others. 2000. "The Community Reinvestment Act after Financial Modernization: A Baseline Report." U.S. Department of the Treasury.

———. 2001. "The Community Reinvestment Act after Financial Modernization: A Final Report." U.S. Department of the Treasury.

Lore, Kenneth G., and Cameron L. Cowan. 2001. *Mortgage-Backed Securities: Developments and Trends in the Secondary Market.* St. Paul, Minn.: West Group.

Macey, Jonathan R., and Geoffrey P. Miller. 1993. "The Community Reinvestment Act: An Economic Analysis." *Virginia Law Review* 79: 291–348.

Mahoney, Peter, 1998. "The End(s) of Disparate Impact: Doctrinal Reconstruction, Fair Housing and Lending Law, and the Antidiscrimination Principle." *Emory Law Journal* 47: 409–526.

MBS Disclosure Report. 2003. "Staff Report: Enhancing Disclosure in the Mortgage-Backed Securities Markets, A Staff Report of the Task Force on Mortgage-Backed Securities Disclosure" (www.treas.gov/press/releases/docs/disclosure.pdf [August 2003]).

Ordover, Janusz, and Andrew Weiss. 1981. "Information and the Law: Evaluating Legal Restrictions on Competitive Contracts." *American Economic Review Papers and Proceedings* 71 (2): 399–404.

Pennington-Cross, Anthony, and Anthony Yezer. 2000. "The Federal Housing Administration in the New Millennium." *Journal of Housing Research* 11 (2): 357–72.

Petersen, Mitchell A., and Raghuram G. Rajan. 1995. "The Effect of Creditor Competition on Firm-Creditor Relationships." *Quarterly Journal of Economics* (110): 407.

Plous, Scott. 1993. *The Psychology of Judgment and Decisionmaking.* New York: McGraw-Hill.

Primus, Richard A. 2003. "Equal Protection and Disparate Impact: Round Three." *Harvard Law Review* 117: 493–587.

Quercia, Roberto G., Michael A. Stegman, and Walter R. Davis. 2002. "The Impact of North Carolina's Anti-Predatory Lending Law: A Descriptive Assessment." Center for Community Capitalism, University of North Carolina at Chapel Hill (www.kenan_flagler.unc.edu/assets/documents/CC_NC_Anti_Predatory_Law_Impact.pdf).

Renuart, Elizabeth. 2003. "Toward One Competitive and Fair Mortgage Market: Suggested Reforms in a Tale of Three Markets Point in the Right Direction, Commentary." *Texas Law Review* 82 (2): 421–38.

Ross, Stephen, and John Yinger. 2002. *The Color of Credit.* MIT Press.

Schill, Michael H., and others. 2002. "Revitalizing Inner-City Neighborhoods: New York City's Ten-Year Plan." *Housing Policy Debate* 13 (3): 529–66.

Schwartz, Alan, and Louis L. Wilde. 1979. "Intervening in Markets on the Basis of Imperfect Information." *University of Pennsylvania Law Review* (127): 630–81.

Stanton, Thomas H. 1999. *Credit Scoring and Loan Scoring: Tools for Improved Management of Federal Credit Programs.* Arlington, Va.: PricewaterhouseCoopers Endowment for the Business of Government.

Stegman, Michael A., Roberto G. Quercia, and Walter R. Davis. 2003. "North Carolina's Anti-Predatory Lending Law: Doing What It's Supposed to Do: A Reply." www.responsiblelending.org/pdfs/Stegman_reply_to_Litan11.pdf.

Stigler, George. 1961. "The Economics of Information." *Journal of Political Economy* 69 (3): 213–25.

Stiglitz, Joseph E. *Economics of the Public Sector.* 3rd ed. New York: W.W. Norton & Co. 2000.

Stiglitz, Joseph E., and Andrew Weiss. 1981. "Credit Rationing in Markets with Imperfect Information." *American Economic Review Papers and Proceedings* 71 (3): 393–410.

Tesler, Lester G. 1973. "Searching for the Lowest Price." *American Economic Review* 63 (2): 40–49.

Turner, Margery Austin, and Felicity Skidmore, eds. 1999. *Mortgage Lending Discrimination: A Review of the Existing Evidence.* Washington: Urban Institute.

Wartell, Sarah Rosen. 2002. "Single-Family Risksharing: An Evaluation of Its Potential as a Tool for FHA." Paper prepared for Millennial Housing Commission.

White, Lawrence J. 1993. "The Community Reinvestment Act: Good Intentions Headed in the Wrong Direction." *Fordham Urban Law Journal* 20: 281–92.

———. 2003. "Focusing on Fannie and Freddie: The Dilemmas of Reforming Housing Finance." *Journal of Financial Services Research* 23 (1): 43–58.

Willis, Lauren E. 2004 (forthcoming). "Decisionmaking and the Limits of Disclosure: The Problem of Predatory Lending." Draft on file with author. Loyola Law School.

U.S. Department of Housing and Urban Development. 2001. Overview of the GSE's Housing Goal Performance, 1993–01 (www.huduser.org/datasets/GSE/gse2001.pdf [August 2003]).

———. 2003. Fiscal Year 2004 Budget Summary 13 (www.hud.gov/about/budget/fy04/budgetsummaryu.pdf [February 3, 2003]).

———. 2004. Proposed Housing Goal Rule–2004 (www.hud.gov/offices/hsg/gse/summary.doc).

U.S. Department of Treasury. 1996. *Government Sponsorship of the Federal National Mortgage Association and the Federal Home Loan Mortgage Corporation.*

———. 2000. "Summary of GSE Affordable Housing Performance," Office of Government Sponsored Enterprise Policy. September 15.

U.S. Department of Treasury and U.S. Department of Housing and Urban Development. 2000. *Curbing Predatory Home Lending: A Joint Report.* U.S. Department of Housing and Urban Development.

Zigas, Barry, and Paul Weech. 2001. "The Rise of Subprime Lending: Causes, Implications, and Proposals, Lending to Borrowers with Blemished Credit: Challenges and Opportunities." Draft paper circulated by Fannie Mae.

Zinman, Jonathan. 2002. "The Efficacy and Efficiency of Credit Market Interventions: Evidence from the Community Reinvestment Act 2." Working Paper CRA02-2. Harvard University Joint Center for Housing Studies.

10

Accuracy in Credit Reporting

MICHAEL E. STATEN AND FRED H. CATE

The accuracy of consumer credit reports was among the most prominent issues in the congressional debate over amending the Fair Credit Reporting Act (FCRA) during the summer of 2003. This came as no surprise to observers of the credit reporting industry and its evolution since the original FCRA was passed in 1970.[1] One of the primary impetuses for passage of the FCRA was to enhance accuracy in credit report content. The act explicitly requires credit bureaus to follow "reasonable procedures to assure maximum possible accuracy" of the information in their credit reports.[2] This language reflects the fact that a hallmark of the U.S. reporting system is its reliance on voluntary reporting from thousands of furnishers of credit-related information. The voluntary nature of the reporting process makes it particularly sensitive to the costs imposed by regulatory and legislative mandates. The legislative balancing act undertaken in crafting the original FCRA was intended to foster accurate reports without discouraging reporting. Consequently, since implementation of the act in 1971, accuracy in credit reporting has been a perennial issue, but Congress has been notably cautious about imposing new requirements on

---

1. Fair Credit Reporting Act of 1970, P.L. 91-508, 84 Stat. 1114 (codified at 15 U.S.C. 1681 1681t).
2. 15 U.S.C. 1681e(b).

either credit bureaus or data furnishers without a clear indication of a problem that required legislative intervention.[3]

During the summer of 2003, testimony before Congress juxtaposed contrasting views of how well the U.S. credit reporting system is performing. Consumer advocacy groups cited credit report inaccuracies in calling for legislation that would impose new procedures and legal liability on both credit bureaus and furnishers of credit report information. In making their case, these groups correctly pointed out that an inaccurate depiction of a consumer's credit history not only can trigger a rejection of a loan application, but with advent of risk-based pricing can also lead to overpricing loans for which the borrower is approved. Moreover, borrowers may not realize that the interest rate or fees they pay may be inflated due to inaccurate information from the borrower's credit report. One advocacy group asserted that inaccuracies in credit reports could cause at least 8 million Americans to be miscategorized as subprime risks, and pay tens of thousands of dollars in excess interest payments over the term of a thirty-year mortgage loan (Brobeck, 2003).

In contrast to assertions of widespread problems in credit files, congressional testimony also documented that the United States has become the world leader in competitive consumer and mortgage credit markets. In 2001, 75 percent of U.S. households participated in the consumer credit markets and held some type of debt. Sixty-eight percent of all U.S. households owned their homes, and nearly two-thirds of these homeowners has some type of mortgage loan. About 72 percent of all households owned at least one general-purpose credit card (for example, Visa, MasterCard, Discover, American Express) (Durkin, 2002, p. 202). The average U.S. consumer-borrower had 10.4 credit accounts (Avery and others, 2003, p. 51). By comparison, European consumers have access to one-third less credit, as a percentage of gross domestic product, than do American consumers (Cate and others, 2003, p. 12). Compared to the vast majority of other countries, U.S. creditors have managed to extend substantially more credit per capita much further down the income spectrum, at the same time maintaining relatively low delinquency rates. In the second quarter of 2000, only 2.8 percent of all mortgage holders in the United States were delinquent more than thirty days.[4] Only 4.6 percent of all credit card borrowers were more than thirty days delinquent on their accounts.[5] In short, Americans enjoy the remarkable

---

3. See, for example, Consumer Credit Reporting Reform Act of 1996, enacted as title II, subtitle D, chap. 1 of the Omnibus Consolidated Appropriations Act for fiscal year 1997, P.L. 104-208, 104 Cong. 2 sess. 2401-2422 (September 30, 1996) (codified at 15 U.S.C. 1681-1681t). The legislative history of the 1996 amendments is documented in Seidel (1998).

4. Authors' calculations using TrenData, an aggregated credit report database product of TransUnion, LLC.

5. Authors' calculations using TrenData.

combination of: 1) widespread access to credit across the age and income spectrum, 2) relatively low interest rates on secured loans (for example, home mortgages, home equity lines of credit, automobile loans), 3) exceptionally broad access to open-end, unsecured credit card products, and 4) relatively low default rates across all types of loans. It seems highly improbable that all of this could be accomplished if the underlying credit reporting system were fraught with serious errors.

To help resolve the conflicting information concerning accuracy, Congress directed the U.S. General Accounting Office (GAO) to undertake a review during 2003 of available studies and databases to determine the frequency, type, and cause of credit report errors. The GAO concluded that "the lack of comprehensive information regarding the accuracy of consumer credit reports inhibits any meaningful discussion of what more could or should be done to improve credit report accuracy" (GAO, 2003, p. 17). In the Fair and Accurate Credit Transactions Act of 2003 Congress continued its cautious approach to new credit reporting requirements. But at the same time, Congress signaled its growing interest in measuring and ensuring the accuracy of credit reports. Specifically, Congress directed the Federal Trade Commission (FTC) to undertake a long-term study of credit reporting accuracy.[6]

In this chapter we survey the available evidence on credit file quality and attempt to assess the strengths and weaknesses of the system as it functions today, as well as identify any changes over time. We conclude by addressing the challenges to the regulatory framework presented by recent credit market developments such as risk-based pricing, and offer some observations about proposed solutions.

What Is an Accurate Credit Report?

A review of various reports and studies that examine credit report accuracy suggests that at the heart of the conflicting assessments of how the U.S. credit reporting industry is doing under FCRA are fundamental differences in the interpretation of accuracy. Accuracy is a stated goal of the reporting system, but exactly what does that mean?

The FCRA itself is not clear on this point. It states that consumer-reporting agencies must "follow reasonable procedures to assure maximum possible accuracy."[7] Accuracy is not defined, nor is it clear what we should expect about the quality of credit files once the upper limits of reasonable procedures are reached.

---

6. Fair and Accurate Credit Transactions Act of 2003, P.L. 108-159, 117 Stat. 1952, 319 (codified at 15 U.S.C. 1681-1681t).
7. 15 U.S.C. 1681e(b).

In its 2003 report to Congress on credit report accuracy, the GAO found that the "available literature and the credit reporting industry strongly disagree about the frequency of errors in consumer credit reports, and lack a common definition for 'inaccuracy'" (GAO, 2003, Highlights).

During congressional testimony in 1991, the president of Consumer Data Industry Association (CDIA)—the credit reporting industry's primary trade association—offered a useful insight that provides a metric for assessing accuracy. He remarked that "the mission of the consumer reporting industry is to serve as an objective third-party provider of information to the companies and consumers involved in credit transactions. Our members are libraries that make it possible for credit grantors to provide consumers with the opportunities they seek" (Kurth, 1991). Ultimately, this general statement may be the key to judging the accuracy of files. The question of how well the reporting system is performing turns on the issue of whether credit files contain sufficient information to allow creditors and other authorized users to assess the eligibility of consumers for the services they seek.

Files can contain factual errors (for example, misspelled name; incorrect old address; misspelled current street, and so on), but still be accurate representations of a consumer's credit history. Conversely, files can be factually correct but not provide an accurate representation of a consumer's credit history because of missing accounts, accounts listed as open but that are long inactive, or old derogatory information that has been rolled off the file. And files may—in fact, almost always—contain stale or outdated information (for example, outstanding balances that are thirty to sixty days old, and so on). Most stale information was accurate at the time it was submitted, but with continued activity on an account (charge activity, payments), the information can become outdated very quickly.

Further reflection suggests that the degree of accuracy of a credit file is entirely dependent on the purpose to which the information will be put. All the information in a file may be factually correct, but the file might be missing key pieces of information about a consumer's past or current credit experience that are important for predicting the consumer's future behavior, rendering the file of little value. Arguably, for millions of consumers in the United States, conventional credit files are missing entire categories of relevant information, such as a history of rent or utility payments. For these people, the files are not accurate representations of the existing information that is helpful for predicting future payment risk.

Complicating the goal of achieving a higher degree of accuracy in credit files are reasons that we may want to and often do compromise accuracy in the files. Our legal and regulatory system has intentionally limited the reporting of old derogatory information as part of a consumer's credit profile. Specifically, old derogatory information (for example, delinquencies, charge-offs, repossessions, collection activity) cannot be reported after seven years (ten years for personal bankruptcy). So some degree of inaccuracy is mandatory under the FCRA.

So it seems that the accuracy of a given credit file is partly dependent on each of the following: what is in the file; what is missing from the file; and the use to which the information will be put. Credit file "quality" may be a better term for assessing how well the FCRA performs in facilitating opportunities for consumers, where quality refers to the predictive value of information contained in the file. The significance of these distinctions will become apparent in the following sections, which examine how the FCRA is structured to promote accuracy, and assess the law's effectiveness.

FCRA and Production of Accurate Credit Files

To understand how the regulatory approach adopted in the FCRA promotes the assembly of credit files that are both accurate and relevant within a voluntary reporting system, it is helpful to think of credit reporting as a problem of information production. For example, in the context of loan decisions, creditors (and consequently credit bureaus) wish to acquire better information about borrowers so long as the extra value (from better risk assessment) exceeds the extra cost.

Constraints that affect any system for producing credit history information (voluntary or compulsory) include the following:

Accuracy is costly. That is, the cost of producing a credit file rises with the level of accuracy (for example, factual accuracy of contents; frequency of data updates; completeness of the consumer's current credit usage profile; depth of historical detail; inclusion of all relevant information useful for assessing credit risk).

The consumer is in the best position to know when a credit file is accurate and complete, across all trade lines. But, the consumer also has an incentive to portray his or her credit history more favorably in order to obtain credit (the problem of moral hazard). So, creditors must verify the credit history from an independent source.

By specializing in central storage of credit histories, a credit bureau can produce accurate reports at lower cost than individual lenders. A centralized data warehouse is less expensive to operate compared to a system in which each potential creditor contacts other creditors with each new application, duplicating each other's storage efforts. Bulk transmittal to a bureau of one month's credit experience for all its accounts is cheaper for a creditor than making and responding to multiple calls on behalf of its customers who are making applications elsewhere.

The market will reward the production of accurate files. A credit bureau's customers will pay more for accurate reports (or buy them more frequently), and pay less as accuracy declines. Self-interest on the part of wealth maximizing credit bureaus in a competitive reporting environment creates a powerful force for improving the quality of files.[8]

An important problem hinders the construction of accurate credit histories under any system. Neither the credit bureau nor the purchaser of a credit report (the credit grantor) can easily judge the accuracy of a consumer's credit file. The creditor only knows its own experience with a customer. The bureau only knows what creditors tell it. Mistakes can be made by either party in data transmittal and file assembly. The consumer knows his or her complete credit history, but has some incentive to misrepresent it out of self-interest.

Given the extensive, voluntary reporting system that had already evolved in the United States in the absence of federal regulation, two fundamentally different regulatory avenues were available for incorporating into the FCRA, the preventive approach and remedial approach. By taking the preventive approach, Congress could have authorized specific and mandatory procedures (either directly within the language of the FCRA or indirectly by granting rule-writing authority to a federal agency such as the FTC) for submitting, verifying, matching, and reinvestigating information on the credit files. In essence, the regulators would stipulate how to run the credit reporting process. Alternatively, the FCRA adopted a remedial approach, which harnessed the incentives for producing accurate reports inherent in a competitive credit reporting market, but also established an error detection and correction mechanism initiated by the consumer. Consumers would be permitted (and encouraged) to monitor their own files, and to dispute items perceived to be incorrect.

The preventive and remedial approaches differ in their impact on the costs of producing accurate credit files. Arguably, the FCRA incorporates the least costly means of using the comparative advantage in the production process of each of the system's participants to improve the accuracy of the end product.

An analogy to other industries illustrates the difference. Manufacturers of complex consumer goods such as automobiles, computers, and electronic equipment face similar quality control problems. For these items, it is expensive for both producers and consumers to detect all errors or defects before purchase. Many potential defects are either so easy to spot or have such serious implications for the end user (and the manufacturer's brand reputation) that the manufacturer invests in processes to detect them before the item is sold. But, with complex goods, some defects will remain. Of course, the customer who purchases and uses a new computer will inspect it on an ongoing basis after the sale.

---

8. Competitive market forces give the bureaus an incentive to improve the quality of information that is predictive of risk. This gives focus to their efforts and affects the resulting content of the file. So, for example, bureaus will not devote effort to update information contained in credit files that creditors once found helpful but no longer utilize (for instance, place of employment). The quality of the file for assessing borrower risk does not suffer, even as some of the information contained in the file becomes outdated.

So, instead of going to the expense of inspecting the computer for all defects twice (once by the producer on the assembly line and once by the consumer as it is used), computer manufacturers shift some of the inspection duties onto the consumer, and promise to repair or replace defective products. The product warranty effectively designates the consumer as a quality-control inspector. Consequently, the manufacturer incurs lower costs of production (relative to more rigorous inspection on the assembly line), the product price is lower, customers incur lower search costs before purchase since they have the assurance that they can return defective merchandise, and everyone enjoys greater gains from trade.[9]

The remedial approach taken by the FCRA resembles the extension of a product warranty (although for credit reports the law mandates the warranty). As noted above, the consumer is the only person who knows the true credit history that the credit file attempts to describe. Essentially, the FCRA designates the consumer as the quality-control inspector with the authority to mandate reinvestigation (and alert potential purchasers) of credit information when errors are detected. By doing so, it places the responsibility for monitoring file accuracy on the party who can determine accuracy at the lowest cost.[10]

It would be incorrect to conclude that the FCRA's remedial approach leaves the credit bureau with no incentive to prevent errors. Although there is no explicit dollar fine imposed when a consumer detects an error, the mandatory reverification process is costly for both bureaus and creditors.[11] Like the automaker that must reimburse dealers for warranty work to repair defective

9. For a more detailed discussion of how the transaction costs associated with measuring quality influence the organization of markets, see Barzel (1982).

10. It is clear from thirty years of commentary on the FCRA that the FTC recognizes the important role and responsibility that consumers play in facilitating the system's production of accurate credit reports. For example, see Noonan (1991).

11. All parties share in the costs of preventing and detecting reporting errors. The remedial approach imposes some additional costs on the consumer as well, most notably in the event that an erroneous credit report leads to rejection for credit, insurance, or employment. The FCRA, as amended in 2003, gives consumers the opportunity to avoid the higher cost of rejection by obtaining one free copy of their credit report each year and purchasing additional copies of their credit report, at any time, as a preventive measure. The 1996 FCRA amendments placed a ceiling of $8 on the price bureaus could charge consumers for a copy of their credit report. Responding to swelling consumer interest in detecting fraud and preserving the integrity of their credit files, by 2002 all three of the major U.S. repositories (Equifax, Experian, and TransUnion) had begun offering services to consumers who wish to monitor their credit files on a regular basis. Consumers who place a lower value on the content of the file (perhaps because they do not anticipate a transaction that would require a credit report) can choose not to incur the cost of checking their file. For all consumers, the FCRA mandates a "quality alert" notice in the form of an adverse-action notice sent to consumers whenever information in the credit report has contributed to a negative decision on an application for credit, insurance, apartment rental, or other credit-related products. This provides additional impetus to check the file. The FCRA also explicitly recognizes that some types of errors may be more costly to the consumer than others. For example, while the FCRA applies a strictly remedial approach to reports used for credit or insurance applications, it incorporates a

vehicles, both creditors and the bureaus would like to reduce the costs they will be required to incur if a consumer finds an error. They will invest in reporting and updating procedures that eliminate most errors. Bureaus have an additional, powerful incentive to invest in procedures that eliminate problems in matching new information to files: the creditors are their customers and they pay for accuracy. A bureau with a reputation for file errors will suffer lost sales in a competitive market for credit reports as creditors shift their business to vendors that establish a reputation for greater reliability.

However, notwithstanding the oft-repeated goal of error-free reports, the reality of matching over 2 billion trade line updates, 2 million public record items, and an average of 1.2 million changes of household address, from 30,000 different furnishers, to the proper consumer files each month is that the resulting files will still contain some errors, although the bureau will not know their location.[12] At some achieved degree of accuracy, it becomes cheaper to correct the error the consumer finds, rather than adopt procedures that would scrutinize every item in every file in an attempt to detect potential errors prior to release. By assigning consumers the legal role of quality inspector, the FCRA reinforces the financial incentive for bureaus to invest in accurate reporting and prevent those errors for which it has a comparative advantage. But for the law to require bureaus to eliminate those errors entirely—that is, to rely exclusively on the preventive approach—would make the system substantially more expensive to maintain and operate, with negative implications for the price and availability of credit and related products. The FCRA's reliance on the remedial approach instead of the more expensive preventive approach is yet another example of the careful balance struck in the statute in the interest of expanding consumer credit opportunities.

Efforts to Measure How Effectively the FCRA Promotes File Quality

As noted above, credit file errors have concerned policymakers and consumers for the past thirty years. Yet, reliable measures of credit file accuracy are surprisingly scarce. Simple barometers of the performance of the credit reporting system can be misleading. For example, the number of complaints received by the FTC involving consumer reporting agencies (that is, credit bureaus) grew from 1,300 in 1997 to nearly 12,000 in 2002 (GAO, 2003, pp. 15–16). However,

---

more preventive approach if a report is requested by a potential employer. If a report for delivery to an employer has any (negative) public record items, the FCRA requires the credit bureau to notify the consumer that such information is being reported, or to take extra steps to ensure the accuracy of the information before reporting it.

12. Consumer Data Industry Association, letter to the National Center for State Courts, April 18, 2002, on file with the authors.

the FTC has stated that it could not determine how many complaints involved alleged errors in reports (versus other issues such as CRA conduct). And, the FTC staff has cautioned that it should not be inferred that an increased volume of complaints indicates a rise in errors, since the former could be due to greater consumer awareness of the FTC's role with respect to credit reporting and rising general awareness of the existence and importance of credit reporting and scoring.

At the request of Congress, the GAO undertook a review during 2003 of available studies and databases to determine the frequency, type, and cause of credit report errors. It concluded that "the lack of comprehensive information regarding the accuracy of consumer credit reports inhibits any meaningful discussion of what more could or should be done to improve credit report accuracy. Available studies suggest that accuracy could be a problem, but no study has been performed that is representative of the universe of credit reports" (GAO, 2003, p. 17). After reviewing the available evidence, we agree.

Inaccuracies can turn up in credit files in many ways. At the risk of oversimplifying, consider two categories of file inaccuracies or errors. Errors of commission consist of items or events included in the file that should not be there (for example, accounts and public record items that do not belong to the borrower, or delinquencies that never occurred). For most consumers, errors in credit reports probably connote an image of errors of commission. This is especially true for victims of mismatched files, or identity theft. In contrast, errors of omission are items or events associated with the consumer that do not appear in the file, for instance, existing but unreported accounts, missing balances or credit limits, and records of prior payment history on accounts, both positive and negative. Both types of errors reduce file accuracy, and may or may not reduce a file's quality in terms of its value for assessing risk.

Most of the limited evidence available on credit file accuracy that is statistically representative consists of studies of file inconsistencies. Such studies pose fewer obstacles for researchers because they do not require the consumer's participation. It is much easier to identify information in a single credit file that is either missing or inconsistent with other information in the file, or is inconsistent with a credit file on the same consumer from another bureau, than it is to determine whether a specific item in the file is correct. A review of available data from both types of studies follows.

Federal Reserve Board—Findings

A 2003 report from the research staff at the Federal Reserve Board examined a large, nationally representative random sample of individual credit reports supplied by one of the three major credit repositories (Avery, Calem, and Canner, 2003). The study's purpose was to assess the suitability of credit bureau data as a source of detailed and timely information, at the regional or national level, on consumer debt status, loan payment behavior, and overall credit quality. Specifically, the researchers examined the detailed (anonymous) credit files for a nationally representative sample of 248,000 consumers as of June 1999. Each record contained approximately 350 variables that described credit usage and performance. In total, the sample contained information on 2.58 million accounts, from more than 23,000 furnishers of information. The authors note that the sample is somewhat dated, so that the findings may not reflect current circumstances.

This type of analysis generally cannot identify whether any particular item in a file is erroneous, such as a delinquency appearing on an account that does not belong to the borrower. However, it is quite effective in identifying patterns of missing data and inconsistencies in the files.

The authors concluded that "although credit reporting company data are extensive, they are not complete. First, information on some credit accounts held by individuals is not reported. Some small retail, mortgage, and finance companies and some government agencies do not report to the credit reporting companies. Loans extended by individuals, employers, insurance companies, and foreign entities typically are not reported. Second, complete information is not always provided for each account reported. Sometimes creditors do not report or update information on the credit accounts of borrowers who consistently make their required payments as scheduled. Credit limits established on revolving accounts are sometimes not reported. Creditors may not notify the credit reporting company when an account is closed or undergoes other material changes" (Avery, Calem, and Canner, 2003, p. 50).[13] They also noted that credit report information is perishable—some pieces of information (for instance, outstanding balance on revolving credit card accounts) become outdated the day after the information is sent to the credit bureau. All of these issues make credit files merely an approximation of the borrower's credit profile. Avery, Calem, and Canner (2003) note issues of particular concern, which are discussed below.

MISSING CREDIT LIMITS. About one-third of the open revolving accounts in the sample were missing information on the account's credit limit. Consequently, about 70 percent of all consumers in the sample had a missing credit limit on one or more of their revolving accounts. Missing credit limits are a con-

13. We note here that although U.S. credit reports do not always reflect all past and current credit obligations for consumers, the United States is a world leader in the reporting of accounts that are not delinquent. Failure to report so-called positive credit information (that is, accounts in good standing, or accounts that were paid as agreed and closed) is the norm overseas. Indeed, several jurisdictions (for instance, France, Australia, Hong Kong) prohibit the reporting of positive credit information in the name of protecting consumer privacy. Research has demonstrated that positive information significantly improves the predictive power of risk scoring models, effectively giving the borrower an opportunity to demonstrate responsible payment behavior, and giving lenders a means of estimating the borrower's total debt usage. For more details see Barron and Staten (2003).

cern because the credit limit on a revolving account is used to calculate revolving account utilization (how much of an available credit line the consumer has utilized), which is an important determinant of overall credit score. A higher utilization rate correlates to higher risk. On accounts missing the credit limit, creditors will typically substitute the highest previous balance (if available) in place of the actual account limit. This typically will overstate utilization and, therefore, overstate risk.

Further analysis showed that the missing limits were mostly attributable to a small group of creditors (12 percent of all creditors accounted for 74 percent of all missing limits) who reported limits on fewer than 5 percent of their accounts (that is, they were apparently routine nonreporters of limits). The authors also found that, for the most part, the nonreporting of limits affected prime and subprime consumers equally. There was no strong evidence of discriminatory underreporting on subprime accounts (to shield them from competition). However, there was a small group of creditors (5 percent of all creditors in the analysis), all of whom specialized in subprime lending (more than 50 percent of their accounts), who reported credit limits more selectively, reporting 77 percent of limits for prime customers versus 40 percent for subprime customers. Avery, Calem, and Canner (2003) note that their findings on missing limits are especially sensitive to the period in which the sample was drawn (June 1999). In the late 1990s several large credit card issuers had stopped reporting account limits for competitive reasons.[14] Pressure from credit bureaus and the banking regulators substantially reduced the problem, so that by 2003, industry officials were reporting that credit limits were missing on only about 13 percent of accounts (Avery, Calem, and Canner, 2003, p. 73).

BALANCE INFORMATION SIGNIFICANTLY OUT OF DATE. One of the useful dimensions of a comprehensive credit report is that it allows calculation of a borrower's total outstanding debt. This requires accurate and up-to-date information on outstanding balances. Three-quarters of all accounts in the sample reported balances without ambiguities, that is, the accounts were listed as open and updated within two months of the sampling date, or the account was reported as closed and had a zero balance at time of last reporting. An additional 18 percent of accounts were dormant, that is, last reported more than two months earlier and showing no outstanding balance. Consequently, creditors could determine balance unambiguously on 92 percent of accounts. However, 8 percent of all accounts showed positive balances but had no recent reporting of activity (last report was more than two months prior to sample date). And, these balances accounted for more than 25 percent of total balance dollars (many of these were

14. Lisa Fickenscher, "Credit Bureaus Move against Lenders That Withhold Info," *American Banker*, December 30, 1999, p. 1; Heather Timmons, "Putting Borrowers in a Bind: Fearful of Competition, Lenders Won't Divulge Credit Records," *BusinessWeek*, March 20, 2000, p. 110.

mortgages). In addition, nearly 60 percent of all accounts that indicated a major derogatory item at last reporting were among these 8 percent of accounts for which the actual balance was questionable. The analysis by Avery, Calem, and Canner (2003) indicates that many of the nonderogatory accounts (especially mortgages and installment loans) in this group were likely closed or sold to other companies, but were not reported as such. Recognizing this problem, the credit repositories have developed stale account rules that will reset balances to zero and mark an account closed under certain conditions. However, accounts with a major derogatory and an outstanding balance listed as the last reported status can have a significant negative impact on consumers applying for credit.

NEGATIVE-ONLY REPORTING. About 1-2 percent of all accounts were reported by creditors who only report negative information. These creditors do not report accounts in good standing. This is common in many other countries, and remarkably low, by comparison, in the United States. Negative-only reporting poses two problems: 1) because some consumer accounts and balances are not reported, it masks overindebtedness problems that may develop into payment problems, leading to erroneously positive risk assessment for some borrowers, and 2) some consumers miss out on the positive effects on creditworthiness of well-handled accounts, because their accounts in good standing are not reported.

NONREPORTING OF MINOR DELINQUENCY. About 11 percent of all accounts are reported by creditors who do not report delinquencies of less than 120 days. An additional 12 percent of all accounts were reported by creditors that do not report delinquencies of less than sixty days. In other words, there is a significant amount of underreporting of delinquency in the system, even though data on payment problems have been shown to be the most predictive factor in scoring models.[15] As a consequence, the credit scores of many borrowers are higher (better) than they would otherwise be.

INCONSISTENT REPORTING OF PUBLIC RECORDS, COLLECTION AGENCY ACCOUNTS, AND INQUIRIES. For consumers with derogatory public record information or collection agency activity in their files, about 40 percent have more than one such record. Analysis suggests that for many of these consumers, the multiple listings are associated with the same episode (for example, one record posted when collection action initiated, another record posted when account paid.) To the extent the creditor risk assessment tools count these flags as separate incidents when they are actually not, it could erroneously penalize consumers. But, there were no codes in the data to allow a creditor to distinguish multiple

---

15. For more detail on the relative weighting of credit report variables in determining a borrower's credit score, and the potential impact of scores on loan interest rates, see the Fair Isaac and Company website at www.myfico.com.

events associated with the same incident from multiple incidents. The same was generally true of multiple inquiries in a credit file: creditors failed to provide the appropriate code for their inquiry in 98 percent of the inquiry records. Consequently, a creditor examining multiple inquiries in a credit file would not be able to determine if multiple inquiries reflected shopping around for the best loan to finance a single purchase, or applications for multiple loans. The first interpretation would have much less impact on risk assessment than the second.

Discussion

The problems identified in the FRB report involve credit file information that is missing, clearly outdated, or ambiguous. Systematic correction of the data shortcomings in each of these categories (if it were feasible) would unambiguously improve the performance of risk models by providing a more accurate picture of each borrower's credit profile. Interestingly, the authors note that the resulting improvement in clarity would not unambiguously help consumers. It would help some consumers and harm others. For example, some consumers with unreported accounts in good standing are harmed by not getting credit for building a good credit record. Others are helped because creditors do not see the full extent of their indebtedness. Similarly, more complete reporting of revolving account limits helps those whose balances are well below limits and harms those with balances at or near the limits.

Most of these problems stem from nonreporting in a voluntary reporting system, or from the failure of data furnishers to use available codes to clarify the information being reported. Avery, Calem, and Canner (2003) suggest that creditors and the credit repositories could jointly develop better codes and reporting protocols for public records and inquiries and encourage their use. The repositories could also expand and refine their stale account rules and flag the accounts from creditors that are no longer reporting information. These steps would clean up some of the ambiguities in the data. In the meantime, most of these problems are well known to creditors and require them to modify the models and rules they use to make decisions.[16]

Consumers could eliminate many of these problems by taking a more active role in reviewing their files. But, vigilant consumers will not correct all of the problems. The authors observe that if consumers did take a more active role, they would introduce their own bias into the error correction process, stemming from their own self-interest. That is, those consumers who find problems in

16. For example, mortgage lenders now commonly require a consolidated credit report on borrowers that merges information from all three of the major repositories. This reduces the risk posed by data missing from a single repository's file. Regarding ambiguous creditor inquiries, Fair Isaac has indicated that it modified its FICO risk scoring algorithm to recognize multiple inquiries from the same type of lender within a short time period as related to a single transaction (for instance, multiple inquiries from auto dealers or auto finance companies.)

their files for which correction will help them will likely report them. Those for whom corrections would harm them likely will not. Missing information, ambiguous information, and outright incorrect data would remain in files whenever resolution would identify the consumer as higher risk.

Consumer Federation of America Study—Findings

A second recent study was sponsored by the Consumer Federation of America (2002) (CFA) and jointly conducted with the National Credit Reporting Association. The CFA report resembles the Federal Reserve Study in that it identifies and tabulates discrepancies and inconsistencies in credit reports, but it adds a new dimension by comparing reports for each consumer across all three repositories. The study focuses on the magnitude of differences in consumer credit scores across repository files. Given the pervasive use of credit scoring across all segments of the consumer loan industry, including mortgage lending, large differences in scores based on variance in file content can have serious implications for consumers. Of course, the problem stems from the variance in content of the underlying credit files and not the scoring models *per se*. Differences in content across files have always existed to some degree, and mortgage decisions in the days before scoring had to take them into account just as they do now. Nevertheless, critics of automated underwriting in mortgage lending worry that the acceleration of the underwriting process that credit scoring has made possible may be causing some lenders to give short shrift to investigation of differences in credit scores for an applicant, especially in regard to the pricing of the loan.

To determine the frequency with which file discrepancies across the repositories generated relatively large differences in credit scores, the CFA report undertook a manual review of a sample of 1,704 combined credit files for consumers who had applied for mortgages during June 2002. The sample was drawn from the archives of three credit reporting agencies (not the three major credit repositories) that collectively served consumers in twenty-two states. The combined files (which consolidate separate credit reports from each of the three major repositories) had been requested by mortgage lenders, along with calculated FICO risk scores from each repository, in conjunction with mortgage applications.[17] The CFA study also conducted a more intensive review of a 10 percent random sample of the combined credit files supplied by one of the participating agencies (a total of fifty-one files). As was the case with the FRB study, the CFA approach cannot identify whether information is correct or incorrect. It can identify inconsistencies and missing data. The CFA sample is not a representa-

17. A FICO credit score is a widely used statistical risk-scoring product sold by Fair Isaac. In drawing the sample, the report states that the participating agencies took "consecutive archived files dating from June 17 to June 20, 2002" (CFA Report, 2002, p. 15). One agency that served multiple time zones selected every second file generated over the four-day period to ensure representation of consumers across all regions.

tive national sample of all borrowers, but for this sample of mortgage applicants it provides intriguing information on the differences in file content across the major repositories. The results included the following:

SCORE DIFFERENCES. Twenty-nine percent of consumers had a range of 50 points or more between their highest and lowest FICO scores. Five percent of consumers had a range in excess of 100 points.

FRAGMENTED AND MISMATCHED FILES. About 10 percent of borrowers had multiple files returned from a single repository. Some were attributable to credit accounts under the applicant's nickname that had not been matched with the applicant's other file. Others had a transposed Social Security number but had sufficient other information in common to determine it was the same person. Still others appeared to represent different people, with no common credit experience between them.

TYPES AND FREQUENCY OF INCONSISTENCIES. The in-depth review of fifty-one combined files quantified the inconsistencies that undoubtedly led to the variance in FICO scores. The report divided these into two categories, errors of omission and errors of commission:

The term *errors of omission* includes:

—One-third of combined files had a mortgage reported by one repository but not all.

—Two-thirds of files had an installment loan reported by one repository but not all.

—Seventy-eight percent had a revolving account reported by one repository but not all.

—Negative information was missing less often than positive information. This is not surprising, given the worldwide tendency of data furnishers to report negative information more readily than positive information. For example, 12 percent of combined files had a revolving account with late payments reported by one repository but not all. Eight percent had a revolving account with a charge-off reported by one repository but not all. Twenty percent of files had a medical account collection reported by one depository but not all. Twenty-five percent of files had some kind of collection omitted by one or more repositories.

These findings serve as a reminder of the voluntary nature of the credit reporting system in the United States. They also highlight the fact that the credit histories for most adults today (certainly all those over the age of forty who have been active in credit markets for the majority of their adult lives) still reflect the regional roots of the reporting industry. All credit bureaus evolved from local operations. The companies that eventually became the three major repositories had recognized regional strengths and weaknesses as recently as a decade ago, when even medium-size banks, retailers, mortgage companies, and other creditors would deal with one, but not all, of the repositories. Some of that reporting heritage remains in the credit files of older adults. Moreover, the lack of universal reporting persists today for many public record items, including collections associated with local doctors, hospitals, and other businesses that extend credit. The fact that such differences exist explains why mortgage lenders want combined reports from all three repositories, in order to catch missing information. In all likelihood, these differences will slowly fade over time as younger consumers obtain credit in an increasingly national market and the repositories devote resources to capturing public record items in all localities.

The term *errors of commission* was used in the CFA report when the repositories reported conflicting information on the same account. For example,

—43 percent of combined files had conflicting information across repositories about the number of times an account was thirty-plus days late. However, the authors do not report how many of these could be differences of only one instance, which could result from a delinquency in the most recent period that is reflected in one depository but not yet in another due to different reporting/loading timelines. The report mentions that this may have occurred in some instances, and notes that it also occurs on reports of older delinquencies, but does not provide details as to how often.[18]

—23 percent of files had conflicting information on the number of times an account had gone to ninety days late.[19]

—Account balances had inconsistencies on 82.4 percent of combined files. Inconsistencies on reported limits occurred in 96 percent of files. The authors of the CFA study admit that their view of credit limits is restricted by the software that was employed to review the reports, which lumps credit limit and high credit into one field.

Discussion

The CFA findings echo the central results from the FRB study: information about various elements of a consumer's credit experience is frequently missing from credit files, a fact that becomes even more apparent when credit file content is examined and compared across three repositories instead of just one. Notwithstanding the claim regarding errors of commission, the CFA study is unable to quantify how often reported information is erroneous.

---

18. Fair Isaac responded by noting that it recognizes the potential for differences in the number of reported delinquencies on the same account, so it does not include this in its models. It does include the number of different accounts on which the consumer has been delinquent. See St. John (2003).

19. This rate seems extraordinarily high, given that the nationally representative FRB study found that 85 percent of all accounts had no record of late payment at any time, and that only 8.7 percent of all accounts had ever experienced a delinquency of ninety or more days. It is all the more striking since the sample consists of mortgage applicants, who would tend to have better credit histories, on average, than the population of all borrowers. This may signal a problem with the sample.

The CFA report begins with an implicit assumption that a consumer's credit report should look the same across all three repositories, and expresses alarm over the degree of inconsistency, and the resulting large variance in credit scores for some consumers. We would expect some inconsistencies, however, given the voluntary nature of reporting in the United States and the participation of 30,000 furnishers of information, many of whom report to only one or two repositories. Add to that the logistical differences in timing across the three repositories as to when information is received and posted to a file. The CFA report admits that some unknown number of the errors of commission likely reflect differences in timing of the updates posted at the repositories. Consequently, any assessment that tabulates errors based on finding inconsistencies across reports from the three repositories (as the CFA report does) will find plenty of supporting evidence.

Because of differences in file content across bureaus, a single consumer's credit score will differ depending upon which bureau file is used. Creditors have long known that the depth of credit files differed across the repositories, depending upon the geographic location of the consumer, and have adjusted their decisions to purchase credit reports accordingly. Of course, these potential differences are the primary reason why mortgage underwriting typically requires a consolidated report based on reports from all three repositories. Other types of lenders (credit card, auto) may still use only one or two reports, but may select the repository believed to have more comprehensive files in the geographic region where the consumer resides.

Perhaps the most interesting insight from the CFA study is the frequency of multiple (but different) files returned for a given consumer. This cuts to the heart of the repositories' biggest challenge: matching billions of pieces of incoming data (per month) to the correct file in order to create a comprehensive picture of a consumer's credit history. Obstacles abound. Application information sent with the initial account opening may contain variations of a consumer's name, and contain small but potentially vexing inconsistencies in the address.[20] Some will occasionally have errors in the applicant's Social Security number. Forty-two million Americans move each year and information with new addresses has to get properly matched to the preexisting file.

The repositories developed matching algorithms to handle these problems. A multiple or fragmented file was created when a repository could not achieve a

---

20. Jane Smith's name may be recorded in a variety of different ways on different accounts depending upon what she used at the time the account was opened (for instance, J. Smith, J. Q. Smith, Jane Q. Smith). Jane may have changed her name when she was married. She may have listed the same address on all of the accounts, but with slight differences (for instance, "123 Main," "123 Main Ave." "123 S. Main Ave." "123 Main, Apt. B"). If Jane is one of 6 million Americans who own vacation homes, she may have opened an account once on vacation and used the vacation home address.

reliable match. Rather than discard new data (error of omission), or add it to an existing file without a reliable match (error of commission), the repository would open a new file with the new data. The fragmented file problem eventually led to consumer alarm about the accuracy of credit reports and a series of congressional hearings to deal with accuracy issue beginning in the late 1980s.[21] However, the repositories' primary customers, the major national credit grantors, were already applying market pressure for better solutions. Beginning in the late 1980s, the repositories' degree of success in solving these problems became an important source of competitive advantage as they competed for commercial customers.

Fragmented files created an acute operational problem for creditors when many credit card issuers began relying heavily on prescreened solicitations in their national marketing campaigns to obtain new cardholders.[22] After observing higher-than-expected delinquencies on new cardholders obtained through prescreened offers, creditors discovered that some of the credit reports used to generate the prescreened lists were incomplete. In these partial (or fragmented) files, a customer's credit history was split between two or more separate files. Consequently, neither file on the consumer reflected a full credit history. One file might pass a prescreen test, despite the presence of negative information in a separate file elsewhere in the database.

To counter higher than expected delinquencies among new cardholders, many national credit grantors began postscreening the applications received from the prescreened customers. That is, a full credit report was routinely purchased after receipt of the application to determine if the customer were indeed creditworthy. Because the application typically contained the cardholder's Social Security number and other identifying information, the various fragmented files were usually linked in response to the creditor's request. Having to postscreen raised the issuer's cost of acquiring new accounts. The value of an accurate prescreen rose further, as did the market pressure on the repositories to reduce fragmented files, when the FTC sharply limited postscreening in 1991.[23]

The credit reporting industry began adopting and expanding a series of procedures to improve the accuracy of files, including 1) development of new algorithms to improve file matching, 2) creation of a standardized reporting format to be used by creditors when supplying data to the bureaus, and 3) voluntary cooperation among the three major repositories to share information on correc-

21. See *Oversight Hearing on the Fair Credit Reporting Act*, hearings before the Subcommittee on Consumer Affairs and Coinage of the Committee on Banking, Finance, and Urban Affairs, U.S. House of Representatives, September 13, 1989.

22. In preparing a prescreened card offer, a creditor asks a credit bureau to provide a screened listing of candidates for credit offers who meet the creditor's specific standards for acceptable risk. Consumers that pass the screening test receive direct mail or telephone solicitations that invite them to apply for a preapproved card.

23. For more on creditor frustration with the fragmented file problem, see Daly (1991).

tions.[24] By 1996, more than 95 percent of all data reported to bureaus was received in the standardized "Metro" format.[25] By 2003, over 99 percent of the total volume of 2 billion records reported per month were received in Metro 1 or Metro 2 format (GAO, 2003, pp. 12–13). However, given the CFA's finding that multiple files were returned on 10 percent of consumers in their sample, a problem with fragmented files still remains, despite the repositories' efforts.[26]

Actual Disputes as a Proxy for Errors of Commission—Findings

As the GAO report noted, statistically representative studies that quantify the frequency of errors of commission (that is, the inclusion of items in a credit file that do not belong to the consumer) are rare. In large part this is because they require 1) a sample of consumers representative of some larger population, 2) their cooperation in examining credit reports for discrepancies, 3) reinvestigation of alleged discrepancies to determine whether the items needed correction, and 4) the involvement of an independent arbiter to determine which of the corrected discrepancies are relevant to the credit-granting decision.

To our knowledge, no study has been conducted that incorporates all of the attributes listed above.[27] We are aware of only one study that approximates these conditions. In 1991 the credit reporting industry trade association, Associated Credit Bureaus (now known as Consumer Data Industry Association, or CDIA), commissioned Arthur Andersen and Company to conduct a Credit

24. For an extended discussion of nonlegislative, self-regulatory measures that had been implemented or were being discussed by the industry in 1991, see Spurgin (1991).

25. "Both the original (Metro) and the new Metro 2 formats are maintained by an industry committee of volunteers from each of the national credit reporting systems. This group meets on a regular basis to develop industrywide responses to questions from data furnishers and create new codes or fields as necessary" Pratt (2003, p. 17).

26. Keep in mind that these multiple files may be the legacy of less-efficient matching routines in the past. Even if matching algorithms today have significantly reduced the creation of new instances of fragmented files, some old fragments remain in the system. The only additional empirical evidence we have found on this point is that the frequency of multiple files in the CFA study was somewhat lower than what was reported in a study conducted by Visa U.S.A. of fragmented files based on 1995 data. That study examined the credit files of applicants who had been selected for credit card solicitations based on a prescreening process with the repositories and who had subsequently applied for the card. The study found that multiple files were returned on 9-14 percent of the applicants. See Visa USA (1997).

27. Two widely publicized studies conducted during the late 1990s by USPIRG (1998) and Consumers Union (2000) sought to identify the frequency of errors of commission. However, their samples were not representative (they sampled organization employees who verified the accuracy of the information in their own files). Moreover, the GAO noted that the studies counted any inaccuracy as an error, regardless of its potential impact, used varying definitions in identifying errors, occasionally provided obscure explanations of how they carried out their work, and did not consult with industry representatives for guidance or clarification on interpreting the data. See GAO (2003, p. 9).

Report Reliability Study.[28] Rather than selecting a representative sample of all consumers and asking them to review their credit files, the Andersen study focused on a random sample of 15,703 consumers who had applied for and been denied credit during a sixty-day period in 1991. As required under FCRA, each of these consumers had received adverse action notices alerting them that they had been turned down based on information in their credit report and that they could request and review their credit report free of charge.

The Andersen study tracked the number of consumers who responded, and subsequently disputed information on the report. It found that 1,223 (7.7 percent) consumers requested a copy of their credit file. Of these consumers, 304 (2.5 percent) disputed information in the file. Reinvestigation was conducted as required by FCRA and the creditors were asked to reevaluate the original application based on the outcome of the reinvestigation. By the time the study was published, reinvestigation had been completed on 267 of the 304 cases, yielding thirty-six cases in which the original decision to deny credit was reversed based on the new information. Andersen concluded that "of all those consumers (1,223) who requested to review their file, the results of the study indicated that less than 3 percent of these consumers for which this study has been completed would have achieved a different credit decision than was originally rendered by the credit grantor after initial review of the information contained in the credit report."[29]

Further reflection indicates that 3 percent is likely an upper bound on the rate at which file errors caused an adverse credit decision, and that the actual percentage could be substantially lower. Only 7.7 percent of consumers who were denied credit bothered to request their credit report. There are at least two potential explanations for what appears to be a strikingly low incidence of follow-up to the denial. One explanation could be consumers' lack of awareness of credit reports, their importance in the credit-granting process, or that the reports could contain errors that would generate an adverse credit decision. Another explanation could be that many, if not most, customers turned down for credit were not surprised at the turndown because they were already aware of problems with their credit history that were likely reflected in their credit report. To whatever extent the latter statement characterizes a segment of the sample, it is clear that by focusing on consumers who respond to adverse action notices the study methodology was biased toward finding a higher error rate than that which characterized the entire population for two reasons: 1) those consumers who receive an adverse action notice are more likely to have data in their file that trigger a negative decision than those who do not receive notices, and 2) those consumers who requested their reports after a turndown were more likely

28. Arthur Andersen and Company, Credit Report Reliability Study (1992).
29. Arthur Andersen and Company (1992).

to turn up errors than those who did not.[30] It should also be noted that the Andersen study was conducted at a time when risk-based pricing was in its infancy (and virtually nonexistent for mortgages), so that a study focused on recipients of adverse action notices would come closer to identifying the proportion of all consumers who had been penalized by credit report errors than would be the case today.

The Andersen study was based on the reporting system of a dozen years ago. We simply do not know how such a study would turn out today, and none has been conducted since. Contemporary evidence on the quality of credit reports is suggestive, but indirect. For example, the CDIA presented some related statistics during its testimony at FCRA Senate hearings in the summer of 2003 (Pratt, 2003). As part of its fraud assistance services, CDIA members provide credit reports to consumers who request them because they suspect they may be at risk or have already become victims of identification theft and fraud. CDIA members provide approximately 100,000 credit reports a month for this purpose. On average, they receive 10,000 follow-up contacts from recipients per month on their toll-free numbers. These contacts do not necessarily equate to disputes as the consumer may simply be calling with questions on a number of issues. In other words, in this group of people who inspect their credit reports because they have prior reason to be concerned about fraudulent activity, no more than 10 percent ended up disputing any items in the report.

Additional information was supplied by one or more of CDIA's members in the form of summary statistics on credit reports delivered to subscribers to one of the "alert" services marketed by the repositories. As part of these services, consumers receive alert bulletins from the repository if their files indicate a certain triggering level of inquiry activity (indicating someone may have been applying for credit in their name) or had additional adverse information added to the file. On average, such fraud alerts resulted in about 180,000 credit files issued to subscribers a year over a two-year period. Subsequently, about 5 percent of consumers contacted the bureaus with a question or dispute. Apparently, the other 95 percent were not surprised by the information in their files.

The reporting industry estimates that approximately 16 million credit reports are issued to consumers a year. About 84 percent of these are free disclosures in response to consumers' requests following adverse action. Another 10 percent are provided in response to a fraud claim. Between 5 and 6 percent are sold to consumers who request them out of curiosity. Across all these issued reports,

---

30. To illustrate, if we made the extreme assumption that none of the reports contained errors that would have changed the credit decision for the 92.7 percent of consumers who did not request a credit report following their adverse action notice, then the incidence of erroneous credit decisions caused by credit report errors would fall to 0.2 percent, that is, two-tenths of 1 percent of all credit denials in the sample attributable to credit file errors. The true percentage likely falls somewhere between this figure and the Andersen study estimate.

Table 10-1. *Dispute Resolution Results, CDIA Members, 2003*

Type of result based on dispute submitted	Percentage
Information verified as reported	46
Data modified per data furnisher's instructions[a]	27
Data deleted per data furnisher's direction	10.5
Data deleted due to expiration of the thirty-day reinvestigation period and no response received from data furnisher[b]	16

Source: Pratt (2003).

a. Note that data may have been modified due to an update of information, rather than a dispute about accuracy of the data as of the date originally reported.

b. It cannot be determined whether the data were accurate as of the date reported.

about 50 percent of the recipients call the bureaus' toll-free numbers with a question or dispute. This is a substantially higher contact rate than was found in the Arthur Andersen study a decade earlier. It is not possible to determine from the reported data whether this is due to heightened consumer awareness of the importance of credit reports, a greater demand for accelerated updates of information contained in the file (perhaps as a consequence of greater reliance on credit scoring in the mortgage granting process), a higher incidence of disputable items, or a combination of these and other factors. Table 10-1 reports the CDIA's industrywide breakdown of results of the dispute resolution process.

CDIA emphasizes that many times disputes evolve over information that was accurate at the time it was reported. In these cases, consumers who dispute an item are actually seeking to update the item. For example, to complete the qualification process for a mortgage loan the consumer may be seeking to update the information sooner than the regular thirty-day reporting cycle in order to document lower balances, closed accounts, or delinquencies that have been resolved. In other cases, a consumer may dispute an account that is not recognized because it has been inactive for several years, or has been sold to a creditor whose name the consumer does not recognize (common with mortgage loans and retail credit card accounts). Consequently, in table 10-1, the items that result in changes to the file do not necessarily reflect instances in which the data were inaccurate at the time initially reported. And, to repeat a point made earlier, not every change to information in the file involves an item that would have a material impact on the consumer's creditworthiness or credit score.

Discussion

Errors of commission do occur in credit reports, but the available evidence does not support a firm conclusion as to the frequency in current files. Available information suggests that such errors do not occur any more frequently today than a decade ago, but the evidence is limited. A statistically valid study demonstrated that in 1991 less than 3 percent of loan application denials were the result of erroneous information contained in credit reports. More recently, over the past two years, we know that for two groups of consumers who had reasons (other than adverse action from creditors) to believe there might be problems with their credit reports, and were given an opportunity to review their reports, only 5-10 percent of them made a follow-up contact with the bureau with a question or dispute. Since not every callback involved a dispute, and not every disputed and corrected item would have affected a consumer's qualification for a loan, these percentages seem at least roughly consistent with the 1991 results.

We also know that, in comparison with 1991, a significantly higher proportion of consumers who received credit reports in 2002 (approximately 50 percent) contacted the credit bureau with questions or to dispute information in the report. Of course, the higher contact rate does not necessarily imply a higher frequency of identified problems. Indeed, to the extent that education efforts on the part of the FTC, consumer groups, and the industry have been successful in encouraging consumers to do their part in quality control, we should expect a higher rate for both credit report requests and callbacks.

For those consumers that called to dispute items, we know that 46 percent of all disputes in 2002 were resolved with no change to the credit file. But for the remaining 54 percent of disputes, we do not know the proportion that arose from information being posted to the credit file that was inaccurate at the time of posting. In 37 percent of all disputes, we know that a change was made to the file as a result of the consumer's intervention, but in two-thirds of these cases the furnisher instructed the bureau to modify the data in the file (as opposed to delete items), suggesting that the change may simply have been an update rather than the correction of an initial error. Clearly, consumer intervention is improving file quality. But it is not clear whether this is due to accelerated posting of information versus correction of erroneously posted items.

Another (and more disturbing) point is that 16 percent of all disputes resulted in data being deleted from the file due to expiration of the mandatory thirty-day reinvestigation period under the FCRA. CDIA has testified that a common tactic of so-called credit repair clinics is to flood the bureaus with disputes on multiple items in a consumer's file, in hopes of getting items deleted because the dispute resolution process becomes overloaded and exceeds the allowed thirty days.[31] On the other hand, it is possible that some of these disputes are cleaning up old accounts for which the original creditor no longer

31. "Note that credit repair can have a deleterious effect on the completeness of a consumer's credit report and, thus where third-party file comparisons identify absences of data between files, this is in part attributable to credit repair. One of our members testified that more than 30 percent of all consumer disputes were generated by credit repair agencies, which commonly dispute accurate, derogatory information with the sole intention of having that information deleted from the file." Testimony of Stuart Pratt (2003, p. 4). In 1996, Congress took steps to criminalize credit repair tactics with the enactment of the Credit Services Organization Act, P.L. 90-321, 82 Stat.164.

exists. The latter outcome is a positive development for file quality while the former outcome erodes file quality. The available data simply do not support an assessment of how often each is occurring.

Role of Consumers

Much of the FCRA's effectiveness hinges on consumer willingness to exercise the power to monitor their reports. Given the heightened consumer awareness of credit scoring (especially for mortgages), concerns over identity theft, and media focus on credit reporting, it seems likely that consumers would request their reports more often than was the case ten or fifteen years ago. In congressional hearings a decade ago, the credit reporting industry trade association (then known as Associated Credit Bureaus) testified that consumers in 1989 requested about 9 million credit reports a year (based on an underlying pool of approximately 150 million files on consumers). About 90 percent of these requests were free disclosures following adverse action taken on the basis of data in the report. The remaining 10 percent apparently stemmed from curiosity about the file. Bureaus received about 3 million requests (33 percent) for reverification a year.

By comparison, we saw above that as of 2002 about 16 million credit reports were issued to consumers annually (based on an underlying pool of approximately 200 million files on consumers). Of those reports, about 84 percent were free disclosures in response to consumer requests following adverse action, 10 percent were provided in response to a fraud claim, and between 5-6 percent were sold to consumers curious about their file. About 50 percent of report recipients contacted a bureau with a question or dispute.

Despite the increased public awareness of credit reports and scores, these numbers are strikingly similar. Between 1989 and 2002, the number of credit reports distributed to consumers, as a percent of total consumer credit files, rose only slightly from 6 to 8 percent.[32] But this seemingly low percentage of inspected files is somewhat misleading. Every application for credit creates an opportunity for detecting a serious error in the file. If the applicant was unexpectedly turned down, an error could well have been the culprit, and the mandatory adverse action notice would likely trigger a request from the consumer to see a report. The relatively small number of requests could simply be signaling that accepted applicants had feedback that there were no serious problems in their files, and that rejected applicants were well aware of their troubled payment history and did not need to see a credit report to confirm it. Thus the adverse action notice feature of the FCRA provides an ongoing monitoring and

---

32. Total requests for credit reports were spread across all three major repositories and some consumers undoubtedly requested reports from all three repositories. Consequently, the number of requests overstates to some degree the number of consumers who actually reviewed their files.

alert service, giving consumers a basic signal and the option to investigate further or not based on their own private information.

We expect that the number of reports requested by consumers will grow. There is ample evidence that a segment of the U.S. population is willing to pay for various alert services and enhanced disclosures of credit file characteristics and credit scores. All three of the major repositories offer an array of such products on their websites, some of which cost over $100 a year.[33]

Indeed, it seems that the repositories are increasingly recognizing product sales to consumers as an important source of revenue growth. That trend seems likely to accelerate, and is a positive development in terms of improving credit file quality. As bureaus compete and acquire hundreds of thousands (perhaps millions) of new consumer customers, they will revamp and upgrade their customer service operations. More importantly, the growing demand for dispute resolution from the growing number of informed consumers will require the repositories to develop new processes to minimize the costs of resolving disputes, and to prevent problem items from appearing in files. These actions in response to market incentives benefit the rest of us who choose not to subscribe to one of the alert services or inspect our own credit report.

Conclusions

Used broadly, as has been typical in the public debate over credit report accuracy, the term "credit report error" is not particularly helpful when evaluating how well the credit reporting system is meeting the goal of enhancing credit and economic opportunities for consumers. Certainly, the reporting industry bristles at the suggestion that information that is missing from a file should be counted as an error, since a credit bureau cannot report information that it never receives. The equating of missing information with error rankles all the more because the FCRA itself requires mandatory rolloff of older derogatory information that may still be predictive.

Moreover, greater file accuracy is valued only to the extent that it improves the ability of file users to assess borrower risk. Some missing information is important for assessing risk, but other missing information is irrelevant. The same can be said for information included in the file that was never correct, or that was once correct but is now out of date. Not all errors are equal, so equating accuracy to lack of errors is misleading.

We have seen that there are relatively few representative data on the frequency with which specific items contained and reported in a file are wrong. But, there is ample evidence that, detailed as they are, credit files do not represent an

33. A recent survey by Privacy and American Business along with Harris Interactive found that 33.4 million Americans have purchased a privacy product to avoid identity theft, check their credit report, or surf or shop online.

exhaustive listing of all past credit experience for many borrowers. Yet, despite missing some elements of borrowers' past credit history, the credit files produced by the voluntary reporting system in the United States are among the most comprehensive produced by any reporting system globally. More importantly, U.S. credit files support risk assessment tools (for example, scoring models) that are able to rank borrowers according to likelihood of repayment with remarkable precision. The Federal Reserve Board study concluded that "[o]verall, research and creditor experience has consistently indicated that credit reporting company information, despite any limitations that it may have, generally provides an effective measure of the relative credit risk posed by prospective borrowers" (Avery, Calem, and Canner, 2003, p. 51).[34] The authors further observe that:

> Available evidence indicates that these data and the credit-scoring models derived from them have substantially improved the overall quality of credit decisions and have reduced the costs of such decisionmaking. Almost certainly, consumers would receive less credit and the price of the credit they received would be higher, if not for the information provided by credit reporting companies (Avery, Calem, and Canner, 2003, p. 70).

That said, it is also clear that there is room for improvement in making consumer credit reports more complete representations of each consumer's past and current credit experience. The problem, of course, is that steps to further reduce credit report errors or inconsistencies impose costs on the credit reporting system. For example, in 2003 Congress required national credit bureaus, upon request, to provide consumers with one free credit report annually. Similarly, proposals are circulating to require bureaus to ensure even better matching of new information to files and to mandate more detailed reinvestigation of disputed information. Each of these marginal steps is expensive. Each imposes new costs on consumers as well as businesses. Not all of these costs are obvious (for example, mandatory tougher matching criteria may result in more frequent turndowns on instant credit applications). And, depending upon where the regulatory burden is placed, these steps could lead to dropout by data furnishers, thus reducing the completeness and predictive value of credit reports.

Ultimately the consumer pays. How much accuracy are we willing to buy? Prescriptions involving more regulatory requirements on furnishers and bureaus are offered up easily by industry critics, but every one of them involves a trade-off—imposes a cost—that is rarely articulated. The FCRA is all about balancing these trade-offs. This chapter has not attempted to consider every complaint or proposal to change the FCRA, but is intended to highlight the fact that trade-offs are inherent in any reporting system, especially the U.S. system, which owes

---

34. See also Avery and others (1996).

so much of its effectiveness to reliance on voluntary reporting and competitive incentives to innovate new products and risk management services.

The solutions to the file quality problems identified in both the FRB and the CFA studies that appear to offer the greatest promise for boosting quality with the least risk of creating new problems may be divided into two categories. The first and most important category would include measures to encourage greater consumer vigilance in examining their credit reports at all three of the major repositories. Despite the 1970 FCRA's elevation of the consumer to a prominent role in quality control (reinforced by the 1996 FCRA amendments), this seems to us to be the weak link in the current system's operation. As we have seen, comparatively few consumers access their credit reports and those that do tend to seek access only when making a major purchase requiring credit. This could reflect confidence that inspection of a report will reveal no surprises, but it may also reflect lack of awareness of the importance of the credit report and cost of errors. There are encouraging signs over the past several years that consumer awareness is growing, as judged by the success of online credit report and scoring products being marketed to consumers. Nevertheless, the consumer's inspection of his or her own report remains the most underutilized of all the existing tools for improving file quality.

Expanding consumer access to free credit reports alone is unlikely to be the most useful or cost-effective method of enhancing consumer vigilance, especially given how few consumers take advantage of their existing rights to access credit reports and dispute information contained in them. The fact is that consumers have always had an opportunity under FCRA to monitor their own reports on a regular basis. The cost of requesting a report, capped under the 1996 FCRA amendments, is dwarfed by the potential savings from detecting errors prior to applying for large loans like automobile and mortgage loans. With so much at stake in terms of the loan price, the notion that a $9 credit report (or even a $30 fee for disclosure and analysis of the borrower's credit score) would be an obstacle to a home purchase seems absurd. We suggest that the problem is more likely that consumers do not fully appreciate the financial implications of inaccurate or obsolete information in their credit file. Effective appeals to borrowers' self-interest can convey the importance of inspecting one's own credit report (for example, detect errors and pay a lower interest rate on loans). Coupled with an explanation of the substantial rights and opportunities of consumers to dispute inaccurate information, this approach seems more likely than the right to a free annual credit report to motivate consumers to request their report and find out what all the fuss is about. Facilitating online access and simpler dispute resolution mechanisms would also help. The point here is to highlight the importance of encouraging consumers to play the critical role that Congress envisioned for them in ensuring the accuracy of credit reports.

The second category of promising approaches to improving credit report accuracy includes measures to enhance the quality, timeliness, and comprehensiveness of the information furnished to credit bureaus. These steps would not compel reporting, but would lower the cost of providing data, and explicitly raise the cost of withholding data. For example, the credit reporting industry and federal regulators could develop and urge furnishers to use less ambiguous codes in reporting public record information. Congress could amend the antitrust laws to allow the credit reporting industry trade association the flexibility to promote uniform reporting requirements and reciprocity agreements for all members, so as to more directly impose a cost on a furnisher who chooses to withhold data.

The current system under which furnishers voluntarily report information to competitive credit bureaus has proved extraordinarily successful and generated benefits for U.S. consumers, far greater than the benefits enjoyed by consumers in countries with less well developed or more restricted credit reporting systems. But the U.S. credit reporting system is sensitive to regulations that impose burdens on furnishers, increase their liability, create higher compliance costs, or otherwise raise the cost of participating in the system. By highlighting the trade-offs in regulating a voluntary reporting system, this chapter emphasizes that attempts to further enhance credit file quality must be examined closely to ensure that they do not do more harm than good by discouraging participation.

References

Avery, Robert B., Paul S. Calem, and Glenn B. Canner. 2003. "An Overview of Consumer Data and Credit Reporting." *Federal Reserve Bulletin* (February): 47–73.

Avery, Robert B., and others. 1996. "Credit Risk, Credit Scoring, and the Performance of Home Mortgages." *Federal Reserve Bulletin* (July): 621–48.

Barron, John M., and Michael E. Staten. 2003. "The Value of Comprehensive Credit Reports: Lessons from the U.S. Experience." In *Credit Reporting Systems and the International Economy*, edited by Margaret Miller, pp. 273–310. MIT Press.

Barzel, Yoram. 1982. "Measurement Cost and the Organization of Markets." *Journal of Law and Economics* (April): 27–48.

Brobeck, Stephen. 2003. Testimony of executive director, Consumer Federation of America at a hearing on HR 2622, "The Fair and Accurate Credit Transactions Act of 2003," before the U.S. House Committee on Financial Services," Washington, July 9.

Cate, Fred H., and others. 2003. *Financial Privacy, Consumer Prosperity, and the Public Good.* Washington: American Enterprise Institute-Brookings Joint Center for Regulatory Studies.

Consumer Federation of America and National Credit Reporting Association. 2002. "Credit Score Accuracy and Implications for Consumers."

Consumers Union. 2000. "Credit Reports: How Do Potential Lenders See You?" ConsumerReports.org (July).

Daly, James J. 1991. "The Brewing Battle for Better Data." *Credit Card Management* 3 (January): 46–52.

Durkin, Thomas A. 2002. "Consumers and Credit Disclosures: Credit Cards and Credit Insurance." *Federal Reserve Bulletin* 88 (April): 201–13.

General Accounting Office. 2003. "Consumer Credit: Limited Information Exists on Extent of Credit Report Errors and Their Implications for Consumers." GAO-03-1036T. July 31.

Kurth, Walter. 1991. Testimony of president, Associated Credit Bureaus, at a hearing before the Subcommittee on Consumer Affairs and Coinage of the Committee on Banking, Finance, and Urban Affairs, U.S. House of Representatives, 102 Cong. 1 sess., June 6.

Noonan, Jeanne. 1991. Testimony of associate director for credit practices, Federal Trade Commission, at a hearing before the Subcommittee on Consumer Affairs and Coinage of the Committee on Banking, Finance and Urban Affairs, U.S. House of Representatives, 102 Cong. 1 sess., June 6.

Pratt, Stuart K. 2003. Testimony of president, Consumer Data Industry Association, at a hearing on the Accuracy of Credit Report Information and the Fair Credit Reporting Act, Committee on Banking, Housing, and Urban Affairs, U.S. Senate, July 10.

Seidel, Joseph L. 1998. "The Consumer Credit Reporting Reform Act: Information Sharing and Preemption." North Caroline Banking Institute.

Spurgin, Ralph E. 1991. "The Times They Are a Changin.'" *Credit World* 79 (November/ December): 10–16.

St. John, Cheri. 2003. "What the CFA Got Right—and Wrong—About Credit Score Accuracy." *Viewpoints* (January-February): 14–16.

USPIRG. 1998. *Mistakes Do Happen: Credit Report Errors Mean Consumers Lose.* (March).

Visa USA. 1997. *File Fragmentation and Delayed Reporting Analysis.* March.

11

Cost-Benefit Analysis of Debtor Protection Rules in Subprime Market Default Situations

DUNCAN KENNEDY

Debtor protection rules ought to influence debtor/creditor interaction in the residential real estate market at three points: post-default pre-foreclosure negotiations, the rate of default, and the cost of credit. Their cumulative impact should be different for "high road" than for "low road' subprime creditors. High road creditors make money through loan performance, invest in minimizing default, and lose money when they have to foreclose. Low road creditors also make money through loan performance, but invest in quick, low-cost foreclosure, and anticipate sometimes being able to appropriate some or all of the debtor's equity. Enforced nonwaivable debtor protection would likely significantly increase low road but not high road costs, and shift market share from low to high roaders, possibly putting the low road out of business. This might well be desirable from an efficiency point of view, given the tendency of borrowers to underinsure against default, and from the point of view of distributive equity, as well as avoiding adverse neighborhood effects of current low road practices.

Post-Default Negotiation

Residential mortgages generally provide that if the debtor is in even minor default, the creditor has the option of accelerating the debt. The debtor then has a short time to cure by paying arrears and penalties, after which point the debtor must pay the full amount outstanding (plus penalties) within a short grace period or be subject to foreclosure. In practice, after default the parties are likely to engage in some kind of negotiation. I will outline the stakes in the negotiation, the bargaining tools of the parties, the range of outcomes, the high road versus low road distinction, and the likely effects of different regimes of debtor protection.

Before beginning this exercise, there are two aspects of the subprime market to keep in mind. The first is that the subprime industry is highly segmented: mortgage brokers, loan initiators, syndicators, the secondary lenders, loan servicers, and, finally, actors who specialize in handling loans in default, are likely to be distinct entities, although related through the prices they pay one another for their pieces of the business. I assume initially, counterfactually, that we can treat the creditor as a single entity that controls every stage from mortgage brokering through foreclosure. I switch to assumptions that are more realistic when analyzing the impact of debtor protection on high road and low road market shares.

The second point is that while the market is segmented as above, a single economic entity can engage, through distinct subsidiary entities, in many different parts of the business and can own subsidiary entities that pursue different strategies. Thus a bank can engage in high road subprime lending while owning or financing other entities that take the low road. At the end of this chapter I speculate on the significance of this possibility.

Stakes and Tools in the Post-Default Negotiation

The stakes in the post-default negotiations are heterogeneous for both debtor and creditor, and require each to make complicated trade-offs. The parties pursue stakes using different bargaining tools, each of which will have a different degree of efficacy according to the specific circumstances.

STAKES BETWEEN DEBTOR AND CREDITOR AFTER DEFAULT. The debtor may want to: retain possession (quantifiable as the asking price of the premises, which is the home value as opposed to the market price); retain whatever equity he may have in the property; avoid a deficiency judgment (meaning liability for the difference between the loan and what the creditor recovers in the foreclosure sale); and minimize future payments. It is also possible that the debtor knows that his income has fallen so far that he has no chance of avoiding foreclosure, so that the stakes are limited to retaining equity, protracting possession, and avoiding a deficiency judgment.

The creditor wants to maximize profit through some combination of: cash payment of arrears; extraction of credible promises of future payments; loan recovery by foreclosure; and, possibly, appropriation of all or part of the debtor's equity in the foreclosure process. But the creditor must take into account the impact of the way it handles foreclosures on the rate of default, and on market share through the impact of foreclosure policies on the rate the creditor can charge for loans.

BARGAINING TOOLS AVAILABLE TO THE PARTIES. The debtor refuses to pay arrears, threatens to refuse future payments, to cease all maintenance, to retain possession until evicted, to challenge the foreclosure in court (for example, asserting technical defects, raising innovative defenses), and to join local antiforeclosure activism. The creditor threatens to accelerate the debt, to unilaterally preserve the property at the debtor's expense, to foreclose immediately, forcing resale at a depressed price, to evict as quickly as possible, to pursue a deficiency judgment if the sale price is less than the debt, and to damage the debtor's credit rating.

Range of Post-Default Outcomes

Some of these threats on each side involve imposing losses that exceed the threatening party's gain. If the creditor evicts, the debtor will lose the asking price (or home value) of possession, while the creditor acquires only the auction price. Foreclosure will destroy a part of the debtor's equity through the legal and intangible costs of the legal proceeding. The lost credit rating benefits neither party. On the other side, stopping maintenance threatens permanent damage to the collateral, the expense of foreclosure diminishes the value of the creditor's asset, and debtor activism threatens the creditor's reputation. Strategic behavior in using these threats to increase shares in some number of cases will lead to a failure to reach agreement and the inefficient carrying out of threats (of eviction, destruction of collateral, and so on) that are pure waste. The fear of outcomes of this kind is a spur to settlement and complicates the possible outcomes of bargaining (Leff, 1970).

RUTHLESS PURSUIT OF CREDITOR REMEDIES. In many cases, however, the result is less dramatic. The debtor pays arrears and a penalty that compensates the creditor for the cost of administering the default, and the mortgage is reinstated (if it has been accelerated). In other cases, the creditor accelerates the debt and proceeds to foreclose, sell at auction, and the buyer (often the creditor) evicts, all in the shortest time that is legally possible. Creditor representatives sometimes assert that when this happens, it is inevitably bad for the creditor as well as for the debtor. But this is highly implausible. It is more plausible that in cases of rapid and ruthless pursuit of creditor remedies there are at the least the following possible outcomes.

Variable outcomes of ruthless pursuit. The creditor's remedy may yield a recovery equivalent to the loss of the loan, because the resale value of the property exceeds the debt by enough to cover the creditor's costs, and the recovery is reinvested at least as profitably (even after transaction costs) as was the initial loan amount. The creditor may end up with a remedy worth less than the lost loan, because the resale value does not cover the outstanding balance plus transaction costs, and the debtor cannot be made to pay a deficiency judgment (no assets, or deficiency judgments legally prohibited).

There is a particularly important third possibility, to wit, that the creditor ends up, in this case of ruthless pursuit of remedies, with a recovery greater than the lost loan. This will occur when the creditor can appropriate all or part of the debtor's equity. This possibility, well canvassed in the legal literature (for example, Mattingly, 1996), tends to be ignored or downplayed in economists' and bankers' discussions of foreclosure (personal observation).

Creditor appropriation of debtor equity in the foreclosure process. In order for this to happen, the mortgaged property must be worth significantly more than the outstanding balance. The two cases in which this is likely to be true are where the debtor has paid off most of the mortgage with stable property values, and where there has been significant appreciation in the value of the property (either because of debtor improvements or because of a general upward trend in values in the neighborhood). In these cases, it may be that after a default and acceleration of the debt by the creditor, the debtor is able to mobilize his equity in the property to pay off the balance (which may have been significantly increased by interest, penalties, and fees).

But it may also be the case that the debtor is unable to do this. First, the debtor may not have cash resources, or resources available from friends or relatives. Second, the state may permit foreclosure in such a short time that the debtor is unable to arrange a commercial loan. Third, the debtor, particularly if elderly, may not be competent to pursue his interests. Fourth, the debtor's credit rating may have deteriorated since the initial loan to such an extent that he cannot obtain commercial credit.

When, for whatever reason, the debtor is unable to pay the accelerated balance, the creditor will have the property sold at auction. The creditor (or another buyer specializing in equity appropriation) will usually acquire the property at the auction for a price below the market value. First, the market for foreclosed properties is highly restricted. Debtor protections, particularly a debtor right to pay off the balance and redeem the property for some period after sale, are a factor in some states. More significantly, the foreclosing creditor has a vast information advantage over competitors over the short time period between the announcement and auction (so-called market for lemons effect). Second, the creditor can usually bid the amount of the unpaid balance at the auction, without putting up any cash.

A creditor who purchases at auction below market price must pay the debtor whatever difference there may be between the amount of the debt and auction price. But the creditor will then hold the property until title is cleared, resell at market price, and thereby appropriate the difference between market and auction price (less expenses), which may be all or merely some of the debtor's equity. In this case, the outcome of the post-default non-negotiation is that the creditor ends up in a better position than it would have been in had the loan been performed.

PRESERVATION OF THE LOAN POST-DEFAULT. Ruthless pursuit of creditor remedies is only one possible outcome of default. It may happen that the creditor negotiates with the debtor in an attempt to secure payment of arrears and credible promises of future performance. The creditor may also renegotiate the loan on more favorable terms, in the hope that this will make it possible for the debtor to perform, saving the expense of foreclosure. Here again, it is important to note that the creditor may end up with the equivalent of the loan pre-default, with a less valuable asset post-default, or with a more valuable asset. The creditor will agree to an outcome that is worse than the original when the alternative of foreclosure is even worse (for example, where the amount of the balance is greater than the market value of the property). The creditor will end up better off than if there had been no default where the debtor, to avoid foreclosure, agrees to terms for reinstatement of the loan that are worse for him or her than the original terms.

Determinants of Outcomes of Post-Default Negotiation

If one asks what are the likely general determinants of post-default negotiations, general market conditions seem likely to have a large influence. Where residential property values in a region or neighborhood are in decline, defaulting debtors are in a good position to obtain concessions because they may well be in a negative equity position, making foreclosure less desirable for the creditor than accepting credible promises of future payment. Where local real estate values have been increasing, creditors have the possibility of appropriating equity and so ending up better off post- than pre-default. Where the mortgage is fixed rate (or otherwise not able to be refinanced) and rates have declined, the creditor has a motive to preserve the loan rather than collecting through foreclosure.

It is also plausible that specific strengths and vulnerabilities of debtors will affect their success in the negotiation. Age and incompetence, bad credit rating, unemployment, and so forth, make the debtor more likely to lose out, likewise the extent to which the debtor has made improvements that increase the home value (asking price) without concomitant increase in market value. But there are less obvious determinants in the nature of modifiable background conditions, which are likely to be ignored. I focus first on the tendency of creditors to choose either ruthless pursuit of remedies or a loan preservation strategy. I then turn to the impact of the legal rules governing creditor remedies on the choice of strategy.

HIGH ROAD AND LOW ROAD IN THE SUBPRIME MARKET. What I will call a "high road" strategy in the subprime market is one of making money through loan performance. A "low road" strategy in the subprime market involves making money either through loan performance or through rapid and cheap foreclosure and resale of properties in default.

High road. On the high road, the creditor eschews predatory lending in part because it increases the likelihood of default. It uses point-scoring systems or nonpoint screens that attempt to eliminate borrowers likely to default. It sets up early warning and other intervention systems to identify loans that are in trouble before default. And after default the creditor invests money in procedures designed to permit loan salvage, including renegotiation and counseling. The high road creditor uses the sticks of threatened foreclosure, eviction, and adverse credit rating, but with the goal of inducing the debtor to take steps to improve ability to pay, and to make credible (enforceable) promises of future payment. It employs staff, particularly legal staff, that is relatively high priced and oriented to ethical performance of job duties, and never deliberately appropriates a debtor's equity.

In line with all of these practices, the high road creditor prices its product on the assumption that foreclosure will be relatively rare, and that when it happens it will be expensive. It will be expensive because it will involve wasted salvage attempts and high priced and slow legal procedures, without hope of equity appropriation.

Low road. Like the high road, the low road is based on making money in part through performance. The difference is that the low road strategy is much more willing to make loans that are likely to default. It makes money off such a portfolio by pricing on the assumption that foreclosure will be common, but rapid and cheap rather than rare and expensive. It will be rapid and cheap because the low roader enforces creditor remedies ruthlessly, using cheap legal services, and spends nothing on the various loan preserving tactics of the high roader. Rapid and cheap exercise of remedies has three effects: where the loan is not salvageable, it reduces the cost of terminating it and maximizes the proceeds; the threat of ruthless enforcement may induce the debtor to settle on terms favorable to the creditor; where the property is worth more than the loan, ruthless enforcement will sometimes permit appropriation of the debtor's equity.

Low road in the subprime market. There are at least two reasons why it seems plausible that the low road strategy might be more common in the subprime than in the prime market. First, borrowers who do not have equity substantially greater than their outstanding balance are less likely, in the subprime than in the prime market, to be good candidates for loan salvage. They will have trouble making promises of future performance credible because they are more likely to be unemployed, disabled, incompetent, or employed in the low wage, secondary labor market without benefits or job security. They are more likely to have no other assets than the property in question, and so to be judgment proof in the case of a deficiency judgment (where deficiency judgments are allowed).

Second, subprime debtors who have substantial equity in their properties are less likely to be able to defend it, against a low road strategy of appropriating it, than are prime market debtors. After the creditor accelerates the debt, the subprime debtor is likely less able to mobilize his own or family network assets to pay off the balance, less competent at handling the situation, and less able, because of unemployment, or credit history, or both, to borrow commercially.

The profitability of the low road depends on general economic conditions. We might speculate that it will be most profitable during a period combining sustained increases in residential real estate prices, sustained increases in the availability of subprime credit, increasing unemployment, and a restricted social safety net for low income subprime borrowers. Under these conditions, there should be a high rate of default, weak bargaining power for defaulters, and large amounts of debtor equity to appropriate in the foreclosure process.

Debtor protection and low road subprime profitability. The profitability of low road strategies in the subprime market is a function not only of the characteristics of subprime debtors and of general economic conditions, but also of the legal rules governing what the parties can do to one another in the post-default negotiation. This point is central to the remainder of this chapter and so requires some elaboration.

Legal Rules Governing Post-Default Interactions

The most striking thing about the legal regulation of post-default interactions is that different states today, and individual states over time, have adopted very different regimes. Setting up such regimes requires the policymaker to make numerous small choices about apparent details. These, and regimes as a whole, may be more or less favorable to the defaulting debtor, with considerable consequences. Some of the most important policy choices embedded in the post-default legal regime follow.

WHAT SAFEGUARDS FOR THE DEBTOR'S INTERESTS IN THE AUCTION PROCESS? A first question is whether the creditor can declare the loan in default, accelerate it, and then organize and carry out the sale of the property (often to himself) on his own initiative, all without ever going to court for a judgment that he is acting within his rights. Other questions have to do with how much time there is between default and sale, notice and place of sale, and so forth. Then there is the question whether the creditor should be permitted to bid the amount of the outstanding balance without putting up some cash, as opposed to a sale by a public officer with all potential buyers having to put up cash.

HOW TO DEFINE THE DEBTOR'S EQUITY ON FORECLOSURE? Most states define the debtor's equity as the difference between the auction price and the balance of the debt, minus the creditor's expenses. But some states have sometimes defined it as the difference between the fair market value of the property and the balance, on the ground that the procedural measures described above do not work to guarantee a realistic sale price and so further creditor appropriation of debtor equity (Mattingly, 1996).

WHETHER OR NOT TO PERMIT DEFICIENCY JUDGMENTS? Some states prohibit deficiency judgments so that the creditor has to be satisfied with whatever the property brings at auction. The prohibition eliminates the possibility of going beyond mere appropriation of equity: where the creditor buys the property at the auction for less than the outstanding balance, even though the market value is larger than the balance, and then collects a deficiency judgment, the debtor ends up worse off than if he or she had never bought the property in the first place.

NONWAIVABLE EQUITY OF REDEMPTION OR NOT? A nonwaivable equity of redemption means that the debtor whose debt has been accelerated can, for some period, up to or after foreclosure, pay the balance due and reclaim the property. All states allow some type of redemption but the provisions vary widely (Schill, 1991).

CAN THE DEBTOR ASSERT FLAWS IN THE MORTGAGE ORIGINATION IN THE FORECLOSURE PROCEDURE? In the area of consumer credit, a major 1960s reform was to eliminate the so-called holder in due course defense when a holder of consumer paper (usually a bank) was confronted with a claim by the consumer that he had been cheated in the transaction with the seller of the consumer good. Contrary to predictions, the consumer credit market did not collapse. A similar proposal here would allow the debtor to assert in the foreclosure action that the underlying loan was predatory or otherwise questionable.

Predicting the Impact of Debtor Protection: Low Road and High Road

Whether it is the prohibition of deficiency judgments, allowing a strong equity of redemption, or whatever, protective rules reduce the bargaining power of the creditor by reducing its ability to make credible threats to injure the debtor. This effect will have little significance during periods when foreclosure is rare. It is likely, when foreclosure rates are high, to be more important in the subprime than prime market. A higher proportion of subprime loans is likely to be in default. Low road subprime creditors are likely to be sensitive to the legal rules and motivated to evade or game them, because their practices of ruthless enforcement depend on the vulnerability of subprime debtors in a way that is not true for creditors oriented to performance.

Debtor Protections and Default Rates: Low Road and High Road

Precisely because they favor the debtor in the post-default negotiation, debtor protections ought, other things being equal, to increase the default rate. By reducing creditor bargaining power, they reduce the expected cost of default to debtors, which should make them more willing to default. Of course, the size of the effect depends on the extent to which default is typically chosen based on a rational calculation, rather than imposed by necessity (for example, unemployment, uninsured illness, family emergency). It also depends on the extent to which debtors are aware of the regime, and on their susceptibility to moral hazard in relation to their obligation to the creditor (Schwartz and Wilde, 1983).

The impact of debtor protection on the default rate ought to be greater for low road than for high road subprime creditors. On the low road, the main deterrent to default is the likelihood that the creditor will foreclose and evict as quickly as possible, with maximum damage to the debtor. Increased debtor protections reduce low road creditor power where loan salvage is unfeasible by slowing the process and giving the debtor more opportunity to obstruct it. More important, they should reduce the debtor's fear of equity appropriation, because many of the protections are specifically aimed at that danger (banning deficiency judgments, equity of redemption). It is at least possible that vigorous enforcement of a strong debtor protection regime would not only increase low road default rates, but also significantly reduce overall profitability (longer to foreclose bad loans and less equity appropriation).

On the high road, creditors invest in early warning, pre-default intervention, post-default counseling, and renegotiation. They have lower default and foreclosure rates than low roaders. Increased debtor protection reduces high roader bargaining power in all these situations, and so should increase the default rate for them, as well as for the low roaders. But the impact on high road profitability should be small by comparison. The legal rules will come into play less often if default rates are low. High roaders can reduce the impact of rules by investing more in their current antidefault practices. And, most important, high roaders are not making money by appropriating equity.

Debtor Protections and Price Effects: Low Road and High Road

Debtor protections ought, other things being equal, to increase the cost of subprime mortgages. Standard analysis says that terms unfavorable to creditors are costly, and the cost must be distributed between buyers (debtors) and sellers (creditors) through higher prices, and reduced margins and volume. Some debtors, in the standard analysis, are priced out of the market. Some of these would have performed and gained equity. Others would have defaulted and been foreclosed, perhaps losing equity but also perhaps having lived at submarket rents while they were performing (Schwartz and Wilde, 1983).

LOW ROAD PRICE EFFECTS. It seems plausible that these price effects will be quite different for the low road and high road. Low road creditors would likely lose significant revenues from debtor protection and have to raise their prices significantly in response. This will reduce the welfare of their performing debtors. It will also increase the default rate with attendant increase in the appropriation of the equity of low road debtors. But it will also deter some potential borrowers from taking a low road mortgage, saving them from the danger of equity appropriation in the event of default, while denying them the chance to build equity through ownership.

HIGH ROAD PRICE EFFECTS. On the high road, debtor protections should not significantly reduce post-default revenues, because high roaders already minimize default. The protections therefore should induce only a small increase in the price of high road credit, with minimal effects on low road debtors.

DEBTOR PROTECTION SHOULD EXPAND THE HIGH ROAD AT THE EXPENSE OF THE LOW ROAD. At first blush, it might appear that legal measures increasing the costs of low roaders, without significantly affecting high roaders, ought to force price increases on low roaders, that would then cause an increase of the market share of the high road at low road expense. This initial impression may be quite wrong, given the peculiar conditions of the subprime market. In that market, it seems to be the consensus (amply supported by the chapters in this volume) that borrower behavior is strikingly unresponsive to the price and terms of mortgage credit.

Information asymmetry in the subprime market. A substantial segment of subprime borrowers do only minimal shopping, and are unable to understand the real terms of the transactions they enter. This applies both to price terms and the virtually incomprehensible boilerplate that lays out the legal position of the parties in case of default. This segment of the market is also ignorant of the distinction between low road and high road post-default practices. The upper limit on creditor pricing has to do either with legal restrictions or with debtor substitution of other commodities for credit, when the apparent monthly cash cost of credit becomes too high.

To the extent low roaders specialize in the least informed segment of this market, forcing higher costs on them may not affect the prices they charge, since price is determined by what the uninformed borrower will pay, and will instead affect volume by making the business less profitable at any given price. Its effect should also be to increase the total payments of performing debtors, increase the default rate, and improve the bargaining position of defaulting debtors (conserving some equity from low roader appropriation) (Schwartz and Wilde, 1979).

Syndication and specialization in the subprime market. There is, however, another characteristic of the subprime market that suggests that debtor protection could indeed reduce low roader market share. The vast majority of sub-prime loans are syndicated, securitized, and sold into the secondary market. The servicing of these loans is performed by banks or other entities that typically have no connection with the origination of the loan before securitization. The servicers in turn may sell their defaulting loans to specialists who make their money through collections.

If the analysis above is accurate, debtor protection should have a significant impact on servicers and collection specialists who take the low road, but not on those who take the high road. The market in which specialists purchase rights to collect from defaulters, unlike the market in which homeowners purchase mort-gages, is relatively competitive and transparent. If low road collection specialists lose revenue because of debtor protection, they will have to bid less for col-lectibles, and should lose market share to high road specialists. It is worth noting that increasing the market share of high road collection specialists might reduce their unit costs, and multiply their advantage over the low road—as well as reducing the default rate and saving debtor equity.

There should be price effects, because what the servicer can sell collectibles for will affect what servicers charge syndicators, what syndicators offer to origi-nators, and thus indirectly, the cost of credit. But to the extent that high roaders displace low roaders, the price increase should be small, since the impact of debtor protection on high road costs should be, according to the analysis above, quite small. In the extreme case, enforced high levels of debtor protection might shut down low road post-default operators altogether, with only a very small increase in the cost of credit.

Unanswered question: organizational structure of the low road. In speculating about the impact of strong, enforced debtor protections on the post-default low road, there is major uncertainty as to who owns the collection industry, and as to its internal cost structure. Here are three dramatically different hypotheses, not meant to exhaust the possibilities.

First, perhaps the low road collection industry is the extension of a low road origination industry that is sharply distinct from the legitimate high road, with manipulative mortgage brokers, predatory mortgage companies, "tin men" who push home improvement on credit, second mortgage "scam-mers," and ruthless foreclosers linked in a chain (and linked culturally) as unethical, low-cost "chiselers." In this hypothesis, the bad loans of the preda-tory lenders go to debtors with high default rates, get syndicated with an ele-ment of fraud into the secondary market, and then foreclosed by low road ser-vicers or collection specialists. These acquire them well understanding their suspect (predatory) origins, and that their debtors will either be bad candi-dates for loan preservation or particularly vulnerable to equity appropriation. On this basis they rationally (though unethically) engage in ruthless pursuit of creditor remedies.

Second, perhaps the low road collection industry is largely owned by mainstream institutions which pursue the low and high roads simultaneously, practicing price discrimination as originators and market segmentation post-default, in each case through intermediaries whose function is precisely to allow the mainstream institutions to deny their involvement. Of course, the degree of mainstream institutional involvement can vary across a spectrum from the pure case of outright (but disguised) ownership, to providing lines of credit to low road originators and low road collectors, preserving deniability about how much they know of the practices they are financing.

Third, perhaps collection is done by specialized firms connected neither to predatory low road originators nor to mainstream institutions, pursuing profit-maximizing strategies based on triage, going for fast foreclosure, to cut losses or appropriate equity, or high road loan preservation, according to which they think will be most profitable in the class of cases to which the debtor belongs. Such companies might be arrayed on a low road to high road spectrum, each with a different internal culture.

Standard analysis suggests that under conditions of perfect competition, perfect information, and zero transaction costs, whichever of these arrangements is most transactionally efficient should eliminate the others. But under conditions of imperfect competition, uncertainty, information asymmetry, and path dependence, it is of course perfectly possible that all three patterns, and others as well, could coexist and compete indefinitely (Schwartz and Wilde, 1979).

Public choice theory might, at first, seem to suggest that mainstream ownership, or at least involvement, is the most likely pattern. Were the mainstream uninvolved, we would expect it to lobby for closing down the low road. But this intuition is counteracted by the thought that a mainstream committed only to the high road still has a powerful interest in forestalling regulation across the range of issues in finance. The mainstream industry might be willing to tolerate low road survival as a cost of maintaining an across the board stance in favor of freedom of contract.

Uncertainty about the organization of the low road would be troublesome if its resolution made a big difference to the expected effect of debtor protection. But as far as I can see, enforced high level debtor protection should induce a shift from low road to high road in each of these organizational patterns. This is, nonetheless, an obvious domain for further empirical research, which might unsettle the analysis above.

Efficiency Effects of Favoring the High Road

The efficiency effects of regulations favoring the high road would be numerous. I organize my speculations according to the scheme of post-default, rate of default, and price effects.

Post-Default Stage

In the post-default negotiation, the great danger is that the parties will end up executing their threats to impose losses on their bargaining partners that exceed their own gains. Debtor protection functions to reduce this danger on one side: it reduces the chances that the creditor will accelerate, foreclose, and evict where the asking price, or home value, of possession is far greater than what the creditor collects in the process. (Note that appropriation of equity is not in itself inefficient, since it is simply a transfer.) Reducing the share of the low roaders would lead to higher expenditures on early warning, counseling, and workout (Leff, 1970). It seems plausible to me that these costs would be less than the benefits to debtors through higher rates of loan preservation and reduced equity appropriation.

Default Stage: Neighborhood Effects

The optimal rate of default is an empirical matter of hopeless complexity. Law and economics provide no categorical solution as to what legal rules are best in the abstract, let alone in practice. It does suggest that debtor protection has countervailing impacts. It should increase default rates by reducing the costs of default. But in so much as it shifts market share from low roaders to high roaders, it should reduce the rate of default because high roaders invest in preventing it. It seems plausible that the default reducing effects would be far larger than the default increasing effects, especially if the increase in enforced debtor protection were accompanied by effective measures against predatory lending.

NEIGHBORHOOD EFFECTS OF DEBTOR DECISIONS TO DEFAULT. If it is the case that debtor protection would reduce default rates, there might be significant external beneficial neighborhood effects. First, debtors deciding whether or not to default, or to passively accept foreclosure, do not take into account the effects of their decisions on their neighborhoods. But subprime defaults are likely to be geographically concentrated, because of the class and race segregation of American homeownership, and because the economic downturns that generate high default rates are often regionally specific. High default rates that are geographically concentrated threaten downward spirals, as the literature since the 1970s has amply demonstrated (for example, Kennedy, 1987, 2002b).

NEIGHBORHOOD EFFECTS OF RUTHLESS PURSUIT OF CREDITOR REMEDIES. Subprime lenders are nationally organized, and may well spread their loans across many markets, thereby reducing their vulnerability to local fluctuations in loan viability. It is quite possible that low road collections by different entities in a single neighborhood will cumulate beyond the threshold at which neighborhood effects emerge. In this case, a collective action problem leads to a reduction of the value of creditor collateral by reducing neighborhood property values across the board—with negative consequences for nondefaulting neighbors—because low road creditors do not calculate the interaction of their ruthless pursuit of their remedies with similar strategies of other low roaders in the vicinity. Debtor protections that squeezed out the low road, thereby reducing the default and foreclosure rates, might significantly reduce this risk.

Ex Ante *Stage: Price Effects*

The two main efficiency issues in the pricing of subprime credit are whether debtors underinsure against default and whether weak debtor protection creates an incentive for predatory lending.

DEBTORS UNDERINSURE AGAINST DEFAULT. From the point of view of the borrower, debtor protection rules function as insurance against the adverse consequences of default. In other words, because there is an equity of redemption, the debtor is less likely to suffer equity appropriation than if the creditor could take the property finally in response to a minor default (Schill, 1991). Debtor protection has to be nonwaivable to work, not only because of information asymmetry, but also because sellers (lenders) have an interest in concealing the costs of default associated with their products (both in order to maintain market share vis-à-vis one another, and in order to maintain the competitiveness of credit vis-à-vis other products) (Kennedy, 1983). Because the protections are not waivable, this is an example of compulsory insurance paid for through the price and administered by the seller (creditor).

The standard efficiency analysis of this kind of compulsory insurance applies (Abraham, 1986). First, the insurance may correct a market failure if debtors as a class tend to underestimate the value of this kind of insurance to them. Second, the risks may be uninsurable in the free market for insurance because of transaction costs (particularly market for lemons information problems). Because the insurance is compulsory, and the rational expectations and risk preferences of debtors are highly variable, some debtors who would not have bought as perfectly informed buyers in a competitive market will have to buy as part of the price of credit.

Overall, there will be efficiency gains if the benefits to those consumers who would have bought (had third-party insurance been available and had they been well informed) outweigh the losses to those forced to buy insurance they neither want nor need. Schill's path-breaking statistical study, done prior to the rise of the subprime market, suggested that debtor protection costs debtors overall far less than they receive in benefits (Schill, 1991). In the subprime market today, one can identify characteristics of debtors that point toward greater efficiency gains and others that point the other way.

Subprime debtors are likely even less informed than Schill's prime market debtors, and they will often have even more to lose from foreclosure. On the other hand, they are likely poorer, and possibly have higher risk preference, and so might be more likely to forgo insurance if fully informed. It seems implausible to me that debtor protection enhances efficiency in the prime market but not in the subprime market.

DEBTOR PROTECTION AND PREDATORY LENDING. One form of debtor protection at the default stage would directly impede predatory lending—the abolition of the holder in due course defense for the entity doing collection. Defects at the origination stage could then be raised at foreclosure even though the debt had been sold numerous times since origination. But increasing and enforcing other nonwaivable protections at the default stage could also reduce the incentives for predation.

It seems possible that predatory mortgage brokers and loan originators generate a disproportionate share of loans that have the two characteristics of equity that can be appropriated and a high probability of default. In the anecdotal typical case, an elderly, minority homeowner has largely paid off a mortgage (often initially a subsidized mortgage), lives in a neighborhood where home values have recently increased, has little income, no assets other than the residence, and needs a loan to pay for maintenance. In this situation, the value of the loan will be greater, and therefore the incentive to make it at any given (predatory) rate will be greater, the easier it is to appropriate the equity on default.

Increased enforced debtor protection should make the payoff from predation smaller by reducing the equity appropriation component of the value of a predatory loan. This will be true even if predation is initially the work of mortgage brokers and only secondarily the work of initiators and those who provide them working capital. These actors have eventually to price collectibles. That pricing affects what they will accept from brokers and what they will get from the secondary market. Again, further empirical work seems highly desirable, but there is at least a presumption based on abstract modeling that if debtor protection shifts market share from low road to high road creditors at the default stage, there should be a reduction of predation at origination.

In conclusion, with respect to the efficiency consequences of debtor protection, it is important to keep in mind that the overall cost-benefit outcome has to include all the stages of the transaction. There are costs and benefits at the post-default stage (for example, reducing deadweight losses from failure to settle and execution of threats of destruction), another set at the default stage (for example, neighborhood effects), and yet a third set at the *ex ante* stage (optimal insurance issues and the effects on predation). How to add up all the elements is inevitably speculative. But the case for debtor protection on efficiency grounds seems to fall somewhere between plausible and highly convincing, depending on one's intuitions about the underlying unresolved empirical questions.

Distributive Effects of Favoring the High Road

The preceding efficiency analysis identifies most of the relevant distributive considerations (Kennedy, 1983), supposing that debtor protection had the effects I have been modeling. As between debtors and creditors as groups, it seems likely that debtors will be better off and creditors (along with their employees and stockholders) worse off. As between different classes of creditors, high roaders should gain (increased market share outweighs marginal reduction of their post-default bargaining power) at the expense of low roaders.

The more complex distributive question concerns effects as between debtors. The choice of a more or less vigorous debtor protection policy is an aspect of a larger and important policy choice between favoring a) low-cost, low-protection credit with high rates of borrowing, high default, and foreclosure, or b) higher-cost, better-protected credit with lower participation, lower default, and lower foreclosure rates. The high-risk strategy permits many to enter the lottery, with the chance of becoming homeowners and accumulating equity, but imposes high costs on the losers. If the strategy is generally successful it has the good neighborhood effects of high homeownership rates, but if it does not work it imposes the bad neighborhood effects of high foreclosure rates.

Debtors in the subprime market are likely those that incur the highest risks from the high-risk strategy. The loss of equity is likely to wipe out their assets. The loss of home value through eviction is likely to lead to a sharp fall in standard of living by forcing a move into high-cost rental housing. The neighborhood effects of high foreclosure rates are likely to be much greater in poor neighborhoods than middle-class or affluent ones. The high-risk strategy is based on the idea of triage—in order for the largest number to enter the middle class, it is acceptable to sacrifice, rather brutally, those who miscalculate their ability to perform.

In practice, debtor protection regimes fall toward the middle of a spectrum. At one extreme, the legal regimes could (but do not) actively encourage equity appropriation in every case of default, no matter how minor, in order to subsidize the cost of subprime credit and maximize participation. In this case, defaulting debtors would cross-subsidize those who perform. At the other extreme, the regimes could (but do not) force substantial cross-subsidies from performing to nonperforming loans, making foreclosure rare, subprime credit expensive, and participation much lower than it is.

Both the existing regimes and the regime of more vigorous debtor protection discussed here fall in between the extremes. It seems plausible that the change under consideration, if it switched market share from low road to high road post-default practices, would reduce the availability of the high-risk option without significantly reducing participation. High roaders with increased market share would not have to increase their prices significantly because they already eschew ruthless pursuit of creditor remedies and invest in loan preservation instead. Moreover, cutting back the low road should reduce predation *ex ante*, making high participation rates less risky for low-income borrowers than they now are.

Of course, this leaves unresolved the larger question of the extent to which policy should push toward high participation when it inescapably increases the risks for losers in the lottery. But that is a subject for another paper (for preliminary considerations, see Kennedy, 2002a).

Conclusion

The analysis of the costs and benefits of post-default debtor protection in the subprime market suggests that there is a case for measures designed to shift market share from low roaders to high roaders, and even a case for putting the low road out of business altogether. It suggests considerably more strongly that, in the absence of a more elaborate model and a good deal of new empirical information, there is no basis for a policy presumption against nonwaivable debtor protections.

References

Abraham, Kenneth. 1986. *Distributing Risk: Insurance, Legal Theory, and Public Policy.* Yale University Press.

Kennedy, Duncan. 1983. "Distributive and Paternalist Motives in Contract and Tort Law, with Special Reference to Compulsory Terms and Unequal Bargaining Power." *Maryland Law Review* 41: 563–642.

———. 1987. "The Effect of the Warranty of Habitability on Low Income Housing: 'Milking' and Class Violence." *Florida State Law Review* 15: 485–533.

———. 2002a. "The Limited Equity Cooperative as a Vehicle for Affordable Housing in a Race and Class Divided Society." *Howard Law Journal* 46: 85–131.

———. 2002b. "Legal Economics of U.S. Low-Income Housing Markets in Light of Informality Analysis." *Journal of Law in Society* 4: 71–119.

Leff, Arthur. 1970. "Injury, Ignorance, and Spite: The Dynamics of Coercive Collection." *Yale Law Journal* 80: 1–56.

Mattingly, Basil. 1996. "The Shift from Power to Process: A Functional Approach to Foreclosure Law." *Marquette Law Review* 80: 77–133.

Schill, Michael. 1991. "An Economic Analysis of Mortgagor Protection Laws." *Virginia Law Review* 77: 489–538.

Schwartz, Alan, and Louis Wilde. 1979. "Intervening in Markets on the Basis of Imperfect Information: A Legal and Economic Analysis." *University of Pennsylvania Law Review* 127: 630–96.

———. 1983. "Imperfect Information in Markets for Contract Terms: The Examples of Warranties and Security Interests." *Virginia Law Review* 69: 1387–467.

PART 5

Working toward Solutions

KEN WADE

In the 1970s, when the Neighborhood Reinvestment Corporation and its nonprofit NeighborWorks network were in their early stages, the driving issue in neighborhoods was redlining—lenders simply were not making loans available for buying or renovating homes predominately occupied by low-income and minority families. Across the country, hundreds of community development organizations formed to harness the resources of local governments, financial institutions, and community residents to create access to credit for underserved areas. Thankfully, the market has changed dramatically in the last twenty-five years. Through the efforts of the Community Reinvestment Act, along with advances in technology and innovative public-private partnerships, communities today have an abundance of capital available. But even in this environment, credit challenges remain critical to the work of the more than 230 Neighbor-Works organizations. The explosion of aggressive loan products combined with automated underwriting systems, risk-based loan pricing, and third-party loan originations have created an almost bewilderingly complex marketplace. As a result, NeighborWorks organizations have shifted from helping families access capital to helping families understand when to borrow and how to get a loan at a fair price. In many ways, community leaders, policymakers, and regulators face more difficult—and more nuanced—challenges than ever before.

The demands on community development professionals have expanded from creating affordable housing and lending to building personal assets and connecting underserved families to broader financial services. The recipe for vibrant neighborhoods today combines a broader set of products and services, beyond loan pools and "bricks and mortar" real estate development. The chapters in part 5 examine three significant issues related to the environment facing community development practitioners this decade: savings, financial services, and preserving homeownership.

The first chapter, by Sherraden and Barr, reinforces a time-honored notion: savings matters. From buying a car needed for employment, to storing savings for emergencies, to investing for retirement, the importance of savings for low-income households is obvious. Sherraden and Barr point out that policymakers, practitioners, and researchers have not placed enough emphasis on incentives for saving, or even analyzed how households save. The authors suggest while much effort has been expended to expand the credit side of the household balance sheet, the savings side of the balance sheet needs more attention. Many existing government programs and institutions targeted to low-income households in practice actually force families to spend savings to qualify for programs, rather than encourage asset accumulation. The authors suggest structures with restrictions, such as those common among retirement plans for middle- and upper-income workers, are critical for encouraging savings. The experiences of the NeighborWorks network buttress this view; programs such as Financial Fitness and individual development accounts are helping even very-low income families build financial assets. Sherraden and Barr emphasize policymakers and practitioners need to redouble efforts to encourage savings behavior. If more families increase their savings, communities would benefit from more opportunities to qualify for prime-quality credit, increasing opportunities for homeownership and even providing a cushion to preserve ownership for low-income families when emergencies do occur.

Seidman and Tescher's chapter focuses on an issue introduced by Sherraden and Barr—the role of basic banking services in building access to credit. Seidman and Tescher suggest there are more than 10 million households in the United States without any basic banking relationship. Without a bank account, individuals must conduct checking transactions outside of traditional financial institutions and have few options to store deposits. The article reviews the forces shaping the provision of basic financial services in the last decade, including the important role of government electronic benefit programs and new technologies. The authors suggest the growth of the so-called alternative financial services, such as check-cashing outlets and paycheck advance lenders, demonstrates the potentially profitable market for products and services targeted to low-income consumers. The growth and popularity of alternative services should be instructive for policymakers. Stored value cards, credit cards, and ATM transactions are examples of products with still untapped potential in this market. Partnerships between government, nonprofit organizations, and the financial sector are overcoming many of the challenges facing unbanked households. However, the regulatory system, designed for last century's depository banking system, must rapidly adapt to the marketplace, including the growth of alternative providers obviously tapping into an unmet need among consumers. Innovative programs show it is possible to connect low-income consumers with mainstream financial institutions, but more work needs to be done.

The final chapter by Crews Cutts and Green examines changes in mortgage loan servicing and loss mitigation efforts. Like all aspects of the mortgage industry, servicing has changed in recent years, driven by technological advances and consolidation. The authors discuss the efforts by servicers to use technology to analyze and predict loan repayment behavior in order to optimize interventions for delinquent loans. By testing the efficacy of various strategies, and providing highly customized outreach and payment options, lenders are able to provide delinquent borrowers more options to remain in their homes, while also reducing the costs of default for investors. Advances in home-retention workout options may serve to preserve ownership for millions of first-time homeowners added in the last decade. Examining Freddie Mac's loss-mitigation systems, the authors suggest repayment plans for low-income delinquent borrowers result in a 68 percent reduction in the likelihood of home loss. The authors suggest credit scoring tools and loan workouts have encouraged home retention instead of foreclosure. This appears to represent a mutually beneficial outcome—homeowners stay in their homes, neighborhoods are saved from the blighting impacts of foreclosed properties, and the revenue to lenders is maximized. Just as the underwriting and origination process has had a profound impact on the mortgage origination marketplace, careful servicing is having profound impacts on families and neighborhoods with high probabilities of delinquent loans.

The benefits of helping families build, maintain, and preserve their assets are as central as ever. Applied research, combined with the experience of community development professionals, can expand understanding of the need for better products and services. Neighborhood Reinvestment Corporation, working with its public sector, nonprofit community development, and financial industry partners, aims to address the challenges facing low-income and minority communities today.

12

Institutions and Inclusion in Saving Policy

MICHAEL SHERRADEN AND MICHAEL S. BARR

C redit is important, especially for purchasing a home, but credit is only one pathway to asset accumulation—the other is saving. The poor must save, not only to qualify for and pay off credit, but also for key purchases such as clothing for the start of a child's school year; life course events, such as births, weddings, and funerals; and emergencies, such as car repair, illness, or job loss.[1] Saving and credit are complementary, often intermingled, and both are important. For most households, including low-income households, asset accumulation requires saving as well as credit.[2]

Recent applied research has contributed to our understanding of the potential importance of saving by low-income households. Caskey (1994) carried out pioneering studies of alternative financial services, such as pawnshops and check-cashing outlets, with important implications for saving policy for the poor (Caskey, forthcoming). Barr (2004) provides an extensive analysis of how changes in the alternative financial sector, banking sector, and payment and dis-

---

1. Rutherford (1998, 2000) provides an excellent study of saving purposes and practices among the poor in developing countries. To our knowledge, no one has done this type of study as carefully in the United States, though Caskey's research (1994, forthcoming) is an important contribution.

2. See Rutherford (2000) and Consultative Group to Assist the Poorest (2002), for excellent discussions in the context of developing countries, and Schreiner and Morduch (2003) for the U.S. context.

tribution networks could increase opportunities for the poor to get access to the mainstream financial sector and save. Stegman (1999) recognizes that electronic banking may provide opportunities to make individual development accounts available to the poor. Beverly, Tescher, and Marzahl (forthcoming) find that recipients of the Earned Income Tax Credit (EITC) can be encouraged to save, at least for the short term, upon receipt of their tax refund. Smeeding (forthcoming) finds that EITC recipients think of their lump sum payment differently from their ordinary income—they tend to use it for larger payments or purchases. The EITC, due to its large size and lump sum distribution, could be a significant source of financing for saving and asset building. In the individual development accounts research we discuss below, low-income households were able to save.

Yet saving by the poor is a largely overlooked topic in the United States. This may be understandable because savings deposits by the poor are often small, perhaps easy to dismiss as unimportant. The explosion of credit availability has rightly garnered attention, though available credit, especially predatory lending, does not always help low-income households. Means-tested income support and other policies often play a negative role in saving, because of asset limits that discourage saving (Ziliak, 1999; Hurst and Ziliak, 2001). In addition, some supporters of means-tested programs have feared that a focus on asset building might weaken political support for income transfers and the social safety net. This stance is well intentioned, but has contributed to keeping asset-building policies for the poor off the political agenda.

As a result of these and other factors, U.S. public policy has largely ignored or marginalized saving policy for the poor. This is particularly striking given the recent rhetoric of the Bush administration about the "ownership society" (discussed later in this chapter). The administration has proposed a dramatic expansion of tax-preferred savings vehicles, but this expansion largely benefits the highest-income taxpayers whose net saving behavior is least likely to be influenced by the policies. The administration has included a small proposal that would expand saving opportunities for the poor, but the overall thrust of the plan is highly regressive. Instead of focusing on additional saving proposals that benefit the upper end of the income scale, public policy should focus on building wealth among the least well off. A sound policy would aim for inclusion of everyone in saving and asset accumulation.

In this chapter we first develop an institutional theory of saving, which is provisional and in need of more empirical testing. We then explore in practice how existing institutions promote dissaving among the poor. We also look at how policies to change these institutional structures could promote saving among these households.

Toward an Institutional Theory of Saving

Basic assumptions about how people behave shape our understanding of economics and our views about the role of law. Traditional economic models of rational choice view decisions as made by optimizing rational agents with perfect foresight. Research in psychology and behavioral economics provides alternative explanations for decisionmaking, such as the importance of default rules, framing, and heuristics. By contrast, the public debate is largely consumed by "culture of poverty" theories of social deviance, laziness, and imprudence as describing the poor. These differing frameworks affect how one views a wide range of phenomena, including saving. The behavioral economic insight can be used not only to understand individual choice, but also, perhaps, to design institutions to influence individual decisionmaking. Our task in this chapter is to explore the contours of an institutional theory of saving and to relate such a theory to the reality of the lives of poor people.

Are the Poor Different?

Are the poor different from the nonpoor? We ask this question because it is fundamental to thinking about options for inclusive saving policy. A great deal of social science theory and political discourse, explicitly or implicitly, treat the poor as different from the nonpoor. Conservatives tend to see the poor as deficient in ability, motivation, and morals, to be corrected by greater individual responsibility. Liberals tend to see the poor as victims of social and economic circumstances, who require special programs to cope with these circumstances.

We take a somewhat different approach. We acknowledge that the poor are different, at least insofar as they do not have as much money, and that many poor people have myriad problems that may have pushed them into poverty or keep them poor. However, in contrast to much of social science theory and political discourse, our view in this discussion of saving is that many of the poor are not different from many of the nonpoor. We take this perspective as a normative stance, and as a practical position. The normative stance is that, until everyone has the same institutional opportunities and public subsidies for asset accumulation, it is not possible to know whether their reactions to institutional structures would be different from others. For example, it is a disservice to an employed yet impoverished single mother who is not offered a 401(k) in the workplace to suggest that she is different from the nonpoor because she does not have retirement savings. Our practical position is similar. It may be possible to create inclusive policies and products for saving that are successful for many low-income households (indeed, we think this is highly possible). If this is the case, there would be little need to focus on how the poor might be different from the nonpoor, as it relates to saving, because it would not matter.

Model of Institutions and Saving

Our theoretical perspective places primary emphasis on purposeful institutional arrangements that structure and support asset accumulation.[3]

Research on saving is extensive but inconclusive (Korczyk, 1998; Carney and Gale, 2001).[4] No theoretical perspective has been found to have strong and consistent empirical support. Neoclassical theories, represented by the life cycle hypothesis (Modigliani and Brumberg, 1954) and the permanent income hypothesis (Friedman, 1957), assume that individuals and households are focused on expected future income and long-term consumption. Many variations have been developed. For example, "buffer-stock" models of saving (Carroll, 1997; Caroll and Samwick, 1997; and Ziliak, 1999), emphasize a precautionary motive for saving, particularly for younger households and for those facing income uncertainty. Overall, these economic theories assume that people are forward-looking and concerned about consumption patterns, preferences are stable, people have perfect information, and everyone makes rational decisions.

Behavioral theories emphasize financial management strategies and self-imposed incentives and constraints (for example, Shefrin and Thaler, 1988). These theories modify conventional economic models in two ways. First, behavioral theories do not assume that wealth is completely fungible. Shefrin and Thaler (1988) propose that individuals use systems of mental accounts and that propensity to spend varies across accounts. Second, behavioral theories do not assume that individuals have perfect information and always behave rationally. Instead, these theories suggest that individuals sometimes have trouble resisting temptations to spend. Therefore, individuals may create their own behavioral incentives and constraints (Shefrin and Thaler, 1988), such as a Christmas Club saving account.

Behavioral theories suggest that saving is likely to increase when precommitment constraints are available. Such mechanisms make it difficult to choose current consumption at the expense of future consumption (Maital, 1986; Maital and Maital, 1994; Shefrin and Thaler, 1988). A common precommitment constraint is payroll deduction. When pension plan contributions are deducted from an individual's paycheck, temptations to spend that money in the short term are almost eliminated. The individual no longer has to make, on a monthly or biweekly basis, a conscious decision to postpone consumption. Other precommitment constraints include overwithholding of income tax (Neumark, 1995) and undertaking home mortgages (Maital and Maital, 1994).

3. The following discussion builds on an emerging body of work at the Center for Social Development at Washington University. The role of institutions in saving by the poor was initiated by Sherraden (1991); detailed in Beverly and Sherraden (1999), and Schreiner and others (2001); and extended in Sherraden, Schreiner, and Beverly (2003).

4. This review of saving theory and research borrows from Beverly and Sherraden (1999).

Psychological and sociological theories do not assume that consumer preferences are fixed, but rather change with economic and social stimuli (for example, Duesenberry, 1949; Katona, 1975; Cohen, 1994). Katona (1975) has noted that saving is a function of two sets of factors: ability to save and willingness to save. As in standard economic theory, the emphasis on ability to save acknowledges that some individuals, because of limited economic resources or special consumption needs, find it more difficult to defer consumption than others. At the same time, the decision to save also requires willpower (in contrast to standard economic theory, where people figure out the optimal plan and then implement it). Psychological theory focuses primarily on this choice, as influenced, for example, by families (Cohen, 1994), peers (Duesenberry, 1949), and past saving experiences (Furnham, 1985; Katona, 1975).

Turning to empirical evidence, life cycle and permanent income models have mixed support, but they especially fail to explain patterns of saving in low-income households. Few behavioral, psychological, or sociological propositions have been rigorously tested. Overall, evidence is mixed and incomplete.

For the purposes of this discussion, we offer a simple institutional model of saving. In our simple model, institutions are the products of laws and other formal mechanisms. Institutions, which are formal and purposeful, have a defined structure and rules, designed to alter behaviors and outcomes for individuals.[5]

Individuals in this model reflect all of their cultural and social background and context, sociodemographic characteristics, and particular experiences. In neoclassical economic terms, individuals are fully informed and rational actors. In behavioral economic terms, humans are viewed as more complex, more like real humans, and they are sometimes irrational actors (Thaler, 2000). We lean toward the behavioral understanding. Also, we do not view preferences or abilities as fixed. In studies of saving behavior it will be important to measure individual characteristics. However, in the present formulation, we do not focus on changing individual characteristics, but on changing institutions.[6]

5. The term "institution" is often used in the social sciences in general, unspecified ways, to mean something like social organization, both informal and formal, above the individual level. Some discussions focus on the emergence of institutions out of culture, or in some cases, out of individual cognition. Most influential in recent years has been the "new institutional economics," with origins in the transaction cost economics of Coase (1937) and led today by North (1990). See also Powell and DiMaggio (1991), and Smelser and Swedberg (1994).

6. In neoclassical theory, people have preferences and then make decisions in the context of constraints and prices. This is a simple theory, widely applicable, and has proven to be enormously successful. Behavioral economics has recently reconsidered this view. According to the behaviorists, individuals are not always all-knowing, not always rational, and preferences are not fixed. Essentially, behavioral economics is specifying new aspects of the individual for study. In this chapter, we are trying to do something similar, but with the other half of neoclassical theory. We are trying to specify the vague area with which individuals interact, known as "constraints." We aim to describe a richer, more detailed understanding of factors that individuals face in making choices. In economic reasoning, individual preferences (neoclassical view) or cognitions and emotions (behavioral

In the model, actions result from individuals interacting with institutions. Similar analyses of institution-individual interaction occur commonly in economic analysis of markets, as well as in social psychology, anthropology, and other fields of study. In this chapter, as a simplification, we take the typical approach used in economics and assume that the interaction occurs. Just as supply and demand reach equilibrium in microeconomics, the market of institutional-individual interaction finds its own equilibrium.[7]

Framework for an Institutional Theory of Saving

From an institutional perspective, saving and asset accumulations are in large part the result of structured mechanisms involving "explicit connections, rules, incentives, and subsidies" (Sherraden, 1991, p. 116). For the nonpoor, these mechanisms include deductions for home mortgage interest and property taxes, exclusions for employment-sponsored pension contributions and earnings, tax deferments for Individual Retirement Accounts and Keogh Plans, and employer contributions and tax deferments for employee pension plans. People with higher marginal tax rates are more likely to participate in tax-deferred savings programs (Joulfaian and Richardson, 2001).[8] Low- and moderate-income households, with little in existing saving, do not have the same access or receive the same incentives from institutions that promote and subsidize asset accumulation (Sherraden, 1991; Howard, 1997; Seidman, 2001). For example, the poor are less likely to have jobs with pension benefits. Even if they do, they receive few or no subsidies because they have low or zero marginal tax rates and the tax benefits are not refundable.

Institutions that influence saving consist of formal laws and regulations, financial enterprises, and financial products. One way to look at what institutions do is that they reduce the cost of saving (a neoclassical view). Another is that institutions reduce levels of cognitive processing on the part of individuals (a behavioral economics view; see Thaler, 2000). In some cases, for example, when firms provide automatic direct deposit of a portion of income into a retirement account unless the employee opts out, institutions may reduce trans-

---

view) determine action. But it can work the other way around. Sometimes an institution will change the action of an individual, and then she changes her preferences. For example, participation in a 401(k) plan will result in accumulating balances that can change a participant's time horizon and assessment of possibilities regarding the future. This is the opposite of the standard economic understanding, which is that future orientation leads to saving. Both views are probably correct to some extent, that is, forward-looking cognition causes saving, and savings cause forward-looking cognition, a virtuous circle (Sherraden, 1991; Yadama and Sherraden, 1996).

7. In fact, we think this market interaction is important and necessary to study. What conditions do institutions offer in the market? How is it that individuals make decisions to participate? Behavioral economics is beginning to shed important light in this area.

8. For many middle- and upper-income households, participation in tax-preferred saving plans may simply shift savings assets from non–tax-advantaged to tax-preferred plans.

action costs to close to zero, and obviate the need for any cognitive processing. In this case, the institution is doing all of the choosing and acting and the individual is essentially passive.

Individuals in the model consist of all of their sociodemographic characteristics, accumulated culture and experience regarding saving, cognitive capacity for financial matters, and emotions regarding money and saving. In this discussion, the target of intervention is not the individual. However, this does not mean that knowledge of individuals is irrelevant. Knowledge of individuals can lead to design of institutions that are more effective in causing saving behavior. For example, we know that individuals overall feel losses more strongly than they feel gains, which would suggest a bias toward security of saving balances rather than always aiming for high returns. Institutions cannot be equally successful with all individuals. The design task is to cause the most saving behavior by the most individuals who are targeted under a particular policy.

Action in the saving model results from the interaction of institutions and individuals (Schreiner and others, 2001). Outcomes are savings and other forms of asset accumulations that are, in turn, likely to lead to other outcomes—economic, social, and psychological—for individuals and families.

Elements of an Institutional Theory of Saving

Institutional perspectives are not new in the social sciences (for example, Gordon, 1980; Neale, 1987), but they are usually not well specified. We offer seven constructs that we believe are important aspects of institutions designed to promote saving and asset accumulation: access, information, incentives, facilitation, expectations, restrictions, and security. These seven constructs have emerged from our research on individual development accounts (IDAs).[9]

IDAs are saving programs targeted to people with low incomes, with subsidies in the form of matching funds upon withdrawal (Sherraden, 1988, 1991). Matched uses of IDA withdrawals typically include homeownership, postsecondary education, and microenterprise. IDAs have become more common during the past decade. More than forty states have an IDA policy of some type, and there are perhaps 400 community-based IDA programs. At the federal level, IDAs were included as a state option in the 1996 Welfare Reform Act, and a federal IDA demonstration created by the Assets for Independence Act began in 1998. Despite this policy activity, coverage is quite limited; the total number of IDA participants in the United States at this writing is less than 50,000. IDAs

---

9. The first four of these—access, information, incentives, and facilitation—were identified by Sherraden and appeared in Beverly and Sherraden (1999). Expectations later emerged from qualitative research on IDAs (Sherraden and others, 2000). In Sherraden and others (2003), we added limits, which we now call restrictions. Security is emerging in IDA qualitative research (Sherraden and others, 2003), and in savings programs in developing countries (Rutherford, 2000; Schreiner and Morduch, 2003).

are in the early stages of development, and much remains to be learned about whether and how they can be effective in building assets of the poor.

The results we discuss here are from a study of IDAs in the American Dream Demonstration (ADD).[10] In presenting findings on IDAs below, we emphasize that this is not a study of total household saving, but only IDA saving. The possibility exists that IDA saving can increase while total household saving or net worth does not increase. In the current study, we cannot test for reshuffling of savings and other forms of assets. Nonetheless, the results may be suggestive for theory about household savings, especially because these are low-income households with, on average, few other financial assets, and thus little to reshuffle.[11] We turn now to the meaning and explanatory potential of these constructs.[12]

ACCESS. Access refers to eligibility and practicality. To take current examples, only a small number of low-income people can participate in IDA programs, and few low-income households have access to 401(k) plans at work.[13] Regarding practicality, distance is a major barrier to financial services in rural areas. Differential access to asset accumulation by race is the central theme in Oliver and Shapiro (1990, 1995) and Shapiro (2004). Half the population does not have access to a pension plan in the workplace, and they are not randomly distributed by race and class. In these circumstances, it is not fully informative to interpret saving and asset accumulation outcomes as resulting solely from individual characteristics and choices. Some people have greater access than others.

There is limited economic evidence regarding the effects of access on saving, in part because it is difficult to disentangle the effects of access from the effects of unobserved individual characteristics. For example, if workers consider the availability of pension plans when they evaluate job offers, then those who work for firms that offer pension plans may value retirement saving more than the average individual. This would create a positive association between access and saving, even if access has no independent effect. However, some researchers (Cagan, 1965; Carroll and Summers, 1987) have concluded that institutional-

10. ADD is funded by a consortium of eleven foundations. The Corporation for Enterprise Development (CFED) undertook the demonstration, and the Center for Social Development (CSD) at Washington University in St. Louis designed and is overseeing the research. The saving period for the demonstration was 1997–2001.

11. While reshuffling of assets is less likely among people with few assets, it is nonetheless possible. Schreiner and others (2001) discusses reshuffling in greater detail.

12. The discussion of institutional constructs that follows borrows from Sherraden and others (2003).

13. Some participants in IDAs focus on the institutional nature of the IDA program. During one pre-IDA focus group, one mother who was on welfare said, "Oh, I get it. It's like a 401(k), only for us." Low-income households are more often in disadvantaged positions relative to these saving features (Caskey, 1994; Bernheim and Garret, 1996; Beverly and Sherraden, 1999; Barr, 2004).

ized saving opportunities promote saving by calling attention to the need for and benefits of saving.

INFORMATION. Information refers to knowledge about the policy or product, as well as knowledge that may contribute to successful performance. Bayer, Bernheim, and Scholz (1996) find that more frequent corporate-sponsored retirement seminars were associated with both higher participation and higher levels of contributions to 401(k) plans. Bernheim and Garrett (1996) report that participation rates were 12 percentage points higher for companies that offered financial education, and 20 percentage points higher for employees who chose to attend. Education increased new savings as a percentage of income by 1.7 percentage points. The effects were greatest for people who saved little before they received education. In another study, Bernheim, Garrett, and Maki (2001) report that financial education for teens increases savings rates when they become adults. In research on IDAs, Schreiner, Clancy, and Sherraden (2002) and Clancy, Grinstein-Weiss, and Schreiner (2001) find that up to eight hours of general financial education is associated with strong increases in net savings amounts in IDA programs. Some financial education appears to have a positive payoff, but extensive financial education might not be better. Because financial education is expensive, these data can contribute to resources being used more efficiently.

INCENTIVES. Incentives are financial rates of return, as well as nonfinancial payoffs for participation. In the latter category can be factors such as peer relationships, status, or opportunity to learn. The net effect of financial incentives on saving is a subject of debate. An increase in the rate of return will not necessarily increase saving. There are two key issues. First, changes in the rate of return on savings may simply result in the reshuffling of the form of assets, with no new saving. Second, for net savers, an increase in the after-tax rate of return has two contradictory effects. On the one hand, individuals may choose to save more because the price of current consumption increases relative to the price of future consumption (the substitution effect). On the other hand, with higher rates of return, individuals can save less and still enjoy the same amount of future consumption (the income effect).

Empirical evidence regarding the effect of incentives on saving among the nonpoor is mixed (see Engen, Gale, and Scholz, 1996; Hubbard and Skinner, 1996; Poterba, Venti, and Wise, 1996; Feldstein, 1995; Hubbard, Skinner, and Zeldes, 1995; Powers, 1998). For low-income households, in contrast, reshuffling is less likely because they are less likely to have savings and other assets to reshuffle. Empirical analysis simulating the effects of private pension plans suggests that pensions do not offset personal saving among lower-income (less-educated) workers (Bernheim and Scholz, 1993). Schreiner, Clancy, and Sherraden

(2002) find that higher match rates in IDA programs are positively associated with fewer unmatched withdrawals and staying in the program, but they are not associated with amounts of saving. This latter finding is consistent with data from 401(k)s, where savings amounts do not increase with match rates beyond a low level (Basset, Fleming, and Rodriquez, 1998; Kusko, Porterba, and Wilcox, 1994).[14]

FACILITATION. Facilitation refers to any form of assistance in saving, for instance, when depositing is done for the participant, as in automatic payroll deduction. Direct tests are rare, but one study provides strong, direct evidence that facilitation affects saving behavior. Madrian and Shea (2000) studied 401(k) participation and contribution rates in a company that began automatically enrolling employees in its 401(k) plan. Before the change, employees had to sign up to participate in the 401(k) plan. After the change, employees had to choose to opt out of the plan if they did not want to participate. Although none of the economic features of the plan changed, participation was significantly higher under automatic enrollment. Participants were also likely to stay with the default contribution rate and fund allocation. Other evidence on the importance of facilitation is the common practice of using the income tax withholding system as a kind of saving plan. Millions of households withhold more than the taxes they owe. More evidence is needed to determine whether this is because they plan for a lump sum refund, despite the strong economic disincentive (the cost of forgone earnings on the money), or overwithhold inadvertently. Direct deposit can also be used to facilitate saving. Direct deposit is positively associated with being a saver, that is, staying in the IDA program (Schreiner, Clancy, and Sherraden, 2002), and IDA participants point to positive effects of direct deposit in their saving performance (Sherraden and others, 2005).

EXPECTATIONS. Expectations are embodied in institutional features such as saving targets and social pressure of staff and peers. In saving behavior among the poor, this is largely unresearched. The only data we have are qualitative reports of some IDA participants that they view the match cap as a monthly target savings amount, and that staff and peerd often encourage them to do so. Some IDA participants state directly that they are trying to fulfill these expectations (Sherraden and others, 2005). A large body of social-psychological research confirms that people tend to try to do what others expect them to do.

14. To complicate matters, some types of incentives have limits or caps. For example, participants in 401(k)s may have tax incentives for putting money aside for retirement, but only up to a cap. These caps create analytical challenges in that they may create censoring effects in saving outcomes. Public policy always has caps for saving subsidies, for instance, limits on how much can be deposited annually into a 401(k) account. These caps in fact may decrease savings below desired levels, though these censoring effects are seldom studied.

Schreiner, Clancy, and Sherraden (2002) and Schreiner (2001) report that IDA holders in the ADD who faced higher savings targets or caps were less likely to make unmatched withdrawals and more likely to be successful savers. Under the heading of expectations we also include contracts, or legalized expectations (Vittas, 1992). A growing portion of saving in the United States is contractual, including 401(k)s, 403(b)s, and similar retirement programs.[15]

RESTRICTIONS. Restrictions are likely to affect saving performance. Contrary to neoclassical thinking, savers often prefer restrictions. Restrictions are of two main types: restrictions on access and use. Regarding restrictions on access, there is a growing literature in behavioral economics on the desirability of putting funds out of easy reach. It may be that savers prefer to put money away in places where they cannot get to it because it would be drawn upon by family and friendship networks if it were available. We have heard this often from IDA participants; family and friends may draw down household assets more among the poor and people of color (Stack, 1974; Chiteji and Hamilton, forthcoming). We hear often from IDA participants that they are glad that the savings are out of reach, because otherwise it would be drawn down due to social obligations.[16]

Regarding restrictions on use, most subsidized saving policies specify such restrictions. For example, 529 saving plans are for college education and 401(k) savings are not available until retirement. Such restrictions are a limitation on choice, but there are situations in which the account holder prefers restrictions. In research on IDAs, participants translate such restrictions into goals. For example, if the money is available only for homeownership, then this tends to focus their saving effort toward that goal (Sherraden and others, 2005 and forthcoming).

SECURITY. All families need a safe place to put their money. Rutherford (2000) details examples of savers in developing countries who are willing to accept a negative rate of interest in exchange for security of their savings. In research on IDAs, the security of knowing that savings are safe and available for the future is mentioned by some participants during in-depth interviews (Sherraden and others, 2005 and forthcoming). Other important types of security relate to investment-specific risks, general market risks, macroeconomic risks, and political uncertainties, faced by all savers. Some public policies, such as Social Secu-

15. There are extensive contractual saving policies in some other countries. For example, the Central Provident Fund of Singapore is a mandatory, defined-contribution saving policy for retirement, homeownership, medical care, insurance, education, and investment (Asher, 1991; Sherraden and others, 1995).

16. Restriction on savings being drawn upon by social networks of course may have negative social consequences. We cannot evaluate this, except to report that many IDA participants express appreciation for the restrictions.

rity, can protect extensively against market and macroeconomic risks, though beneficiaries are subject to political risk that their benefits would be cut. Similar protections are uncommon in defined contribution retirement plans, or other forms of asset accumulation held by individuals.

OTHER INSTITUTIONAL ELEMENTS. Lastly, we should note what we do not know. Unobserved factors associated with IDA programs are correlated with saving level. The average monthly net deposit (AMND) in IDAs, controlling for all observed factors, can be as much as $20 per month different across IDA program sites. The overall AMND average is $19, so these differences from unobserved factors across sites are large (Schreiner, Clancy, and Sherraden, 2002). We do not know what the unobserved factors are, or how much each one matters, but the size of the effects strongly suggests that IDA programs probably vary in unobserved ways that affect savings performance. For example, the level of staff commitment, the quality of financial education, or the vision and leadership of the executive director may contribute to saving performance.

Toward Measures

The constructs above are an attempt to begin specifying an institutional theory of saving. This project is in an early stage of development, and much more remains to be done. The aim is to work toward an informative and useful set of institutional constructs that, if supported by research, can help to specify better theory and guide policy. Eventually, constructs can be refined into measures. Measures might then be combined into an index of institutionalization, which could be used to compare various saving policies within a country or in comparative research across countries. Such developments would help change the vague idea of institutions into a tool for analysis, knowledge building, and policy decisions.

An omnibus measure that we call "degree of institutionalization" might also be useful for comparing saving policies. If we imagine saving institutions ranging on a continuum from negative to positive in terms of how much savings they generate, we might have the following seven types: discourage saving; neutral on saving; encourage saving slightly; encourage saving aggressively; contractual saving, opt-in; contractual saving, opt-out; and automatic or mandatory saving.

With respect to the category *discourage saving,* means-tested social programs in the United States have asset limits that are a disincentive for saving among low-income households. Sherraden (1991) argued that asset limits in means tested programs should be abandoned or greatly eased. During the 1990s, almost all states eased asset limits in many programs, but much more can be done to reduce discouragement of saving by the poor.

Neutral on saving refers to public policy that neither discourages nor encourages saving. This is an ideal type, useful in theory, but probably impossible to find in practice. Next are *two levels of encourage saving—slightly and aggressively.* Without specifying the difference, we make the point that the extent of encouragement can matter. Policies can slightly encourage saving, for example, a small interest rate, or aggressively encourage saving, for example, large public subsidies, public information campaigns, and universal direct deposit.

Moving toward the more institutionalized end of the continuum are *contracts, where we identify two levels—opt-in and opt-out.* Individuals may need or want constraints on the ready availability of their money, and are therefore willing to enter into contracts to have the money put out of reach. This is the case, for example, in 401(k)s. The first level of contractual saving is *opt-in,* referring to individuals being asked if they want to participate. The next level is *opt-out,* referring to individuals being signed up automatically, with the option of quitting. Research has reported higher participation rates when 401(k) plans are presented as opt-out rather than opt-in. Automatic or mandatory saving is already a part of U.S. policy in the sense of mandatory contributions toward Social Security.

While the institutional theory of saving we propose, and the measures to test it, are only tentative at this point, we believe they can make useful contributions to saving policy.

Toward a Saving Policy for the Poor

We now explore the existing institutional context for financial decisionmaking by low- and moderate-income households. We contend that institutional constraints facing such households mostly fall into the category "discourage saving" outlined above. We then analyze ways to change those constraints.

Unbanked and Underbanked

The poor, like everyone else, often require a wide range of financial services, including saving services.[17] Some may think that the poor cannot—or even should not—save. After all, when incomes are low, the necessities of food and shelter may take every available dollar. But this is a great misconception of the financial life of the poor. Even people who are poor must save small lump sums for routine payments, including rent, clothing for school, and home or automobile repairs, and occasionally must have larger sums for major life events, such as births, marriage, illness, accidents, and deaths. Many low-income families save for major goals of household development, such as moving to a better neighborhood, purchasing a car to be able to drive to a better job, buying a computer

17. This section builds on Barr (2004) and is adapted with permission.

and Internet access, purchasing a home, or capitalizing a microbusiness. In this section, we illustrate how institutional saving features discussed above in theory can deter or promote saving by the poor in practice.

Today, instead of a regular means to save, the poor largely face institutionalized dissaving from high-cost financial services. Access to basic financial services is critical to success in the modern American economy. Nearly 10 million U.S. households—9.5 percent of all U.S. households—do not own a bank account (Kennickell, 2000; Aizcorbe, 2003).[18] Twenty-two percent of low-income families—over 8.4 million families earning under $25,000 a year—do not have either a checking or savings account (Kennickell, 2000). Most of the unbanked[19] are low-income: 83 percent of the unbanked earn under $25,000 a year (Vermilyea and Wilcox, 2002). The unbanked are more concentrated in low-income neighborhoods (Dunham, 2001).

Households are more likely to be unbanked when they have lower incomes, less wealth, less education, are not working, are younger, have more children, rent their home, and are a racial or ethnic minority.[20] Broadly speaking, the most common reason persons cite for lacking a checking account is not having enough money to be able to afford the costs of account ownership (Caskey, forthcoming).[21] Other unbanked persons said that they distrusted banks, did

18. The General Accounting Office (GAO), using the 1998 and 1999 Survey of Income and Program Participation (SIPP), estimated that "about 11 million benefit recipients, over half of all federal benefit check recipients in 1998, were unbanked. This estimate is substantially higher than Treasury's 1997 estimate, which showed that 24 percent of federal beneficiaries (5.2-6.5 million) lacked bank accounts" (GAO, 2002). GAO extrapolates from its SIPP estimates to suggest that among all U.S. adults, 22.2 million households, or 55.9 million individuals, are unbanked, representing 20 percent of all households and 28 percent of all individuals.

19. We use the term "unbanked" to refer to individuals who do not have an account (savings, checking, or otherwise) at a depository institution. The "underbanked" are those with an account at a depository institution, but who also rely for their financial services on other financial services providers (such as check cashers, payday lenders, and refund anticipation lenders) that largely serve low- and moderate-income neighborhoods. Problems faced by the "unbanked" and "underbanked" overlap significantly, but diverge in important respects that we explore. We use the term "bank" generically to refer to all depository institutions, including commercial banks, thrifts, and credit unions. Where differences among these types of depository institutions matter, we use the specific terms.

20. Findings from demographic surveys of the unbanked vary regionally (Caskey, 1994; Dunham, 2001; Greene, Rhine, Toussaint-Comeau, 2003; Hogarth and O'Donnell, 1999; Hogarth, Lee, and Anguelov, 2004; Rhine, Toussaint-Comeau, and Hogarth, 2001). These descriptions of the unbanked do mask heterogeneity of the population. For example, mentally ill unbanked persons or prisoners face a host of problems, making it difficult to bring them into the banking system, that we do not address here. Nor do we address policy responses to persons who choose not to use banks because the individuals are engaged in illegal activity, or wish to hide their income from spouses, for example.

21. The most commonly cited reasons for lacking a bank account are "do not have enough money" (50 percent of respondents in Booz-Allen Hamilton, Shugoll Research, 1997); "no savings" (53 percent of respondents in Caskey, forthcoming); "do not write enough checks to make it worthwhile" (28.4 percent of respondents in Kennickell and others, 2000); "do not have enough

not want to deal with banks, or had privacy concerns (Rhine, Toussaint-Comeau, and Hogarth, 2001). Families living in neighborhoods with higher concentrations of blacks or Hispanics are less likely to own a checking account. Among the banked, low-income minorities are less likely than whites to have a checking account, but more likely than whites (all else being equal) to have savings accounts. By contrast, proximity to a bank branch seems not especially predictive of being banked (Vermilyea and Wilcox, 2002).[22]

The period 1995 to 1998 marked a decline in the percentage of low-income families who are unbanked from 25 to 22 percent (Kennickell and others, 2000).[23] Economic growth in the 1990s improved the job prospects and incomes of the poor, although these gains eroded significantly in recent years (U.S. Census Bureau, 2002).[24] Policy changes in the EITC increased the take-home pay of low-income workers and helped to increase labor force participation. Welfare reform, beginning with waivers for states to use welfare-to-work strategies and culminating with the 1996 Welfare Reform Law, increased the percentage of welfare recipients entering the workforce. Greater workforce attachment and higher incomes may have increased the benefits of bank account ownership and also may have provided more low-income persons with the wherewithal to meet bank minimums or afford bank fees. Account ownership grew most quickly among groups at or below the poverty threshold and the next largest gains came from those just over the poverty line (Hogarth, Lee, and Anguelov 2005).

Institutional Context for Dissaving

The consequences of not having access to mainstream financial services can be severe. Lack of access to bank accounts and structured saving mechanisms make it more difficult for low-income families to save. The unbanked face high costs for basic financial services, which reduces effective take-home pay.[25] For example, a worker earning $12,000 a year would pay approximately $250 annually

---

money" (12.9 percent of respondents in Kennickell and others, 2000), "bank fees are too high" (23 percent of respondents in Caskey, forthcoming); "bank minimum balance requirements are too high" (22 percent of respondents in Caskey, forthcoming); "high minimum balance requirements and fees" (Vermilyea and Wilcox, 2002). In one study, 62 percent of respondents cited unfavorable account features and costs (Rhine, Toussaint-Comeau, and Hogarth, 2001).

22. Data are insufficient to determine whether the racial neighborhood effect is related to any reluctance by neighborhood merchants to accept checks from minorities or from any person in minority neighborhoods, or is related to consumer preferences (Vermilyea and Wilcox, 2002).

23. The percentage of unbanked families continued to decline somewhat through 2001 (Aizcorbe and others, 2003).

24. Median household incomes dropped, and the poverty rate increased, in 2001 and 2002 (DeNavas-Walt and others, 2003; Proctor and Dalaker, 2003).

25. Total estimated fringe banking transaction costs, including check cashing, payday lending, pawn loans, rent-to-own transactions, and auto title lending are $5.45 billion annually (Carr and Schuetz, 2001).

just to cash payroll checks at a check-cashing outlet (Dove Consulting, 2000), in addition to fees for money orders, wire transfers, bill payments, and other common transactions.[26] Almost all of the checks cashed at check cashers pose relatively low risk: nearly 80 percent of checks cashed at check-cashing outlets are regular payroll checks; another 16 percent are government benefit checks (Dove Consulting, 2000).[27] A large portion of these checks could presumably be direct deposited into bank accounts at relatively low cost—if low-income people had bank accounts.

The costs of these basic financial transactions reduce the effectiveness of federal income transfer programs and may undermine public initiatives to move families from welfare to work. Studies of the EITC suggest that higher take-home pay from the EITC helps to induce labor force participation (Hotz and Scholz, 2001).[28] But high-cost financial services reduce effective take-home pay and thus may also diminish the effectiveness of the EITC. One survey found that 44 percent of a sample of EITC recipients in inner city Chicago used a check-cashing service to cash their government refund check (Smeeding, Phillips, and O'Connor 2000). Nationwide, in 1999, nearly half of the $32 billion in EITC refunds provided to over 18 million low-income families were distributed through refund anticipation loans, costing EITC recipients $1.75 billion for tax preparation services, electronic filing, and loan fees (Berube and others, 2002).

Similarly, some studies suggest that welfare programs that encourage work, coupled with policies that let families keep more of their earnings before benefits are reduced or eliminated, have helped to increase workforce participation and job retention (Blank, 2002). Yet the positive effects of welfare reform may be undermined by high-cost financial services. Although states have switched to the EBT for welfare recipients, once these households begin earning income, or leave the welfare rolls, they often lack access to the banking system, and pay high fees to cash their income checks.[29] Even in the bulk of states that have moved to EBT for welfare payments, welfare recipients may still face high costs for financial services. First, administrative problems in some state programs make it hard to withdraw sufficient funds for bill payment (for example, monthly rent). Second, most EBT programs do not link recipients to bank accounts, which means that these recipients need to find other means to convert

26. The use of check cashers may vary considerably by region, and by urban or rural location (Dunham, 2001; Rhine, Toussaint-Comeau, and Hogarth, 2001; Hogarth, Lee, and Anguelov, 2004; Stegman and Faris, 2001).

27. Check cashers focus on these checks to reduce credit risk. These operations, however, often also require additional efforts to reduce credit and fraud risk.

28. Empirical work is needed on the labor force effect, if any, of high-cost financial services.

29. There is some evidence that check cashers may see the welfare-to-work population as a new market (Fox and Mierzwinski, 2001).

their work income to cash to pay bills, save funds, and access credit. Third, payroll checks and EITC refunds may still push them toward high-cost transaction services. Lastly, welfare recipients may be dissuaded from opening a bank account because they believe that their bank account balances will cause them to exceed state welfare program asset limits (Caskey, 1997; Hogarth, Lee, and Anguelov, 2004).[30]

In addition, low-income families must save if possible to cushion themselves against personal economic crises, such as injury or loss of a job, and for key life events, such as buying a home, sending their children to college, or retirement. Low-income households face key barriers to saving (Banerjee, 2001). Because they are poor, they face higher opportunity costs for putting their funds toward savings rather than current consumption. Because the poor accumulate little, financial institutions face high costs in collecting their savings relative to the amounts saved, and are thus reluctant to expend resources to open accounts for them, and they may offer low returns on savings, further reducing incentives the poor have to save. Low-income families, particularly those without bank accounts, often lack regular mechanisms to save, such as payroll deduction plans, further reducing the likelihood that they will do so (Beverly and Sherraden, 1999).

In a survey of New York and Los Angeles low-income neighborhoods, 78 percent of the banked held some form of savings, broadly defined, while only 30 percent of the unbanked had savings. Obviously, the ability to save is a function of income. But differences hold even across income ranges: being banked is highly correlated with saving (Vermilyea and Wilcox, 2002). This may suggest that bank account ownership makes it easier for households to save. Bank account ownership may be correlated with a propensity to save. That is, households who want to save open bank accounts. Thus one would need to measure differences in propensity to save in order to determine whether account ownership itself is a strong factor in increasing savings.[31]

Bank accounts can be important entry points for the provision of regular savings plans for low-income workers through payroll deduction. Still, most low-income workers work for firms without savings plans or are themselves not covered by such plans even when their employers have savings plans (Ameriks, Caplin, and Leahy, 2002). In addition to the fact that low-income unbanked families lack an easy mechanism for regular savings, the tax system, through which the bulk of government savings benefits are provided, largely subsidizes savings for higher-income households. The Treasury Department estimates that

---

30. In some states, account balances will cause recipients to lose eligibility under some circumstances (Corporation for Enterprise Development, 2002).

31. For evidence that financial planning influences wealth accumulation, see Ameriks, Caplin, and Leahy (2002).

more than two-thirds of tax expenditures for pensions go to households in the top 20 percent of the income distribution, while the bottom 40 percent get only two percent of the tax benefit (Orszag and Greenstein, forthcoming).

Furthermore, without a bank account, it is more difficult and costly to establish credit or qualify for a loan. A bank account is a significant factor—more so, in fact, than household net worth, income, or education level—in predicting whether an individual also holds mortgage loans, automobile loans, and certificates of deposit (Hogarth and O'Donnell, 1999).[32] After controlling for key factors, one study determined that low-income households with bank accounts were 43 percent more likely to have other financial assets than households without bank accounts (Gale and Carney, 1998). Low-income persons without bank accounts face higher costs of credit than low-income persons with accounts,[33] and in any event, low-income households generally face higher costs of credit than households with higher incomes (Banerjee, 2001). Moreover, the savings products that low-income individuals do have access to generally provide low levels of return, and in turn may drag down savings rates. This lower saving rate is a problem itself, and further increases the cost and reduces the availability of credit to these households.

Low-income families find it difficult simply to make ends meet each month and lack access to short-term credit at a reasonable cost to smooth out earnings. The main complaint of low-income families, for example, in Caskey's (forthcoming) study, was the "insecurity and stress associated with living from paycheck to paycheck." Most low- and moderate-income households manage to spend all their income each month (Hogarth, Lee, and Anguelov, 2004; Rhine, Toussaint-Comeau, and Hogarth, 2001). Bank account ownership will not suddenly change that, but account ownership may make it easier for low-income households to manage their finances, save even if in modest amounts, and access lower-cost forms of credit.

It is difficult to untangle causation, but a lack of account ownership is linked to credit problems. Either unbanked low-income persons have lower propensities to plan financially than other low-income households, or lack of a bank account makes it harder to plan and save. In turn, once credit problems emerge, credit-impaired individuals have a harder time getting access to bank accounts. In Caskey's (forthcoming) survey of low-income households, 42 percent of unbanked households were two months late on bills in the last year, compared with 28 percent for banked households, while 41 percent of unbanked house-

32. There may be personal characteristics of those owning bank accounts—such as propensity to plan, budget, be thrifty, and save—that are not fully captured by this analysis and that may account for better savings and credit outcomes.

33. Credit scoring innovations may increase the benefits of account ownership for low- and moderate-income persons. W. A. Lee, "Debit Scores May Gauge Subprime Market," *American Banker*, February 28, 2002, p. 10.

holds were contacted by a debt collection agency in the past year, compared with 25 percent for banked families. When low-income unbanked families need to borrow, they must turn to expensive forms of credit. Only 14 percent of unbanked poor families carry credit cards that might help them smooth out payment for short-term increases in consumption or to weather occasional dips in income, while 59 percent of low-income banked households carry credit cards (Caskey, forthcoming).

Account ownership in and of itself is no panacea. Some low- and moderate-income individuals with bank accounts often lack savings, and may turn repeatedly to payday lenders (who charge, on average, 474 percent APR), and to other forms of high-cost credit (Fox and Mierzwinski, 2001).[34] Given the lack of health insurance, low-income families without savings or access to informal networks of family and friends often use payday loans when faced with expenses related to birth or illness (Rhine, Toussaint-Comeau, and Hogarth, 2001).

Fourth, low-income families who cash their entire paycheck may face high risk of robbery or theft.[35] By transitioning into bank accounts where they can store a portion of their earnings, withdraw funds in smaller amounts, pay for goods or services directly using debit, and withdraw funds outside of the concentrated time periods during which benefit checks and paychecks are commonly cashed, these families can decrease their exposure to risk of crime.

Changing the Institutional Framework of Saving Policy for the Poor

Promoting low-income household savings is critical to lowering reliance on high-cost, short-term credit, lowering risk of financial dislocation resulting from job loss or injury, and improving prospects for longer-term asset building through homeownership, skills development, and education. Savings policy should focus on four approaches—account ownership, employer savings plans, IDAs, and fundamental pension reform. First, bank account ownership can be an important step for low-income families to begin to save, for both shorter-term financial stability and longer-term savings goals. Second, payroll deduction plans need to become critical avenues for low-income savings. Third, for intermediate-term saving needs, such as homeownership, college education, or entrepreneurial ventures, IDAs are providing a new means for low-income households to save. Lastly, fundamental pension reform is required to provide low-income families with the opportunity for tax-advantaged savings that are currently skewed toward the more affluent members of our society.

34. Indiana's Department of Financial Institutions found that consumers took an average of thirteen loans a year, ten of which were rollovers of earlier loans. An Illinois Department of Financial Institutions survey found an average of ten loan contracts over eighteen months.

35. R. Craver, "Safety and Numbers: Hispanics Caught between Risks of Carrying Cash and Banking It," *Winston-Salem Journal*, January 22, 2003. C. Davenport, "Seeking a Secure Financial Foothold; Banking Barriers Leave Area Immigrants Vulnerable to Crime, Economic Disparities," *Washington Post*, November 15, 2001.

Evidence to date suggests that low-income individuals can save if given the opportunity to do so, at least if offered a significant matching contribution. Some 73 percent of federal employees earning $10,000 to $20,000 annually participated in the federal government's Thrift Saving Plan, and over half of those earning under $10,000 also participated (U.S. Department of the Treasury, 1998). Some 60 to 70 percent of families at the poverty level are current or usual savers (Hogarth, Lee, and Anguelov, 2004; Ferguson, 2002).[36] The 2001 Survey of Consumer Finances found that 30 percent of families in the bottom income quintile saved in the prior year, and 53.4 percent of those in the second-lowest quintile saved (Aizcorbe and others, 2003). Savings account features have an appeal for the unbanked. In a Treasury Department survey of unbanked federal check recipients, respondents were aware that an ETA savings feature would only pay a nominal rate of interest (explicitly posed in the survey as "$2 annually on a $100 deposit"), but this feature would account for approximately 25 percent of the typical respondent's decision on whether to enroll in the ETA (Bachelder and Aguerre, 1999).

Some lower-income individuals use alternatives to bank accounts to facilitate savings. Anecdotal evidence exists that low-income people purchase money orders with their paychecks at the beginning of the month and hold them for later use. In so doing, they convert their income and benefits into a less liquid and more protected form, for bill payment later in the month or as savings for planned and unplanned expenditures in the future.[37] Researchers have also found that low-income taxpayers over-withhold on their income taxes more frequently than higher income taxpayers; some economists suggest that these taxpayers use withholding as an automatic savings mechanism. This may suggest that demand for savings products among the poor is high enough that some will accept a zero or negative interest rate (Highfill, Thorson, and Weber, 1998).

The way that employer-sponsored savings plans are set up can matter a great deal (Madrian and Shea, 2000; Choi and others, 2004). Automatic enrollment, in which employees are signed up for regular payroll deduction into 401(k) plans unless they choose to opt out, have been increasingly used in larger companies.[38] For those at the bottom end of the pay scale, and in particular for younger workers, as well as black and Hispanic employees, automatic enrollment in pension plans significantly boosts participation and asset accumulation

36. R. W. Ferguson Jr., "Reflections on Financial Literacy," remarks before the National Council on Economic Education, May 13, 2002 (www.federalreserve.gov/boarddocs/speeches/2002/20020513).

37. Postal savings orders offer protection if lost or stolen and are backed by the U.S. Postal Service.

38. Hewitt Associates reports that 14 percent of companies used automatic enrollment in 2001, up from 7 percent in 1999, driven in part by a desire to meet IRS "top-hat" antidiscrimination rules (Choi and others, 2004).

(Choi and others, 2001). [39] Employer-offered default contribution rates, default investment plans, rollovers into new pension accounts of low-balance accounts for terminated workers, and employer matches can all increase participation and contribution rates (Choi and others, 2004). In order to foster increased asset accumulation over time, without dissuading lower-income workers from contributing at all, automatic enrollment contribution rates for low-income workers can be set low initially, and then can be increased over time as their salaries increase (Thaler and Benartzi, 2004).

Yet few low-income workers have access to employer-sponsored pension or other savings plans. The Internal Revenue Code provides two-thirds of its pension benefits to the top 20 percent of the population, while the bottom 60 percent gets only 12 percent of any tax benefit (Summers, 2000). Most low-income workers work for firms without savings plans or are not themselves covered by the plan that their employers offer to other employees, in part because of the part-time or seasonal nature of their work (Orszag and Greenstein, forthcoming). Low-income employees may be reluctant to save because they need their wage income, and most low-income workers have lower contribution rates than higher-income ones when they are covered by plans. They also are more likely to work in high-turnover, part-time, or seasonal jobs in which it is more costly and difficult to establish savings programs. Existing antidiscrimination rules, which the Treasury Department has announced it may make more lenient still, permit wide disparities in the provision of savings plan benefits among employees.

As indicated above, individual development accounts have been introduced and are becoming more widespread. Most states have some type of IDA policy, and in addition to the American Dream Demonstration, the federal government enacted the Assets for Independence Act in 1998. Despite this policy activity, IDA programs today are small and community based. The next step is to con-

---

39. Automatic enrollment in 401(k) plans significantly boosted participation rates, to rates well exceeding 85 percent, whereas previous rates had ranged from 26 to 43 percent after six months and 57 to 69 percent after three years of employment. However, most participants tended to choose a low default savings rate (2-3 percent) and conservative investment plan (for example, money market fund). Slightly less than half of plan participants continued at the low rate and conservative plan after three years. Thus on average, after three years, given higher participation but lower contribution rates and more conservative plans, there was only a slight positive overall companywide average effect on savings of automatic enrollment. Companies could, of course, set default rates higher (say, equal to rate at which employer match ceases) and let employees switch to lower contribution rates if desired, but there may be some trade-off in terms of opting out early. As noted above, for those at the bottom of the pay and savings spectrum, however, automatic enrollment significantly increased participation rates and asset accumulation. See also Madrian and Shea (2001) (48 percentage point increase in participation among new employees; 11 percentage point increase overall; automatic enrollment particularly helpful in increasing participation among young, lower-paid, and black and Hispanic employees). Automatic enrollment was actively encouraged by the Treasury Department in the late 1990s. See also Rev. Rul. 98-30 (1998), Rev. Rul. 2000-8, Rev. Rul. 2000-33, and Rev. Rul. 2000-35 (2000); Summers (2000); Economic Growth and Tax Relief Reconciliation Act (2001).

nect IDA programs and principles with large policy systems. In this regard, tax credits to financial institutions could help to overcome barriers to widespread adoption of IDAs. The Savings for Working Families Act,[40] first introduced by Senators Lieberman and Santorum, is a promising approach. Under the act, financial institutions offering IDAs would receive tax credits annually offsetting up to $500 in match funds and $50 in account administration costs. The current legislation, drafted with an overall cap on accounts, would provide for up to 300,000 new IDAs at a cost of under $500 million.[41] The cap on the number of accounts may limit financial institution interest in developing the infrastructure necessary to support these accounts, and should be removed. If permitted to operate without a cap, this legislation could help to transform financial services for the poor, by moving from small-scale, nonprofit focused efforts to a large-scale, financial-institution driven financial product that meets the longer-term savings needs of low-income families.[42] As with bank accounts for low-income persons, technology will need to play a central role in driving down the costs of IDA provision.[43]

Directions for a Universal, Inclusive Saving Policy

As indicated above, banking the poor, and giving them access to saving services and products, depends on public policies working in conjunction with private sector financial institutions. So that this discussion of large-scale policy does not seem entirely speculative, we turn to a proposal for a large, inclusive saving plan in the United States, and a universal, progressive child saving policy in the United Kingdom.

PROPOSAL FOR UNIVERSAL SAVING ACCOUNTS IN THE UNITED STATES. President Clinton proposed Universal Savings Accounts (USAs) in his State of the Union address in 1999. In his State of the Union address in 2000, Clinton offered a similar proposal, saying:

> Tens of millions of Americans live from paycheck to paycheck. As hard as they work, they still do not have the opportunity to save. Too few can make use of IRAs and 401(k) plans. We should do more to help all working families save and accumulate wealth. That is the idea behind the Indi-

40. A version of the legislation passed the Senate as Title V of the CARE Act of 2003 on April 9, 2003. See Senate Bill 476, 108 Cong. (Sen. Grassley).

41. See Senate Report 108-011, CARE Act of 2003 (February 27, 2003).

42. The legislation could also be modified to provide for a similar tax credit to financial institutions for providing low-cost electronic banking accounts for low-income persons. Such a tax credit would be the easiest way to bring the First Accounts pilot to scale if the demonstration proves successful (Barr, 2004).

43. The Doorways-to-Dreams test of an Internet-based back office platform for IDA programs will prove instructive in this regard. See www.d2dfund.org.

vidual Development Accounts, the IDAs. We ask you to take that idea to a new level, with new retirement savings accounts that enable every low- and moderate-income family in America to save for retirement, a first home, a medical emergency, or a college education. We propose to match their contributions, however small, dollar for dollar, every year they save.[44]

The 1999 USA proposal did not take off politically, and it was reconceptual- ized as the Retirement Savings Accounts in 2000. The RSA proposal channeled tax credits to financial institutions to cover administrative costs of the accounts, plus match funds deposited by financial institutions into the account. Despite the limited political impact, these proposals elevated the idea of inclusive, pro- gressive saving policy to a new level. Occasions when government leaders have made large and progressive asset building proposals have been few. The USA proposal in 1999, which was like a 401(k) for all workers, with deposits and matching funds for those with lowest incomes, was budgeted at an expenditure level of $33 billion a year (roughly the size of the EITC), and RSAs were even larger, at an estimated cost of nearly $55 billion annually.

These proposals are markedly different from President Bush's saving initia- tives, which are called Lifetime Saving Accounts and Retirement Savings Accounts. The Bush proposals make little effort at inclusion and are aimed at carving up Social Security, rather than adding to it. If enacted as proposed, the Bush proposals would give still greater saving-related tax benefits to the non- poor, and little or nothing to the poor.

CHILD TRUST FUND IN THE UNITED KINGDOM. A serious discussion of asset-based policy began in the United Kingdom in 2000 (Kelly and Lissauer, 2000; Nissan and LeGrand, 2000; Institute for Public Policy Research, 2001). In a major policy development in April 2001, Prime Minister Tony Blair pro- posed a Child Trust Fund for all children in the United Kingdom, with progres- sive funding. He also proposed a demonstration of a Saving Gateway, matched saving for the poor.[45] Blair said:

I believe we have already made important strides in extending opportunity for all—through improving skills and work, through improving living

44. President Clinton, State of the Union Address, Washington, 2000. Barr, who co-authored this chapter, participated in policy development on USAs and RSAs at the Treasury Department. Before Clinton's speech, at the request of the Treasury Department and White House, the Center for Social Development provided data and analyses from IDA research in ADD.

45. The Institute for Public Policy Research (IPPR) has led asset-based policy work in the United Kingdom (for example, Kelly and Lissauer, 2000; IPPR, 2001). Asset-based theory, policy discussion, and IDA research from the United States influenced development of the Saving Gate- way and Child Trust Fund in the United Kingdom (see H.M. Treasury, 2001; Sherraden, 2002).

standards, and through improving the quality of public services. But now we want to add a fourth element: more people getting the benefit of assets and savings, so that we help spread prosperity and opportunity to every family and community. . . . We want to see all children growing up knowing that they have a financial stake in society. We want to see all children have the opportunity of a real financial springboard to a better education, a better job, a better home—a better life. . . .[46]

The Child Trust Fund would be based on the principle of progressive universalism, wherein every baby would receive an endowment, but those in lower-income families would receive a larger lump sum. In the original proposal, every child in the United Kingdom would receive at birth a deposit into an account, and three additional deposits, ranging from fifty to 100 pounds, would be made as the child grows up. Parents, relatives, or friends could make additional contributions. A limited number of investment options would be available (H.M. Treasury, 2001).[47]

In April 2003, Prime Minister Blair announced that he would go forward with the Child Trust Fund. Beginning in April 2005, each newborn child will be given an account, retrospective to children born from September 2002. All children will receive an initial deposit of at least 250 pounds, and children in the bottom third of family income will receive 500 pounds. Additional government deposits are not yet specified (H.M. Treasury, 2003). The Child Trust Fund will provide universal and progressive contributions to the child's account, and lifelong accumulation.[48] As David Blunkett observed in 2000 when he was Secretary of State for Education and Employment "we are on the cusp of a different way of looking at the welfare state—one which focuses on capital and assets."[49]

Conclusion

Perhaps the rudimentary institutional theory of saving outlined in this chapter will be a useful step forward. A focus on saving and asset-based policy is not intended to replace a focus on income support, or to limit support for credit-oriented policy, but rather to complement income and credit policies. It seems likely that more diverse policy responses will be emerging in the years ahead. This chapter adds to a growing body of work in asking whether savings and

46. Tony Blair, "Savings and Assets for All," speech given April 26, 2001, 10 Downing Street, London.

47. Nissan and Le Grand (2000) were influential in the Child Trust Fund proposal.

48. Precursors to this policy concept can be found in Tobin (1968), Haveman (1988), Sawhill (1989), Sherraden (1991), and Lindsey (1994).

49. David Blunketts, "On Your Side: The New Welfare State as an Engine of Prosperity," speech given to Department of Education and Employment, London, June 7, 2000.

assets should play a larger role in public policy, and whether the poor should be included in the saving and asset-based policies that already exist.

In the twentieth century, U.S. public policy extended income supports of many kinds to a larger portion of the low-income population. Public policy and private enterprise have extended credit broadly. The widespread availability of credit in America is a remarkable financial achievement.[50] If the same level of policy commitment and commercial creativity were applied to the goal of extending saving, it is possible that millions of low-income Americans who today have little or no savings would begin to save and accumulate assets.

References

Aizcorbe, A. M., and others. 2003. "Recent Changes in U.S. Family Finances: Evidence from the 1998 and 2001 Survey of Consumer Finances." *Federal Reserve Bulletin* 89 (1): 1–37.

Ameriks, J., A. Caplin, and J. Leahy. 2002. "Wealth Accumulation and the Propensity to Plan." Working Paper 8920. Cambridge: Mass.: National Bureau of Economic Research.

Asher, M. 1991. "Social Adequacy and Equity of the Social Security Arrangements in Singapore." Occasional Paper 8. Centre for Advanced Studies, National University of Singapore.

Bachelder, E., and I. Aguerre. 1999. Dove Associates. ETA Conjoint Research (U.S. Department of the Treasury) (www.fms.treas.gov/eta/reports/conjoint.pdf).

Banerjee, A.V. 2001. "Contracting Constraints, Credit Markets, and Economic Development." Working Paper 02-17. MIT Department of Economics (September).

Barr, M. S. 2004. "Banking the Poor." *Yale Journal on Regulation* 21 (1): 121–237.

Basset, W. F., M. J. Fleming, and A. P. Rodriguez. 1998. "How Workers Use 401(k) Plans: The Participation, Contribution, and Withdrawal Decisions." *National Tax Journal* 51 (2): 263–89.

Bayer, P. J., B. D. Bernheim, and J. K. Scholz. 1996. "The Effects of Financial Education in the Workplace: Evidence from a Survey of Employers." Working Paper 5655. Cambridge, Mass.: National Bureau of Economic Research.

Bernheim, B. D., and D. M. Garrett. 1996. "The Determinants and Consequences of Financial Education in the Workplace: Evidence from a Survey of Households." Working Paper 5667. Cambridge, Mass.: National Bureau of Economic Research.

Bernheim, B. D., D. M. Garrett, and D. M. Maki. 2001. "Education and Saving: The Long-Term Effects of High School Financial Curriculum Mandates." *Journal of Public Economics* 80 (3): 435–65.

Bernheim, B. D., and J. K. Scholz. 1993. "Private Saving and Public Policy." *Tax Policy and the Economy* 7: 73–110.

Berube, A., and others. 2002. "The Price of Paying Taxes: How Tax Reparation and Refund Loan Fees Erode the Benefits of the EITC." Progressive Policy Institute Survey Series. Brookings.

Beverly, S. G., and M. Sherraden. 1999. "Institutional Determinants of Saving: Implications for Low-Income Households and Public Policy." *Journal of Socio-Economics* 28: 457–73.

Beverly, S. G., J. Tescher, and D. Marzahl. Forthcoming. "Low-Cost Bank Accounts and the EITC." In *Inclusion in the American Dream: Assets, Poverty, and Public Policy,* edited by M. Sherraden. Oxford University Press.

---

50. As detailed in other chapters in this volume, not all credit is quality credit. Nonetheless, the sheer availability of credit in the current U.S. political economy may be unprecedented.

Blank, R. 2002. "Evaluating Welfare Reform in the U.S." *Journal of Economic Literature* 40: 1105–66.

Booz-Allen Hamilton, Shugoll Research, U.S. Treasury. 1997. "Mandatory EFT Demographic Study." OMB 1510-00-68.

Cagan, P. 1965. "The Effect of Pension Plans on Aggregate Savings: Evidence from a Sample Survey." Occasional Paper 95. New York: National Bureau of Economic Research.

Carney, S., and W. Gale. 2001. "Asset Accumulation among Low-Income Households." In *Assets for the Poor: The Benefits of Spreading Asset Ownership,* edited by T. Shapiro and E. Wolff, pp. 165–205. New York: Russell Sage Foundation.

Carr, J. H., and J. Schuetz. 2001. "Financial Services in Distressed Communities." Fannie Mae Foundation (August).

Carroll, C. D. 1997. "Buffer-Stock Saving and the Life Cycle/Permanent Income Hypothesis." *Quarterly Journal of Economics* 12 (1): 1–55.

Carroll, C. D., and A. A. Samwick. 1997. "The Nature of Precautionary Wealth." *Journal of Monetary Economics* 40 (1): 41–71.

Carroll, C. D., and L. H. Summers. 1987. "Why Have Private Savings Rates in the United States and Canada Diverged?" *Journal of Monetary Economics* 20: 249–79.

Caskey, J. P. 1994. *Fringe Banking: Check-Cashing Outlets, Pawnshops, and the Poor.* New York: Russell Sage Foundation.

———. 1997. *Beyond Cash-and-Carry: Financial Savings, Financial Services, and Low-Income Households in Two Communities.* Consumer Federation of America.

———. Forthcoming. "Reaching Out to the Unbanked." In *Inclusion in the American Dream: Assets, Poverty, and Public Policy,* edited by M. Sherraden. Oxford University Press.

Chiteji, N., and D. Hamilton. Forthcoming. "Family Matters: Kin Networks and Asset Accumulation." In *Inclusion in the American Dream: Assets, Poverty, and Public Policy,* edited by M. Sherraden. Oxford University Press.

Choi, J. J., and others. 2001. "For Better or For Worse: Default Effects and 401(k) Savings Behavior." Working Paper 8651. Cambridge, Mass.: National Bureau of Economic Research.

———. 2004. "Defined Contribution Pensions: Plan Rules, Participant Decisions, and the Path of Least Resistance." In *Tax Policy and the Economy,* edited by J. M. Poterba, pp. 67–113. MIT Press.

Clancy, M., M. Grinstein-Weiss, and M. Schreiner. 2001. "Financial Education and Savings Outcomes in Individual Development Accounts." Working Paper 01-2. Washington University, Center for Social Development.

Coase, Robert. 1937. "The Nature of the Firm." *Economica* 386 (4): 386–405.

Cohen, S. 1994. "Consumer Socialization: Children's Saving and Spending." *Childhood Education* 70 (4): 244–46.

Consultative Group to Assist the Poorest. 2002. "Savings Are as Important as Credit: Deposit Services for the Poor." Donor Brief 4. Washington: Consultative Group to Assist the Poorest.

Corporation for Enterprise Development. 2002. *Federal IDA Briefing Book: How IDAs Affect Eligibility for Federal Programs.*

DeNavas-Walt, C., and others. 2003. "U.S. Census Bureau, Current Population Reports, P60-221, Income in the United States: 2002." Washington: GPO.

Dove Consulting. 2000. *U.S. Department of the Treasury, Survey of Nonbank Financial Institutions.*

Duesenberry, J. S. 1949. *Income, Saving, and the Theory of Consumer Behavior.* Harvard University Press.

Dunham, C. R. 2001. "The Role of Banks and Nonbanks in Serving Low- and Moderate-Income Communities." Paper prepared for Changing Financial Markets and Community

Development Federal Reserve System Community Affairs Research Conference, Washington, April 5-6.

Engen, E. M., W. Gale, and J. Scholz. 1996. "The Illusory Effects of Saving Incentives on Saving." *Journal of Economic Perspectives* 10 (4): 113–38.

Feldstein, M. 1995. "College Scholarship Rules and Private Saving." *American Economic Review* 85 (3): 552–66.

Fox, J. A., and E. Mierzwinski. 2001. "Rent-A-Bank Payday Lending: The 2001 Payday Lender Survey and Report." Consumer Federation of America (CFA) and the U.S. Public Interest Research Group.

Friedman, M. 1957. "A Theory of the Consumption Function." General Series 63. National Bureau of Economic Research. Princeton University Press.

Furnham, A. 1985. "Why Do People Save? Attitudes to, and Habits of, Saving Money in Britain." *Journal of Applied Social Psychology* 15 (4): 354–73.

Gale, W. G., and S. Carney. 1998. "Asset Accumulation among Lower-Income Households, Benefits and Mechanisms for Spreading Asset Ownership in the United States." Paper prepared for Ford Foundation Conference, New York University, December 10-12.

General Accounting Office. 2002. "Electronic Transfers: Use by Federal Payment Recipients Has Increased but Obstacles to Greater Participation Remain." GAO-02-913. Report to the Subcommittee on Oversight and Investigations, Committee on Financial Services, House of Representatives.

Gordon, W. 1980. *Institutional Economics: The Changing System.* University of Austin Press.

Greene, W. H., S. L. W. Rhine, and M. Toussaint-Comeau. 2003. "The Importance of Check-Cashing Businesses to the Unbanked: Racial/Ethnic Differences." Working Paper 2003-10. Federal Reserve Board of Chicago.

H. M. Treasury. 2001. *Saving and Assets for All: The Modernisation of Britain's Tax and Benefit System, Number Eight.* London.

————. 2003. *Details of the Child Trust Fund.* London.

Haveman, R. 1988. *Starting Even: An Equal Opportunity Program to Combat the Nation's New Poverty.* New York: Simon and Schuster.

Highfill, J., D. Thorson, and W. Weber. 1998. "Tax Overwithholding as a Response to Uncertainty." *Public Finance Review* 26 (4): 8.

Hogarth, J. M., J. Lee, and C. Anguelov. 2005. "Who Has a Bank Account? Exploring Changes over Time, 1989–2001." *Journal of Family and Economic Issues* 26 (1): 7–30.

Hogarth, J. M., and K. H. O'Donnell. 1999. "Banking Relationships of Lower-Income Families and the Government Trend toward Electronic Payment." *Federal Reserve Bulletin* 85: 463.

Hotz, V. J., and J. K. Scholz. 2001. "The Earned Income Tax Credit." Working Paper 8078. Cambridge, Mass.: National Bureau of Economic Research.

Howard, C. 1997. *The Hidden Welfare State: Tax Expenditures and Social Policy in the United States.* Princeton University Press.

Hubbard, R. G., and J. S. Skinner. 1996. "Assessing the Effectiveness of Saving Incentives." *Journal of Economic Perspectives* 10 (4): 73–90.

Hubbard, R. G., J. Skinner, and S. P. Zeldes. 1995. "Precautionary Saving and Social Insurance." *Journal of Political Economy* 103 (2): 360–99.

Hurst, E., and J. Ziliak. 2001. "Welfare Reform and Household Savings." Working Paper 234. Northwestern University/University of Chicago Joint Center for Poverty Research.

Institute for Public Policy Research. 2001. "The Centre for Asset-Based Welfare at the Institute for Public Policy Research." London: Institute for Public Policy Research.

Joulfaian, D., and D. Richardson. 2001. "Who Takes Advantage of Tax-Deferred Savings Programs? Evidence from Federal Income Tax Data." *National Tax Journal* 54 (3): 669–88.

Katona, G. 1975. *Psychological Economics.* New York: Elsevier.

Kelly, G., and R. Lissauer. 2000. *Ownership for All.* London: Institute for Public Policy Research.

Kennickell, A. B., and others. 2000. "Recent Changes in U.S. Family Finances: Results from the 1998 Survey of Consumer Finances." *Federal Reserve Bulletin* 86: 1–29.

Korczyk, S. M. 1998. *How Americans Save.* Washington: American Association of Retired Persons.

Kusko, A. L., J. M. Porterba, and D. W. Wilcox. 1994. "Employee Decisions with Respect to 401(k) Plans: Evidence from Individual Level Data." Working Paper 4635. Cambridge, Mass.: National Bureau of Economic Research.

Lindsey, D. 1994. *The Welfare of Children.* Oxford University Press.

Madrian, B. C., and D. F. Shea. 2000. "The Power of Suggestion: Inertia in 401(k) Participation and Savings Behavior." Working Paper 7682. Cambridge, Mass.: National Bureau of Economic Research.

Maital, S. 1986. "Prometheus Rebound: On Welfare-Improving Constraints." *Eastern Economic Journal* 12 (3): 337–44.

Maital, S., and L. Maital. 1994. "Is the Future What It Used to Be? A Behavioral Theory of the Decline of Saving in the West." *Journal of Socio-Economics* 23 (1/2): 1–32.

Modigliani, F., and R. Brumberg. 1954. "Utility Analysis and the Consumption Function: An Interpretation of Cross-Section Data." In *Post-Keynesian Economics,* edited by K. K. Kurihara, pp. 388–436. New Brunswick, N.J.: Rutgers University Press.

Neale, W. C. 1987. "Institutions." *Journal of Economic Issues* 21 (3): 1177–206.

Neumark, D. 1995. "Are Rising Earnings Profiles a Forced-Savings Mechanism?" *Economic Journal* 105: 95–106.

Nissan, D., and J. LeGrand. 2000. "A Capital Idea: Start-Up Grants for Young People." Policy Report 49. London: Fabian Society.

North, Douglas C. 1990. *Institutions, Institutional Change, and Economic Performance.* University of Cambridge Press.

Oliver, M., and T. Shapiro. 1990. "Wealth of a Nation: A Reassessment of Asset Inequality in American Shows That at Least One-Third of Households Are Asset Poor." *American Journal of Economics and Sociology* 49: 129–51.

———. 1995. *Black Wealth/White Wealth: A New Perspective on Racial Inequality.* New York: Routledge.

Orszag, P., and R. Greenstein. Forthcoming. "Employer-Based Pension Plans: Policy, Inequality, and Recommendations." In *Inclusion in the American Dream: Assets, Poverty, and Public Policy,* edited by M. Sherraden. Oxford University Press.

Poterba, J. M., S. F. Venti, and D. A. Wise. 1996. "How Retirement Saving Programs Increase Saving." *Journal of Economic Perspectives* 10 (4): 91–112.

Powell, Walter W., and Paul J. DiMaggio, eds. 1991. *The New Institutionalism in Organizational Analysis.* University of California Press.

Powers, E. T. 1998. "Does Means-Testing Welfare Discourage Saving? Evidence from a Change in AFDC Policy in the United States." *Journal of Public Economics* 68: 33–53.

Proctor, B. D., and J. Dalaker. 2003. U.S. Census Bureau, Current Population Reports P60-222, "Poverty in the United States: 2002." Washington: U.S. Government Printing Office.

Rhine, S., M. Toussaint-Comeau, and J. Hogarth. 2001. "The Role of Alternative Financial Service Providers in Serving LMI Neighborhoods." Paper prepared for Changing Financial Markets and Community Development, Federal Reserve System Community Affairs Research Conference, Washington, April 5-6.

Rutherford, S. 1998. "The Savings of the Poor: Improving Financial Services in Bangladesh." *Journal of International Development* 10 (1): 1–15.

————. 2000. *The Poor and Their Money*. Oxford University Press.

Sawhill, I. 1989. "The Underclass: An Overview." *The Public Interest* 96 (Summer): 3–15.

Schreiner, M. 2001. "Match Rates and Savings: Evidence from Individual Development Accounts." Working Paper 01-6. Washington University, Center for Social Development.

Schreiner, M., M. Clancy, and M. Sherraden. 2002. "Saving Performance in the American Dream Demonstration." Research Report. Washington University, Center for Social Development.

Schreiner, M., and J. Morduch, eds. 2003. *Replicating Microfinance in the United States*. Washington: Woodrow Wilson Center Press.

Seidman, L. 2001. "Assets and the Tax Code." In *Assets for the Poor: Benefits and Mechanisms of Spreading Asset Ownership*, edited by T. Shapiro and E. N. Wolff, pp. 324–56. New York: Russell Sage Foundation.

Shapiro, T. 2004. *The Hidden Cost of Being Black*. Oxford University Press.

Shefrin, H. M., and R. H. Thaler. 1988. "The Behavioral Life-Cycle Hypothesis." *Economic Inquiry* 26: 609–43.

Sherraden, M., and others. 1995. "Social Policy Based on Assets: The Impact of Singapore's Central Provident Fund." *Asian Journal of Political Science* 3 (2): 112–33.

Sherraden, M., and others. 2005. "Saving in Low-Income Households: Evidence from Interviews with Participants in the American Dream Demonstation." Center for Social Development, Washington University.

————. Forthcoming. "The Meaning of Savings." *Journal of Income Distribution*.

Sherraden, M. 1988. "Rethinking Social Welfare: Toward Assets." *Social Policy* 18 (3): 37–43.

————. 1991. *Assets and the Poor: A New American Welfare Policy*. Armonk, N.Y.: M.E. Sharpe.

————. 2002. "Opportunity and Assets: The Role of the Child Trust Fund." Notes for seminar organized by Prime Minister Tony Blair, 10 Downing Street, London, and dinner speech with Chancellor of the Exchequer Gordon Brown, 11 Downing Street, London, September 19.

————. 2003. "Individual Accounts in Social Security: Can They Be Progressive?" *International Journal of Social Welfare* 12 (2): 97–107.

Sherraden, M., M. Schreiner, and S. Beverly. 2003. "Income, Institutions, and Saving Performance in Individual Development Accounts." *Economic Development Quarterly* 17 (1): 95–112.

Smeeding, T. M. Forthcoming. "The EITC and USAs/IDAs: Maybe a Marriage Made in Heaven?" In *Inclusion in the American Dream: Assets, Poverty, and Public Policy*, edited by M. Sherraden. Oxford University Press.

Smeeding, T. M., K. R. Phillips, and M. O'Connor. 2000. "The EITC: Expectation, Knowledge, Use and Economic and Social Mobility." Center for Policy Research (April).

Smelser, N. J., and R. Swedberg, eds. 1994. *The Handbook of Economic Sociology*. Princeton University Press.

Stack, C. 1974. *All Our Kin: Strategies for Survival in the Black Community*. New York: Harper and Row.

Stegman, M. 1999. *Savings and the Poor: The Hidden Benefits of Electronic Banking*. Brookings.

Stegman, M. A., and R. Faris. 2001. "Welfare, Work, and Banking: The North Carolina Financial Services Survey." The 23rd Annual Research Conference of the Association for Public Policy, Analysis, and Management, Washington, November 2.

Summers, L. H. 2000. Remarks at the Department of Labor Retirement Savings Education Campaign, Fifth Anniversary Event, Washington, July 18.

Thaler, R. H. 2000. "From Homo Economicus to Homo Sapiens." *Journal of Economic Perspectives* 14 (1): 133–41.

Thaler, R., and S. Benartzi. 2004. "Save More Tomorrow: Using Behavioral Economics to Increase Employee Saving." *Journal of Political Economics* 112: S164–S187.

Tobin, J. 1968. "Raising the Incomes of the Poor." In *Agenda for the Nation,* edited by K. Gordon, pp. 77–116. Brookings.

U.S. Census Bureau. 2002. "Historical Income Table-Families (table F-3). Mean Income Received by Each Fifth and Top 5 Percent of Families (All Races): 1966 to 2001." (September).

U.S. Department of the Treasury. 1998. TSP Participation and Contribution Rates Sheet.

Vermilyea, T., and J. A. Wilcox. 2002. "Who is Unbanked, and Why: Results from a Large, New Survey of Low- and Moderate-Income Adults." Federal Reserve Bank of Chicago, Conference on Bank Structure and Competition, May 8-10.

Vittas, D. 1992. *Swiss Chilanpore: The Forward for Pension Reform?* Washington: World Bank.

Yadama, G., and M. Sherraden. 1996. "Effects of Assets on Attitudes and Behaviors: Advance Test of a Social Policy Proposal." *Social Work Research* 20 (1): 3–11.

Ziliak, J. P. 1999. "Income Transfers and Assets of the Poor." Discussion Paper 1202-99. University of Wisconsin, Institute for Research on Poverty.

13

Unbanked to Homeowner: Improving Financial Services for Low-Income, Low-Asset Customers

ELLEN SEIDMAN AND JENNIFER TESCHER

B eing poor at the end of the twentieth century did not necessarily mean having a low income. In 1998, at the height of the most recent economic boom, the official poverty rate for families had fallen to 10 from 12.3 percent at the close of the severe recession of the 1980s. Yet in the same fifteen-year period, asset poverty had risen to 25.5 from 22.4 percent (Haveman and Wolff, 2001).[1]

The asset poor disproportionately belong to minority groups and have lower education levels. In 1998, 45.3 percent of blacks and Hispanics were asset poor, compared to 20.5 percent of white households. Similarly, 26.5 percent of high-school graduates were poor, compared to 15.3 percent of college graduates. Among female-headed households with children, the asset-poverty rate was an astounding 53.7 percent (Haveman and Wolff, 2001).[2] In real terms, these fam-

The Ford Foundation sponsored much of this chapter's research. The authors wish to thank their colleagues at ShoreBank Advisory Services, particularly Lisa Richter, Christopher Tan, Bryant Woods, and Claudia Puentes, for their assistance and insights.

1. The cited number is based on the least-inclusive definition of asset poverty: a family's total net worth, including both liquid and illiquid assets, is insufficient to meet the basic needs of food, clothes, and shelter for three months. A more inclusive, but more realistic, definition of asset poverty that excludes often illiquid home equity from the calculation showed that 36.8 percent of households were poor.

2. Asset-poverty rates were also extremely high among those under age twenty (70.7 percent), ages twenty-five to thirty-four years old (46.8 percent), and without even a high-school degree (40.2 percent).

ilies are living a paycheck or two away from destitution, at risk of not having enough money to feed, clothe, and shelter family members. With the U.S. unemployment rate climbing from 4.5 percent in 1998 (the year of the statistics cited above) to the current rate of 5.2 percent, many asset-poor families have faced this situation (March 2005). Trends in requests for emergency food and shelter bear this out. According to the U.S. Conference of Mayors' (2002) study of hunger and homelessness in American cities, each of the twenty-five cities surveyed saw an increase in requests for emergency food assistance, with an average increase of 19 percent over 2001 request levels. Requests for emergency shelter increased an average of 19 percent in the same period, with all but three cities citing an increase. These increases follow similarly large increases in every year since 1998.

Over the last several years, it has become increasingly recognized that the financial services system can play a major role in the relationship between income and asset building. Lower-income families with deposit accounts are more likely to own other assets, such as savings or retirement accounts, homes, cars, and life insurance, than are those without accounts (Hogarth and O'Donnell, 1999).[3]

According to the 2001 Survey of Consumer Finances, only 11 percent of the total population did not have a transaction account, but this included almost 25 percent of nonwhite or Hispanic households, more than 30 percent of those in the bottom income quintile, and 20 percent of renters.[4] The reasons cited for not having this type of account included not only "do not have enough money," but also concerns about minimum balances and service charges and a simple dislike of dealing with banks (Aizcorbe, Kennickell, and Moore, 2003; Caskey, 2000). Yet even the poorest of the poor have demonstrated they can save and become owners of major assets such as houses when provided with the appropriate structure and incentives (Schreiner, Clancy, and Sherraden, 2002).

A bank account serves many purposes in today's economy. It provides an opportunity to receive a paycheck quickly and safely, along with myriad ways of accessing funds, including checks, ATMs, and debit cards. Particularly important for the purposes of this chapter, however, is that a bank account provides an opportunity to save, including saving in very small increments, and to earn interest on those savings. In turn, a banking relationship established through a checking or savings account can provide the account holder with financial education and high-quality credit products, as well as with positive recognition in a credit report.

3. Lower-income families are defined as those with incomes under 80 percent of the national median, which in 2003 (the latest year for which data are available) was $43,318.

4. Higher-bound estimates of the number of unbanked consumers were developed by the General Accounting Office (GAO) using data from the 1998 and 1999 Survey of Income and Program Participation (SIPP) (GAO, 2002).

In summary, the path from asset poverty to homeownership may well be through traditional financial services providers—but only if that sector can rise to the occasion. This will require new product design, improved marketing and outreach strategies, more welcoming customer service, and, especially, buy-in from bank CEOs. Moreover, banks will have to go beyond persuading low-income customers to open accounts. Banks must also enable and encourage their account holders to make full and effective use of the broader suite of services—including savings and investment vehicles—that traditional financial services providers can offer. Fortunately, developments in demographics, marketing, technology, and public policy all suggest an increase in the sector's interest in and ability to serve many of those in the lower reaches of the income and asset scale.

How We Got Here

During the 1980s, a series of articles in the *Atlanta Journal and Constitution* drew the country's attention to the problems that minorities, particularly African Americans, were having in obtaining the benefits of the modern mortgage finance system.[5] Although there have always been African American homeowners, they and other minority and low-income consumers appeared not to be benefiting from the steady supply of relatively low-cost mortgage money that the mainstream financial services sector, working with the secondary market, was increasingly making available to other borrowers. Over the next several years, many developments combined to significantly increase homeownership rates among minorities and low-income families, including the greater effectiveness of the Community Reinvestment Act (CRA) and Home Mortgage Disclosure Act; the rise of effective advocacy targeting this issue by community-based organizations; and external and internal pressures on Fannie Mae and Freddie Mac.[6]

By the late 1990s, however, new issues and concerns had appeared. Community-based organizations, and then the press and policymakers, became concerned about the quality of the loans supporting those homeownership rates. Predatory lending, in which equity was stripped from homes rather than added to it, first appeared in the press in January 1998 and in congressional testimony in March 1998.[7] Cases against Delta Funding, First Alliance, and Associates

5. Bill Dedman, "The Color of Money," *Atlanta Journal and Constitution,* May 1-4, 1988. The series was awarded the Pulitzer Prize in 1989.

6. Compare U.S. Census Bureau (1999, tables 7 and 8) with U.S. Department of Commerce News (2004, tables 7 and 8).

7. Kathleen Howley, "Borrowers with Credit Problems Have Options: You Don't Need a Perfect History to Obtain a Mortgage Because Banks Are Offering Up a Variety of 'Subprime' Lending Products," *Boston Globe,* January 4, 1998, p. G1. See also congressional testimony presented before the Senate Special Committee on Aging, March 16, 1998, "Equity Predators: Stripping, Flipping, and Packing Their Way to Profits" (http://aging.senate.gov/public/events/hr14.htm).

First Capital Corp. made it clear that the problem was not confined to a small group of fringe players.[8]

A look at the companies charged and the manner in which they did business strongly suggested that technology, which had been critical in expanding home-ownership opportunities, also provided opportunities to find the vulnerable and to fund loans with only the most limited assessment of risk—and with virtually no knowledge of the borrower's circumstances.

The focus on predatory and more costly subprime lending, with their increased risk of foreclosure,[9] in turn spawned a deeper interest in how and why homeownership had become a trap, rather than a benefit, for some low-income families. Initial efforts at foreclosure prevention turned into broader postpur-chase counseling. By 2000, the Joint Center for Housing Studies at Harvard University was asking whether homeownership is always a "good deal" for low-income homeowners (Retsinas and Belsky, 2002). One of the hypotheses explored was that when families become homeowners without any financial cushion on which they can fall back, problems—such as the major repairs needed by the older houses in which low-income families often live—can lead to disaster, in the form either of a predatory-lending spiral or direct and imme-diate foreclosure.

The focus of the banking and bank regulatory communities, at least through 2000, was on assuming low-income consumers and access to credit. Providing low-income and minority consumers with access to a broader array of financial services was not a priority, and the fact that many Americans had no connection to a traditional bank was not part of the national consciousness. The general assumption was that low-income consumers had low account balances and high transaction volumes—an unprofitable combination for a traditional bank. Aside from various state laws requiring lifeline banking accounts for senior citizens and the poor, banking regulators emphasized the importance of providing loans and investments in low-income communities rather than other types of asset-building consumer financial services. Thus there were neither private incentives nor public pressures to adequately serve this market.

A variety of changes in the financial services environment ultimately has led to a greater recognition of the plight of the asset poor and the connection between asset building—including homeownership—and access to financial ser-vices (see table 13-1).

---

8. See *People of the State of New York* v. *Delta Funding Corp.*, 99-Civ.-4951 (E.D.N.Y.); *Federal Trade Commission* v. *Citigroup Inc. Associates First Capital Corporation*, 239 F. Supp. 2d 1302 (N.D. Georgia 2001); *Federal Trade Commission* v. *First Capital*. 00-CV-905C F. 206 F.R.P. 358 (W.D. N.Y. 2001).

9. Foreclosures have increased fairly steadily since 1986, in part because of the increase in the proportion of subprime loans. U.S. Department of Housing and Urban Development (2005, p. 74, table 18).

Table 13-1. *Changes in the Financial Services Industry*

Major changes	Impacts and consequences
Technological advances reach consumer-banking segment.	Reduction in the cost of serving the consumer market. Introduction of more efficient retail products.
Direct deposit of federal payments.	New research to better understand preferences of low-income consumers. Increased recognition of the unbanked.
Expansion of alternative financial services sector.	New concerns over predatory practices. Demonstration of profitability of low-income consumers. Increasing awareness, interest of traditional financial institutions in the market.
Emergence of the Individual Development Account (IDA) movement.	Better understanding of the importance of assets and connection to financial services. Proof that the poor can save.
Major demographic shifts in the United States.	Confirmation of market potential of Latinos, other immigrant groups. Growing interest from banks.

First, the technology boom that had made the increase in homeownership possible began to move more fully into the retail market (Weissbourd, 2002). While Internet banking as a stand-alone business has not met its initial promise, automated teller machines (ATMs) capable of performing an expanding array of functions, direct deposit, online banking and, most recently, all types of electronic payment products, have brought down the cost of serving the retail banking customer and carry the promise of ever-greater efficiencies.

Second, following the passage of the Debt Collection Improvement Act of 1996, which required that all federal payments to individuals (other than tax refunds) be made by direct deposit, the Treasury Department (which was charged with the task) realized that many federal benefit recipients did not have bank accounts. Although there is dispute over the precise number of people involved, it was at least 10 million (General Accounting Office, 2002). To develop a strategy for dealing with this problem, the Treasury Department commissioned research that led to a better understanding of why people did not have bank accounts (Dove Consulting, 2000; Dunham, 2001). Despite this increased recognition of the unbanked, the department's ultimate solution, the Electronic Transfer Account, did little to move significant numbers of benefit recipients to direct deposit (General Accounting Office, 2002).

Third, the alternative financial services sector mushroomed throughout the 1990s and has continued to grow. For example, the number of payday lending stores grew from a few hundred outlets in the mid-1990s to more than 10,000 by 2000. The number of pawnshops increased from about 4,800 in 1986 to more than 11,600 in 2003. Check-cashing outlets (which often also function as payday lenders) proliferated, with especially significant increases in states where payday lending is common, such as Alabama, Kentucky, Mississippi, South Carolina, Tennessee, and Utah (Tanoue, 2000; Caskey, forthcoming). Research focused on substitute financial services providers—check cashers, payday lenders, pawn shops, and rent-to-own stores—and tallied up the toll taken by the use of these providers on the finances of low-income individuals and communities (Carr and Schuetz, 2001). It also became clear that the subprime and alternative financial services sectors could be highly lucrative (Caskey, forthcoming; Dove Consulting, 2000). A few mainstream financial services institutions sought to leverage the growing distribution channel offered by alternative players by buying firms, joining forces in funding (sometimes characterized as "renting their charter"), or adding alternative products to their traditional product lines.

Fourth, the emergence of the Individual Development Account (IDA) movement emphasized the role of assets in poverty alleviation and demonstrated the importance of formal financial mechanisms in facilitating saving (Beverly and Sherraden, 1999). An IDA is a financial tool, typically a savings account held at a depository institution, which matches the savings of low-income families with additional funds in order to facilitate the purchase of an asset, such as a house, post-secondary education, or small business. The IDA concept (see Sherraden, 1991) took hold rapidly with the development, by the end of the century, of a multimillion-dollar national demonstration project organized by the Corporation for Enterprise Development and funded by a group of foundations. Targeted policy work by these groups and others led to the creation of a federally funded IDA program and numerous state programs. By 2003, the number of IDAs was estimated at between 20,000 (New America Foundation, 2003) and 50,000 (see chapter 12 in this volume). These new resources created greater opportunities for understanding how poor people can build assets and how financial institutions might become part of that process.

Finally, and to some extent unacknowledged until the results of the 2000 Census became available in 2001, the United States was undergoing major demographic shifts. Financial services firms began to focus more heavily on the market opportunities implied by these changes. In particular, the Latino population grew by 58 percent in the 1990s and by 2003 totaled 37.4 million, or 13 percent of the U.S. population (U.S. Census Bureau, 2003). Sixty percent of Latinos were born in the United States and 55 percent live in the suburbs. Estimates of Latino purchasing power exceed $600 billion annually. Yet a very large percentage of the Latino population—estimates range as high as 34 percent (53 percent for Latino immigrants)—is unbanked (Jacob and others, 2005). The Asian population also grew very substantially in the 1990s, and the African

American population grew at a rate significantly exceeding that of the non-Hispanic white population. Immigrant and minority populations also tend to be significantly younger than the white population. In combination with ever-increasing information about the profitability of the alternative financial services sector, demographic trends are causing mainstream financial services providers to focus attention on formerly overlooked communities.

Asset Building and Financial Services: Demand

Banks, thrifts, and credit unions can serve the asset-building needs of individuals by providing access to deposit accounts (which are a convenient and safe way to receive and hold money) and to savings accounts (which enable people to save and earn interest and to track their deposits and interest earned). Depository institutions also provide access to the payments system. In addition, many depository institutions provide informal, formal, or both kinds of financial education, usually in connection with a transaction or proposed transaction, such as buying a home. As highly regulated institutions, they are also more likely to provide loans on responsible terms and with reporting that enables consumers to build up positive credit records. Yet a significant number of low-income, low-asset individuals sit on the sidelines of the traditional financial services marketplace, often because their immediate needs are unmet by traditional offerings.

A good deal has been written on this subject over the last several years, most recently in an analysis of the 2001 Survey of Consumer Finances by Aizcorbe, Kennickell, and Moore (2003). They found that of those without checking accounts, 28.6 percent thought they did not write enough checks to make it worthwhile, but a full 22.6 percent simply did not like dealing with banks; 10.2 percent found service charges too high; while only 3.6 percent cited credit problems. However, among the half of the sample currently without a checking account who had had one in the past, 12.8 percent said services charges were too high and 6.3 percent cited credit problems. It is not only self-selection that keeps people who have had difficulty managing checking accounts out of the banking system. Most banks subscribe to and use ChexSystems, a database that tracks individuals who have had problems managing checking accounts, ranging from bounced checks to fraud, over the prior five years. Until recently, being listed on ChexSystems, no matter what the cause, was sufficient reason to deny an individual an opportunity to open a checking account at the nation's largest banks (Park, 2003).[10]

Other studies have expanded on respondents' stated dislike of banks, citing negative experiences in dealing with banks, either in this country or abroad; lack

---

10. See Paul Beckett, "It's Not in the Mail: Bounce a Check and You Might Not Write Another for Five Years," *Wall Street Journal,* August 1, 2000, p. A1.

of proper identification; lack of immediate availability of funds; inconvenient locations and hours; difficulty understanding bank fees (resulting in uncertainty and sometimes prior bad experience in using an account); and lack of the full array of services a customer might want, such as inexpensive money orders to pay rent to landlords, who often will not take checks (Carr and Schuetz, 2001; Bair, 2003; Suro and Bendixen, 2002; Berry, Herman, and Wright, 2003). More subtle factors can also discourage low-income consumers, including: the lack of bilingual frontline and customer service staff; a culture that does not emphasize sales or customer service (and thus is not inclined to reach out either to a stranger walking into the lobby or to someone who does not fully understand the terms of an account); and the intimidating manner in which bank lobbies are physically organized.[11] Finally, surveys and interviews show that privacy concerns keep some low-income families from interacting with mainstream banks. This is a growing area of concern for undocumented immigrants, who worry that their information will be shared with immigration authorities. Immigrants are also concerned about the possibility that bank accounts opened with alternative forms of identification, such as Individual Taxpayer Identification numbers, will not be recognized in the future and they will lose access to their money.

Comparing a typical menu of bank products with the reasons why some Americans choose not to have a banking relationship suggests that the problem may not be lack of demand, but rather the lack of an appropriate and appealing supply. While traditional banking institutions are well positioned to meet low-income families' long-term financial needs, most are ill-equipped to meet their immediate and short-term needs. Traditional checking accounts are predicated on consumer liquidity, a luxury poor people generally do not have. Even banks that have one or two products appropriate for modest-income consumers generally lack a full line of products that would enable consumers to build on their initial successes. In addition, bank branches are often inconveniently located for the poor and do not offer them a comfortable atmosphere. While the financial services industry is quite sophisticated about segmenting upper-income consumers and crafting appropriate marketing messages to reach them, little attention has been paid to outreach efforts at the lower end of the income scale.

Moreover, what is required to encourage asset building among low-income consumers is not merely a more robust set of financial products and services, but a holistic approach to engaging with these customers. Consider, for instance, the Credit Path, a model developed by Alternatives Federal Credit Union in Ithaca, N.Y.,[12] to describe the process by which low-income individu-

---

11. Evan Perez, "Banking on Immigrants," *Wall Street Journal,* May 9, 2003, p. B1.

12. Alternatives Federal Credit Union is a Community Development Financial Institution and participant in the Retail Financial Services Initiative (RFSI). RFSI is a three-year project to expand access to financial services and wealth-building opportunities for low- and moderate-income consumers. Organized by the National Community Investment Fund and funded by the Ford, John

als can progress from meeting immediate transactional needs to building longer-term assets. The model, a metaphor for the progression to financial prosperity, describes a path along which consumers travel, first becoming transactors, then savers, then borrowers, and, finally, owners.

Many low-income families are already savers, whether or not they have bank accounts. Without a connection to a formal financial institution, however, their savings will grow far more slowly and they will face more obstacles along the path to longer-term prosperity. The question is, what can depository institutions, community-based organizations, the government, and others (such as vendors of innovative, cost-reducing products) do to make the financial services system a more fully effective means of asset building for low-income consumers?

Asset Building and Financial Services: Supply

Traditional depositories face a host of financial, structural, and cultural challenges in serving low-income consumers both well and profitably. The trends described earlier, however—rapid technological change, the rise of the alternative financial services sector, an increased focus on assets, and major demographic shifts—are creating new opportunities and incentives for the financial services industry to improve the quality and quantity of financial services available to low-income, low-asset consumers in ways that ultimately may promote asset building. Three recent developments in the marketplace provide a glimpse of the potential, as described below.

The players are changing. The constellation of firms that constitutes the financial services industry continues to grow and shift, creating new opportunities and leverage points. Companies that used to be considered financial services vendors, providing products for banks to use, are now marketing their products directly to consumers or using other nonbank firms (such as retailers or employers) to market them. In addition, a whole new category of technology enablers has emerged, providing enhanced platforms for reaching consumers and moving funds. With the support of the Ford Foundation, in early 2004 ShoreBank Advisory Services launched the Center for Financial Services Innovation to work within this broad marketplace to find promising innovations that will enhance the interest and ability of the financial services sector to build long-term relationships with low-income, low-asset consumers. The center also brokers partnerships and invests in promising products, practices, and partnerships.

D. and Catherine T. MacArthur, Annie E. Casey, and Fannie Mae Foundations, the initiative has as its goal increasing the quantity and quality of financial services for low- and moderate-income consumers by developing, testing, and publicizing replicable business models for serving this market. The initiative was formally launched on January 1, 2003, with a group of twelve community banks and credit unions from across the country. Many of the examples in this chapter come from the work of RFSI participating institutions.

Unconventional partnerships are emerging. The growing variety of firms that now constitute the financial services market has led to new, and often unlikely, partnerships. Firms that were not aware of each other three or four years ago are beginning to form alliances—in some cases, specifically in order to reach low- and moderate-income customers.

Access is growing and changing. New partnerships are both being driven by and resulting in a new array of access points for transacting financial business. The functionality of these delivery channels is increasing over time, offering the potential for integrating both short-term transactional products and longer-term, wealth-building products into a coherent system for low-income, low-asset consumers.

Innovation is occurring throughout the industry, at large banks and small credit unions, retailers and nonbank companies, nonprofits and technology firms. In the last two years alone, new products and delivery channels have emerged for sending money abroad, paying employees, cashing checks, storing funds, and making purchases online. All of these provide potential asset-building platforms for currently underserved consumers.

The market clearly is moving, increasingly serving the low-income community. Moreover, in some areas, enhanced competition has produced not only lower prices but also significant innovation. A scan of the financial services landscape, coupled with dozens of interviews with industry actors, points to five broad strategies that hold significant promise for connecting low-income consumers with asset-building opportunities: the workplace as an access point and distribution channel; remittances; stored-value cards; bank/nonbank partnerships; and self-service delivery.

These strategies speak simultaneously to the immediate and short-term needs of low-income consumers and to the profitmaking motive of financial institutions (see table 13-2). However, additional innovation and experimentation are needed to ensure a link to asset building. They hold promise because they meet five important tests:

—They leverage opportunities to reduce costs and increase productivity through technology, without requiring the expense of entirely new platforms.

—They have demonstrated a potential to reduce customer acquisition costs through partnerships and technologies that facilitate broader access and reach.

—They do not require wholesale government intervention or subsidy (though some regulatory changes could be beneficial in broadening product functionality and speeding wider industry adoption).

—A significant amount of firm-level innovation is already occurring, and both new and existing players have emerged as potential change leaders.

—Low-income consumers have demonstrated early acceptance of these product innovations.

Table 13-2. *Strategies for Closing the Supply Gap*

Strategy	Key opportunities
Workplace as an access point and distribution channel	Provides access to potentially large pools of low-wage workers. Builds on existing platforms (automated payroll savings, retirement accounts). Builds on employers' stake in financial well-being of employees.
Remittances	Provide consumer entry point that could lead to other financial products. Reduce costs for financial institutions, fees for consumers.
Stored-value cards	Meet liquidity needs, transactional preferences of low-income consumers. Reduce typical account costs for depositories.
Bank/nonbank partnerships	Increase the reach of depositories while keeping costs low. Recognize needs, preferences of low-income consumers.
Self-service delivery	Reduces transaction costs while improving consumer access.

Workplace as Access Point and Distribution Channel

As an institution that features regular contact between the mainstream economy and low-income, low-asset workers, the workplace presents tremendous opportunities to help these employees build assets. Indeed, as the locus for automatic payroll savings plans and retirement savings plans, such as 401(k) accounts, the workplace has long been a favored asset-building channel for higher-wage workers. The same technology that has made this possible, coupled with newer technologies such as payroll cards, provides the opportunity to extend these benefits to lower-wage workers.

The employment relationship has changed significantly over the last twenty years, with more people being employed by smaller entities for shorter periods. Moreover, the traditional role many credit unions played for large-scale employers—often providing not only bank accounts and auto loans but also financial education and even emergency loans—is not being replicated among the smaller employers where, increasingly, unbanked individuals and those underserved by the traditional financial services system are employed. At the same time, new research indicates that employers have a stake in the financial well-being of their employees. According to one study, the cost to an employer of an employee who is financially stressed is $400 annually, primarily in time wasted and absenteeism. Other studies suggest that 20-30 percent of low-wage workers are under financial stress great enough to hurt their productivity. While financial literacy programs can help reduce financial stress, employers whose programs go beyond literacy to connect employees to bank accounts, help them save, and even provide for responsible short-term emergency loans have better results (Filene Research Institute, 2002). For example, Legacy Bank in Milwaukee, a Retail Financial Services Initiative (RFSI) participant, has been extremely successful in bringing low-income day care center owners and employees into the financial mainstream through a combination of workplace-based financial education and strong customer service.

The workplace can efficiently bring together three parties—worker, employer, and financial institution—that all have an interest in working together to improve the worker's financial status. For financial services firms, the workplace represents an already heavily automated access point for reaching large pools of underserved consumers. For workers, an employer partnership with a depository institution provides an opportunity to receive earnings quickly and safely, as well as access to the type of structured, automated savings mechanisms that make asset building more likely. For employers, such a partnership provides an opportunity not only to reduce payroll costs, but also to enhance worker productivity and retention.

CHANGING TECHNOLOGY OF THE WORKPLACE. Numerous developments have occurred in the way financial services are delivered in the workplace. Two of the most important are direct deposit and retirement saving.

Direct deposit of employee pay became a reality with the formation of the National Automated Clearing House Association (NACHA) in the mid-1970s. Both employers and financial institutions favor direct deposit because of the cost savings—an estimated $1.25 per paycheck for employers and 70 cents per electronic transaction (in contrast to teller use) for financial institutions. An American Payroll Association (2000) survey of employers showed that 56 percent of employees have their paychecks directly deposited, compared with near-universal usage of this option by workers in Japan and Europe. Half of the employees who refuse direct deposit do so because they have no bank account.

To serve unbanked employees and reduce payroll costs even further, increasing numbers of employers are replacing paper paychecks with electronic payroll cards. A Celent Communications study estimates that 10 percent of unbanked households were using payroll cards in 2002, with usage expected to increase to 30 percent in 2005 (Moore, 2002). Currently, more than 2.2 million payroll cards are used, double the number used a year ago (Mayer, 2004). However, the cards' utility in moving employees toward building assets depends in part on how they are structured (Office of the Comptroller of the Currency, 2003).

Employer-sponsored retirement saving plans also have changed significantly over time. Beyond the shift by many employers from defined-benefit to defined-contribution plans, the systems developed by financial services firms to manage retirement plans have reduced administration costs, increased investment options, and facilitated self-service management for employees through the

Internet. Yet these benefits often do not affect low-wage workers, either because their employers do not offer retirement saving plans or because they choose not to participate. Research on savings behavior suggests that saving is more likely if there are automatic mechanisms to facilitate it. For instance, one study found that automatic enrollment for 401(k) plans boosted participation rates from 37 to 86 percent, with even sharper increases for lower-paid employees (Madrian and Shea, 2000). Furthermore, automatic deduction of funds from an employee's paycheck for placement in a pooled retirement account is feasible whether or not the employee has a bank account.

More recently, a handful of employers have begun experimenting with a new crop of wealth-building products and services for employees. Some are beginning to incorporate college savings plans (known as 529 plans) into employee benefit offerings by holding educational seminars and using payroll deduction to facilitate participation (Clancy and Sherraden, 2003). Others, like Marriott International, have begun offering Individual Development Accounts to qualifying employees through partnerships with nonprofit organizations and state governments. Finally, community groups have begun working with employers to provide their employees with information about filing for the Earned Income Tax Credit (EITC). At the end of 2003, for instance, Corporate Voices for Working Families, a nonprofit corporate membership organization of forty-one large employers, created and distributed an EITC Toolkit to highlight the benefit to employers of helping employees apply for the credit.

LEVERAGING THE EMPLOYMENT RELATIONSHIP TO BUILD ASSETS: MOVING THE MARKET. While much has already occurred in the employer-based market, a good deal more needs to be done. In particular, moving from payroll cards, even when account-based, to true participation in asset building will require both structural changes and, more importantly, additional attention to financial education by both financial institutions and employers. (Such education will be necessary to ensure that fees are reasonably structured and minimally incurred). Also, payroll card functionality needs to be more robust to encourage saving and asset building. For instance, payroll deduction is a powerful mechanism for encouraging retirement savings. It could also be used in combination with a payroll card to facilitate shorter-term saving.

Marketing efforts targeted to low-wage workers by financial institutions and employers also need to be improved. Commercial bankers, who tend to manage employer relationships, need to work more closely with those who know how to market to low-wage workers in order to increase the acceptance rate of direct deposit and payroll-card products. One possibility would be to build on the employee assistance program model, developing a new component to provide financial information and counseling by pairing expensive human intermediaries with other sources of information available via the Internet or kiosk. Also, more employers could market the EITC to their low-wage workers, facilitating quick refund receipt and deposit in the short term—and broader financial engagement in the long term—by linking employees with a bank account, payroll card, or other mechanism.

Remittances

Remittances—vehicles for transferring funds from one country to another—are a major product of financial services systems around the world. The worldwide remittance total, acknowledged to be significantly understated, has been estimated at more than $100 billion annually. In 2002, Latino immigrants in the United States sent approximately $32 billion to their respective home countries, about 2 percent of the region's GDP, with almost one-third of the total going to Mexico (Inter-American Dialogue, 2004). The average remittance amount to Latin America is $260 a month. While the share of an immigrant's income sent home in remittances varies with the length of time he or she is in the United States, it is frequently more than 20 percent, with lower-income Latinos accounting for the bulk of remittances. According to the Inter-American Development Bank, fees earned annually from remittances exceed $3 billion (World Council of Credit Unions, 2003).

Until recently, money transfer agents, such as MoneyGram and Western Union, had an almost complete monopoly on consumer remittances. Fees were high and unfavorable exchange rates in recipient countries made the total cost even higher. Starting in 1996, however, and especially since the election of Mexican President Vicente Fox, banks and credit unions have shown increasing interest in this market, launching a series of cheaper alternatives[13] (Orozco, 2003). In January 2004, following the Special Summit of the Americas, the White House announced its commitment to lower the cost of remittances by half within five years by establishing a regionally compatible electronic payment system.[14] The critical factors encouraging banks and credit unions to move into this market appear to be the demographics of the Latino community, increasing use of ATMs by Latinos in both the United States and Latin America (making technological solutions to cost reduction more feasible), and growing acceptance of alternative forms of identification to support opening bank accounts, in particular the *matrícula consular* offered by the Mexican government.

13. See Manuel Orozco, "Costs, Economic Identity, and Banking the Unbanked," testimony before the Congressional Hispanic Caucus, March 26, 2003 (www.thedialogue.org/publications/country_studies/remittances/econ_identity.pdf). Also Manuel Orozco, "Changes in the Atmosphere? Increase of Remittances, Price Decline but New Challenges," Inter-American Dialogue, 2003.

14. Michelle Heller, "White House Remittance Commitment," *American Banker*, January 14, 2004, p. 14. See also Declaration of Nuevo Leon, paper presented at the Summit of the Americas, Monterrey, Mexico, January 12–13, 2004 (www.summit-americas.org/SpecialSummit/Declarations/Declaration%20of%20Nuevo%20Leon%20-%20final.pdf).

Remittances have the potential to be an important entry point, both for banks and credit unions entering the burgeoning Latino market and for Latinos entering the mainstream financial system. They are heavily used by young, low-income, unbanked Latinos, a customer base that traditional banks have had a hard time attracting. Technology is allowing banks to offer remittances more cheaply than their nonbank competitors, reducing both production and customer acquisition costs. Once these new Latino customers are in the door, firms have the opportunity to provide additional products and services.

As banks and credit unions have entered the remittance market over the past twenty-four to thirty-six months, prices have dropped significantly. From November 2001 to November 2002, the average cost of a remittance to Latin America fell from $17.46 to $16.02, a 9 percent decline (Orozco, 2003). In general, bank remittance products fall into one of the following models, in order of lowest to highest cost:

—dual ATM or debit cards for the sender and receiver, with funds available via ATM;

—banks operating as the money transfer agents, in partnership with Mexican banks acting as the receivers;

—traditional wire transfer; and

—through Automated Clearinghouse (ACH) services, which the Federal Reserve system extended to Mexico in 2004.

Numerous banks, large and small, have created dual ATM card accounts with the expectation that one card will be sent to relatives abroad, who will be able to use the ATMs in their home country.

REMITTANCE TO RELATIONSHIP: MOVING THE MARKET. External factors have encouraged new market entrants, increasing the supply of less costly remittance products for Latinos. To move the market further, additional experimentation is needed to translate that first product—a remittance—into a broader financial relationship. The addition of a structured savings feature would turn what is a purely transactional product into an asset-building opportunity. When loading an ATM card with funds to be sent abroad, the consumer should also be able to designate a portion of the funds to be diverted to a savings or investment product.

Partnerships between large financial services firms that have developed low-cost products and other institutions trusted by Latinos are a way of building a broader financial relationship with consumers while simultaneously reducing distribution costs. JP Morgan Chase is using its existing payroll platform to offer a card-to-card remittance product for members of the United Farm Workers of America and other labor union members through a partnership with the AFL-CIO. Union members who sign up receive two cards, one to keep and one to send to family members in other countries, who can use the card to access, via ATM, funds transferred by the worker to the card.

While the remittance market appears to be a perfect example of competition at work to the benefit of all, challenges remain, both to the ability of banks and credit unions to offer the basic product, and, more particularly, to the broader goal of using remittances as a path to asset building. In particular, the USA Patriot Act and concerns about illegal immigration are putting pressure on the use of the *matrícula* and raising questions about ongoing acceptance by banks and credit unions of alternative forms of identification from undocumented immigrants. Conversations with policymakers concerning the implications of the Patriot Act for the ability of banks and credit unions to serve this market will be needed. These conversations should be aimed at ensuring that the laws are designed and interpreted in ways that balance concerns about national security and fraud with the need to provide immigrants with increased access to full financial services.

Stored-Value Cards

The first stored-value cards were transit-fare cards and electronic gift certificates. They were, in essence, electronic cash: they could be spent, but not reloaded, and if lost or stolen the owner had no recourse. The next iteration arrived with electronic-benefits transfer: welfare recipients (and, later, recipients of food stamps and other government benefits) received cards instead of checks. These cards, unlike the original stored-value cards, do not contain the value; instead, they are used to access electronic networks, through which the funds are tracked and stored. The cards are used for both one-time payments, such as insurance claims, and recurring payments such as payroll (discussed above) and child support. Today, there are a variety of stored-value cards, including general spend cards. These cards can be either signature- or PIN-based and can be used for a variety of functions (such as to access cash, pay bills, and buy goods), and many cards can be reloaded in a variety of ways at a range of locations.

At a minimum, stored-value cards provide financial services firms with a less costly mechanism for offering consumers a basic transaction vehicle and a safe place to store funds, merging the payment and saving applications into one product. These cards appeal to cash consumers who prefer a pay-as-you-go structure without the uncertainty of overdraft and bounced-check fees. The portability of stored-value cards and the variety of distribution channels available for selling and loading them provide increased opportunities to reach low-income consumers.

The stored-value card market has exploded in recent years. Hundreds of product marketers, issuers, distributors, and providers have issued millions of general spend, payroll, and other types of stored-value cards. For traditional depositories, these cards offer a promising way to reach a new consumer segment. According to the 2002 ABA Bank Card Survey Report, 21 percent of bank issuers of debit cards planned to offer stored-value cards in 2003, compared with 8 percent in 2002 (American Bankers Association, 2002). For non-bank firms, the cards broaden their typical product offerings, enabling them to offer a quasi-savings vehicle. For instance, the nation's two largest tax preparation firms recently established partnerships with stored-value card vendors to enable their customers to receive their tax refunds electronically. H&R Block has partnered with Bank of America, which added functions like remittances and in-branch transactions to its existing card product. The company began piloting the card in three U.S. markets during the 2004 tax season. Jackson Hewitt, the country's second-largest tax preparation company, has joined forces with Rush Communications (run by rap music impresario Russell Simmons) to offer its customers the Rush Card.

An important distinction among the various kinds of stored-value cards is whether they are linked to pooled accounts, in which the funds of individual cardholders are commingled, or to separate bank accounts owned by individual consumers. Individually owned accounts are more expensive to provide and maintain, but they offer FDIC insurance and greater consumer protections against loss or theft.[15] They also afford consumers a potentially tighter connection to asset-building opportunities, although few of the existing individual-account products actually leverage this possible advantage. In 2004, the Federal Reserve Board issued a request for comments on how Regulation E, which implements the Electronic Funds Transfer Act (EFTA) and provides protections to consumers using electronic fund transfer (EFT) systems, should apply to payroll cards. In the same year, the FDIC issued a request for comments on the definition of deposit and the application of FDIC insurance to stored-value cards (Federal Deposit Insurance Corporation, 2004; Federal Reserve System, 2004).

FROM CARDS TO SAVINGS: MOVING THE MARKET. The lower cost of stored-value cards relative to traditional bank accounts, coupled with the increasing automation of the payment-system environment, has led to significant product innovation. Stored-value cards have important potential benefits for low-income, low-asset consumers. The cards enable customers to move out of the cash economy, using a safer medium of exchange that also makes available to them innumerable products and services that are almost impossible to access with cash. These benefits, however, are only modestly linked to asset building. They may even have the opposite effect, because stored-value cards may carry high initiation and transaction fees, and may also encourage increased consumption by facilitating purchases that typically require a credit or debit card (such as those made over the Internet). If the cards are truly to mimic bank

---

15. Stored-value cards in which the funds are held in a single pooled account with subaccounts may qualify for pass-through FDIC insurance if the subaccounts are administered properly.

accounts and start low-income, low-asset consumers on the asset-building path, even greater card functionality is needed. Some potential strategies are to:

—Broaden the methods and locations available to consumers for loading additional funds on stored-value cards. This could increase competition between banks and nonbanks, creating additional opportunities for low-income consumers.

—Add a longer-term savings component to stored-value cards, which are currently designed only as short-term storage vehicles. Develop a partnership between a card vendor and a low-cost mutual fund provider to enable customers to move funds electronically from the card into an investment account in small increments. Alternatively, set up a structured savings mechanism that automatically sweeps money each month from the card to a savings or investment account.

—Work with regulators as they explore issues such as the application of Regulation E and FDIC insurance for stored-value cards, to make sure that they are sensitive to consumer protections that encourage innovation. In addition, work with credit bureaus to include ownership of a stored-value card as a positive indicator in credit-scoring models, even if the card itself is not backed by an individually owned account. Today, credit bureau scoring models in the United States are not set up to accept transactions made with stored value or general debit cards. However, some companies, such as NetSpend Corporation, one of the largest stored-value card providers in the country, have expressed interest in and have experimented with ways to link their customers to the credit reporting system. Moreover, in 2005, NetSpend announced a new program that will enable card holders to link to interest-bearing savings vehicles through their cards.

Bank and Nonbank Financial Services Providers: Blurring the Lines

Some of the most promising—and most controversial—strategies to enhance asset-building opportunities through financial services come in the form of partnerships between banks and nontraditional partners, such as check cashers, retailers, and community-based organizations.

These partnerships illustrate an important paradigm shift in which function is emphasized over form. More financial services providers of all kinds are beginning to focus on the methods needed to deliver the right product functionality to low-income consumers, breaking free of the constraints of legacy systems and conventional wisdom in order to better meet customer needs. In some cases, banks are recognizing that they may be better suited to a back-end role, such as processing payments and moving money, rather than the front-end job of attracting low-income customers. In other cases, banks and credit unions are making dramatic changes in product mix and branch operations to better reach the market. While such partnerships present opportunities to better reach and serve low-income consumers, they also require careful strategies to ensure reasonable and transparent pricing and to facilitate true asset-building opportunities.

NEW PARTNERSHIPS TO BUILD ASSETS: MOVING THE MARKET. Accompanying the rapid growth of the nonbank financial services sector has been a growing recognition that check-cashing outlets and similar businesses represent a powerful distribution channel for reaching lower-income consumers. Moreover, a 2000 industry survey of check-cashing customers showed that 49 percent would use savings accounts if they were available from their regular check-cashing outlets (Eric Mower Associates, 2000). It is the potential combination of transactional and asset-building products and services that holds the greatest promise for meeting the needs of low-income consumers. The most well-known example of this is Union Bank of California's Cash 'N' Save division. Conceived more than ten years ago and championed by the firm's vice chairman, this banking/check-cashing hybrid operates both in Union Bank branches and retail locations, offering reduced-fee check cashing and specialized starter bank account products. The bank reports a 40 percent rate of converting check-cashing customers to bank account use. This does not mean that consumers stop using check-cashing services; rather, many continue to use both check-cashing and banking services—an important insight when developing new business models for serving low- and moderate-income consumers. Several other banks, including the $86 billion KeyBank, are replicating this model to reach out to unbanked customers.

Technology is an important ingredient in many bank/nonbank partnerships. For instance, a unique payment terminal called a Point of Banking (POB) machine is what facilitates the partnership between Bethex Federal Credit Union, an $11 million low-income credit union in the Bronx, New York, and RiteCheck, a check-cashing chain with fourteen outlets in the Bronx and Manhattan.[16] Bethex customers can complete transactions (including deposits, withdrawals, transfers, and balance inquiries) at RiteCheck locations through the POB, which functions like an ATM with a human teller to accept and dispense cash. Currently, POBs are supported only in the New York area, but a joint industry committee of credit unions and check cashers has been formed to support expansion of the service. POB service is now provided to clients of other credit unions, such as Actors Federal Credit Union, and is available in more than 100 check-cashing outlets. A national expansion could facilitate additional partnerships (Jacob, 2004).

For transaction-based partnerships to lead to asset building, it is critical that nonbank financial services providers be linked to the broader credit-reporting system, such that nonbank financial activity is captured in credit reports and credit-scoring models. For instance, timely repayment of payday loans should be considered an indication of positive credit behavior, so that the consumer can eventually qualify for a more traditional loan.

16. Bethex Federal Credit Union is an RFSI participant.

The current regulatory framework can create obstacles to implementing partnerships between banks and nonbanks. This in part happens because banks tend to be regulated at the federal level, while nonbank financial service providers are largely regulated at the state level. Moreover, state regulations vary widely. Conversations between industry players and both federal and state regulators could help increase understanding of the opportunities and challenges in this arena, leading to new interpretations that will ease partnership formation. It is critical that, in the course of promoting partnerships with alternative services providers, all parties focus on asset building and avoid predatory practices.

Self-Service Delivery: Balancing High-Tech and High-Touch

The lure of self-service delivery of financial services to low-income consumers is the vastly reduced cost of such transactions. While an account withdrawal at a teller costs a bank approximately $1.07, a similar transaction at an ATM costs only $0.27; over the Internet, it costs a mere $0.015 (Weissbourd, 2002). Today, the attractiveness of self-service delivery has been enhanced by the advent of advanced-functioning ATMs, Internet transactions, and computer kiosks that offer the vision of greater penetration into the low- and moderate-income community.

While the number of ATMs has nearly quadrupled over the past decade to 384,000 nationwide, the number of monthly transactions per machine has been cut in half since 1997[17] and the machines have become less profitable to operate. Eager to find other ways to generate fees, ATM operators have been experimenting with dispensing a variety of other financial and nonfinancial products and services. These include selling postage stamps, phone cards, and airline tickets; paying bills; offering overdraft protection; and even sending flowers or buying music CDs. While some of the experiments have been mildly successful, the industry has yet to find a new business model that is as popular with consumers as cash dispensing.

There has been a growing realization, however, that (with the addition of a cash acceptor) ATMs could offer a variety of transaction services for people without bank accounts. ATM functionality continues to expand and today includes coupons, maps, mobile phone services, ticketing, and loyalty programs. Moreover, NCR Corp. has developed an ATM that revolutionizes the deposit-taking function, and Bank One has piloted the machines in Kentucky and Indiana. Deposits, made without envelopes, are scanned by the machine and partially processed, reducing costs for financial institutions, and providing the consumer with immediate availability of cash deposits—an important selling point for many low-income consumers. Some analysts expect deposit automa-

---

17. Michelle Higgins, "Automated Teller Machines Soon Will Be Dispensing a Lot More than Cash," *Wall Street Journal,* June 6, 2002, p, D1.

tion at ATMs to expand significantly in the next few years. Unbanked consumers can use a variety of self-service financial services kiosks to cash checks, pay bills, purchase additional cellular phone minutes, and conduct other basic transactions. Today, companies that provide kiosks that once only handled check cashing or bill payment are beginning to bundle these services together with reloadable stored value cards, phone cards, wire transfer services, and even online shopping capabilities.

One interesting example of kiosks with bundled services is 7-Eleven's Vcom kiosk, which began as a pilot in 2002. Check cashing is the most popular service offered through the machines, but consumers can also use the kiosks to transfer money abroad, buy car insurance, access phone cards, reload 7-Eleven E-Cash prepaid MasterCard cards, pay bills, and buy money orders. (7-Eleven sells $5 billion in money orders annually). Today, 7-Eleven's Vcom, which is offered in partnership with NCR, CashWorks, American Express, and several other third-party service providers and financial institutions, is the nineteenth-largest financial kiosk deployer in the country, with 1,050 machines. The fee structure is similar to that of a typical check casher.[18] This program, while promising, has experienced some challenges. 7-Eleven stopped placing new kiosks in July 2003, having installed only 1,050 kiosks out of the planned 3,500. While the company says that it still plans to install a Vcom kiosk in every store, at this point the kiosks are not available in all 7-Eleven locations, nor are they concentrated in a specific market. If this strategy is ultimately successful, the initiative could increase competition and ultimately bring down costs for consumers.

The Internet is also an increasingly important self-service channel. Efforts by community groups, technology firms, and the federal government to increase computer and Internet access for lower-income consumers have led to the creation of hundreds of community technology centers (CTCs) in low-income communities nationwide.

Along with the Internet, however, has come the recognition that most consumers still want access to a range of delivery channels, as well as some human interaction for certain transactions. This is particularly true for the low-income market. For instance, the Latino Community Credit Union in Durham, North Carolina, which has had enormous success in opening accounts for recent immigrants, has used both individualized instruction and incentives (such as raffles in which the prize can only be claimed by using an ATM machine) to convince customers to try the machines and thus reduce teller lines. Conversely, the credit union recently decided to close down the drive-through lane at a new

---

18. Cherie Jacobs, "7-Eleven Unveil ATMs 'On Steroids,'" *Tampa Tribune,* December 11, 2002, p. 1; David Brietkopf, "Latest Kiosk Pitch from 7-Eleven: Bill Payment," *American Banker,* June 19, 2003, p. 1.

branch it had acquired because it would have compromised the strength of face-to-face interactions with customers.

SELF-SERVICE THAT IS MORE THAN TRANSACTIONAL: MOVING THE MARKET. Self-service financial technology is expensive, and it is unlikely that new functionality will be developed or deployed just for low-income consumers. Those who do choose to deploy it are often focused on new fee revenue opportunities or efficiencies rather than on the opportunity to link consumers with broader wealth-building opportunities. For example, as 7-Eleven and its partners reach out to the unbanked, advocates for lower-income consumers need to reach out to 7-Eleven to ensure that transactions are fairly priced and that the machines will provide access to a broader range of wealth-building products and services.

The nation's banks have been slow to deploy multifunction ATMs that provide both traditional offerings and cash transaction services, and to increase the presence of such machines in low- and moderate-income communities. Most ATMs run on the outdated IBM OS/2 operating platform. As six of the ten largest U.S. banks upgrade their machines to the Microsoft NT operating system, they are also expanding machine functionality, offering an opportunity to influence what the machines can do and where they are placed.

It is also important to continue to experiment with Internet and kiosk delivery (tailored for low- and moderate-income consumers) by improving content and linking information and education with the ability to register for products and conduct transactions. Products built on Internet access offer the lowest-cost delivery method, in part because they can leverage existing computers by linking content providers, financial services firms, and the many libraries and community technology centers (CTCs) that provide free or low-cost access to computers and educational programming. An example of this strategy is One Economy, a nonprofit organization working to connect subsidized housing residents with computers and unique, multilingual Internet content geared to lower-income consumers. The organization has developed a new website for consumers, the Beehive, and is working with financial services partners to transform the site from a passive purveyor of information to an enabler of transactions.

Better data on the nature and extent of low-income consumer demand for self-service delivery could highlight the potential for additional products and services and help firms develop new business models that support their provision. The experience of financial services and technology providers in moving low-income consumers to self-service delivery has been mixed. Finding the right balance between high-tech delivery and high-touch service, while also keeping costs low, will be important.

Table 13-3. *Barriers to Closing the Supply Gap*

Barriers	Key issues
Cultural barriers	Conservative culture in banking industry. High level of risk aversion toward low-income consumers. Conventional business model may not be appropriate to underserved customers.
Lack of market data	Insufficient information about needs and preferences of low-income consumers. Scarce information inhibits the development of profitable, non-predatory financial products. Partnership among government, foundations, and private sectors can increase research.
Need to find volume	Typical business models need large volume of customers to compensate for small transaction sizes and low balances. Despite the decrease in costs, outreach to low-income consumers needs large volumes to be an attractive business strategy.
Finding appropriate partners	Outreach partnerships with trusted intermediaries. Technology partnerships with vendors. Service partnerships with alternative financial service providers.
Improving regulatory system	Improve consistency of different sources of regulation (federal and state levels) for different layers and products in the market.

What Is Missing?

Changes in the financial services landscape have led to significant innovation that has the potential to increase asset-building opportunities for low-income, low-asset consumers, many of whom are unbanked or underserved by traditional financial institutions (see table 13-3). A number of barriers remain, however, including:

—cultural and structural barriers within financial institutions;

—a lack of the market data needed to make a business case for outreach;

—business models that require large volumes of customers;

—the need to identify appropriate partners; and

—a regulatory system that does not always keep pace with market change.

Cultural and Structural Barriers

This chapter addresses some of the cultural barriers facing low-income consumers as they contemplate participation in the financial mainstream. Cultural barriers, however, also exist within financial services firms. The banking industry is highly regulated, and has long had a very conservative culture. Banks have a level of risk aversion that can lead to blanket-refusal policies rather than careful risk management.[19] These policies tend to have a disproportionately negative impact on low-income consumers. Furthermore, in a regulated industry, when a new idea (particularly a new product idea) is proposed, the first question asked often is not "will it sell?" or "will it be profitable?" but "what will the regulators say?" Despite the successes of CRA, the financial services regulatory environment is designed primarily to emphasize safety and soundness rather than community reinvestment.

Firm-level structural issues also come into play. The underlying business model for conventional banking—whose organizing unit is the account—may be antiquated, particularly for serving lower-income consumers. For example, bank structures in which outreach to low-income customers is not aligned with responsibility for profitability can lead to situations in which products are inappropriately promoted to maximize revenue, with little concern about the impact of such products on the asset-building opportunities of low-income customers.[20] The recent controversy over "bounce protection" is an example of this problem. Moreover, established firms with large investments in technology and legacy systems are less likely to choose to innovate in order to better reach the low-income market, because the additional cost of systems change makes it harder for initiatives to meet internal hurdle rates.

As the examples in this chapter demonstrate, however, ten years of bank deregulation, the pressures of CRA (and the threat of CRA on the credit union side), the demographics of the immigrant market, and the support of senior bank regulators are definitely eroding this barrier. Speeding up its elimination

19. The use by banks of ChexSystems (a listing of people who have had accounts closed during the prior five-year period for repeated overdrafts, unpaid overdrafts, or fraud, and used to deny those people checking accounts) is a good example of this problem. Risk management with respect to checking accounts is important to depository institutions, as nearly $700 million in bad checks was lost in 2001. ChexSystems was being used by banks as the solution. Following a public outcry that started with an article in the *Wall Street Journal* in August 2000, many banks modified their use of the system. (See Paul Beckett, "It's Not in the Mail: Bounce a Check and You Might Not Write Another for Five Years," *Wall Street Journal,* August 1, 2000, p. A1; and Paul Beckett, "Banks to Rethink System Used to Approve Applicants Opening Checking Accounts," *Wall Street Journal,* August 17, 2000, p. A12.) Moreover, in a number of cities, nonprofit entities and banks have joined together in the Get Checking program, a second-chance program that mitigates risk through education, a requirement that balances outstanding on closed bank accounts be repaid, and a modified checking or savings product that enables a new bank to assess the customer's current behavior before deciding whether to allow the customer a full-service checking account. Get Checking, which started in Milwaukee, is now operating in thirty-seven communities (Fannie Mae Foundation, 2003). Nevertheless, ChexSystems is still used by many with minimal, if any, analysis of the actual risk being avoided by refusing to open accounts (Park, 2003).

20. Alex Berenson, "Banks Encourage Overdrafts, Reaping Profits," *New York Times,* January 22, 2003, p. A1. For an industry defense, see Paul Nadler, "In Defense of Overdraft Protection," *American Banker,* January 29, 2003, p. 7.

will require resolution of the other issues discussed here—especially the paucity of market information.

Lack of Information about the Market

Despite a growing awareness of the unbanked and their general demographic characteristics, little specialized industry information exists detailing the financial needs and preferences of these and other low-income consumers. Even firms already serving low-income consumers say they lack the kind of attitudinal and behavioral data they need to better customize their products and services. The surprise with which the 2000 Census was greeted is a surface manifestation of this problem. Moreover, market research about low-income consumers is woefully behind that available for middle- and upper-income consumers and those living in suburban communities. For example, Claritas, the country's leading market research firm, classifies the country's households into sixty-six "clusters," groupings of consumers whose needs, capacity, and behavior are similar enough that businesses depend on them to develop and market products and services. Only three of those groupings cover central cities, where much of the unbanked and underserved population lives. Moreover, Claritas's coverage of rural America is also thin.

Beyond market data, the industry lacks information on the cost structures involved in serving low-income consumers in ways that also promote asset building. Despite significant innovation in the marketplace, much of the experimentation is at too early a stage to yield solid results that could guide the development of new business models. Without this information, it is difficult to make the business case for developing new products to market to and serve unbanked and underserved populations, particularly within institutions that want to make certain that they can make a profit without being accused of predatory pricing.

With time, the results of innovations should lead to a growing understanding of the business models that reach consumers most successfully and are also financially viable. The key will be developing mechanisms for sharing this information among the wider financial services industry, because success often breeds competition. The combined efforts of the government, foundations, and private sector are beginning to make a major improvement in this situation. One example is MetroEdge, a market research firm created with the support of foundations and ShoreBank.[21] MetroEdge developed specialized analytical techniques to uncover business opportunities in often-overlooked urban and ethnic markets.[22] The Retail Financial Services Initiative (discussed earlier) will make pub-

21. In early 2005, the financial services work of MetroEdge was absorbed back into ShoreBank Advisory Services.

22. Claritas has partnered with MetroEdge to serve clients interested in both suburban and inner-city markets.

licly available its analyses of the efforts of participating institutions to serve this market.

Need to Find Volume

Typical business models for serving low-income consumers require large volumes of customers in order to compensate for what are generally believed to be smaller transaction sizes. Entrepreneurs and established firms alike, however, are struggling to find large-enough pools of low- and moderate-income customers to make their models work—particularly as some Internet-based strategies have failed to attract adequate numbers of customers.

Many bank costs are essentially fixed on a per-transaction or per-account basis. Thus administering a savings or checking account has certain fixed costs related to opening the account, maintaining records, and sending statements. If the account is large and transactions few, the funds in the account, which often earn no or low rates of interest, can be an important source of relatively inexpensive funding for the institution. If balances are low and, in particular, if low balances are combined with frequent transactions, the account is less profitable. The technological innovations of the past ten years, including those discussed in this chapter (such as ATMs, direct deposit, Internet banking, and the use of debit cards), have the potential to reduce costs significantly, thereby making accounts profitable at lower balance levels. However, the smaller margins still demand larger volume to make outreach to low-income consumers an attractive business strategy.

The role of bank legacy systems should not be underestimated. These systems, which are embedded in bank operations, not only make the creation of new types of products difficult and expensive but, perhaps more importantly, make it difficult to accurately track the profitability of innovative products and services. For example, many banks still use systems that evaluate the profitability of a checking account of a given size without differentiating whether the account owner uses a teller or an ATM to transact business (even though it is clear that ATM transactions are far less expensive). Even more sophisticated systems rarely evaluate customer profitability over time, or consider reduced marketing expenses when customers are reached through word-of-mouth or by other inexpensive means. Because it can take several years for low-income, low-asset consumers to be ready for the credit products banks consider most profitable, and, conversely, because word-of-mouth can be a highly successful marketing strategy in low-income communities, these failings of legacy systems can be significant barriers unless a bank believes it is guaranteed a large market.

The workplace and bank/nonbank partnership strategies described above are the most likely to be able to overcome the customer volume hurdle, as they both present opportunities for reaching large numbers of consumers through established nonbank platforms. Moreover, the high level of interest of banks in serving the Latino market (after the 2000 Census revealed the market's large size and high rate of growth) demonstrates that this barrier can be overcome with the right data. The challenge will be to move the products, strategies, and enthusiasm shown for the Latino market into other underserved markets with less dramatic size and growth potential.

Finding Appropriate Partners

Some of the most promising strategies for serving the low-income, low-asset population involve bank/nonbank partnerships. These can include outreach-focused partnerships with trusted intermediaries such as employers, community-based organizations, unions, educational institutions, and churches; technology partnerships with vendors; and service partnerships with alternative financial service providers who have been offering some products—such as non–account-based check cashing—that meet the needs of the low-income population, but are not normally considered bank products.

Each of these three types of partnerships presents special challenges. The issues regarding trusted intermediaries revolve around interest, competence, scale, and culture. Simply put, the intermediary must be trusted by both sides. Not only do consumers need to believe in the intermediary's good faith—the bank also needs a demonstration that the intermediary is actually able to successfully perform the outreach function that will bring good customers to the bank. This often requires not only good intentions but, increasingly, the ability of the intermediary to effectively perform such services as financial education, credit counseling, and mortgage origination. Particularly when the intermediary is a not-for-profit entity, developing such skill, especially at scale, requires funding on other than a per-closed-transaction basis. Investments in groups able to perform well for both the community and the bank, essentially through more effective deployment of the funds invested by banks to meet CRA requirements, could help overcome this partnership challenge.

Vendor partnerships present a different kind of challenge. Here, the issue is frequently that the innovation occurring at the vendor level cannot find the right audience within the bank. This results, in part, from a lack of understanding on both sides of the possibilities of new technology; it also is because those in the bank most interested in serving low-income consumers often have little interaction with the bank's retail activities. Even when such contacts are made, those in retail banking may have little interaction with the areas of the bank responsible for operations and technology. This is a challenge that requires both better internal communications within the bank and a fuller understanding, by champions of outreach, of the importance of systems and operations.

Finally, partnerships with alternative financial services providers raise difficult challenges with respect to understanding, culture, and community relations.

Many alternative service providers have established niches in financial services areas that banks find excessively risky (such as check cashing) or too expensive on a transaction basis (such as small loans). Yet, these providers have proven themselves exceptionally profitable because of sophisticated risk-management systems, lower cost structures, and an ability to charge prices that, for both regulatory and cultural reasons, banks do not find appropriate. The latter practice, of course, has earned alternative providers the enmity of community groups and, often, the disdain of bankers. Learning how to partner with high-quality alternative providers whose systems can help banks expand their suite of products for the low-income community while avoiding the negatives (including pricing above the appropriate risk-adjusted level) could make an important contribution to successfully moving low-income, low-asset consumers to an asset-building path.

Improving the Regulatory System

The regulatory system that governs retail banking at depository institutions (and parallel activities at alternative financial services providers) is a complex combination of federal and state regulation. Even if it were perfectly attuned to the needs of low-income, low-asset consumers (which it is not), the current system is extremely difficult for financial institutions, consumers, and entrepreneurial technology providers to navigate.

The pieces of the system that are particularly in need of attention in this context are the laws and regulations governing consumer protection and related issues at the federal and state levels and the differential manner in which they are enforced with respect to different types of providers. For example, although the USA Patriot Act has imposed new identification requirements on banks and credit unions (as well as securities firms) for people opening accounts, these requirements do not apply to check cashers. The manner in which usury ceilings and other interest-rate based regulations are established and enforced is the genesis not only of very different patterns of payday lending across the country (Caskey, forthcoming), but also of the entire controversy about whether banks are improperly "renting their charter" when they fund third parties engaged in payday lending.

Perhaps even more important to regulatory consistency is the differential manner in which enforcement of identical laws occurs. Depository institutions are subject to regular examination by federal (and frequently state) regulators, during which their compliance with consumer laws and regulations is assessed. Although the bank regulators have a bias toward requiring an institution to fix problems when they find them rather than punishing wrongdoers, the relatively constant oversight and scrutiny (plus the threat of the occasional spectacular enforcement action when things have gone very wrong) tend to keep depository institutions on the conservative side of the limits of consumer protection laws. On the other hand, enforcement of consumer protection and licensing regulations with respect to alternative financial services providers is, in most states, a complaint-based system. Relatively small budgets in both the state enforcement agencies and, at the federal level, the Federal Trade Commission, mean that complaints must reach a very high level before meaningful action is likely to be taken. Although class-action lawsuits and lawsuits brought by state attorneys general fill some of the gap, they too require a high volume of problems in a single entity to be cost-effective.

Another area where clarification, and perhaps revision, is needed relates to the definition of an "account" for deposit insurance purposes. The tension is between the cost-effectiveness of the use of subaccounts for such purposes as payroll cards and Individual Development Accounts and the desire to make certain that the beneficiaries of such subaccounts have the same protections and opportunities as other full-fledged account holders.

Conclusion

The success of alternative providers has demonstrated that there is a large market for financial services within the low-income community and that it is possible to tap into it profitably with the right combination of products, services, and marketing. At the same time, a confluence of demographic, technological, competitive, and public policy events has made the mainstream financial services community more interested in serving this market with an array of products beyond credit. Despite these positive developments, however, many barriers remain to asset building by the unbanked and underserved. These include outdated banking regulations, the conservative culture of traditional institutions, a need for better market data, and the lack of business models that adequately address the true potential of the lower-income market. A number of innovative programs have shown that it is possible to overcome these problems, especially by focusing on creative strategies such as workplace distribution and education, remittance provision, stored-value cards, bank/nonbank partnerships, and self-service delivery.

This is, therefore, a good time to be hopeful about market opportunities to put low-income, low-asset consumers on an asset-building track with mainstream financial institutions. Furthermore, the positive developments described in this chapter—already under way in the market—can be greatly encouraged by initiatives that will improve the regulatory system, assist providers in forming creative partnerships, provide better market data, and help the mainstream financial services industry to understand the challenges and opportunities presented by the unbanked, underserved, and lower-income market.

References

Aizcorbe, Ana M, Arthur B. Kennickell, and Kevin B. Moore. 2003. "Recent Changes in U.S. Family Finances: Evidence from the 1998 and 2001 Survey of Consumer Finances." *Federal Reserve Bulletin* 89 (January): 1–32.

American Bankers Association. 2002. "ABA Bank Card Survey Report" (www.aba.com [January 2004]).

American Payroll Association. 2000. "1998/99 Pay Media Survey" (www.americanpayroll.org/paymed02.html).

Bair, Sheila C. 2003. "Improving Access to the U.S. Banking System among Recent Latin American Immigrants." Multilateral Investment Fund (www.iadb.org/mif/v2/files/28doca.pdf).

Berry, Chris, Shelly Herman, and Darice Wright. 2003. "Financial Services Demand in Lower-Income Areas: A Three-City Survey." Paper presented at Building Assets, Building Credit: Symposium at the Joint Center for Housing Studies. Cambridge, Mass., November 18–19.

Beverly, Sondra, and Michael Sherraden. 1999. "Institutional Determinants of Saving: Implications for Low-Income Households and Public Policy." *Journal of Socio-Economics* 28: 457–73.

Carr, James H., and Jenny Schuetz. 2001. "Financial Services in Distressed Communities: Issues and Answers. Fannie Mae Foundation" (www.fanniemaefoundation.org/programs/financial.PDF).

Caskey, John. 1997. "Lower-Income Americans, Higher Cost Financial Services." Publication 1752-22. Madison, Wisconsin: Filene Research Institute, Center for Credit Union Research.

———. Forthcoming. "Presented in Land Sharks: Predatory Financial Practices and the Community Response." In *Credit Markets and the Poor*. Russell Sage Foundation.

Clancy, Margaret, and Michael Sherraden. 2003. "The Potential for Inclusion in 529 Savings Plans: Report on a Survey of States." St. Louis: Washington University, Center for Social Development (gwbweb.wustl.edu/csd/Publications/2003/ResearchReport-529savingsplansurvey.pdf).

Dove Consulting. 2000. "Survey of Nonbank Financial Institutions." Study prepared for the U.S. Department of Treasury (April) (www.treas.gov/press/releases/reports/nbfirpt.pdf).

Dunham, Constance. 2001. "The Role of Banks and Nonbanks in Serving Low- and Moderate-Income Communities." In *Changing Financial Markets and Community Development; Proceedings of a Federal Reserve System Community Affairs Research Conference,* edited by Jackson L. Blanton, Alicia Williams, and Sherrie L. W. Rhine, pp. 31–58. Chicago: Federal Reserve Bank of Chicago.

Eric Mower Associates, Marketing and Research Services Division. 2000. "FiSCA (Customer Satisfaction Research) Final Report." September 26.

Fannie Mae Foundation. 2003. "Get Checking, Innovations in Personal Finance for the Unbanked: Emerging Practices from the Field" (www.fanniemaefoundation.org/programs/pdf/fscs_GetChecking.pdf).

Federal Deposit Insurance Corporation. 2004. "Definition of 'Deposit'; Stored Value Cards." *Federal Register* 69 (April 16): 74.

Federal Reserve System. 2004. "Electronic Funds Transfer." *Federal Register* 69 (September 17): 180.

Filene Research Institute. 2002. "Financial Stress and Workplace Performance: Developing Employer-Credit Union Partnerships." Paper prepared for colloquium at the University of Wisconsin-Madison.

General Accounting Office. 2002. "Electronic Transfers: Use by Federal Payment Recipients Has Increased but Obstacles to Greater Participation Remain." (September).

Haveman, Robert, and Edward Wolff. 2001. "Who Are the Asset Poor? Levels, Trends, and Composition, 1983–98." Discussion Paper 1226-01. Institute for Research on Poverty, University of Wisconsin.

Hogarth, Jeanne M., and Kevin A. O'Donnell. 1999. "Banking Relationships of Lower-Income Families and the Governmental Trend toward Electronic Payment." *Federal Reserve Bulletin* 85 (July): 459–73.

Inter-American Dialogue Task Force on Remittances. 2004. "All in the Family: Latin America's Most Important International Financial Flow." *Inter-American Dialogue* (January).

Jacob, Katy. 2004. "The PayNet Deposit Program: Check Casher-Credit Union Partnerships and the Point of Banking Machine." Chicago: Center for Financial Services Innovation.

Jacob, Katy, and others. 2005. "Stored Value Cards: Challenges and Opportunities for Reaching Emerging Markets." Chicago: Center for Financial Services Innovation.

Madrian, Brigitte, and Dennis Shea. 2000. "The Power of Suggestion: Inertia in 401(k) Participation and Savings Behavior." Working Paper 7682. Cambridge, Mass.: National Bureau of Economic Research (May).

Mayer, Caroline E. 2004. "From Paycheck to Plastic: More Companies Opt for Cards as Cheaper, Paperless Process," *Washington Post*, January 6, p. E1.

Moore, Ariana-Michelle. 2002. *Payroll Cards: A Direct Deposit Solution for the Unbanked.* Boston: Celent Communications.

New America Foundation. 2003. "Introduction to Asset Building" (www.newamerica.net/index.cfm?pg=DocRelated&DocID=164 [August 2003]).

Office of the Comptroller of the Currency. 2003. "Payroll Cards: An Innovative Product for Reaching the Unbanked and Underbanked" (www.occ.treas.gov/cdd/payrollcards.pdf).

Park, Esther. 2003. "Risk Management Strategies for New Accounts: RFSI Participants Share Their Experiences." Chicago: Retail Financial Services Initiative, National Community Investment Fund (www.cfsinnovation.com/managed_documents/ncif_risk.pdf).

Retsinas, Nicolas P., and Eric S. Belsky. 2002. "Examining the Unexamined Goal." In *Low-Income Homeownership: Examining the Unexamined Goal,* edited by Nicolas P. Retsinas and Eric S. Belsky, pp. 1–14. Brookings.

Schreiner, Mark, Margaret Clancy, and Michael Sherraden. 2002. "Saving Performance in the American Dream Demonstration." St. Louis: Washington University, Center for Social Development (gwbweb.wustl.edu/csd/Publications/2002/ADDreport2002.pdf).

Sherraden, Michael. 1991. *Assets and the Poor: A New American Welfare Policy.* Armonk, N.Y.: M.E. Sharpe.

Suro, Robert, and Sergio Bendixen. 2002. "Billions in Motion: Latino Immigrants, Remittances, and Banking." Washington: Pew Hispanic Center and Multilateral Investment Fund (November).

Tanoue, Donna. 2000. Remarks presented by chairman, Federal Deposit Insurance Corporation, at the Seventh Annual Greenlining Economic Development Forum, June 16.

U.S. Census Bureau. 1999. "Housing Vacancies and Homeownership, Fourth Quarter 1998."

U.S. Conference of Mayors. 2002. "A Status Report on Hunger and Homelessness in America's Cities" (www.usmayors.org/uscm/news/press_releases/documents/hunger_121802.asp).

U.S. Department of Commerce News. 2004. "Census Bureau Reports on Residential Vacancies and Homeownership."

U.S. Department of Housing and Urban Development. 2005. "U.S. Housing Market Conditions, Fourth Quarter 2004." (February).

Weissbourd, Robert. 2002. "Banking on Technology: Expanding Financial Markets and Economic Opportunity." Paper prepared for Financial Services Roundtable, Brookings Institution and Ford Foundation (www.brook.edu/es/urban/publications/weissbourdopp.pdf).

World Council of Credit Unions. 2003. "CU Remittances Have a World of Potential" (www.woccu.org/press/press_rel/pressr.php?pressr_id=404).

14

Innovative Servicing Technology: Smart Enough to Keep People in Their Houses?

AMY CREWS CUTTS AND RICHARD K. GREEN

The advent of automated credit-scoring evaluation tools in the mid-1990s has led the mortgage industry through a major technological revolution. The impact of credit scoring and automated underwriting in the loan origination process and on homeownership has received much attention (see, for example, Avery and others, 2000; Straka, 2000; Gates, Perry, and Zorn, 2002; and Gates, Waldron, and Zorn, 2003); innovations in loan servicing have received relatively little (for a rare exception, see Stegman, Quercia, and Davis, 2003). Yet it is the case (as shown in figure 14-1) that foreclosure rates have stayed below their 1998 levels throughout the 2001 recession and subsequent two years of job-loss recovery. At the same time, the mortgage servicing industry has undergone dramatic changes, emphasizing the use of credit-scoring tools and home-retention workouts to try and keep people in their homes.[1] This chapter focuses on the impact of the servicing of delinquent loans on the likelihood of home loss through foreclosure. We believe this is the first empirical study to focus on the issue.

---

1. According to the Mortgage Bankers Association National Delinquency Survey, quarterly foreclosure rates in 1998 varied between 0.58 and 0.69 percent. The peak foreclosure rate during the 2001 recession and subsequent recovery period (as of June 2003) was 0.56 percent—over that same time there were nine consecutive quarters of losses in nonfarm payroll employment, totaling 2.6 million jobs. During the 1990–91 recession and recovery period, foreclosure rates peaked at 0.83 percent, with 1.5 million jobs lost over four quarters.

Figure 14-1. *Foreclosure Rates of Prime Conventional Loans Compared to Employment, 1998–99*

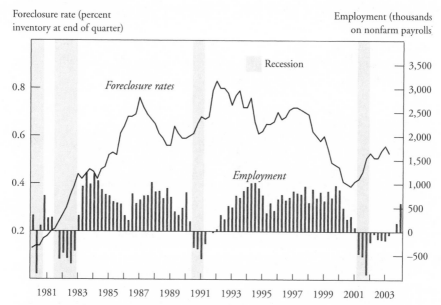

Foreclosure rate (percent
inventory at end of quarter)

Employment (thousands
on nonfarm payrolls)

Sources: Mortgage Bankers Association of America, Freddie Mac, National Bureau of Economic Research, Bureau of Labor Statistics.

The economics literature on mortgage defaults has long focused on two borrower options: payment of the mortgage obligation, or default (generally interpreted as the borrower handing over the keys to the property in exchange for cancellation of the mortgage obligation—the borrower exercises the put option). Often, default and foreclosure are used interchangeably to imply the borrowers lose their homes. Recently, the literature has started to consider default and foreclosure separately from delinquency, but the papers are limited in scope regarding the variety of options that borrowers hold both in delinquency and foreclosure, and none are fully modeled empirical studies.

LaCour-Little (2000) provides an excellent history of the evolution of technology in the mortgage industry. His focus is primarily on origination and data management, however, and provides little on the innovations in mortgage servicing. We extend the work of LaCour-Little (2000) by documenting the innovations in mortgage loan servicing and loss mitigation. We focus in particular on Freddie Mac's innovations in these areas, and examine whether two programs in particular have helped stave off foreclosure and, as such, have kept people in their homes.

We begin by developing a taxonomy of servicing, default, and workout options, then review the default literature as it pertains to the innovations in loan servicing and loss mitigation. We follow with a description of technological innovations in problem loan servicing, including Freddie Mac's Early Indicator® tool and workout programs, and provide some descriptive statistics that suggest they have been successful in mitigating home loss. We close with an empirical model of foreclosure conditional on delinquency that attempts to quantify the extent to which a workout program can prevent foreclosure, with attention to U.S. Department of Housing and Urban Development–defined low- and moderate-income and underserved borrowers.

Taxonomy of Servicing and Default

Before engaging in a discussion of the implications of servicing innovations and economic models of mortgage default, it seems sensible to start with a discussion of what loan servicing entails and what constitutes borrower default.

Servicing

Mortgage servicing, at its most basic level, is the collection of mortgage payments from borrowers and disbursement of those payments to lenders, local governments, and insurers.[2] Servicers also: send payment notices and year-end tax statements to borrowers and tax authorities; report to investors; administer escrow accounts maintained to pay real-estate property taxes and hazard insurance; contact borrowers when payments are overdue and begin foreclosure procedures on delinquent accounts; and otherwise enforce lender policies. They collect and report information on the borrower's payment history to national credit bureaus, act as the customer support agent for the lender, and handle interest-rate adjustments on adjustable-rate mortgages.

Because loan servicing depends little on external information beyond the interactions between the borrowers and servicers, Fabozzi and Modigliani (1992), among others, have argued that the business contains economies of scale. Loan servicing firms have started to capture economies of scale through consolidation in recent years, as shown in figure 14-2. In 1989, the five largest servicers held less than 10 percent of the market share of total single-family mortgage dollars outstanding in their servicing portfolios. Today, they control almost 40 percent. Among the twenty-five largest servicers, market share has grown from less than 20 percent to nearly 65 percent.

To date, few studies have been done on the impact of consolidation in the servicing industry, and even fewer have appeared in the academic literature. Rossi (1998) examined the cost structure of the mortgage banking industry and found that scale economies were not yet exhausted, even at the largest output sizes. One industry study, completed by KPMG Consulting and summarized in

2. The terms *lender* and *investor* are used interchangeably hereafter; the investor may be a secondary-market player or the lender who originated the loan.

Figure 14-2. *Market Shares among Top Servicers Compared to Loan Costs, 1989–2003*

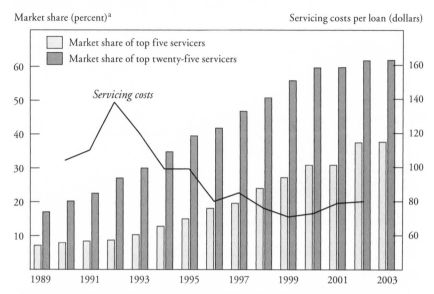

Market share (percent)[a]   Servicing costs per loan (dollars)

☐ Market share of top five servicers
■ Market share of top twenty-five servicers

Servicing costs

Sources: Inside Mortgage Finance Publications (2001, 2004); Mortgage Bankers Association.
a. Fraction of total single-family mortgage dollars outstanding.

Oliver and others (2001), found that servicing costs at the megaservicers (those that service more than 1 million loans annually) were more than 20 percent lower than the industry average cost, and these cost advantages held across all measures they examined. For example, the direct servicing costs, which exclude technology investments and corporate overhead costs, were just $36 per loan at megaservicers in 2000. The industry average for that year was $47 per loan. Similarly, megaservicers had lower technology costs at $9 per loan versus $12 for the industry average, and lower general and administrative costs at just $13 per loan versus $17 for the industry average.

According to the Mortgage Bankers Association (MBA), annual servicing costs per loan in 2001 averaged $79 and each servicing employee annually processed an average of 1,034 loans.[3] Costs in the early 1990s averaged about $120 per loan, falling to around $85 by 1996–97, and have remained below $80 since 1998. Each servicing employee processed just 938 loans on average in 1998, the first year the MBA collected this information. MBA attributes these lowered costs to both technological developments and the use of outsourcing (or specialization) for some servicing activities.

3. See Mortgage Bankers Association, "Refi Boom Drives Up Servicing Costs in 2001 According to Most Recent MBA Cost of Servicing Study" (www.mbaa.org/news/2002/pr0808a.html [December 30, 2002]). See also Walsh (2002).

Default, Delinquency, and Foreclosure

Borrowers are technically in default on their mortgage when they fail to meet any of the obligations of the mortgage contract. Therefore the term "default" can imply any failure to pay, from minor delinquency to loss of the home through foreclosure. Legal payment default occurs when one payment has been completely missed and a second is due and payable.

Delinquency is typically measured in thirty-day intervals for the first three months of the default, for example, thirty-, sixty-, and ninety-day periods. State laws govern foreclosure processes, and the time when the foreclosure process can start varies by state.[4] Industry practice is to consider loans that are more than ninety days late as "in foreclosure" for standard statistical purposes. Loans that are at least ninety days late or in the foreclosure process are considered seriously delinquent.

Foreclosure implies the lender has used its legal rights to take possession of the property under state law; a foreclosed property is referred to as real estate owned (REO). This is an involuntary transaction on the part of the homeowner in that a court order or similar decree has forced the owner to give up his or her rights to the property.

For a lender, costs accumulate as the seriousness of the contractual failure increases. These costs include the opportunity cost of principal and income not yet received, servicing costs, legal costs, costs of property preservation and costs of property disposition. Although foreclosure is a rare event, the costs of foreclosure are enormous. For example, Focardi (2002) estimated that for a sample of loans that went through the full formal foreclosure process, the total cost—including lost interest during delinquency, foreclosure costs, and disposition of the foreclosed property—was $58,759, and the process took an average of eighteen months to resolve. Voluntary title transfer alternatives to foreclosure were less expensive and less time consuming, but still had average costs in excess of $44,000 and took nearly one year to conclude.

State laws also affect foreclosure costs because not all legal foreclosures are the same. In states that allow nonjudicial foreclosure or power-of-sale foreclosure, title to property can be obtained relatively quickly, within two to four months. In states that require judicial foreclosure, title claims can take six months or longer, sometimes even years.[5] Disposition of the property then takes additional time once the lender has secured title. Additionally, most, but not all, states allow a lender to try to recover monies owed on the mortgage in excess of the

---

4. For a summary of foreclosure laws in the United States, see Dunaway (2002). A current synopsis is also available at www.myhousesaver.com/state.html, or in current HUD FHA *Mortgagee Letters*, such as ML 2001-19 (www.hud.gov/offices/hsg/mltrmenu.cfm).

5. See Dunaway (2002) for a summary and analysis of the impacts of state foreclosure laws on default timelines.

property value from other assets a borrower holds. A summary of state foreclosure law characteristics and foreclosure time frame is provided in table 14-1.

Taxonomy of Workout Options

Regardless of lender policy, the borrower can simply fully reinstate (or cure) the mortgage by paying all the past due amounts and fees owed, and thus retain ownership interest in the property. The borrower can do this at any time before the finalization of the foreclosure and even after foreclosure sale in states that allow redemption.[6] But there are many different alternatives or workouts to foreclosure once a borrower is in default of the mortgage contract; many of these alternatives are relatively recent innovations in loan servicing. One class of workouts allows the borrower to reinstate the mortgage over time and keep the home. The second class of workouts results in voluntary title transfers if a borrower has a demonstrated involuntary inability to pay.[7] These options are examined below.

Home Retention Workout Options

One workout option is partial reinstatement. This is when the borrower resumes regular monthly payments and agrees to a repayment plan over a period of up to twelve months for the remainder due. In this case, the borrower's credit record will indicate that the borrower is meeting his or her obligation and that a repayment plan is in place. Nevertheless, the number of months for which the borrower was delinquent and the severity of the delinquency will continue to appear on the borrower's credit report.[8] If the borrower partially reinstates the mortgage but does not enter into a repayment plan, then his or her credit record will indicate a continuation of the delinquency for the number of months due in arrears, for example, the borrower would remain two or three months at "sixty-days delinquent" status, also known as 2x60 or 3x60 days delinquent.

Short-term forbearance allows for the suspension of up to three payments or a reduction in payments for up to six months with a repayment plan to follow at the end of the forbearance period. Long-term forbearance allows for the suspen-

6. Some states, known as presale redemption states (specifically Kansas, Wisconsin, and Vermont), allow reinstatement only up to a stated number of days before the foreclosure sale of the property. Redemption clauses allow a borrower to reclaim the foreclosed property by essentially buying it back from the lender for the amount due rather than reinstating the loan. During the redemption period the lender cannot sell the property.

7. The options described here are available from the Seller/Servicer Guides from Freddie Mac, among other places. Involuntary inability to pay is discussed in more detail later in this chapter.

8. Freddie Mac and Fannie Mae policy is for the servicer to report repayment plans and to note the status of the amount owed on the plan, such as how many months of originally past-due payments are covered by the plan, and to have the borrower reinstated as current and paying as agreed going forward.

Table 14-1. *Foreclosure Characteristics and Time Frame by State*

State	Security instrument	Foreclosure type	Initial step in process	No. of months to start	Redemption period	Deficiency judgment
Alabama	Mortgage	Nonjudicial	Publication	1	12 months	Allowed
Alaska	Deed of trust	Nonjudicial	Record notice of default	3	None	Allowed
Arizona	Deed of trust	Nonjudicial	Record notice of sale	3	None	Allowed
Arkansas	Mortgage	Judicial	Record notice of default	4	None	Allowed
California	Deed of trust	Nonjudicial	Record notice of default	4	None	Prohibited
Colorado	Deed of trust	Nonjudicial	File FCL documents with public trustee	2	75 days	Allowed
Connecticut	Mortgage	Judicial	Complaint to sheriff	5	None	Allowed
Delaware	Mortgage	Judicial	Complaint	3	None	Allowed
District of Columbia	Trust deed	Nonjudicial	Record notice of default	2	None	Allowed
Florida	Mortgage	Judicial	Complaint	5	None	Allowed
Georgia	Security deed	Nonjudicial	Publication	2	None	Allowed
Hawaii	Mortgage	Nonjudicial	Publish notice of intent	3	None	Allowed
Idaho	Deed of trust	Nonjudicial	Record notice of default	5	None	Allowed
Illinois	Mortgage	Judicial	Complaint	7	None	Allowed
Indiana	Mortgage	Judicial	Complaint	5	3 months	Allowed
Iowa	Mortgage	Judicial	Petition	5	6 months	Allowed
Kansas	Mortgage	Judicial	Complaint	4	6–12 months	Allowed
Kentucky	Mortgage	Judicial	Complaint	6	None	Allowed
Louisiana	Mortgage	Judicial	Petition for executory process	2	None	Allowed
Maine	Mortgage	Judicial	Complaint	6	None	Allowed
Maryland	Deed of trust	Nonjudicial	File order to docket	2	None	Allowed
Massachusetts	Mortgage	Judicial	File complaint relative to S&SR Act	3	None	Allowed
Michigan	Mortgage	Nonjudicial	Publication	2	6 months	Allowed

State	Security	Process	Notice	No.	Redemption	Deficiency
Minnesota	Mortgage	Nonjudicial	Publication	2	6 months	Prohibited
Mississippi	Deed of trust	Nonjudicial	Publication	2	None	Prohibited
Missouri	Deed of trust	Nonjudicial	Publication	2	None	Allowed
Montana	Deed of trust	Nonjudicial	Record notice of sale	5	None	Prohibited
Nebraska	Mortgage	Judicial	Petition	5	None	Allowed
Nevada	Deed of trust	Nonjudicial	Record notice of default	4	None	Allowed
New Hampshire	Mortgage	Nonjudicial	Publication	2	None	Allowed
New Jersey	Mortgage	Judicial	Complaint	3	10 days	Allowed
New Mexico	Mortgage	Judicial	Complaint	4	None	Allowed
New York	Mortgage	Judicial	Complaint	4	None	Allowed
North Carolina	Deed of trust	Nonjudicial	Notice of hearing	2	None	Allowed
North Dakota	Mortgage	Judicial	Complaint	3	60 days	Prohibited
Ohio	Mortgage	Judicial	Complaint	5	None	Allowed
Oklahoma	Mortgage	Judicial	Petition	4	None	Allowed
Oregon	Deed of trust	Nonjudicial	Record notice of default	5	None	Allowed
Pennsylvania	Mortgage	Judicial	Complaint	3	None	Allowed
Rhode Island	Mortgage	Nonjudicial	Publication	2	None	Allowed
South Carolina	Mortgage	Judicial	Complaint	6	None	Allowed
South Dakota	Mortgage	Judicial	Complaint	3	180 days	Allowed
Tennessee	Deed of trust	Nonjudicial	Publication	2	None	Allowed
Texas	Deed of trust	Nonjudicial	Post and file notice of sale	2	None	Allowed
Utah	Deed of trust	Nonjudicial	Record notice of default	4	None	Allowed
Vermont	Mortgage	Judicial	Complaint	7	None	Allowed
Virginia	Deed of trust	Nonjudicial	Publication	2	None	Allowed
Washington	Deed of trust	Nonjudicial	Record notice of sale	4	None	Allowed
West Virginia	Deed of trust	Nonjudicial	Publication	2	None	Prohibited
Wisconsin	Mortgage	Judicial	Complaint	Varies	None	Allowed
Wyoming	Mortgage	Nonjudicial	Publication	2	3 months	Allowed

Sources: U.S. Department of Housing and Urban Development, *Mortgagee Letter 2001–19*; (www.myhomesaver.com/state.html [December 2002]).

sion or reduction of payments for a period of four to twelve months with a corresponding repayment plan for full reinstatement or payoff within twelve months of the end of the forbearance.[9] If the borrower seeks forbearance prior to delinquency, his or her credit report will only indicate the presence of a repayment plan; otherwise, such as with the case of partial reinstatement, if the borrower pays as agreed under the repayment plan, he or she limits the damage to his or her credit history from the delinquency.

A loan modification is a permanent change in one or more terms of a borrower's loan that allows the loan to be reinstated and results in a payment the borrower can afford. A loan modification is negotiated when a cooperative borrower has indicated a desire to retain ownership of the property, a capacity to support a mortgage under the new terms, and does not qualify for a refinance of the loan under lender/investor policies. Under a loan modification, a borrower's credit record is restored to "currently paying as agreed" status.

A partial claim workout is offered under the Federal Housing Administration (FHA) loan loss mitigation program, and it is a workout in which the lender will advance funds on behalf of the borrower in an amount necessary to fully reinstate a delinquent loan (not to exceed twelve months of principal, interest, taxes, and insurance, or PITI). The borrower, on acceptance of the advance, will execute a promissory note and subordinate mortgage payable to HUD.[10] Currently, these promissory, or partial claim, notes carry no interest and are not due and payable until the borrower either pays off the first mortgage or no longer owns the property.

Voluntary Title Transfer Workout Options

In addition to the involuntary transfer of title through foreclosure, there are several options under which the borrower can voluntarily transfer title if regular sale would be too burdensome and home retention is not possible. A deed-in-lieu of foreclosure is the simplest case, and involves the borrower forgoing any continued ownership interest in the house in exchange of the cancellation of the mortgage obligation—essentially the borrower just hands over the keys. A short sale (or short payoff), or preforeclosure sale, is a negotiated and lender-approved sale where the borrower has found a buyer for the property, but the sale proceeds are less than the amount owed inclusive of sale costs and other fees. In this case, the lender either negotiates an unsecured repayment plan with the borrower for the additional amount owed or forgives the remaining debt.

A workout mortgage assumption permits a qualified applicant to assume title to the property and the mortgage obligation from a borrower who is currently

---

9. FHA terminology is a "special forbearance," without distinction between short term and long term.

10. See in particular *FHA Mortgagee Letter* 00-05, (www.hud.gov/offices/hsg/mltrmenu.cfm) for details on partial claims and other foreclosure alternatives in the FHA program.

delinquent or is in imminent danger of default because of involuntary inability to pay. Some mortgage contracts have assumption terms already in place; a workout assumption can occur regardless of whether the initial contract has an assumption stipulation.

Moral Hazard and Other Risks

If borrowers simply walk away from the mortgage obligation because the property is worth less than the mortgage balance, even though they have not experienced an event that reduces their ability to pay the debt (as is frequently modeled in the economics literature), then there is a moral hazard if home values fall or grow too slowly.[11] The borrowers have no incentive to maintain the property and can live in the home rent-free while the foreclosure process unfolds. Or alternatively, the borrowers can purchase a nearby home at depressed prices while their credit rating is intact, stipulating that the old home would become an investor property, and then default on the original mortgage and give up that property in foreclosure.

Deficiency judgments can mitigate moral hazard caused by falling house prices. In states that allow them, other borrower assets can be claimed by the mortgage lender to cover losses incurred through the foreclosure (and foreclosure alternatives) process, and thus discourage borrowers from reneging on their obligations. Most lenders require an involuntary inability to pay before workouts are approved, meaning the borrower does not have the capacity to fully reinstate and carry the mortgage due to illness, job loss, significant property damage or depreciation, or other significant economic shock.

Only six states currently prohibit the lender from seeking a deficiency judgment recourse against a foreclosed borrower (table 14-1 lists deficiency judgment allowances by state). In the early 1990s, California, a nonrecourse state, and Massachusetts, a recourse state, suffered similar declines in house prices and job losses. In 1995, the peak default year in both places, Fannie Mae saw more than seven times the REOs and foreclosure sales in California than in Massachusetts, but had only five times more credit-risk exposure (see Inside Mortgage Finance, 1995). Although only anecdotal evidence exists of California borrowers ruthlessly using their option to default through moral hazard rather than involuntary inability to repay, the Fannie Mae experience suggests that allowing deficiency judgments at least reduces the incidence of foreclosure when home values decline.

Some properties, such as those that contain an environmental hazard, carry a liability risk. In such cases, the lender can decide that the debt is uncollectable,

---

11. An excellent study on moral hazard and mortgage default is Riddiough and Wyatt (1994), which examines the effect of whether the lender is a "wimp" (offering forbearance) or "tough guy" (aggressive in pursuing foreclosure) on borrower propensity to default, and finds significant borrower behavior elasticities with respect to lender behavior.

Figure 14-3. *Growth of Home Retention Workouts, 1997–2003*

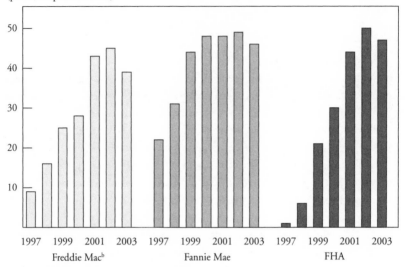

Home-retention workout ratio
(percent of problem loans)ᵃ

Sources: Freddie Mac, Fannie Mae, and HUD.
a. Problem loans are those that are 60 days delinquent or worse that did not reinstate on their own.
b. Freddie Mac ratios do not include repayment plans or forbearances prior to 2001.

and elect to charge off the debt and terminate the mortgage lien rather than acquire the property through foreclosure. This last option does not transfer title of the property. Additionally, borrowers can also exercise an option to declare bankruptcy, which could limit the lender's ability to negotiate workouts or the impact of a lender's threat to force foreclosure.

Workout options have been widely adopted throughout the mortgage industry, and home retention workouts have risen dramatically in recent years. Figure 14-3 shows the share of problem loans held by Freddie Mac, Fannie Mae, and the FHA that were worked out using home retention options. Workouts have risen dramatically in all three cases. In 1997, roughly 10 to 20 percent of problem loans (sixty days delinquent or worse that did not reinstate on their own) at Fannie Mae and Freddie Mac were resolved with a home-retention workout alternative.[12] By 2002, the two companies resolved about 50 percent of problem loans via workouts.

In the FHA program, the number of loans resolved with some form of workout has risen from just over 5,000 in fiscal year 1997 to just over 73,000 at the end of fiscal year 2002. Home-retention workouts account for all the growth in

12. That is, the percentages represent the number of loans that got home retention workouts divided by the number of loans that got home retention workouts or became REO properties. This is known as the workout ratio in servicing industry terminology.

the workout numbers—770 loans (15.3 percent of workout alternatives) in 1997, and 68,755 loans (94.1 percent) in 2002. Voluntary title transfers barely grew from 4,249 loans in 1997 to 4,327 in 2002. Moreover, in fiscal year 2002, workouts outnumbered foreclosures for the first time.[13]

State of the Literature

The standard way to think of the default option in the economics and finance literature is to examine a borrower's propensity to exercise a put option when the value of the mortgage becomes greater than the value of the underlying asset (the property) (see, for example, the survey by Kau and Keenan, 1995). Some models also include a trigger event, such as illness, job loss, or divorce, that leads the borrower to default on the mortgage (see, for example, Deng, Quigley, and Van Order, 2000). It is nearly always assumed (or modeled) that the borrower's choice is between keeping and losing the home. These standard models, therefore, equate any mortgage default with foreclosure, and the implied form of the foreclosure is a deed-in-lieu transfer of title to the lender—that is, the borrower stops by the bank and hands over the keys.[14]

Vandell (1993) observed that the state of the literature at that time was woefully behind industry practice. In particular, he noted that the then current literature on both commercial and residential mortgage default failed to consider: 1) transaction costs to the borrower from default including effects on future credit availability; 2) recourse considerations that allow the lender to seek other assets of the borrower if the proceeds from the sale of the foreclosed property do not cover the outstanding principal balance; 3) the magnitude and timing of the revenues and the losses associated with default; and 4) the possibility that a workout or loan modification could occur.

Little has changed in the years since Vandell (1993). However, a series of papers has improved the state of the literature on residential defaults. Among them are Ambrose and Capone (1996, 1998, 2000), Ambrose, Buttimer, and Capone (1997), and Ambrose and Buttimer (2000). Two other notable studies are Pence (2001) and Stegman, Quercia, and Davis (2003).

Ambrose and Capone (1996) examine the theoretical costs and benefits of four single-family residential mortgage foreclosure alternatives—loan modifications, preforeclosure sales, deed-in-lieu transfers, and lender forbearance. Using a parameterized simulation model, the authors conclude that such alternatives

---

13. We have been unable to obtain detailed home retention workout data prior to 2000. However, recent data are available at (www.hud.gov/offices/hsg/comp/rpts/com/commenu.cfm).

14. These papers do not explicitly state whether the foreclosure is voluntary or involuntary; however the terms are often couched as a borrower decision to pay-as-agreed or default and lose the house, which is tantamount to voluntarily handing over the keys in a deed-in-lieu transfer, rather than a legal taking of the home by the lender.

can be successful at mitigating expected default costs, but, because the results depend on probabilities, the risks are better carried by large, well-diversified national mortgage insurers or secondary-market agencies such as Fannie Mae and Freddie Mac. The authors infer that these types of institutions have invested in loss mitigation practices because they are best able to take advantage of such practices.

Ambrose, Buttimer, and Capone (1997) recognized that default (meaning delinquency) and foreclosure are distinct events and made that distinction in their purely theoretical model. They concluded that increases in the delay between default and foreclosure reduce the value of the mortgage and increased the likelihood of default (foreclosure). They also explicitly demonstrate the effects of transaction costs on the likelihood of default (foreclosure), including the possibility of lenders recouping losses from borrowers through postforeclosure deficiency judgments.

Their analysis had, at the time, significant implications for the FHA and Veterans Administration (VA) loan programs. Under those programs, lenders and servicers, as a matter of policy, were not to pursue deficiency judgments from borrowers who were foreclosed upon. They cited the practice of conventional mortgage investors and mortgage insurers seeking deficiency judgments as the most important reason why loss rates in the FHA and VA programs were relatively high.

Ambrose and Capone (1998), in a very detailed and careful investigation, examine model misspecification resulting from differences in borrower motivation for default and find that negative equity has less influence on borrower default (delinquency) than was previously thought. Specifically, they propose that some borrowers may use the default option to temporarily fund other critical expenditures and are not, *ex ante*, intending to exercise their put option, suggesting that there are at least two types of defaulting borrowers.[15] They conclude that pricing models with decision rules or boundary conditions that generate defaults solely from borrowers with negative equity are therefore prone to misspecification. They note that the likelihood that a foreclosure alternative will be successful depends on the borrowers' individual motivations for default. They further suggest that rules for offering loss-mitigation foreclosure-avoidance options should be limited to true trigger-event defaulters who have demonstrated economic hardship and commitment to the property. Their conclusions are consistent with industry practices implemented in the early to mid-1990s.

Ambrose and Buttimer (2000) develop a theoretical option-pricing model that explicitly allows borrowers to reinstate their mortgage out of default. They

15. Cutts and Van Order (2005) posit that this behavior is likely more prevalent in the subprime market because the credit-damage cost is lower for those borrowers than for prime borrowers and subprime borrowers may have few other options for obtaining credit other than to "borrow" their mortgage payment.

conclude that the optimal loss-mitigation program in areas with stable house prices is to provide an economic incentive for the borrower to cure (proxied by waiving default penalties) in conjunction with seeking deficiency judgments. However, they find that overall, providing incentives for borrower reinstatement (again by waiving default penalties) by themselves are not effective in reducing foreclosure costs. Nevertheless, if borrowers know that default and foreclosure affect future credit availability, they will default less. It is thus in the lenders' interest to reinforce the impression that default is costly to borrowers.

Ambrose and Buttimer (2000) rely on parameters not supported by empirical evidence to reach this finding. For example, default penalties are only one barrier to reinstatement; borrower capacity to reinstate and willingness to keep the home are the others. As an example, in the event of divorce the home is sometimes used for revenge, to deprive the other spouse of the asset, and perhaps to ruin the spouse's credit rating. If borrowers suffer a sufficiently adverse economic shock they may not be able to afford the burden of a repayment plan, but may be eligible for a home retention workout. The relative likelihood of these alternatives is a function of their simulations, but cannot be known without estimation.

Last in this series of papers is Ambrose and Capone (2000), which looks at the propensity for redefault among borrowers who have agreed to a home-retention workout plan. Using a hazard-rate model for predicting defaults, the authors find that the risk of redefault is significantly higher than the risk of a first default, especially within two years of the initial default. They also conclude that economic factors helpful in predicting first defaults are not helpful in predicting subsequent defaults.

This study asks a very important question regarding recidivism rates and the ability of servicers and investors to predict future redefault. Knowing that a borrower has gone delinquent on a mortgage in the past is a highly predictive indicator that a loan will default in the future, which is why this information is used in both manual and automated underwriting systems, and why loans are re-underwritten at the time a home-retention workout is considered. The conclusion in Ambrose and Capone (2000) that factors useful in predicting likelihood of first default are not useful in predicting second default is predicated on the fact that they only have data from loan origination, not current credit, collateral, and capacity data from the time of the loan reinstatement. Therefore their principal conclusion may well be that it is important not to use (just) origination data when evaluating troubled loans. In fact, this very issue provides the centerpiece for our empirical results below.

Finally, Pence (2001) examines the impact of state foreclosure laws on loan origination terms. Many housing market shocks are local in nature, and the author argues that ignoring these shocks may incorrectly lead to the interpretation of a local shock as due to differences in foreclosure laws. Pence controls for these regional characteristics by comparing mortgage applications in different census tracts that border each other but are located in different states and thus are subject to different foreclosure laws. She finds strong statistical evidence that the generosity of state foreclosure laws to borrowers is negatively related to loan size and suggests that policymakers should carefully consider borrower and lender reactions to foreclosure statutes.

The Pence study, however, does not examine what happens after loan origination. We cite it here because it is an innovative approach to determining what impact various foreclosure laws and deficiency judgment statutes might have on mortgage markets. Her approach could be used to do a similar study using, for example, the FHA data used by Ambrose and Capone (2000).

Stegman, Quercia, and Davis (2003) examine the efficacy of loss mitigation programs for affordable mortgage programs—those characterized by below-average loan balances and disproportionately large numbers of low- and moderate-income borrowers—and note the special challenges posed by this market segment. They conclude that the affordable side of the mortgage market has not yet fully adopted the technological innovations that have made their way into the mainstream portion of the prime market, but these tools could be very effective at loss mitigation in this market.

State of the Industry

At best, the studies mentioned in the previous section indicate that workout alternatives are good *sometimes*, such as when house prices are stable or when borrowers perceive their ability to borrow in the future will be adversely affected by a foreclosure today. But workout policies set by lenders need to be consistently effective to be profitable. Given that the trend in the industry has been wider adoption of workouts, particularly home retention workouts, they are almost certainly more consistently successful than the current literature would imply.

Technological innovations have occurred in (prime) mortgage servicing, and they have come along at the same time that home retention workouts have exploded. That the two have happened simultaneously is not by accident.

LaCour-Little (2000) describes how rapid consolidation in mortgage servicing has made the industry much more cost driven, forcing servicers to find ways to reduce costs and streamline processes. He notes that big breakthroughs in servicing were introduced by automated voice response (AVR) systems and network integrated voice response (NIVR) systems introduced in the early to mid-1990s. Under both systems customers inquire and companies respond to the most commonly asked questions using touch-tone telephones. These systems dramatically reduced the costs of maintaining customer service operations, especially for around-the-clock services, since they addressed basic borrower questions without requiring a live servicing agent on the other end of the call. The LaCour-Little study does not investigate servicing technologies any further.

Two other significant technological innovations revolutionized loan servicing in the 1990s. The first innovation was the development of performing loan servicing management tools, which took the regularly occurring reporting, remitting, and tracking tasks and automated them. The second innovation is in the form of automated credit-scoring-based servicing tools that emerged in wide use in the late 1990s. These tools risk-rank delinquent accounts to identify loans that are likely to benefit from early interventions to avoid foreclosure. The tools also are used to underwrite loan workouts, helping borrowers keep their homes. Below we discuss data-tracking and credit-scoring tools in a bit more detail for the purposes of documenting the history of these innovations and their role in facilitating successful home-retention workout options.

Data-Tracking and Management Tools

Innovations in the management of performing loans have been rapid and far-reaching. LaCour-Little (2000) presents a chart of the activities that occur in loan servicing. This chart is reproduced in figure 14-4, with our addition of reporting to national credit repositories and mortgage insurance providers. For every arrow spanning from the center box in the diagram there are technological innovations used by servicers to streamline reporting and increase accuracy. The savings in servicing costs are enormous when taken in aggregate, from the elimination of postage costs through automated electronic data deliveries, to lower labor costs due to automation of database updating and standardization of procedures. Independent financial-technology vendors, such as ALLTEL (now Fidelity) Information Services and Fiserv, and large servicers, such as Wells Fargo, developed many of these servicing innovations. Niche vendors and industry consortia are being continuously developed, pushing servicing innovations even further as better technology develops.

Innovative Credit-Scoring-Based Servicing Tools

Automated credit-scoring-based servicing tools emerged in wide use in the late 1990s. They serve three very important purposes: 1) to streamline collection call campaigns by risk-ranking delinquent accounts to identify loans that are likely to benefit from early interventions to avoid foreclosure; 2) for loans past the early stages of delinquency, to identify loans most likely to create a loss without an intervention and to direct servicer attention and resources toward resolving these loans; and 3) to underwrite delinquent loans for a workout. In the first two cases, the scoring tools also allow servicers to target resources much earlier in the delinquency process to contact troubled borrowers much earlier than was done before, thus reducing the time and cost of loss mitigation. In the latter case, higher success rates—defined as borrowers keeping their homes—among

Figure 14-4. *(Mostly) LaCour-Little's (2000) Simplified Flow of Loan-Servicing Activities*

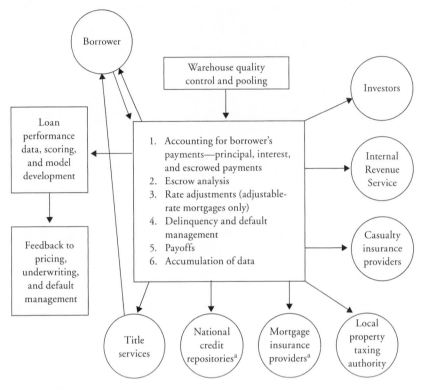

a. Added by authors.

loans in a repayment plan or other home retention workout are achieved by using scoring tools in workout underwriting.

The first widely used collections scoring tool was Strategy, developed by Jim Carroll and Associates. It used patterns of the timing of a borrower's previous mortgage payments as an indicator of economic distress. In 1996, Freddie Mac and the Mortgage Guarantee Insurance Corporation jointly developed Early Indicator (EI), which incorporated the Strategy tool and launched it in 1997 in a pilot program involving Wells Fargo Bank.[16] This tool relied on the credit scoring technology already used in automated underwriting models. In 1997, Fannie Mae launched Risk Profiler®. Today, servicing scoring tools are used on

16. See Comeau and Cordell (1998) for more on the testing and launch of Early Indicator. Within the Early Indicator system, two scores are produced. EI Early Collections scores range from 000 to 099, with lower scores indicating higher likelihood of worsening delinquency beyond the first month. EI Loss Mitigation scores range from 100 to 399, with lower scores indicating a higher likelihood of a loss-producing outcome. The score ranges are deliberately set to avoid confusion with FICO credit bureau scores, which range from 400 to 900.

Table 14-2. *Early Indicator® Loss-Mitigation Scores Rank Loans Accurately by Risk of Home Loss*

Score range	Number of loans scored	Borrowers retain homes	Borrowers lose homes	Odds ratio of borrowers retaining to losing homes
101–200	14,321	2,675	8,587	1:3
201–250	6,923	2,566	2,184	1:1
251–310	13,181	6,365	2,149	3:1
311–360	28,770	16,001	2,329	7:1
361–390	83,471	53,122	2,512	21:1
391–400	143,790	110,047	1,045	105:1
Total	290,456	190,776	18,806	10:1

Source: Authors' calculations on a sample of delinquent Freddie Mac loans scored in 4Q 1998. Performance measured through 4Q 2000.

over 80 percent of mortgages in the $8 trillion single-family mortgage market, with EI being the dominant tool.

Early Indicator and Risk Profiler have been highly successful in helping servicers focus attention on borrowers who are at high risk of losing their homes. Table 14-2 shows that borrowers who achieve high EI Loss Mitigation scores are at very low risk of losing their homes—on average just one in 105 will end up losing their homes. Moreover, roughly half of the loans scored by Early Indicator are viewed as low risk, even though they are currently delinquent on their mortgage. Figure 14-5 shows similar ability by Risk Profiler to identify delinquent loans likely to go on to foreclosure and ultimately REO.

The primary purpose of tools such as Early Indicator is to identify which borrowers are in most need of servicer attention. However, servicers must follow the guidelines set by investors in determining which borrowers should be offered home retention workouts and what type of workout would be the best option for each borrower's circumstances. Turning to the same technology and modeling techniques applied in automated underwriting, Freddie Mac and Fannie Mae developed tools specifically for use in underwriting workouts—Freddie Mac's Workout Prospector® was launched in 1996 and Fannie Mae's Workout Profiler® in 2002. These tools greatly increase the chances that a workout will result in the desired outcomes of keeping borrowers in their homes and reducing costs to the investors.

Taken together, the servicing tools created by Freddie Mac, Fannie Mae, and others have greatly increased the chances that a delinquent borrower will have the option of a home retention workout, and that a workout will be offered earlier in the process. This latter effect is important in ensuring that a workout will result in the borrower fully reinstating the loan and keeping his or her home. In a recent review of the FHA program, a servicer was reported to have found that the success of a workout in the FHA program decreased from a peak of more

Figure 14-5. *Default Rates of Loans with Risk Profiler®—High- versus Low-Risk Scores*

Percent

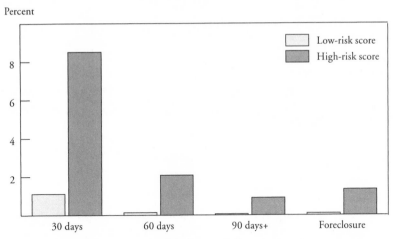

Source: Fannie Mae; based on 10.6 million loans scored.

than 45 percent if the workout were processed in the first one or two months of delinquency, to less than 10 percent if the workout were not accomplished within seven months.[17]

Model, Data, and Results

One valid concern, of course, is whether workouts work. That is, are borrowers with workouts more likely to reinstate or "cure" than borrowers who do not get into a workout plan? We turn now to this question.

Economic Theory

Unlike the origination decision, which is a decision about whether to enter into a contract with a borrower based on incomplete and asymmetric information, the decision of whether to offer a workout involves an alignment of economic incentives. Specifically, the lender wants to get its money back under the contract terms (that is, the interest rate and amortization term) and the borrower wants to keep his or her home. Once a borrower becomes delinquent, the investor faces a potentially lengthy and costly process to foreclose on the house and evict the borrower. Focardi (2002) estimates that foreclosure costs average $58,792 and take eighteen months to resolve.[18] The borrowers face a loss of dig-

17. Department of Housing and Urban Development, "Office of the Inspector General Audit Report: Follow-Up Nationwide Review Department of Housing and Urban Development's Loss Mitigation Program" (www.hud.gov/oig/ig280001.pdf [December 21, 2002]).

18. Note that Focardi's (2002) estimates apply to the entire first-lien mortgage market, not just the conventional, conforming market segment.

nity, severe damage to their credit rating (and thus damage to their future ability to obtain credit), and the loss of their home and any equity they may have in it.

Even if it is inevitable that the borrower will lose his or her home, alternatives to foreclosure where the borrower gives up the home are also incentive compatible. According to Focardi (2002), voluntary title transfers such as short sales and deed-in-lieu transfers cost more than $44,000 on average and take twelve months to resolve—a savings to the lender of $14,000 over foreclosure. For the borrower, avoiding the indignity and credit damage that results from foreclosure makes these options preferable. Thus it is in neither party's interest to continue down the path to foreclosure if another option is available.

Empirical Model

The hypothesis we are attempting to test is whether entry into a repayment plan reduces the likelihood of home loss from the default. For now, we approach this using a simple Cox proportional hazard model:

$$H(t) = h_0(t) \exp(x, \beta).$$

This model has been widely used in the literature (see Kiefer, 1988 for a survey). The model attempts to explain the likelihood and timing of a failure, which in our context is any loan that terminates as an REO, deed-in-lieu transfer, short sale, third-party sale, charge-off, or lender repurchase. The $h_0(t)$ component of the equation gives a baseline hazard function for failure when all covariates are zero. The covariates shift the baseline up and down: a negative coefficient means that an increase in the explanatory variable will lead to a reduction in the probability of failure at any point in time.

Our hypothesis is that, conditional on entry into delinquency, households in a Freddie Mac repayment plan will fail at a lower rate than households that are not. We therefore specify a model that models the probability of failure as a function of characteristics about the loan at the time it enters our sample and whether the borrower is put into a repayment plan.

Data

Our estimation data include 148,050 complete observations on loans owned by Freddie Mac that entered into sixty-, ninety-, or 120-day delinquency between January and September 2001.[19] We follow each loan for eighteen months after inflow into the sample.

---

19. The raw data sample contained 344,422 observations, including both duplicate entries as loans worsened (or improved) in their delinquency status, and loans that in-flowed into a repayment plan. We used only one entry per loan, and chose the worst delinquency status if more than one delinquency in-flow was observed. Repayment plan inflows were ignored because repay plans are used as an independent variable in our regressions.

Table 14-3. *Fail and Cure Rates by Inflow Delinquency Status*

	Time since entry into sample			
Rate	*Inflow sample*	*6 months*	*12 months*	*18 months*
Fail rates[a]				
Repayment plan	48,962	1.1	3.0	4.2
60 days late	182,829	2.5	6.2	7.8
90 days late	75,043	8.1	15.8	18.7
120+ days late	37,588	13.3	24.1	27.6
Cure rates[b]				
Repayment plan	48,962	71.6	85.4	89.7
60 days late	182,829	72.8	83.6	87.0
90 days late	75,043	57.1	68.4	72.6
120+ days late	37,588	46.1	56.9	61.3

Source: Authors' calculations on a sample of delinquent loans owned by Freddie Mac; inflow into delinquency or repay plan occurred between January 2001 and September 2001.

a. Loans fail when the borrower loses the property through foreclosure REO, deed-in-lieu transfer, short sale, or the loan is a charge-off or lender repurchase.

b. Loans cure when the borrower fully reinstates the loan, the loan is prepaid, modified, or assumed.

Simple summary analysis on these data suggests that workouts are effective at keeping borrowers in their homes. If we define as a cured loan any loan that either fully reinstates, gets modified, is assumed by a new borrower, or is paid off, and a failed loan as any loan that results in the loss of the home through foreclosure or foreclosure alternative, then from table 14-3 we see that roughly 90 percent of loans that start repay plans will cure within eighteen months compared with 73 percent for loans that are ninety-days delinquent or just 61 percent of loans that are 120-days or more delinquent. When viewed from a fail-rate perspective the results even more strongly support the effectiveness of repay plans. Of loans that get to 120-days delinquent status, 28 percent will fail, but just 4 percent of loans in repay plans will end in home loss for the borrower.

The dependent variable in our model is the time at which the loan fails, as defined in table 14-3. There are two important adjustments we need to make in creating this variable: we must deal with the fact that some observations in our sample exit without foreclosing (that is, some observations cure), and that some observations are censored (that is, reach the end of the sample period without either failing or curing). We use a standard competing risks model within STATA, the program used for the estimation, which identifies the exit time for each observation and incorporates censoring.

Our covariates are:

—length of delinquency at time of entry into sample;

—loan-to-value ratio at time of entry into sample;

—unpaid balance at time of entry into sample;

—Early Indicator Loss Mitigation score at time of entry into sample;

—current coupon rate;

—FICO score at origination;

—whether the borrower is in bankruptcy at time of entry into sample;

—whether the loan qualified as a HUD low- to moderate-income goal loan at origination;

—whether the loan qualified as a HUD underserved area goal loan at origination;

—whether HUD goal information was missing;

—whether the loan was modified in a workout before entering sample;

—whether the borrower entered a repayment plan or the loan was modified in a workout after entry into sample; and

—interaction variables between repayment plan and HUD goal status.

We describe each variable in a bit more detail below.

LENGTH OF DELINQUENCY AT TIME OF ENTRY. We have flags for whether loans are sixty-days or ninety-days delinquent at the time they enter the sample. The omitted category is 120-days delinquent. Loans deeper into delinquency are likely more troubled, and therefore more prone to fail.

CURRENT LOAN-TO-VALUE RATIO AT TIME OF ENTRY. Current loan-to-value (CLTV) ratio gives a proxy for how "in the money" the default option is.[20] We would expect higher loan-to-value loans to have higher incidence of failure. That said, over the sample period, house prices were generally rising, so there are relatively few loans where the default option was deeply in the money. Consequently, it might be difficult to identify the effect of this variable on failure.

UNPAID PRINCIPAL BALANCE AT TIME OF ENTRY. For very low balance loans, it is generally in everyone's interest to cure the loan, and we would rarely expect to see them fail. We otherwise have no particular prior belief on the relationship between unpaid principal balance and propensity to fail.

EARLY INDICATOR SCORE AT TIME OF ENTRY. Early Indicator Loss Mitigation scores are used here as a proxy for current credit condition. EI values range from 100–400, with high scores corresponding to lower risk of home loss.

CURRENT COUPON. The coupon rate gives us a proxy for the value of the competing risk to default—the prepayment option. High coupon mortgages have an incentive to prepay. Higher current coupons also offer more room to negotiate a

---

20. We use the standard economics terminology of "default option" here to denote the borrower's option to "put" the loan, that is, to exchange the loan obligation for the collateral.

loan modification in the event that the borrower would be unable to refinance the loan. On the other hand, households may become delinquent because they do not have access to the refinance market. It is therefore possible that a high coupon rate, conditional on delinquency, reveals information about the borrower not captured by such things as the EI score, and therefore could be positively related to failure.

FICO SCORE AT ORIGINATION. This variable has been used in past studies (see Ambrose and Capone, 2000). We include it to test our view that it has little impact on failure probabilities conditional on delinquency. We also perform regressions omitting it, because we have many observations where it is missing. Loans originated before 1994 do not have FICO scores since Freddie Mac did not use credit scores as an underwriting criterion before then.

BANKRUPTCY AT TIME OF ENTRY. Ironically, bankruptcy reduces the probability of failure at any point within the eighteen months that we follow the loans, because foreclosure proceedings may not take place until after bankruptcies are settled.

HUD AFFORDABLE GOAL QUALIFYING MORTGAGE. The focus of the conference for which this study was prepared is wealth accumulation for underserved areas and low- and moderate-income households. HUD has developed standards for identifying loans that go to low- and moderate-income borrowers, underserved neighborhoods, or both. We use these standards in our empirical model to set up underserved and low- and moderate-income flags, and then we interact these dummy variables with the existence of a repayment plan, which will be described below. The interaction terms will tell us the effectiveness of the repayment plan for these special areas and households relative to other areas and households.

PREVIOUS LOAN MODIFICATION AT TIME OF ENTRY. Recidivism is a concern with home retention workouts, and some of the loans in our sample (4,399) were previously modified. At issue is whether loans that previously have been modified have a higher propensity to fail than loans that have not. Unfortunately, data on whether the borrower previously entered a repayment plan or other workout besides a loan modification are not available in our sample. However the structure of our data sample will allow this question to be examined in the future once a longer time series is available.

HOME-RETENTION WORKOUT AFTER ENTRY. This is the featured variable. We use indicators of whether a borrower entered a repayment plan, ignoring other workout options, or entered a repayment plan or loan modification to identify impacts of home retention workouts on failure propensities among delinquent borrowers. In theory, repayment plans and loan modification will always extend the time to failure, but the proportional hazard allows us to evaluate their impact on the overall rate of failure—we expect the workout options to prevent failure and therefore shift the baseline hazard function downward.

Results

Results are presented in table 14-4. For the models that include FICO as an explanatory variable, we have 63,613 observations;[21] for those that do not, we have 148,050 observations.

The results are remarkably robust. We find:

—loans arriving sixty-days delinquent are less likely to fail than those arriving later;

—high CLTVs lead to slightly higher failure probabilities;

—unpaid principal balance has no impact (statistically or otherwise) on failure probabilities;

—Early Indicator Loss Mitigation score is a powerful predictor of failure;

—high current coupon sometimes reduces failure probability a little;

—goal-qualifying loans are more likely to fail; and

—we are less likely to observe failure among those in bankruptcy.

None of these results surprise us.

What is interesting is the coefficient on FICO score for those regressions that include it. Higher FICO scores at origination have a statistically significant but small impact on failure probability—they push it upward. We speculate that because we control for current FICO score to some extent by including Early Indicator Loss mitigation score, people with high origination FICOs in the sample saw their circumstances change markedly, and therefore are more likely to fail.

The coefficients on previously modified loans in all model specifications strongly indicate that these loans are less likely to fail, even though they became delinquent after modification. One reason for this may be that these borrowers have identified themselves as being experienced with the options available to them if they cooperate with servicers.

We now turn to our featured variable: whether the borrower is in a repayment plan. Our results are robust—for all four model specifications, the probability of failure drops sharply when borrowers get into a repayment plan. And while such plans are not quite as effective for low- and moderate-income borrowers or for those who live in underserved areas, they are nevertheless still very effective. At sample means, being in a repayment plan lowers the probability of

---

21. The lack of FICO scores is almost always attributable to loan origination prior to 1994, the year in which Freddie Mac made credit scores part of its underwriting criteria for loans it would consider investment quality and therefore eligible for purchase by the company under its charter.

Table 14-4. *Time to Default Survival Function Estimates*

Variable	Description	Model A		Model B		Model C		Model D	
		Hazard ratio	t statistic	Hazard ratio	t statistic	Hazard ratio	t statistic	Hazard ratio	t statistic
Inflow60	Loan was delinquent 60 days at inflow into sample	0.516	−13.134	0.298	−41.645	0.509	−13.380	0.296	−41.761
Inflow90	Loan was delinquent 90 days at inflow into sample	1.034	0.636	0.799	−12.099	1.012	0.229	0.802	−11.895
CLTV	Current LTV at inflow into sample ($)	1.007	4.565	1.019	28.894	1.008	5.027	1.020	29.757
UPB	Unpaid principal balance on delinquent loan ($)	1.000	−0.731	1.000	−7.987	1.000	−0.346	1.000	−6.742
EI Score	Early Indicator score at inflow into sample	0.991	−20.954	0.995	−21.380	0.991	−20.644	0.995	−20.675
Coupon	Current interest rate on delinquent mortgage (%)	0.998	−0.090	0.967	−3.978	0.997	−0.130	0.972	−3.416
FICO score	Borrower FICO score at origination	1.002	6.204	...		1.002	6.026	...	
Bankruptcy	Borrower in bankruptcy	0.504	−12.202	0.672	−14.813	0.492	−12.651	0.655	−15.778
Low-Mod	At origination, loan qualified for HUD GSE low- and moderate-income goal	1.001	0.024	0.997	−0.089	1.005	0.129	1.003	0.098
Underserved	At origination, loan qualified for HUD GSE underserved area goal	1.152	3.653	1.162	4.306	1.152	3.642	1.161	4.277
HUD_Missing	Pre-1993 origination or loan missing information on HUD affordable goal status	2.022	1.217	1.321	9.470	2.026	1.220	1.326	9.577

PreviousLoanMod	Loan modification prior to inflow into sample	0.458	−7.614	0.537	−14.154	0.480	−7.156	0.552	−13.537
Repay	Borrower entered home retention workout (repayment plan) post-inflow	0.234	−15.533	0.209	−48.095	...	...	...	...
LowMod_Repay	Interaction variable: low- or moderate-income borrower loan enters home retention workout (repayment plan)	1.367	2.654	1.553	4.792	...	...	...	...
Underserved_Repay	Interaction variable: HUD underserved area goal loan enters home retention workout (repayment plan)	1.055	0.444	1.119	1.065	...	...	...	...
Workout	Borrower entered home retention workout (repayment plan or loan modification) post-inflow	...	...	...	...	0.203	−17.061	0.174	−53.755
LowMod_Workout	Interaction variable: low- or moderate-income borrower loan enters home retention workout (repayment plan or loan modification)	...	...	...	...	1.366	2.648	1.580	4.952
Underserved_Workout	Interaction variable: underserved loan enters home retention workout (repayment plan or loan modification)	...	...	...	...	1.054	0.439	1.132	1.173
No. of observations		63,613		148,050		63,613		148,050	

failure by 68 percent for low- and moderate-income borrowers. While this is not quite as impressive as is the result for borrowers that are not low- and moderate-income (where failure probability is reduced by almost 80 percent), it remains nevertheless remarkable. Based on the results from our analysis, we believe that repayment plans are both statistically significant and economically important—that is, they work very well at keeping delinquent borrowers in their homes.

Our result becomes even stronger when we recognize that the majority of loans in our sample did not have the benefit of being underwritten with state-of-the-art automated underwriting since more than 58 percent of the loans evaluated in our data were originated prior to 1998—automated underwriting for mortgages was introduced by Freddie Mac in 1995, but it was 1998 before automated underwriting was a significant contributor to the mortgage origination process.[22] This helps clarify that it may well have been the servicing process rather than initial loan quality that led to surprisingly low default rates in the early 2000s, which featured high job losses during the recession and eighteen months into the economic recovery. It is important to note that selection bias might be an issue—although we have controlled for a number of important borrower characteristics (especially borrower credit condition using the Early Indicator score), there could be omitted characteristics among those in repayment plans that vary substantially from those that are not.

Conclusions

The mortgage literature is vast—it contains many papers on mortgage originations, prepayment, and default (meaning foreclosure). Despite its vastness, it has nearly ignored an event that happens more often than foreclosure itself—delinquency without failure. This study is among the first studies to explore empirically the transition between delinquency and foreclosure, and investigate home-retention workout options that can reduce failure probabilities conditional on delinquency.

We know that automation has brought tremendous benefits to the loan origination market, particularly among borrowers previously believed to be too high risk for prime credit. For example, Straka (2000), Gates, Perry, and Zorn (2002), and Gates, Waldron, and Zorn (2003) demonstrated that significant gains in underwriting accuracy using automated systems (specifically Freddie Mac's Loan Prospector) have both expanded homeownership opportunities for borrowers targeted by affordable loan programs (such as first-time homebuyers,

---

22. Loan Prospector reviewed 38,248 loans in 1995; 203,424 in 1996; 528,809 in 1997; 2.1 million in 1998; 3.0 million in 1999; 3.8 million in 2000; 7.4 million in 2001; 8.2 million in 2002; and 9.5 million loans in 2003. See "Freddie Mac's Loan Prospector Service Reviews 9.5 Million Mortgage Loans in 2003" (www.freddiemac.com/news/archives/lp/2004/lps_2003_volume_020304.html [February 16, 2004]).

low- and moderate-income borrowers and minority households) and reduced credit risk for investors.

There is a *prima facie* case that improvements in servicing are important innovations, and parallel many improvements in the underwriting and origination process. Just as the underwriting and origination process has had a profound impact on the market for new mortgages, so it would seem that the servicing process has had a profound impact on the disposition of delinquent loans. The mortgage origination market has become much more sensitive to interest rate cycles, while the share of delinquent mortgages that result in home loss has become much less sensitive to the business cycle (see figure 14-1). Despite serious job losses in the early 2000s, mortgage foreclosure has risen by only half as much as it did in the early 1990s—in fact, by the peak in serious delinquencies in 2003, ninety-day delinquency and foreclosure rates in the prime market had only risen back to 1998 levels.

We have identified one potential reason for this: the institution of credit scoring tools for identifying at-risk loans and underwriting workouts, and policies that encourage home-retention workouts. Owners of mortgages can now better identify which borrowers have the capacity to repay their loans, and then to make appropriate arrangements to allow them to do so. We have found that across a variety of specifications, delinquent borrowers, and among them low- and moderate-income borrowers and borrowers in underserved areas, are less likely to lose their home if they are in a repayment plan or other workout. We need to be a bit careful about our interpretation of these results because it is possible that borrowers in repayment plans have unobserved characteristics that differ from other borrowers.

Nevertheless, it is heartening to note the large correlation between the likelihood of not failing and being in a repayment plan, even after controlling for variables that by themselves are important predictors of default and foreclosure.

References

Ambrose, Brent W., and Richard J. Buttimer Jr. 2000. "Embedded Options in the Mortgage Contract." *Journal of Real Estate Finance and Economics* 21 (2): 95–111.

Ambrose, Brent W., Richard J. Buttimer Jr., and Charles A. Capone Jr. 1997. "Pricing Mortgage Default and Foreclosure Delay." *Journal of Money, Credit, and Banking* 29 (3): 314–25.

Ambrose, Brent W., and Charles A. Capone Jr. 1996. "Cost-Benefit Analysis of Single-Family Foreclosure Alternatives." *Journal of Real Estate Finance and Economics* 13: 105–20.

———. 1998. "Modeling the Conditional Probability in the Context of Single-Family Mortgage Default Resolutions." *Real Estate Economics* 26 (3): 391–429.

———. 2000. "The Hazard Rates of First and Second Defaults." *Journal of Real Estate Finance and Economics* 20 (3): 275–93.

Avery, Robert B., and others. 2000. "Credit Scoring: Statistical Issues and Evidence from Credit-Bureau Files." *Real Estate Economics* 28 (3): 523–47.

Comeau, Phil, and Larry Cordell. 1998. "Case Study: Beating the Odds. Loss Mitigation Scores Helped Wells Fargo Save Resources, Assist Borrowers in Avoiding Foreclosure." *Servicing Management* (June): 70.

Cutts, Amy Crews, and Robert A. Van Order. 2005. "On the Economics of Subprime Lending." *Journal of Real Estate Finance and Economics* 30 (2): 167–97.

Deng, Yong Heng, John Quigley, and Robert Van Order. 2000. "Mortgage Terminations, Heterogeneity, and the Exercise of Mortgage Options." *Econometrica* 68 (2): 275–307.

Dunaway, Baxter. 2002. *The Law of Distressed Real Estate,* vols. 1–5. New York: Clark Boardman Callaghan/West Group.

Fabozzi, Frank J., and Franco Modigliani. 1992. *Capital Markets: Institutions and Instruments.* Englewood Cliffs, N.J.: Prentice-Hall.

Fannie Mae. 2002. "Fannie Mae Single Family Guide."

Focardi, Craig. 2002. "Servicing Default Management: An Overview of the Process and Underlying Technology." *TowerGroup Research Note* 033-13C. November 15.

Gates, Susan Wharton, Vanessa Gail Perry, and Peter M. Zorn. 2002. "Automated Underwriting in Mortgage Lending: Good News for the Underserved?" *Housing Policy Debate* 13 (2): 369–91.

Gates, Susan Wharton, Cynthia Waldron, and Peter M. Zorn. 2003. "Automated Underwriting: Friend or Foe to Low-Mod Households and Neighborhoods." Paper presented at the Symposium on Improving Financial Services in Low-Income Communities, Harvard University Joint Center for Housing Studies, November 18–19.

Inside Mortgage Finance. 1995. "Federal National Mortgage Association: California REO Surges, Other States Mixed." *Seller/Servicer Update (*now called *Mortgage Market Update)* 8 (9): 9-12.

———. 2001. *The 2001 Mortgage Market Statistical Annual,* vol.1. Bethesda: Inside Mortgage Finance Publications.

———. 2004. *Inside Mortgage Finance.* February 6.

Kau, James, and D. C. Keenan. 1995. "An Overview of Option-Theoretic Pricing of Mortgages." *Journal of Housing Research* 6 (2): 217–44.

Kiefer, Nicholas M. 1988. "Economic Duration Data and Hazard Functions." *Journal of Economic Literature* 26 (2): 646–70.

LaCour-Little, Michael. 2000. "The Evolving Role of Technology in Mortgage Finance." *Journal of Housing Research* 11 (2): 173–205.

Pence, Karen. 2001. *Essays on Government Policy and Household Financial Decisions.* Ph.D. dissertation, University of Wisconsin.

Oliver, Geoffrey A., and others. 2001. "Profitable Servicers in the New Millennium." *Mortgage Banking* 61(9): 32–41.

Riddiough, Timothy J., and Steve B. Wyatt. 1994. "Wimp or Tough Guy: Sequential Default Risk and Signaling with Mortgages." *Journal of Real Estate Finance and Economics* 9 (3): 299–321.

Rossi, Clifford. 1998. "Mortgage Banking Cost Structure: Resolving an Enigma." *Journal of Economics and Business* 50 (2): 219–34.

Stegman, Michael A., Roberto G. Quercia, and Walter R. Davis. 2003. How Technology Is Making Servicing Even Smarter: Affordable Lending and Default Management. Working Paper. Center for Community Capitalism, Frank Hawkins Kenan Institute of Private Enterprise, University of North Carolina at Chapel Hill.

Straka, John W. 2000. "A Shift in the Mortgage Landscape: The 1990s Move to Automated Credit Evaluations." *Journal of Housing Research* 11 (2): 207–31.

U.S. Department of Housing and Urban Development. 2002a. "FHA Comptroller's Reports to the Commissioner: FHA Portfolio Analysis" (www.hud.gov/offices/hsg/comp/rpts/com/commenu.cfm [December 2002]).

——. 2002c. *Office of the Inspector General Audit Report: Follow-Up Nationwide Review, Department of Housing and Urban Development's Loss Mitigation Program*, 2002-DE-0001 (www.hud.gov/oig/ig280001.pdf [December 21, 2002]).

——. 2005. *FHA Mortgagee Letters*, various dates (www.hud.gov/offices/hsg/mltrmenu.cfm [April 2005]).

Vandell, Kerry D. 1993. "Handing Over the Keys: A Perspective on Mortgage Default Research." *Journal of the American Real Estate and Urban Economics Association* 21 (3): 211–46.

Walsh, Marina. 2002. "Servicing Costs up in 2001 Refi Surge." *Mortgage Banking* 62 (12): 66–74.

Contributors

William C. Apgar
Joint Center for Housing Studies
Harvard University

Michael S. Barr
University of Michigan

Eric S. Belsky
Joint Center for Housing Studies
Harvard University

Christopher Berry
Kennedy School of Government
Harvard University

Raphael W. Bostic
University of Southern California

Stephen Brobeck
Consumer Federation of America

Allegra Calder
Joint Center for Housing Studies
Harvard University

Paul S. Calem
Board of Governors of the Federal
Reserve System

Karl E. Case
Wellesley College

Fred H. Cate
Indiana University

Yan Chang
Freddie Mac

J. Michael Collins
Neighborhood Reinvestment
Corporation

Amy Crews Cutts
Freddie Mac

Allen J. Fishbein
Consumer Federation of America

Hollis Fishelson-Holstine
Fair Isaac

Edward Golding
Freddie Mac

Edward Gramlich
Federal Reserve Board

Richard K. Green
George Washington University

Duncan Kennedy
Harvard Law School

George McCarthy
Ford Foundation

Frank E. Nothaft
Freddie Mac

Nicolas P. Retsinas
Joint Center for Housing Studies
Harvard University

Ellen Seidman
ShoreBank Advisory Services

Michael Sherraden
Washington University

Michael E. Staten
Georgetown University

Jennifer Tescher
ShoreBank Advisory Services

Susan M. Wachter
University of Pennsylvania

Ken Wade
Neighborhood Reinvestment
Corporation

Index